GESTURE AND POWER

THE RELIGIOUS CULTURES OF AFRICAN AND AFRICAN DIASPORA PEOPLE

Series editors:
Jacob K. Olupona, Harvard University
Dianne M. Stewart, Emory University
and Terrence L. Johnson, Georgetown University

The book series examines the religious, cultural, and political expressions of African, African American, and African Caribbean traditions. Through transnational, cross-cultural, and multidisciplinary approaches to the study of religion, the series investigates the epistemic boundaries of continental and diasporic religious practices and thought and explores the diverse and distinct ways African-derived religions inform culture and politics. The series aims to establish a forum for imagining the centrality of Black religions in the formation of the "New World."

GESTURE
AND POWER

RELIGION, NATIONALISM, AND
EVERYDAY PERFORMANCE IN CONGO

Yolanda Covington-Ward

DUKE UNIVERSITY PRESS   DURHAM AND LONDON   2016

Library of Congress Cataloging-in-Publication Data
Covington-Ward, Yolanda, [date] author.
Gesture and power : religion, nationalism, and everyday performance in Congo /
Yolanda Covington-Ward.
pages cm—(The religious cultures of African and African diaspora people)
Includes bibliographical references and index.
ISBN 978-0-8223-6020-9 (hardcover: alk. paper)
ISBN 978-0-8223-6036-0 (pbk. : alk. paper)
ISBN 978-0-8223-7484-8 (e-book)
1. Kongo (African people)—Communication. 2. Body language—Congo (Democratic
Republic) 3. Dance—Social aspects—Congo (Democratic Republic) I. Title. II. Series:
Religious cultures of African and African diaspora people.
394—dc23
2015020742

Cover art: Weighing of the spirit (bascule) in worship service,
DMNA Church, Luozi, 2010. Photo by Yolanda Covington-Ward.

To my grandmother Nene and my sister-in-law Dell Olivia Attoh

CONTENTS

ACKNOWLEDGMENTS

First, I must thank God for bringing me this far. Next, I thank my family for supporting me, from CES 110X in the Bronx all the way to the tenure track at the University of Pittsburgh. My grandmother Nene; my mother, Diane Covington, and father, Roger Dixon; my siblings: Tavi, Dana, Nyesha, Brandon, Michelle, Taurean, and Tristan; all my aunts and uncles, especially Sony, Audrey, Danny, Tony, Shirley-Mae, JoAnn, Abby, Duke, and Dionne; all my many cousins, especially Chris and Leisa; my mother-in-law, Teeta, and sister-in-law Dell—indeed, the whole village.

I must thank many people who have contributed to the book's development: my dissertation committee at the University of Michigan: Elisha Renne, Kelly Askew, Tata Mbala Nkanga, Maxwell Owusu, and Julius Scott. I also thank the Department of Anthropology, especially Laurie Marx, and the Department (then Center) for Afroamerican and African Studies, especially Kevin Gaines, Mamadou Diouf, Devon Adjei, Beth James, and Chuck Phillips. My fellowship at the Institute for the Humanities enabled me to complete the writing of my dissertation. I am grateful to all my colleagues (past and present) in the Department of Africana Studies at the University of Pittsburgh: Brenda, Jerry, Christel, Michael, Oronde, Michele, Cecil, Joseph, Kwame, and Vernell for their support.

There are so many people that impacted and facilitated my research in the Congo: Tata Fu-Kiau Bunseki, may he rest in peace; Professor Kimpianga Mahaniah—a great resource and support to me both in Luozi and Kinshasa. Ne Nkamu Luyindula—thank you for the Kikongo, drumming, and dance lessons and the late-night debates. In Luozi: Pere Blaise and the Catholic mission; the Luyobisa family (Pa Luyobisa, Ma Suzanne, and the children); the

DMNA church (Dibundu dia Mpeve ya Nlongo mu Afelika); Charles Mayangi Masamba; the members of BDK (Bundu dia Kongo) in Luozi; the Communauté Evangelique du Congo (CEC) churches and mission; Ma Jackie; Reagan, my little brother; Eric and Yannic; Ma Marcelline, my sister; Tata Zam. Ma Muniangu; Ton-Ton Niki Niki; Ma Mambweni; Ma Sylvie; Ma Virginie; Jose Dianzungu and his wife; Papa Leon, everyone who allowed me to interview them—I cannot thank you enough. I just hope my work does justice to what I learned from all of you.

In Kinshasa: Papa Jean Kambayi Bwatshia and Mama Angelique; Mama Annie Meta, may her soul rest in peace. Thank you to the public affairs section of the American Embassy in Kinshasa; Tata Nzuzi and Tata Ndundu, Abbe Ngimbi, Frederick Ngandu. I must thank the staff at the National Archives in Kinshasa; the librarian at CEPAS (Centre d'Etudes pour l'Action Sociale), and Pere Body at Scholasticat. I had many friends in Kinshasa; within the diasporic community—Jill and Anthony, Aleathea, Patsy and Marco, S.T., Mike, Ray, and any others I forgot here; thank you. In Gombe and other parts of Kinshasa—Christian, Bolene, and everyone else—thank you for the great times and stimulating conversation. Ma Helen, Ma Patricia, Pere Matota, Pere Alain Nkisi, and friends at the Liberian embassy in Congo, thank you.

I would also like to thank the staff at the Tervuren Museum and the African Archives in Belgium, the American Baptist Historical Society, and the Angus Library for all their help. I can't forget my community of Congo/ Central Africa/Africa researchers: Wyatt MacGaffey (thank you for your comments), Ira Dworkin, Nichole Bridges, John Nimis, Ed Davis, Bruce Whitehouse, David Eaton, John Cinnamon, Jeremy Rich, Charles Tshimanga, Bennetta Jules-Rosette, John Janzen, Bob White, Cécile Fromont, John Thornton, Linda Heywood, Alma Gottlieb, Paul Stoller, Mwenda Ntarangwi, Nicole Eggers, T.J. Desch-Obi, Jessica Krug, Jemima Pierre, and anyone I may have forgotten. I also want to thank my Black Performance Theory Community; Thomas DeFrantz, E. Patrick Johnson, Stephanie Batiste, Jennifer Devere Brody, Anita Gonzalez, Jeffrey McCune, and many others. Thank you also, to Biza and Titos Sompa and Bichini bia Congo for giving me the embodied knowledge of Kongo performance.

For funding, I must thank the Institute of International Education (IIE) Fulbright program, Rackham Graduate School, Center for African and AfroAmerican Studies (CAAS) Africa Initiatives, Center for World Performance Studies, Institute for the Humanities, Department of Anthropology, Council of Alumnae Women, Richard D. and Mary Jane Edwards Endowed Publication Fund, International Institute, the Ford Foundation

Fellowship Program, African Studies Program and Global Studies Center at Pitt, and the Dietrich School of Arts and Sciences for funding my project.

I am grateful to my research assistants Siatta Dennis and Loretta Agyemang for their help. I must also thank my friends here in the United States who have supported me throughout my graduate career and after. My writing group members, Patricia Moonsammy, Shanesha Brooks-Tatum, and Menna Demessie; Grace Okrah for all the support and encouragement (keep at it); my cohort and other anthro folks—Xochitl, Britt, Henrike, Sergio, Marisabel, Cecilia, Sonia, Lara, and others. My writing partners in Pittsburgh, especially Renä Robinson. My best friend Chidimma, thank you for everything, Chi! My Ford family: David, Koritha, Aisha, Tyson, Tene, Laurence, and others who have been supportive. The Ford postdoctoral fellowship allowed me to complete my book revisions. In Pittsburgh, I must thank Edda Fields-Black for her guidance and feedback, Alberta Sbragia, Pat Manning, Macrina Lelei, Lara Putnam, Joyce Bell, Waverly Duck, and all my other colleagues—you know who you are. I also want to thank Miriam Angress, associate editor at Duke; the series editors, Jacob K. Olupona, Dianne M. Stewart, and Terrence L. Johnson; my project editor, Susan Albury; and the two anonymous reviewers for their feedback and encouragement.

To ma fille, Leyeti, I love you dearly; you forced me to keep pushing harder. To my baby son Lincoln, welcome to our family. Last but not least, I must thank my husband, Lincoln Ward, for standing by my side through all these years. He often tells me, "you can't see yourself swimming." Your encouragement and support mean the world to me. If there is anybody that I did not mention here—thank you all the same.

Earlier versions of sections of chapters three and four previously appeared in "Threatening Gestures, Immoral Bodies: The Intersection of Church, State, and Kongo Performance in the Belgian Congo," in *Missions, States, and European Expansion in Africa*, edited by Chima Korieh and Raphael Njoku (2007). An earlier version of the short background section on ABAKO in chapter seven appeared in Joseph Kasa-Vubu, ABAKO, and Performances of Kongo Nationalism in the Congolese Independence Movement," *Journal of Black Studies* (2012). Throughout the manuscript I have done the translations from French to English and take full responsibility for any errors. Mfiaukidi!

Introduction

Gesture and Power

May 11, 1921. Léon-Georges Morel, the territorial administrator for the Southern Cataracts Territory in the Lower Congo of colonial Belgian Congo,[1] is heading to the town of Nkamba. He is investigating the activities of Simon Kimbangu, a man who local Kongo people are calling a prophet. Many people are flocking to Nkamba, leaving jobs, carrying sick relatives for healing, and rapidly increasing the anxiety of Belgian colonial authorities. Morel arrives at Nkamba in the company of two soldiers, estimating the crowd in Nkamba at around eight hundred people. As he continues on the road into town, he encounters Kimbangu, who is accompanied by two men and two women. Kimbangu is wearing red pants and a white flannel shirt and is carrying a stick shaped like a bishop's staff. Morel observes his behavior. "The person of interest," he writes, "was agitated by a general trembling of his body." His companions, Morel notes, were "all agitated by the same trembling and making bizarre shouts." They make a circle around him, and Morel tries to speak to the group, but they do not respond. After the trembling subsides, Morel sets up his tent in the town. Simon Kimbangu approaches the tent and, after reading the story of David and Goliath from the Bible, comes forward to shake Morel's hand. "I notice that his hand is icy," Morel writes, "a reaction following the period of nervous shaking. I take advantage of this period of calm to ask Kimbangu the reason for this not very suitable and grotesque manner of receiving me. He responds that: 'It is God that ordered him to come to meet me in that way and that the bizarre shouts are nothing but his conversation with God. It is God that orders him and his apostles to tremble in this way.'" During Morel's visit to Nkamba, Kimbangu, his disciples, and the assembled crowd largely ignore and openly challenge Morel's orders, probing questions, and authority as a representative of the colonial administration. Consequently, Morel advised his superiors in the colonial government for urgent and immediate action to suppress the movement because "the natives will say they have found the God of the Blacks . . . it is certain that he [Kimbangu] could direct the spirit of the natives toward hostility to the White race."[2]

October 1, 2005. I am staying in the town of Luozi in the westernmost province of Bas-Congo, Democratic Republic of Congo (DRC). The town is the administrative center of Luozi territory, which is a largely rural area covered with green rolling hills, mountains, and wide plots of cassava, soybeans, and other agricultural crops. I am walking down the red dirt road next to the soccer field that doubles as an airplane landing strip, an area locals jokingly refer to as Luozi's airport. My friend Tanu[3] and I were invited to attend an event organized by Bundu dia Kongo (BDK), a nationalist movement seeking to address the political and economic marginalization of Kongo people by combining religion, politics, and cultural revitalization.[4] The larger goal of BDK was to gain autonomy by restoring the precolonial Kongo Kingdom in the present day. Their members were becoming increasingly active in Luozi and other parts of the Lower Congo, as well as Kinshasa. Because of their emphatic rejection of Christianity as the "White man's religion," and advocating their own religion (called BuKongo) instead, BDK members were often in conflict with local churches. This particular event was to honor members of the group killed in 2004 in a confrontation with both local law enforcement and members of the major missionary-founded Protestant church in Luozi. Tanu and I meet a small group of BDK members on the road to the cemetery, where they are singing and waving small green branches. As we join the group, one of the local leaders tells me a young White missionary wanted to see the ceremony and they denied her access. Looking at me fiercely, he says, "We can't reveal all our secrets. But you, you are our sister, so you can come." After the ceremony ends, I am introduced to another man representing the regional leadership of the group. I reach out my hand for a handshake in greeting, and he just looks down at it, unmoving. I stand there with my hand outstretched, completely embarrassed, until Tanu quickly reminds me to use the *bula makonko* gesture, where the hands are cupped and clapped together three times. I clap my cupped hands. Finally, the man, who I will call Ne Tatu, physically responds in kind, saying, "This is the proper form of greeting in Kongo culture, dating back to the Kongo Kingdom. That is why in Bundu dia Kongo we greet each other in this way. Kongo people need to let go of the White man's ways and honor their own culture. That is how things will change for us."

While separated by more than eighty years, both of these incidents illustrate the importance of microinteractions of the body in framing and staking political claims in the Lower Congo. Nationalist movements for people of the Kongo ethnic group have often taken religious forms over the past century. Different ways of using the body in social interaction, with multivalent meanings, play a large role in these nationalist movements. In the case of Kimbangu, the spirit-induced trembling he experienced (caused by the Holy Spirit[5]) started a region-wide Christian prophetic movement that threatened the hegemony of Western missionaries and Belgian colonial administrators alike. This messianic movement, inspired by prophecies of independence and a reversal of the world order, blended Kongo traditional embodied movements and ritual with mission-inspired Protestant Christianity, including hymns, social conduct, and biblical interpretation.[6] Looking at the colonial suppression of the movement through arrests, interrogations, violence, and imprisonment in penal labor camps, the Belgians, including Morel, clearly believed their authority, in both religious and political matters, was being threatened. Likewise, my own embodied interactions with Bundu dia Kongo reveal the importance of gesture for fostering ethnic nationalist sentiment and taking an active role in everyday struggles for power and authority. This bula makonko greeting has become emblematic of the Bundu dia Kongo movement itself as its leaders try to wed a new religion and revitalization of traditional culture with strategies to capture more political power and representation. Moreover, as an African American woman, my own physical body and embodiment became part of a larger discourse of religious prophecy, Kongo identity, and Kongo nationalism during my time in the Congo, especially in 2005–6.

Gestures and spirit-induced trembling are two of several important types of everyday cultural performances that are sites of struggles for power and authority in daily life in the Congo. But how can the physical body do so much? What is the relationship between everyday embodied cultural performances and power, and what role do these performances play in legitimizing competing forms of spiritual and political authority? How are these claims then used to support nationalist movements?

In this book I argue that everyday cultural performances in interpersonal encounters are crucial sites for making political claims used to legitimize and inspire larger social movements. More specifically, I am interested in how the body is used to bolster religious claims to authority that can either challenge or support existing structures of power. Using the BisiKongo ethnic group in the Democratic Republic of Congo as a case study, I illustrate that performances in daily life at the micro level can have a decisive effect on macrolevel systems of power and structures of authority, and also be impacted by those same societal structures.[7] My monograph blends history and ethnography to explore how everyday cultural performances of the body such as gestures (*bimpampa*), dances (*makinu*), and spirit-induced trembling (*zakama*) are used to create, confirm, and contest authority in daily life. I build on previous studies of power and performance in Africa, but I shift the focus from performances framed as separate events (for example, on a stage) to performances in everyday life. This shift is important because it demonstrates how seemingly mundane interpersonal relations at the micro level can have much larger consequences.

I also take a chronological approach to show the importance of daily performances in shaping the social and political lives of the BisiKongo, and the connections between these performances and larger social changes. Other studies have fruitfully used nontraditional sources such as language, objects, or foods to analyze historical transformations (Appadurai 1988; Fields-Black 2008; Mintz 1986). My focus on everyday performances from the early twentieth century to 2010 illuminates the agency of Kongo people in engaging with and redefining themselves in relation to transformative events such as European colonialism and the expansion of Christianity, postcolonial dictatorships, and present-day social and political marginalization.

In analyzing these periods of social change, I am not attempting to write a complete and exhaustive history. Rather, I place the body at the center of my analysis and focus on specific and significant "performative encounters" that best illustrate how everyday cultural performances are affected by and have an impact on larger social transformations. Before going any further, let me clearly define how I am using several terms while also situating my work within existing scholarship.

Over the last few decades, there has been a resurgence of interest in the body in anthropology and the social sciences and humanities more generally (Csordas 1999; Farnell 1999; Lock 1993; Strathern 1996; Van Wolputte 2004). Embodiment is one concept that has received increased attention. Following anthropologist Thomas Csordas, I understand *embodiment* as "our corporeality or bodiliness in relation to the world and other people" (2011, 137). Csordas also privileges embodied experiences as the basic starting point for understanding human culture and life (1993, 135). Embodiment encompasses perception and engagement; feeling with, being in, and using one's body. I shift the focus in studies of embodiment from affective states and feelings to how bodies are actually used in everyday life. A number of terms could be used to describe how people use their bodies. While *movement* captures the act of moving all or a part of the body,[8] this term is so general that it groups involuntary twitches along with choreographed dances. A term that better captures the phenomenon of interest in this book is *performance*.

Performance is an "essentially contested concept" that has been used in the humanities and social sciences to describe and analyze a wide variety of human activity.[9] Theories of performance have emerged from anthropology, linguistics, oral interpretation, theater, folklore, and sociology, among other disciplines, all eventually shaping the field of performance studies. While many related definitions of performance exist, performance as a general concept has proven useful for capturing the ongoing processes of social life. I combine several approaches to define *performance* as restored behavior enacted with a heightened awareness, consciousness, and/or intention, with the capacity to transform social realities. I will examine each of the components of this definition in turn.

Restored behavior conveys the idea that what we do with our bodies is never for the first time, as these movements are "twice behaved behavior" based on past actions and observations, learned both consciously and unconsciously in our social environments (Schechner 1985, 35–41). For example, the vigorous trembling that came to define the prophetic movements of the colonial era in the Lower Congo region had its origins in the embodiment of traditional priest-healer-ritual specialists (*banganga*) in and near the Kongo Kingdom before the arrival of Europeans. Trembling of the body that signified the presence of territorial or other spirits in the precolonial era was embodied in a similar manner yet redefined as an index of the Holy Spirit in the Kongo Christian prophetic movements in colonial-era Belgian Congo.

Another component of performance is heightened awareness, which demonstrates that performance is reflexive and involves manipulation of behavior, based on the awareness of being observed (Bauman 1989, 266). As Marvin Carlson states, "performance is always performance for someone, some audience that recognizes and validates it as performance even when . . . that audience is the self" (1996, 6).

Consciousness and/or intention is another part of my understanding of performance. Performance is always conscious and can be but is not always explicitly self-conscious. The definition of consciousness I am using here draws on the work of philosopher John Searle, who sees consciousness as a biological feature of humans and certain animals consisting of inner, subjective (what-it-feels-like) qualitative states that are first-person experiences. These conscious states, among other characteristics, always have a content, vary in degrees (have a center and periphery), and are mostly intentional (1992). Here, intention is not just about intending to do something, which is one among many forms of intention. Rather, intentionality is about directedness or aboutness, so belief, hope, fear, and desire are also forms of intentionality (Searle 1983, 1–3). Thus, performance is intentional in the sense it is directed toward and in engagement with someone or something. Searle also describes consciousness as having a center and a periphery, so a person's attention can be focused on one thing or task, yet the person still remains simultaneously aware of other sensations, feelings, and stimuli. Thus, many states that other scholars might call unconscious Searle locates at the periphery of everyday consciousness. With his approach, unconscious mental states are always potentially conscious (1992). Intentional conscious states function within what Searle calls the "background,"[10] a set of capacities (assumptions, expectations, know-how, ways of doing things) that are not themselves intentional (175–79). Searle's approach to consciousness, especially as being centered in physical bodies, is echoed by his predecessor, Maurice Merleau-Ponty, who defined consciousness as "being-towards-the-thing through the intermediary of the body" ([1962] 1981, 138). Thus, the body is the means of acting on, understanding, and engaging with the world.

Embracing a broader definition of both consciousness and intention (Searle 1992) allows us to better understand how Kongo conceptions of the body challenge Western ideas of body, mind, and intentionality. Who is actually moving or affecting the body? Studies of Kongo cosmology and conceptions of the self, along with my own research experiences, support the idea that many (although not all) Kongo people think of humans as consisting of three (or more) parts (Jacobson-Widding 1979, 307–24; Laman 1962).[11] In one conversation during my field research, the parts were described as *nsuni* or *nitu* (body), *mpeve* (spirit), and *moyo* (soul) (Ne Nkamu Luyindula, September 23, 2005). Mpeve is the metaphysical dimension and also means "wind" or "breath" and is present throughout the body (Laman 1962, 1). The Holy Spirit is a powerful, greater mpeve that comes to inhabit the body. As Tata Kizole explains, "it is the spirit that animates the person so that they enter into trance" (July 20, 2010). Here, Kongo conceptions of spirit possession suggest a copresence such that otherworldly spirits (whether nature spirits or the Holy Spirit, among others) move the body with varying degrees of awareness by the person who is possessed (Janzen and MacGaffey 1974, 144–45; W. MacGaffey 1983, 70–71). To further complicate matters, Kongo conceptions of witchcraft (*kindoki*) allow for people to use the nonphysical parts of their selves to harm others in a social unit with either *conscious or unconscious* jealousy; willful intention is not needed (W. MacGaffey 1986b, 161). All of this suggests that Kongo conceptions of the self and spirit possession engender a more expansive understanding of intentionality and consciousness that goes beyond Western approaches and views spirits and spirit selves as actors using and affecting physical bodies in everyday life.

My study presents a varied array of concrete examples of these aspects of performance, all of which exhibit heightened awareness and different degrees of consciousness. Reflecting the explicit self-consciousness of performance, rural Kongo women forced to dance in local animation troupes in the 1970s during President Mobutu Sese Seko's regime consciously manipulated their movements under the watching eyes of visiting government and provincial officials. However, the trembling of many Kongo prophets and their followers is also an example of conscious performance because while the Holy Spirit is causing the physical trembling, people are often aware of their subjective feelings and sensations when the Holy Spirit possesses them.

The last major characteristic of performance, as I define it, is its potential to transform social realities. In general, when people think of performance, especially staged performances, they see them as representing or reflecting reality. "From Plato and Aristotle forward, theorists have agreed that theatre 'imitates,' 'reflects,' 'represents,' or 'expresses' individual actions and social life. As Hamlet told the Players, the purpose of theatre is 'to hold the mirror up to nature.' Representational art of all kinds is based on the assumption that 'art' and 'life' are not only separate but of different orders of reality: life is primary, art secondary" (Schechner 2013, 131).

However, many scholars of performance now recognize that performances can also transform reality as well. Victor Turner, the most influential pioneer of studies of performance in anthropology, described the possible power of cultural performance in the following way: "cultural performances are not simple reflectors or expressions of culture or even of changing culture but may themselves be active agencies of change" (1987, 24). Edward Schieffelin best elaborates on this idea when he writes, "performance deals with actions more than text: with habits of the body more than structures of symbols, with illocutionary rather than propositional force, with the social construction of reality rather than its representation. . . . Performances, whether ritual or dramatic . . . alter moods, social relations, bodily dispositions, and states of mind" (1997, 199). The vignette about Bundu dia Kongo and its emphasis on using specific greetings to recreate the former Kongo Kingdom in the present is an illustrative example of the transformative capacity of performance. Their efforts created an influential movement that led to their spiritual leader being elected to the country's national assembly both in 2006 and 2011. Overall, the transformative potential of performance is the most important defining characteristic for this study.

Additionally, to more fully capture its transformative potential, my understanding of performance incorporates everyday interactions as well as performances that are more clearly bounded or set apart from everyday life (that is, on a stage).[12] In this, sociologist Erving Goffman's studies of performances in everyday social interactions have influenced my approach.[13] Goffman studied performances in everyday encounters, which are largely enacted according to a "working consensus" (1959, 10). In this regard, Goffman's work largely avoids looking at interpersonal encounters as sites of social conflict, as people for the most part stay within their roles, adhering to well-defined scripts (Denzin 2002, 107). I build on Goffman's ideas but refocus attention on the less often studied moments when everyday interactions veer from their norm, creating ruptures and challenges in struggles for power and authority placing the body at the center.

I am looking at specific types of performances I am calling *everyday cultural performances*, which I sometimes also call *embodied performances*. These interchangeable terms are both ways of defining specific bodily movements enacted with a heightened awareness while drawing on culturally and historically grounded restored behavior. These particular performances are very specific units of analysis because they have cultural relevance and significance for Kongo people over time. What I mean is, these cultural performances are embodied ways of being-in and engaging-with the world that people in this region of Central Africa have been enacting for centuries. They are part of a corpus of body techniques, "ways in which from society to society people use their bodies" (Mauss [1934] 1979, 97). French sociologist Marcel Mauss's study of "body techniques" was one of the first to outline how cultural norms of movement that differ from society to society are unconsciously learned. He discusses differences in digging, marching, walking, and other actions of various societies, concluding that each society has its own personal habits, which have ancient histories and are transmitted from adults to children through the process of enculturation. Csordas's concept of "somatic modes of attention" expresses a similar idea.[14] The cupped hand clapping, bula makonko, which I mention earlier in this chapter, is one such example of an everyday cultural performance. It has its origins in the everyday greeting and court ritual practices of the precolonial Kongo Kingdom and continues to be used in modern-day Lower Congo but was redefined as a form of spiritual expression and a symbol of group identity in the context of the Bundu dia Kongo movement. Thus, my focus is not on all possible performances of the body, but on specific ones rooted in the culture and history of the Lower Congo region.

But the body is not just a means of learning or expressing social norms or conventions; it is also a means of doing, creating, and transforming the world around oneself. This is reflected in Mauss's assessment that "the body is man's first and most natural instrument" ([1934] 1979, 104). In my research, I start with the premise that control of the body is *always already* a site of struggle in social conflict and political negotiations. Performances, like many other forms of embodied movement, can thus prove a critical site of inquiry for examination of struggles for power and authority in multiple settings. Moreover, performances can also play a key role in the constitution of self and larger group identities. A number of theorists have used linguist J. L. Austin's (1962) concept of performative utterances (where saying something is actually doing something) to describe situations where performances are in fact performative—where performing something brings it into being. Gender theorist Judith Butler applies Austin's idea to argue that gender is constituted through daily, repetitive, performative acts, so one is not born a woman but becomes a woman through many performances (2004, 154). Building on Butler's ideas, anthropologist Paulla Ebron discusses gender as both consciously and unconsciously performed in West African contexts, constituting subjects but also providing a means of understanding other social distinctions such as age and lineage (2007). Anthropologist John L. Jackson Jr. argues for understanding race as performative, even within Black communities where "whiteness" and "blackness" are enacted as behaviors in everyday life (2001, 188–89). Performance studies scholar E. Patrick Johnson echoes the importance of racial performativity but also urges a focus on the real, everyday consequences of race and the dialogic relationship between race and performance in the construction of identity (2003, 9). In his many studies of performances in everyday life, Erving Goffman defined the basic unit of study as the encounter, which he defined as "the natural unit of social interaction in which focused interaction occurs" (1961, 8).

By combining Austin's and Butler's concepts of performatives with Goffman's concept of encounters, I coined the term *performative encounters* to describe situations when the body is used strategically in everyday life to transform interpersonal social relationships in meaningful ways, impacting the social and political positions of the people interacting.[15] For performative encounters then, *doing something is doing something more.* In Goffman's studies of social encounters, most encounters reinforce the existing status quo. On the contrary, performative encounters are transformative—they change the existing social relationship in a manner that did not exist before, such as when handshakes are rejected and greetings are vigorously negotiated; when spirit-induced bodily trembling interrupts the proceedings of a court trial; when a walk down the street is suddenly interrupted by the expectation that you clap when the presidential motorcade passes. These examples and others that I explore demonstrate that some social interactions have much larger consequences than others, illuminating the multiple ways that everyday cultural performances are engaged in the active construction of social life.

Four main points frame this book: First, I advocate placing the physical, moving body at the center of analysis—an approach I call the *body as center*. The human body is our first and most important means of engaging with and impacting the world around us. Critical insights can be gained if we pay attention to what people do with and through their bodies in their everyday lives.

Second, the human body is an important site for affecting group and individual subjectivities and identities, and everyday performances such as gestures and other movements of the body can be used to strategically engender social action—either to unify groups of people in concerted action, or even to foster dissent. This is what I call the *body as conduit*. While *subjectivity* and *identity* are terms often used interchangeably, subjectivity refers more so to inner states, emotions, feelings, and thoughts, while identity is based not only on how you see yourself but also on how others see you. My interest centers on how individual and subjective embodied performances become shared by members of a group and then become the foundation for a shared group identity. So, for example, while spirit possession by the Holy Spirit during the colonial-era prophetic movements was an individual experience, it was also an experience that many people shared in common, even in the same space and time as shown by Léon Morel's account of his first encounter with Simon Kimbangu. Moreover, the colonial state similarly persecuted people possessed by the Holy Spirit, who shared experiences of harassment, imprisonment, violence, and exile—all of which impacted their growing nationalist sentiment. However, it is also because of the potential transformative power of moving bodies that they are specifically targeted to both create and maintain the status quo (Bourdieu 1977; Mitchell 1988). By this I mean that the process doesn't move just from individual subjectivity to group identity, but also from a larger group identity down to individual embodiment. This is best shown with the example of *political animation* in postcolonial Zaire, based on a forced, shared, and embodied group experience that was to impact the individual subjectivity of each participant. Indeed, in both instances the body acts as a conduit and plays a critical role in subjectivity and identity on both individual and group levels.

Third, performance, as the "social construction of reality rather than its representation" (Schieffelin 1997, 199), what I call *body as catalyst*, is a process that takes place not only in set-apart events onstage, but also in bodily encounters in everyday interactions. These encounters could be with other people or even spiritual entities. Thus, even spirit possession can then be seen as an everyday cultural performance rather than a special event occurring only in ritual spaces. Such an assertion is supported by the work of scholars such as Adeline Masquelier (2001) in her study of Mawri spirit possession in Niger.

Fourth, as one particular dimension of the social construction of reality through performance, authority is both made and unmade through these everyday performances. *Authority* is a term that evades any set, agreed-on definition.[16] For the purposes of this project, I define *authority* as the ability to influence or determine the conduct of others within a hierarchy of statuses in a group, in which that authority may be more or less legitimate, and the members of the group may or may not recognize the rights of this authority to exercise power. The recognition and reception of others in everyday interactions (following Erving Goffman) are necessary for relations of authority to function but also present a site for resistance and challenge. The spiritual realm often provides access to an alternative form of authority through which people can upset the prevailing social order through effective use of their bodies.

While focusing on the BisiKongo, *Gesture and Power* has larger implications for humankind in general. It provides a theoretical framework for understanding how the micropolitics of the body in interpersonal encounters can affect macro-level social and political structures. Such a framework can even be applied to our own society, with examples such as the considerable criticism that followed President Obama's bow to the king of Saudi Arabia in 2009, or the larger impacts of oppressed Black southerners refusing to step off of the sidewalk for White pedestrians in the 1960s (Berrey 2006; Wesley 2009). This study has broader relevance than just for the United States, but for people in societies across the world as it explores both politicized embodiment and how people use religion to both challenge and create social structures. My work also provides a method for examining the interplay of embodiment, spirituality, and power. An analytical approach that examines performative encounters can be applied to examples ranging from the display of spirit possession by Malay women on the shop floors of Japanese factories (Ong 1987) to baptism and healing as political acts in the Watchtower movement of colonial-era Malawi (Fields 1985). Overall, the body can be a powerful and effective tool for social and political transformation, especially when buttressed by spiritual claims. Bodies, however, are also vulnerable—to dismemberment, disappearances, arrests, floggings, and other forms of physical violence, and even death. My point here is to show that, regardless of the risks, bodies are often used as tools for social change.

Bodies, Performance, and Embodied Histories

November 2005. After an extended stay in the town of Luozi, I came back to Kinshasa briefly before heading back to the United States for a week for Thanksgiving. However, Luozi remained with me, not only in the red dirt hiding in the creases of my suitcases and in the soles of my sneakers, or the *madeso* (beans) that I brought back to my host family to cook and eat, but also in the genuflection of my knees that happened almost involuntarily when I greeted someone, or the bula makonko that accompanied the greeting, along with a slight bow of the head and the feedback sound that came from my throat to indicate that I was actively listening. My host family and neighborhood friends in Gombe, a high-end residential neighborhood in Kinshasa, remarked that I had become a girl of Luozi in my mannerisms, moving in a way they considered *très poli* like Ma Josephine, the MuKongo domestic worker who prepared daily meals and cleaned the home of my host family.[17] When I later returned to the United States, I had to retrain my body as I often unwittingly found myself continuing to exhibit these same embodied practices, ways of moving that had not been a part of my body before my time in Luozi.

I open this section with this story to demonstrate the importance of bodily movement for carrying cultural ideals and histories and acting as a type of performance in everyday life. The genuflections and hand clapping that I first imitated and then unreflexively embodied reflect a long history of hierarchal societies in the Lower Congo, going back to the precolonial Kongo Kingdom and also encompass the embodiment of gender and age. Both consciously and unconsciously, the body plays a huge role in capturing beliefs, values, categories, and histories that have deep meaning for members of a cultural community. Although most historical studies continue to privilege written texts, many scholars now recognize that history also exists in the body through embodied practices (Shaw 2002; Stoller 1995). Scholars have been interested in not only the body as a way of knowing, but also the body as a way of remembering. How are memories and histories embodied and passed on to others?

In *Outline of a Theory of Practice* (1977), French sociologist Pierre Bourdieu addresses memory through embodied practice, where practice can be understood as anything people do. He defines habitus as a set of generating principles that produce practice based on the structures within itself, which were passed on from previous generations (72). Moreover, these generating principles, based on both past action and the objective conditions of the present, guide practice. Bourdieu connects the habitus to the body with his concept of the body hexis, one of the many ways that the habitus is passed on and reproduced, most often by children imitating the actions of adults. "Body hexis speaks directly to the motor function, in the form of a pattern of postures that is both individual and systematic, because linked to a whole system of techniques . . . and charged with a host of social meaning and values" (87). In his discussion of habitus and body hexis, Bourdieu points out that embodied practice is a form of mnemonics as well, invoking social and cultural values. Bourdieu demonstrates this point in his discussion of male and female embodiment in Kabyle society in Algeria: "Body hexis is political mythology realized, em-bodied, turned into a permanent disposition, a durable manner of standing speaking, and thereby of feeling and thinking. . . . The manly man stands up straight and honours the person he approaches or wishes to welcome by looking him right in the eyes. . . . Conversely, a woman is expected to walk with a slight stoop, looking down, keeping her eyes on the spot where she will next put her foot. . . . In short, the specifically feminine virtue, lahia, modesty, restraint, reserve, orients the whole female body downwards, towards the ground, the inside, the house, whereas male excellence, nif, is asserted in movement upwards, outwards, towards other men" (94).

Bourdieu emphasizes the importance placed on these values being embodied, because in this Kabyle example, the very principle of feminine virtue seen as appropriate for women is most aptly demonstrated by the way in which a woman uses, orients, and moves her body. In this way, the gendered values of Kabyle society are actually embodied by women and men in everyday posture, movement, and life. The significance of values embodied in such a way explains why embodied practices are targeted when people, organizations, and institutions seek to transform the values, belief systems, and behavior of groups of people and individuals alike. This becomes especially clear in situations where institutions (for example, prisons, churches, governments, and moral reform associations) want to "produce" new subjects. The prime example within my own study is political animation, forced nationalistic singing, and dancing under President Mobutu. The body is targeted precisely because "treating the body as a memory, [institutions] entrust to it in abbreviated and practical, that is, mnemonic, form the fundamental principles of the arbitrary content of the culture. The principles em-bodied in this way are placed beyond the grasp of consciousness" (1977, 94). Thus, correctives and etiquette reinforce social values and become forms of "an implicit pedagogy, capable of instilling a whole cosmology, an ethic, a metaphysic, a political philosophy, through injunctions as insignificant as 'stand up straight' or 'don't hold your knife in your left hand'" (94).

According to Bourdieu, for all societies, emphasis is placed on embodying its core values because of the subtle persuasiveness of ideologies that become so embedded in one's body that they seem natural. As a result, "every group entrusts to bodily automatisms those principles most basic to it and most indispensable to its conservation" (1977, 218n44). This becomes even more important for societies without an extensive history of writing or inscribing. While Bourdieu's work on the habitus and body hexis is highly influential, some criticisms and lingering questions remain. First, the habitus that structures practice seems so restrictive that individual agency and creativity seem to disappear. What is the role of human agency in the habitus? Second, what happens to the habitus in periods of massive social transformation and in the context of encounters between different groups? Third, if the habitus is outside the realm of consciousness (or, in Searle's terms, at the periphery of consciousness), how can it be intentionally targeted for change? It is in these areas of inquiry that Bourdieu's theory can be expanded on and improved.

Along with Bourdieu's writing, Paul Connerton's seminal work *How Societies Remember* (1989) has also been very influential on studies of the body across disciplines. Connerton outlines personal, cognitive, and habit memory as the three classes of memory (21) but emphasizes the role of the body in habit memory especially: "In habitual memory the past is, as it were, sedimented in the body" (72). To further distinguish how the body works in the service of memory and history, Connerton differentiates two types of social practice: incorporating practices—intentional or unintentional bodily activity done in the presence of others—from inscribing practices—devices or media used for storing and retrieving information (for example, newspapers, computers, photos) (72–73). Incorporating practices are transmitted through the body, and habitual behavior reminds us that "all habits are affective dispositions; that a predisposition formed through the frequent repetition of a number of specific acts is an intimate and fundamental part of ourselves" (1989, 94). Thus, through the repetition of certain acts laden with cultural significance, these acts become a part of one's daily routine and the values and meanings associated with these acts unconsciously become a part of one's cultural ethos. "Incorporating practices therefore provide a particularly effective system of mnemonics" (102), meaning that bodily practices can activate and create cultural memories. Connerton thus supports Bourdieu's own assertions about embodied memory and also categorizes different approaches to passing on and storing memory and history.

In her influential work *The Archive and the Repertoire* (2003), performance studies scholar Diana Taylor makes an argument that is very similar to Connerton's in regard to the modes of transmission and storage of communal memories. "Archival memory," she writes, "exists in documents, maps, literary texts, letters, archaeological remains, bones, videos, films, CDs, all those items supposedly resistant to change. . . . Archival memory works across distance, over time and space." On the other hand, the repertoire "enacts embodied memory: performances, gestures, orality, movement, dance, singing—in short, all those acts usually thought of as ephemeral, nonreproducible knowledge. . . . The repertoire requires presence" (19–20). Taylor's archive is very similar to Connerton's idea of inscribing practices, while the repertoire seems to have much in common with incorporating practices. However, she takes theories of memory even further with her idea of the scenario, which is a recurring plot, storyline, or framework derived from either the archive and/ or the repertoire. Taylor uses the scenario to highlight how social knowledge is both constituted and transmitted (the scenario of European "discovery" of indigenous Americans for example). By analyzing many examples of scenarios in the Americas in multiple genres, from performance art to graffiti, and how scenarios are both reinforced and challenged, Taylor provides a fruitful starting point for the examination of embodied memory in the context of performances.

Thus, Bourdieu, Connerton, and Taylor have all made the case that embodied practices are immensely critical to transmitting and activating social values, ideals, and cultural history. Indeed, many scholars working within Africa have either applied their ideas or made similar claims in studies ranging from Anlo-Ewe conceptions of bodily senses in Ghana (Geurts 2002) to bodily comportment in Sierra Leone (M. Jackson 1989) to masked and danced histories in Nigeria (McCall 2000). Attention to embodiment offers another perspective on collective memory, with larger implications for how the history of Africa is written (Jewsiewicki and Mudimbe 1993). My own research in the Congo also supports the importance of embodied performances in everyday life in the Lower Congo. The ways of moving that I learned through my interactions with others are similar to the embodied performances children in the Lower Congo learn in their everyday lives. Along with explicit correctives and directions, children unconsciously imitate the behaviors of adults in their households, schools, markets, community gatherings, and churches. *Gesture and Power* builds on the existing literature by also advocating for the importance of embodied performances in understanding Kongo culture and history. However, I push the research even further by looking not just at what the body represents, but at what the body does, by examining performances in everyday life rather than only in "set-apart" events, and by showing how the meanings and uses of these embodied performances have changed over time, while simultaneously scrutinizing the larger social and political contexts in which they are embedded and engaged. My approach privileges African agency, showing that whether the subject is a rural, illiterate farmer who self-identifies as a prophet in the face of European missionaries or a postindependence violent dictator seeking to quell dissent, everyday cultural performances are key to their engaging with and transforming the world around them. Thus, while the body is indeed a means of passing on memory and history, it is also a means of *challenging, creating, and redefining* memory and history.

With my work, I am also trying to challenge notions that a focus on performance is very limited in what it can tell us about a society, and that performances themselves have an insignificant impact on the world around us. Some past critiques of both studies of performance and microsociological studies caution that focusing on individual performances (both as bounded events and as interactions in everyday life) can lead to a lack of historical context and minimal attention to the relationship between performances/interactions and larger social structures (Bronner 1988; see also list of critiques in Adler and Adler 1987).[18] For example, in his work on performances in daily life, Goffman does not analyze the potential impact of these everyday performances on larger social structures or organization; in fact he argues for seeing the interaction order (the domain of activity of face-to-face interaction) as a completely separate sphere of activity (1983, 2). Further, Goffman believes that in the vast majority of cases, the interaction order is not "somehow prior, fundamental, or constitutive of the shape of macroscopic phenomena" (9). I seek to challenge this assertion by showing that such a perspective decontexualizes performances from larger social and political moorings—rather, the micro and the macro mutually influence each other. In her review article "The State of Research on Performance in Africa," Margaret Thompson Drewal advocates analyzing performance as part of temporal processes to address some of these shortcomings. She writes, "Adopting a temporal perspective means following repeated performances of the same kind by the same people and between different groups of people. It means focusing on individuals in specific performances as they *use* structure and process and then locating that performance within a larger body of performances and in history, society, and politics" (1991, 37). I take up Drewal's challenge by exploring the interaction between everyday performances and larger social structures, while also charting the historical development of transformations in the uses and meanings of several Kongo everyday cultural performances in struggles for power and authority.

Everyday Cultural Performances in Kongo Culture and History

Everyday cultural performances acts as an umbrella term to encapsulate the three major types of bodily action that I examine: gestures (bimpampa), dances (makinu), and spirit-induced trembling (zakama) (see table 1.1). Robert Farris Thompson is the preeminent trailblazer in studying Kongo bimpampa and makinu and has inspired my own work in many ways.[19] His approach, however, is largely from an art history perspective, usually in relation to static material objects, paintings, and aesthetic concepts, although his studies *African Art in Motion* (1974), *Le Geste Kongo* (2002), and *Tango: The Art History of Love* (2005) are notable exceptions that also incorporate bodily movement and dance. I build on and expand his research by looking at cultural performances in motion and sociopolitical context. In focusing on the performances themselves and how their meanings, uses, and relationship to authority change over time, I hope to provide a socially and historically situated analysis of Kongo performance practice in the Lower Congo. Next, I briefly explore each of these everyday cultural performances in turn.

First, bimpampa are largely understood as gestures.[20] Gesture, as a concept, has been described in a number of ways, with a more common definition being "any kind of bodily movement . . . which transmits a message to the observer" (Thomas 1992, 1). For my own work, I embrace Carrie Noland's definition of gesture as "the organized forms of kinesis through which subjects navigate and alter their worlds" (2009, 4). Her definition is broad enough to embrace gestures both as habit and as intentional strategy, recognizing the importance of culture and social influence on bodily movement while at the same time illuminating human agency and choice. As such, gestures can be voluntary or involuntary, express feelings or ideas, accompany speech, or have aesthetic or instrumentalist aims. The topic of "gesture" has seen a recent resurgence of interest by scholars in a variety of fields, from history to linguistics to cultural and dance studies (Braddick 2009; de Jorio 2000; Noland and Ness 2008).[21] Notable among this emerging literature is Carrie Noland's monograph *Agency and Embodiment* (2009), a groundbreaking theoretical

TABLE I.1 Comparison of Characteristics of Kongo Everyday
Cultural Performances

Type of Performance	Voluntary or Involuntary	Set apart from or existing within daily life	Secular or Sacred	Public or Private
Bimpampa (gestures)	Both voluntary and involuntary	Within daily life	Both secular and sacred	Usually public
Makinu (dances)	Usually voluntary	Usually set apart from daily life	Both secular and sacred	Usually public
Zakama (spirit-induced trembling)	Usually involuntary	Both set apart from and existing within daily life	Sacred	Both public and private

treatise examining how bodily sensations created through gestures are constitutive of the individual subject. Noland views gestures as performative in the sense that they help individuals to come into existence. I take a complementary approach in this book by focusing on gestures in the context of social interaction and struggles for power. I am interested in how gestures are used both for the creation of and as the result of group identities, and how they are used to transform social realities. In exploring the real-life consequences of the intersubjective uses and meanings of gesture in everyday life, I am building on anthropologist Thomas Csordas's approach to intercorporeality (2008). Gail Weiss (1999) captures the importance of intercorporeality in interaction when she writes, "the experience of being embodied is never a private affair, but is always already mediated by our continual interactions with other human and nonhuman bodies" (5). Moreover, because my work also examines spirit possession, I add an additional layer of complexity to the study of gesture. Thus, while individual subjectivity is important, gestures in interactional contexts and in the constitution of group identities are the focus of my own intellectual endeavor.

While a few scholars such as anthropologist Adam Kendon (1997, 2004) have vigorously explored the study of gesture, gesture in anthropology remains marginalized and continues to focus mainly on sign language (Farnell 1995) or the relationship of gesture to verbal expressions and language (Haviland 1998, 1999; Kendon 2004; McNeil 2000). Thus, the study of gesture in anthropology that has not received much attention, similar to the study of dance, which, although less marginalized than gesture, remains on the fringes of anthropological inquiry (Reed 1998, 504). I believe this is the case because, like many other disciplines that have grown out of Western thought, anthropology remains haunted by the Descartian dualism that privileges the mind over the body and often posits the body as the site of irrationality and emotion. In the Kongo cultural context, bimpampa are always understood in the context of communicating something to someone. Art historians have been the most engaged in studying Kongo gestures, including Robert Farris Thompson and Barbaro Martinez-Ruiz (2013). Martinez-Ruiz, in his groundbreaking study of Kongo body language and graphic writing, presents physical evidence from cave paintings that support his assertion that the gestural history of this region of Central Africa goes back for several thousand years (2009). With such a history, gesture is a critical everyday form of communication and interaction for BisiKongo people. "Far more than aesthetic additions to verbal communication," Martinez-Ruiz writes, "gestures among the BaKongo are a form of language and a mode of communication in their own right" (2009). Thus, bimpampa are a crucial part of being-in-the-world for the BisiKongo. Moreover, *bimpampa* as a term doesn't usually stand alone, as the part of the body being used is often indicated (Professor Mbala Nkanga, July 19, 2007). Thus, *bimpampa bia moko* would be gestures of the hands, for instance.

The second everyday cultural performance that I examine is makinu—dances. Makinu comes from the Kikongo verb *kina*, to dance, although music and singing accompanies these dances. Like bimpampa, the term *makinu* is usually used with another term describing the context. Thus, renowned MuKongo scholar Fu-Kiau kia Bunseki describes elders talking about the dances of the Kongo Kingdom in the following way: "They mentioned *makinu ma bakulu* (dances for the ancestors), *makinu ma mfumu* (dances for the king), the related *makinu ma nsi* (dances of the nobility),[22] *makinu ma nkisi* (dances in honor of healing spirits) and *makinu ma soonga* (ecstatic dances, climaxed by the descent of the spirit, from the realm of the ancestors)" (quoted in Thompson 2005, 63). Another type of makinu not mentioned here, but very important in Kongo cultural performance, is *makinu ma luketo* (dances of the hips), which interviewees often called *kisi nsi* (of the land, tradition). This book explores various contexts where dances are politicized in the Lower Congo, from when makinu became a site of contention during the prophetic movements of the colonial period, to how they are again redefined as part and parcel of the nationalist project under Mobutu.

Last, spirit-induced trembling (zakama) is another cultural performance with deep salience in Kongo history, dating back to the precolonial era. The vigorous trembling that would overtake the bodies of different banganga was a sign of territorial or other spirits entering their bodies (Cuvelier 1953b, 135;

Dapper 1686, 336–37). Knowledge of these historical embodied practices led some Western missionaries to quickly categorize Kimbangu's trembling in 1921, in the context of a Christian movement, as "pagan" (Andersson 1958). However, this spirit-induced trembling provided Kongo people with an alternate source of authority from the spiritual realm that enabled political challenges to Belgian colonial hegemony while also shaping a nascent Kongo nationalism. This study aims to demonstrate the usefulness of a focus on everyday cultural performances to the disciplines of anthropology, Africana studies, religious studies, and the field of performance studies, and the unique perspective that such an approach provides to studies of society and history.

Nationalism, Performativity, and Power on and off the Stage

March 17, 2006. After dressing and eating a quick breakfast, I announce my departure to my host mother and close the blue security gate behind me. I step carefully as I walk along the uneven road until I arrive at a busy intersection. I join a small group of people already standing there and begin to move my right hand in a sideways waving motion, indicating to the passing improvised taxis (which are no more than people's personal cars being used for business purposes) that I want to go down Kinshasa's main road, Boulevard du 30 Juin. Kinshasa, Congo's capital city, is a bustling metropolis of an estimated eight million people. However, one of the major infrastructural problems of such a rapidly expanding city, one still recovering from civil war and neglect, is the lack of public transportation. When a taxi slows, I run quickly to grab the door handle so I am one of the first inside the vehicle. Regardless, I end up squished in the backseat with three other people. When I finally arrive at my stop, I pay the driver, cross the boulevard, and walk two blocks to enter the security screening area of the building that houses the American Cultural Center. After running a number of errands over the course of the day, I end up in the information resource library. I am sitting at one of the computers, checking e-mail and generally surfing the Internet. Suddenly, I begin to hear very loud singing outside of the building. When it continues, I become curious and try unsuccessfully to peer through the window. Not able to see much, I leave my spot since the room is basically empty, exiting the library, passing through one set of doors and entering another into the security screening area. One door is held open as several people look outside at the activities across the street. I join the group of curious onlookers. Taking a quick estimated count, I see a group of about 160 people in front of the building of the independent electoral commission. I ask one of the security officers at the door about the event, and he explains that Antoine Gizenga,[23] an eighty-year-old politician, is coming to the building to submit his nomination as a presidential candidate. All the people are singing, and some of them are dancing as well. Many are waving either a cloth or a small branch back and forth in the air, and most of them are dressed in similar party cloth displaying the face of their candidate. As I continue to watch, and even after I eventually collect my belongings and leave the building for another appointment, the crowd of supporters shout slogans and sing song after song together, performing their loyalty and support for their presidential candidate. Although I had only seen examples of it on videos, read about it, and heard about it from people I had interviewed, it seemed political animation, which dated to President Mobutu's era, had resurfaced in the multiparty state.

During President Joseph-Desiré Mobutu Sese Seko's thirty-two-year regime in the Congo (1965–97), he instituted a policy that forced citizens to dance and sing in demonstration of their allegiance to a coercive state. At political rallies and parades, but also in school classrooms and in places of business, movement and song brought people of different religions, ages, and ethnic backgrounds together under the flag of the renamed nation of Zaire. Political animation was clearly an example of state power being imposed through performance. But how can we understand the relationship between power, performance, and individual bodies? Subsequently, what role, then, does civil religion play in the relationship between citizens' performing bodies and political states?

Following Michel Foucault, I see power as something not held, but rather exercised, acting on the actions of others (2000, 340). I differ, however, in how I conceptualize the relationship between power, society, and individual bodies. Foucault recognizes the importance of the body for power relations and the constitution of subjects. He writes, "Let us ask, instead, how things work . . . at the level of those continuous and uninterrupted processes which subject our bodies, govern our gestures, dictate our behaviors, etc. In other words . . . we should try to discover how it is that subjects are gradually, progressively, really and materially constituted through a multiplicity of organisms, forces, energies, materials, desires, thoughts, etc." (1980, 97). Here, then, Foucault presents individual subjects as shaped by larger social forces and relations of power to such an extent that even the "material," the biological, is socially constructed. He reinforces this when he writes, "The body is molded by a great many distinct regimes; it is broken down by the rhythms of work, rest, and holidays; it is poisoned by food or values, through habits or moral laws. . . . Nothing in man—*not even his body*—is sufficiently stable to serve as the basis for self-recognition or for understanding other men" (1984, 87–88, emphasis mine).

However, both Foucault's and Bourdieu's approaches (as previously discussed), place so much emphasis on the constitutive constraints of society—on people acting according to previously established rules, customs, and generative principles—that there is little room for human creativity, especially by and through physical bodies. Indeed, as Brenda Farnell notes, for such social theorists, the body "usually remains a static, more or less passive cultural object of disciplines and representations, separate from the mind" (1999, 348), or in other words, "a mindless, unconscious repository and mechanistic operator of practical techniques" (2000, 409). Farnell advocates understanding the body as a locus of embodied and intentional human action, where human agents produce meaning through actions both "out of awareness through habit or skill or [through] highly deliberate choreographies" (1999, 348). Performance, once again, is the most useful concept for capturing the idea of this intentional embodied action. As Johannes Fabian notes, "performance . . . certainly is action, but not merely enactment of a pre-existing script; it is making, fashioning, creating" (1990, 13). In short, while power is exercised and clearly impacts how we use our bodies in the world, people are not robots following commands. In our everyday performances, we can take preexisting behavior and shape it to meet our needs in that moment; ways of moving and their associated cultural values can also be resignified.

Performances as explicitly intentional acts can be strategically used to try to shape group belonging and affiliation in particular ways and have been useful in shaping sentiments of nationalism especially. I follow Anthony Smith's definition of *nationalism* as "an ideological movement for the attainment and maintenance of autonomy, unity, and identity on behalf of a population some of whose members deem it to constitute an actual or potential 'nation.' (In this sense, one can, and does have nationalism without nations, just as more rarely we can speak about nations without nationalism)" (2006, 175). There is now a burgeoning literature on the relationship between performance and nationalism, and struggles for power between and among citizens and states. Kelly Askew's ethnography *Performing the Nation* (2002) focuses on the role of performance in actually constructing the heterogeneous nation of Tanzania. Using J. L. Austin's (1962) concept of performative statements, Askew successfully shows that the production of a "nation" and national imaginaries through performance is crucial in Tanzania, especially since the nation is composed of two formerly separate countries with different identities (2002, 6).[24] Thus, Askew emphasizes the need for governments and states to continuously perform to solidify national identity. Attention to performance then "can expose the continual performance not only required *by* states but required *of* states. . . . Saying and, notably, *performing* the nation brings it into being. Words alone are insufficient" (292). Singing a national anthem, chanting slogans, and performing in a band at a state-sponsored rally are some of the many ways in which, "through their shared performances, the citizens of a state congeal and bring the nation—however variegated—into being" (290–91). By emphasizing the constant need of states to perform their power and citizens their allegiance, Askew reveals the importance of performances in constituting nations as "imagined communities."

In his groundbreaking work on power and the politics of performance, anthropologist Johannes Fabian shows the inner workings, micro-level decisions, and state interventions that shaped one particular theater performance for a troupe in Shaba, Zaire (1990). His work laid the foundation for scholars who followed, as within the last decade in both anthropology and performance studies, there have been a number of studies of what Jay Straker calls "state scripted nationalism" (2007, 209) in postcolonial Africa. What each of the authors does well is explore the multifaceted relationship between power, performance, and national identity, providing insights that I build on in my own study. For example, in her study of theater troupes in Tanzania, Laura Edmondson goes beyond a resistance/complicity binary and highlights the multiplicity of responses and interpretations of theater performances connected to the Tanzanian state. Such an approach informs my own work on the nuances of citizen-state relations in my examination of political animation in Zaire. Likewise, Bob White's highly relevant study of popular musicians in former Zaire (2008), and other studies of dancing women at political rallies in Malawi (Gilman 2009) and "militant theater" in revolutionary Guinea (Straker 2009) all explore how citizen's bodies were used, both voluntarily and by force, to represent particular ideologies and conceptions of the nation-state. These investigations provide an additional lens on my analysis of state-scripted nationalism in postcolonial Congo. Moreover, Francesca Castaldi's work on national ballets in Senegal (2006) brings attention to the role of ethnicity in state-sanctioned performances of the nation, another relevant theme in my own work.

While all these analyses complicate our understandings of performed nationalisms in Africa, they focus on staged, public performances in spaces usually set apart from everyday life. I argue that nationalism in everyday life settings is just as important for creating a sense of belonging. Inspired by Askew's (2002) observations of the use of *taraab* musical performance to negotiate local social relations, my own focus on everyday cultural performances, with and without music, allows us to examine multiple levels of politics in daily life, so that individual tactics and collective action as well as evolving ideas of BisiKongo ethnicity and ethnic nationalism are all implicated in the performative encounters that are the focus of this study.

Moreover, in this book I discuss the importance of coercion in certain performances of nationalism in Africa—a topic that has been understudied, with some exceptions (for example, Gilman 2009; Mbembe 1992; White 2008). I use the term *coercion* in the sense of one person or group of people using physical force, threats, or sanctions to control the behavior of another person/group such that they act in a manner that they would not without the coercion. While political animation under President Mobutu is the strongest example of coerced performances of nationalism in the book, other instances (such as a colonial administrator's policy of using forced dancing to combat Kongo prophetic movements) reveal how forced embodied performances were expected to have an effect on group subjectivity and identity. I discuss political animation in postcolonial Zaire as part of a larger "civil religion," a public religious dimension that is expressed through a set of rituals, symbols, and beliefs" (Bellah 1967, 4). If we embrace Emile Durkheim's definition of religion as "a unified system of beliefs and practices relative to sacred things, that is to say, things set apart and forbidden—beliefs and practices which unite in one single moral community called a Church,[25] all those who adhere to them" ([1912] 1995, 44), then it is clear that both colonial-era spirit possession and postcolonial civil religion in the Lower Congo qualify as forms of religion. Both are systems of rites, symbols, and beliefs shared by a collective, and while the sacred entity in the *bangunza* movement was the Holy Spirit, the sacred entity in Zaire's civil religion was Mobutu himself. Indeed, gods and spirits are not absolutely necessary in order for a religion to exist (Durkheim [1912] 1995, 27–33). What both religions share is an important emphasis on the body; what differs is who or what is moving that body—from an external spiritual force animating your body, to you yourself animating your body to satisfy the demands of an external force (the political state). Thus, I am interested in understanding the mechanisms and consequences of civil religion and its workings on the body. A focus on everyday encounters reveals that emerging national identities and ideologies in the Congo were often expressed through the embodied performances of the population, by force, a sense of loyalty, and other means.

Performance, Authority, and the Spiritual Realm

July 26, 2010. I am in Luozi, meeting with Ma Kudada for an interview about her experiences in a local African Independent Church.[26] My research assistant Kilanda and I take turns asking her questions. Ma Kudada is a short, slender woman in her late thirties, demure and a bit reserved, wearing a headscarf, tailored top, and long skirt that she made herself using a colorful fabric. As the conversation continues, she becomes more animated. "When I was born, my mother had me baptized in the Catholic Church." She was raised on a Catholic mission in another part of Luozi territory, but her life was completely changed when she underwent her confirmation ceremony as a teen. "When the bishop touched my forehead with the oil, I noticed something had happened in me; a big change as if I saw a big, ferocious animal at the altar that was going to devour me; immediately I fled the church. I trembled, I couldn't see anyone around me." She then explains that the Holy Spirit had descended into her, and this experience led her to eventually become a member of the Luozi DMNA congregation. DMNA (Dibundu dia Mpeve ya Nlongo mu Afelika) is one of many churches of the Holy Spirit with origins in the Kongo prophetic movements of the colonial era, which began with the visions and trembling of the prophet Simon Kimbangu in 1921.

The cultural embodiment of zakama, spirit-induced trembling, dates back to the banganga of the precolonial era. Whether learned explicitly or observed through other experiences, embodied trembling was historically used among the Kongo as an index of the presence of a spiritual force in the body of the trembling person. The uncontrollable trembling that Ma Kudada experienced parallels the embodied trembling of the prophet Simon Kimbangu, who started a region-wide prophetic movement in 1921 that threatened the hegemony of Western missionaries and Belgian colonial administrators alike. Numerous incidents when trembling prophets and their followers openly challenged, publicly defied, or even physically assaulted Europeans in the Lower Congo, demanding that they leave the country, demonstrate the seriousness of such bodily comportment. Zakama allowed access to a spiritual authority that superseded the claims of Belgians and others who sought to legitimize their rule over their African colonial subjects. Spirituality, then, had very significant political consequences, especially as a competing source of authority and power.

In this study, I examine how bodies are used in religious contexts to create a site of authority that undermines existing relations of power. What role do everyday cultural performances in religious contexts have in constituting, confirming, and contesting authority? A clue in the relationship between religion and authority may be found in Max Weber's classic study, where he identifies three major claims to legitimacy made in relation to authority:

traditional, based on belief in the sanctity of traditions; rational, based on legal means and laws; and charismatic, resting on exceptional characteristics of individuals, often based on their connection to the spiritual realm (1968, 215).[27] The supernatural realm (from ancient Egyptian pharaohs to women possessed by Catholic saints in the Kongo Kingdom) was often the source of claims to a special status that set one apart from others.[28] Like power itself, which is continually challenged, legitimacy is disputed as well, leading to contestations over authority. In this project, I use cultural performance to question the fixedness of authority, which is always shifting.

The relationship between religion and politics in modern Africa is an area of study needing further research (Meyer 2004), and one useful approach is to examine the intersection of the body, politics, and authority.[29] In addition, in religious studies more generally, there has been a scholarly shift to examining how religion is embodied and lived in everyday life (P. Brown 1988; Hall 1997; McGuire 1990, 2008; Weisenfeld 2013). A part of this shift is renewed attention to power relations in practices of religion (Edgell 2012). The body plays a significant role in religious practice and can be the foundation of larger claims to power. Paul Stoller's ethnography (1995) of the Hauka movement and spirit possession in a Songhay town in the Republic of Niger explores how spirits of Europeans (called Hauka, a name applied to the spirit mediums as well) possess devotees who then mimic various colonial personages, particularly the military. Through gestures, language, improvised uniforms, wooden guns, and other implements, the Hauka mediums utilize embodied practices to express cultural memories of European colonization.[30] These practices also served to constitute a transethnic, cross gender, transnational group identity of Hauka mediums who resisted the demands of colonization: they refused to pay taxes, trained for guerilla warfare, refused to work, moved their villages into the bush, and advocated subordination of the French. "Through the power of embodiment," Stoller writes, "the Hauka stutter-step over the border separating ritual from political practice" (1995, 7). Similarly, in her study of Pentecostalism in Nigeria, Ruth Marshall highlights the importance of the body in conversions: "the focus of born-again conversions is individual conduct, expressed in the tropes of personal mastery through a variety of techniques of the self, such as bodily asceticism, fasting, prayer, assiduous Bible study, permanent self-examination and public witness" (2009, 12).[31] While in the early decades of the Pentecostal revival in the 1970s, Pentecostal leaders avoided participation in secular politics, by the 1990s Pentecostal churches and their leaders became very politically influential in Nigeria, with pastors elected to government positions and even running for president of the country (214–17). Adeline Masquelier's ethnography (2001) of *bori* possession in a Hausaphone Mawri community in Niger also makes connections between religion and larger political struggles. She describes bori as a site of resistance to some of the major transformations in Mawri society, particularly Islamic suppression and scorn. People possessed by bori spirits present an alternative spiritual authority that clearly challenges the larger religious narrative rooted in Islam. Moreover, bori spirits can appear in everyday life—in markets, on public transport, and so on—outside of ritual contexts (128). An additional key point that Masquelier makes is that bori spirit possession is a means by which Mawri people engage with and impact the world: "Mawri understanding is often embedded in praxis—that is, enveloped in bodily attitudes—rather than enunciated through words, concepts, or formulas. Spirit possession, in general, is a mode of understanding and acting upon the world that is based on bodily practice rather than verbal performance" (185). Likewise, zakama is an embodied mode of understanding, being-in, and transforming the world among Kongo people in the Lower Congo region. All these ethnographies, then, demonstrate how spirituality and religious practice, expressed through physical bodies, can be an important resource for creating new forms of authority.

There is something special about spirits and the supernatural realm. Spirits are elusive—they can be neither shot nor arrested. Because they cannot be physically touched, they often cannot be controlled. It is perhaps this elusiveness that inspires both fear and awe in cases of spirit possession. But religious power also comes from conduct, gestures, and other forms of embodiment outside of spirit possession. My work extends this discussion to look at embodied religion more broadly; considering spirit possession but also civil or secular religion in terms of the worship of political leaders such as President Mobutu Sese Seko;[32] and examining rituals in churches but also in cemeteries, forests, schools, and everyday encounters on the street. Ruth Marshall argues for seeing religion as a site of action, rather than just as a means of creating meaning (2009, 22). Following Marshall, I focus on how religion has been strategically used to motivate and unite large groups of people, moving beyond analyses of meaning and symbolism, to illuminate social transformation caused by concerted action. Further, religious discourse, beliefs, and rituals can be both a weapon of the weak and a tool of those in advantageous sociopolitical positions. Spiritual and political authority can both engender and challenge one another through moving and feeling bodies.

In sum, the study of everyday cultural performances can provide a different perspective on the role of religion and spirituality in struggles for power in the Lower Congo. Most recent studies of performance and power miss the elements of spirituality and religion, partially because of their focus on performance as events set apart from daily life. My study places the body at the center of analysis to help us better understand the role of religion in struggles for power and the creation of nationalist sentiments in everyday life.

There is a need for more anthropological studies of religion that address larger-scale politics and also examine religious practice outside of structured ritual contexts. Attention to performances in everyday life can reveal the countless ways that both authority and nationalism are configured, showing the importance of the body for staking claims that stem from the spiritual realm and are transforming group consciousness and action. Embodied performances can be strategically associated with certain values, beliefs, and ideas—from the Black power fist to the Heil Hitler salute—and because of these associations embodied performances can both challenge and support existing social and political structures. Moreover, social positions are made and unmade through everyday interactions with others; authority depends not only on who you are, what position you occupy, or what you have, but it is also based on your own cultural performances and others' responses to them.

Methods and Travels

My approach to my research project was rooted in anthropological methods such as participant observation and individual interviews, combined with archival documentation. While I left for the Congo with an interest in "Kongo traditional dances," most of the themes that appear in this book arose through an emergent, inductive process rather than being imposed from the start. This is a qualitative study, based on fifteen months of ethnographic and archival research in the Democratic Republic of Congo, Belgium, the United States and the UK between 2005 and 2012, with most of the data collected during a year-long research trip in the Congo from 2005 to 2006 (funded by a Fulbright grant) with a follow-up trip in 2010. To fully research the politics of everyday performances, I employed three main methods.

The first method was based on examining archival materials such as missionary diaries, state reports, travel narratives, accounts of literate Congolese, and performance programs, among others, to illuminate the precolonial, colonial, and postcolonial histories of makinu, bimpampa, and zakama. I approached my use of these multiple archives with an awareness of archives as political institutions and products, in which, as Jacques Derrida notes, "the archivization produces as much as it records the events" (1996, 7). In what anthropologist Ann Stoler calls the "archival turn," scholars in multiple disciplines over the last few decades have begun to see archives not as impartial collections of truthful documents, but as sites of knowledge production, state power, and ethnographic projects in and of themselves (Arondekar 2005;

Mbembe 2002; Stoler 2002). In the particular instance of Western writing about African religions and spiritual practices, V. Y. Mudimbe cautions Africans themselves against the "colonial library," a body of knowledge created by European explorers, travelers, missionaries, anthropologists, and colonial administrators based on negative representations of African practices and beliefs, which were largely seen and defined by the West as "deviant" (1994, xii; 1988, 175–89). Thus, my strategy for engaging with archives was to try to read them both against and along their grain, in order to recognize patterns of misinformation, omission, and negativity that shaped the products—indeed, I tried to remain cognizant of "the power in the production of the archive itself" (Stoler 2002, 101). I consulted multiple archives and libraries in the Democratic Republic of Congo including: the National Museum, the National Archives, the Main Library of the l'Université Pédagogique National (UPN), the National Library, the National Institute of Arts, CEPAS (Centre d'Etudes pour l'Action Sociale), Pere Bontinck's personal library at Scolasticat, Facultés Catholiques de Kinshasa (FCK), the library of College Boboto in Kinshasa, the Jesuit Canisius Library at Kimwnza, the Mayidi Grand Seminary in Bas-Congo, the Library of Luozi, and the museum of the CEC (Communauté Evangelique du Congo) Protestant church in Luozi. In Belgium, I consulted the African Archives of the Minister of Foreign Affairs (which houses the majority of documents from the colonial period in the Congo) in Brussels and ethnographic images and documents of the Royal Museum for Central Africa, in Tervuren. I also collected documents from the archives of the American Baptist Historical Society at Mercer University (Atlanta, Georgia) and the archive of the Baptist Missionary Society at Regents Park College (Oxford, UK).

The second method was based on conducting interviews to investigate the significance and function of makinu, bimpampa, and zakama in both past and contemporary life, the beliefs and worship practices of the DMNA church, personal experiences of political animation, and the mission and practice of Bundu dia Kongo. Like archives, interviews are also influenced by power dynamics. As a federally funded graduate student from the United States, I was in a considerably better financial and social position than most (but not all) of my interviewees. As anthropologist Katherine Ewing notes, interviewing is much more than the collection of information; "an utterance is an index or sign of the relationship between speaker and hearer" (2006, 91). The difference in social position, as well as anxiety about my intentions (especially with regard to my interactions with members of Bundu dia Kongo, who were being persecuted by the local government and law enforcement authorities), surely shaped the responses that interviewees gave to my questions. However, since my larger focus on gesture, dance, and other forms of embodiment was not typically seen as a threatening or invasive subject (with the exception of political animation under Mobutu), most people were eager and willing to speak with me and share their knowledge and experiences. As my topic also focused specifically on embodiment in Kongo culture, many people saw my study as a positive project that valorized Kongo culture within a larger context of BisiKongo political and economic marginalization in the broader country. My topic attracted interest and cooperation because of the role my study could play in the process of staking political claims, especially in the context of the nationalist fervor that groups like Bundu dia Kongo were creating in Luozi at the time. Thus, whether I wanted to be or not, I was implicated in the everyday power dynamics that defined the lives and struggles of my interviewees and interlocutors.

I conducted and recorded sixty-two interviews of dancers, musicians, professors, audience members,[33] pastors, church members, and other people, in both Luozi and Kinshasa, and one interview in Mayidi (all in the Congo). I used nonprobability sampling (Bernard 2011, 145) to select interviewees with the expertise and life experiences most relevant to my research questions. I found participants most often through suggestions from my contacts, who were usually Congolese professors, performing artists, or religious leaders; in this way, I was able to avoid, for the most part, people who did not have the knowledge to answer my questions. I also depended quite a bit on several people with whom I engaged in many dialogues over the course of my stay, including Tata Kimpianga Mahaniah (founder of the Free University of Luozi); Tata Ndundu Kivwila (professor at the National Institute of Arts); and my friend and key cultural consultant, Kikongo teacher, and occasional research assistant, Ne Nkamu Luyindula.[34] I also arranged many interviews myself based on seeing people perform or hearing about their knowledge and skill in particular areas of performance that interested me. I compensated all my interviewees for their time and their travel as well, especially if they came far to do the interview. I conducted my interviews in French, which many people did seem at least moderately comfortable with, especially in Kinshasa. In Luozi, although I used French there as well, I occasionally had to ask a friend or my research assistant to interpret Kikongo for me, especially with a few of the older interviewees. My Kikongo was still not advanced enough to do interviews in, and although I did try to learn as much as I could in everyday interactions, people would sense my weakness in the language and switch to French, which helped me to communicate, but frustrated my developing Kikongo. For most of my interviews, if I was not accompanied by a friend, one or more research assistants were present, helping to take notes or translate as necessary. The study is limited in this regard, as some of the dialogue may have been lost in translation. I worked with four research assistants mainly, three of whom were young men (David, Philippe, Mathieu) and one of whom was a young woman (Kilanda), all in Luozi.

The third method I used was participant observation of performance events. These included weddings, funerals, the construction of tombs, the cleaning of cemeteries, worship services in churches every Sunday and throughout the week, cultural festivals, performance group rehearsals and presentations, rallies and parades, community theater, and other events. For the most part, I depended on friends and others associated with my work to let me know when events were happening, although I did find some events of my own accord. I attended and videotaped many events during my ethno graphic field research, to retain records for further analysis. I always asked permission before recording and was usually granted permission, especially after I began to burn VCDs for the performing groups or participants in the performances as a token of appreciation for their participation.[35] If the events were funerals or weddings, I always brought a small donation in an envelope as well to give to the family. Much of my observation and participation in bimpampa also occurred on a daily basis, as I walked the roads and encountered other people, embodying the proper greetings I had learned.

The BisiKongo, also known as BaKongo, are the ethnic group one finds throughout the Lower Congo, where people speak varying dialects of the same language, Kikongo. While exact estimates are difficult, nearly six million people in the Democratic Republic of Congo, Republic of Congo, and Angola speak Kikongo or one of its dialects as a first language (Lewis 2015) (see map I.1).[36]

Over the course of my research, I divided my time in the Congo between two main sites, including Kongo communities and interactions with Kongo people in the urban metropolis of Kinshasa, and those in Luozi, a rural, agricultural town located in the western province of Bas-Congo. As a brown-skinned African American woman conducting research in post-colonial Congo (a country that lacks a vibrant tourist industry), the position I occupied, not by any choice of my own, hovered in between "native" and "stranger." Because of my skin color and features, I was often seen as one of the "skinfolk," to use a term popularized by Zora Neale Hurston ([1942] 1991, 168). This enabled me to experience many aspects of daily life as many Congolese did, as I was not explicitly marked as a foreigner. Thus, interwoven throughout the manuscript is the narrative of my own experiences. This approach is significant because my social location as a female African American ethnographer shaped unique interpersonal interactions tied to

MAP I.1. Map of the Democratic Republic of Congo, prepared by Bill Nelson.

perceived identity, connected to both past and present nationalist movements in my research site, and informed a more nuanced understanding of daily life in postcolonial Congo.

Chapter Overview

Part I of the book, "Performative Encounters, Political Bodies," continues with chapter 1 to describe my research methodology and my two primary research sites—Kinshasa, the capital city, and Luozi, a small town on the rural periphery of Bas-Congo province. Approached reflexively, this chapter explores how a young woman from the South Bronx ended up in the Congo, and how my own history and body both intersected with and diverged from the experiences and beliefs of the BisiKongo people I interviewed and interacted with on a daily basis.

Part II of the book is "Spirits, Bodies, and Performance in Belgian Congo." Chapter 2 uses documents from the Baptist Missionary Society, American

Baptist Foreign Missionary Society, and Belgian colonial archives, as well as personal interviews to examine spirit-induced trembling (zakama) as a site of moral and political contestation between the church and colonial state, and the indigenous population in the Lower Congo. The chapter focuses on the *kingunza* movements that swept the Lower Congo with the emergence of the prophet Simon Kimbangu in 1921. Through performative encounters, the kingunza movement used a type of spiritual legitimacy gained from the religious realm to subvert Belgian colonial authority, using Kongo bodies as the key weapons of resistance. Chapter 3 examines the kingunza movements after the arrest and imprisonment of Simon Kimbangu, as well as colonial discourses on secular Kongo dances (makinu). Makinu were seen as "indecent" threats to public morality. As the kingunza movements gained strength and Kongo people continued to participate irrespective of persecution, colonial agents visualized the potential of using one form of Kongo embodied practice, makinu, to combat another, kingunza.

Part III of the book, "Civil Religion and Performed Politics in Postcolonial Congo," opens with a chapter that considers the relationship between performance and authority during the postcolonial period under the dictatorial regime of Mobutu Sese Seko. State-scripted dancing and singing, most commonly known as *animation politique*, became part and parcel of daily life for average citizens of Zaire. The adoration of Mobutu became a civil religion as the ideologies of his regime were reinforced through the everyday performances of the citizens, and through Mobutu's own attempts to supplant everyday religious practice with performances in his own honor. This chapter examines yet another shift in the relationship of embodied cultural performances to political authority, in particular from the early 1970s to the 1990s. Using interviews in Kinshasa and Luozi and archival documents retrieved in Kinshasa, I examine the connection between Mobutu's policies and ideologies, ordinary Kongo citizens, dancers and musicians, and their embodied practices. Specifically, I look at the impact of animation politique in three major areas of everyday life in rural Luozi territory: schools, businesses, and churches.

In chapter 5, I examine the localized effects of national policies of animation politique on women from the Kongo ethnic group living in Luozi territory in postcolonial Zaire. My focus on the lived and gendered experiences of animation politique allows me to posit coerced performance as an often overlooked but quite potent governmental technique that not only seeks to shape individual and group subjectivities, but also disrupts the moral order of local communities. I build on Achille Mbembe's work on the banality of power by examining the experiences of women in their engagement with a coercive state—one that demanded specific performances from them, both on and off the stage. Specifically, I illuminate the impact of performative encounters in the bedroom. My interviews show that the sexual exploitation of female dancers, even in the most rural areas, largely created moral disorder and fostered negative sentiments in local communities, thus undermining the nationalist project. I argue the complex engagement of these women with the state under Mobutu was a form of gendered nationalism that differed from the experiences of male performers.

Part IV of the book is called "Re-creating the Past, Performing the Future." Chapter 6 focuses on the movement of Bundu dia Kongo to explore the importance of embodied performances in the current post-Mobutu era for making explicit political statements and mobilizing large groups of people for concerted action. Bundu dia Kongo is a Kongo politico-religious-nationalist group that is fully engaged in a struggle for the political representation and governance of Kongo people, with the ultimate goal of establishing a separate Kongo nation-state. Because of their intense and aggressive activism, the Congolese government has intensely persecuted members of Bundu dia Kongo, leading to the deaths of over two hundred BDK members in clashes with authorities in 2008 and, ultimately, the banning of the group. The chapter examines their ideological beliefs and political goals and then focuses on the ways that Bundu dia Kongo uses the body and the reformation of bodily habits, both in everyday interactions and spiritual worship, as a means of unifying Kongo people around cultural memories of the former Kongo Kingdom. This chapter also considers attempts by the leadership of Bundu dia Kongo to control forms of embodiment that may act as sites from which others may challenge the growing but tenuous authority of the movement.

The conclusion of the book summarizes the major findings, emphasizing the multivalent meanings and uses of bimpampa, zakama, and makinu over time and in different contexts, and noting the importance of embodied performances in everyday social interactions for both constituting and challenging secular and religious authority and supporting nationalism. The chapter returns to three themes in regards to the body in studies of religion and power: the body as center, conduit, and catalyst. I also provide suggestions for future research and lines of inquiry by discussing the significance of this study for research on embodied practices across the Atlantic in the New World.

Part I

PERFORMATIVE ENCOUNTERS,

POLITICAL BODIES

CHAPTER 1

Neither Native nor Stranger

Places, Encounters, Prophecies

Meeting Kimbangu: Everyday Encounters and Embodied Prophecies in Luozi

January 30, 2006. Wearing baggy sweat pants, an old T-shirt and sneakers, and a scarf tied over my hair, I join my friends outside, closing the door of the house behind me.

"Let's go, then," I say.

Kilanda (big sister), Pierre (brother), Suzanne (little sister), Phillipe (Kilanda's baby), and I are headed to one of the family's many fields in Luozi to plant soybeans. Up and down several winding red dirt paths, over rough troughs, past grazing goats, and through thigh-high grass, we walk until we arrive after about ten minutes in a field next to the overgrown cement foundation and half-finished walls of the future site of a bigger and better Kongo DMNA[1] church.

"This is it," Pierre gestures.

I gaze at the site, shading my eyes from the bright sunlight. We put down our water jugs, baskets, and hoes, and Kilanda places Phillipe in the care of his little aunt under the shade of a colorful umbrella. Kilanda and Pierre begin to test my knowledge of plants, which is not too developed, since I am a city girl. Nevertheless, I am determined to show that I had learned something during my time in Luozi. Pierre points to the first plant.

"*Saka-saka*" (meaning cassava-leaves), I say excitedly. He chooses another.
"*Nkovi*" (collard greens—now that was an easy one).
"*Et ca?*" (And this?) Kilanda gestures to yet another plant.
"*Nguba*" (peanuts), I answer.

As they prepare for all of us to plant soybeans, I begin to take photos of the plants and the field. Kilanda notices an older woman at work clearing the overgrowth in one room of the church structure, and so we go over there to say hello. She is a member of the DMNA church and looks to be in her sixties. Her head is covered with a scarf, and she is wearing a beige sleeveless tank top with a *pagne* wrapped around her waist. She is deftly pulling weeds and grass from the ground by hand and wipes the sweat from her brow with her forearm as she stands to greet us as we approach the structure. Kilanda introduces me as a *noire-americaine* (Black American), and the woman smiles, and then spontaneously breaks into song:

> Tata Kimbangu weti zieta kaka mu Afelika
> Weti niku nanga nsi ye kamba vo lusiama.
> Ah Ah Ah lusiama AhAhAh lusiama
> weti niku nanga nsi ye kamba vo lusiama
> Ah Ah Ah lusiama AhAhAh lusiama
> weti niku nanga nsi ye kamba vo lusiama
> Ah Ah Ah tata ye mama nge wabo kulua
> simba sabala kia mpeve ye kota mu mvita

> Papa Kimbangu always walks in Africa
> He moves the world and says to be strong
> Ahhh Be strong, be strong,
> He moves the world and says to be strong
> Ahhh Be strong, be strong,
> He moves the world and says to be strong
> Fathers and Mothers you who are called
> Hold the sword of the spirit and enter the war

Had I experienced this same situation when I first arrived in the Congo, I probably would not have understood the implications of her impromptu song and cultural performance. However, months before this, in September, as I walked through Luozi with Ne Nkamu, my chief cultural consultant, music/Kikongo language tutor, and friend, we passed through the yard of an older couple. When Ne Nkamu introduced us, the elderly gentleman took off his hat, smiled, and said something about the prophecy coming true. A few days later, Ne Nkamu and I crossed the path of a group of men at work on constructing a building. As I introduced myself and tried my fledgling Kikongo by asking them their clans, some of the men responded and then asked me the same question. As Ne Nkamu stepped in to explain that I don't know my clan because of slavery and the slave trade to the Americas, another man chimed in about the prophecy of Simon Kimbangu, and some of the others nodded. Moreover, on my first meeting with representatives of Bundu dia Kongo in Luozi, the same comment was made, and they explained to me that this particular prophecy of Kimbangu was recorded in their sacred book, and they have created a list of regulations to govern the impending return of African Americans to the Congo.

Over and over again, especially during my time in Luozi, people associated my presence, my very body, with the fulfillment of the prophecy of Tata Simon Kimbangu. The prophecy that Simon Kimbangu supposedly made during the colonial period basically said that Black Americans would come back to the Congo to help liberate it, and also teach the Congolese all the technical knowledge and skills they needed to be more successful than their colonial oppressors. Although there doesn't seem to be any text that Kimbangu actually wrote himself proclaiming this, the prophecy has been immortalized in eyewitness accounts, colonial government documents, song lyrics of the Kimbanguist Church, the sacred book of Bundu dia Kongo, and in the memories of Kongo people. What exactly was this prophecy and what did it have to do with me?

An informant told anthropologist Wyatt MacGaffey the following prophecy, saying it dated to 1921: "Pray to your brethren who were sold in the ivory and rubber to the country of the Americans. The Lord will send them to this country to teach crafts and give skills surpassing those of the whites" (1968, 177). Writing from Luozi in June 1921, colonial administrator Léon Cartiaux conveyed the claims of Masamba and Kinko, two BisiKongo carpenters who went to the town of Nkamba and said they heard Kimbangu say publicly that "for so many years the Belgians are our rulers and haven't done anything for us till this day, but before long Americans will arrive here in order to make war with the Belgians and become our rulers."[2] Kimpianga Mahaniah cites Belgian author Maquet-Tombu, who reported a deported prophet as saying that "the black Americans will soon come and conquer the Congo" (1993, 411). Joseph Van Wing, a Belgian Catholic missionary and longtime inhabitant of the Congo, also mentioned a variant of the prophecy when he wrote about Mpadism, another Kongo-based prophetic movement influenced by Simon Kimbangu, which occurred from 1939 to 1946. Clearly drawing on the implications and antagonisms of WWII, the prophecy foretold a war won by the Germans, who will give the Congolese access to arts and sciences, and then, "after twenty or thirty years . . . the German king would make Black Americans come to the Congo. He will kick out all the foreign missionaries and allow the Blacks to pray to God among themselves" (1958, 600). Mac-Gaffey also discusses the prophecy as shown in a hymn of the Kimbanguist Church:

If the King of the Americans comes
To restore the King,
The chiefs of this world shall pass away.
If the King of the Americans comes
The troubles of this world shall pass away
If the King of the Americans comes
The King of the Blacks will return.[3]

This prophecy is notable because it is about not only Americans, but Black Americans in particular, coming (returning) to the Congo with technical know-how and skills, to teach and aid the Congolese in gaining their independence from the Belgians. Several authors have linked this reference to the spread throughout Central Africa of the ideas, publications, and movement of Marcus Garvey. This is particularly poignant because at least one Congolese intellectual, John Panda Farnana, had been identified as a Garveyist agitator, while other Congolese had been found to have Garveyist publications in their possession. Kimbangu himself worked for a time at Huileries du Congo Belge, a British owned oil refinery, alongside Black Americans and Anglophone Africans who discussed ideas of Pan-Africanism (Kodi 1993, 263–88; Mahaniah 1993, 414–16). Thus, Kodi posits Marcus Garvey as the "King of the Americans" who is mentioned in the prophecies (1993, 278). Moreover, both Mahaniah and Kodi link circulating rumors of the arrival of a ship on the Congo River signifying the end of Belgian rule, with the Black Star Lines of Marcus Garvey (Kodi 1993, 279; Mahaniah 1993, 415). The actual presence of African Americans at the Huileries du Congo Belge and their interactions with Europeans there affected Congolese perceptions of African Americans as a group. According to Makidi Kuntilma, an informant that Kimpianga Mahaniah interviewed, even in the 1920s African Americans had a reputation for rebelliousness and had a great influence on his uncle Massamba, who also worked at the oil refinery. "He [his uncle] was so influenced by black American culture that he could speak Pidgin English. Even his temperament was affected. He respected no one, even Europeans, with whom he had many fights. . . . The black American was seen as heroic and was very much admired for challenging Europeans" (Mahaniah 1993, 416).

What also cannot be discounted are shared experiences of discrimination, mistreatment, and denigration. Frantz Fanon's analysis of the "fact of blackness" examines how the colonial context creates both corporeal and historico-racial schemas by which Black people come to understand themselves as objectified, inferior bodies in the gaze of whiteness (1967, 109–40). By highlighting how these schemas work in everyday life in bolstering common oppressive conditions for Blacks living under White domination across the world, Fanon allows us to also consider the role of shared experiences of racial oppression in shaping Simon Kimbangu's prophecies about African American collaborators and saviors fighting with the Congolese against the Belgians. All these factors created a greater sense of connection between Kongo people and African Americans during the colonial period.[4]

These exchanges and encounters that I experienced bring us back to the intersection of embodiment, performance, religion, and Kongo nationalism. The fact that I was a brown-skinned African American conducting research in a West Central African country affected the reception that I received and the development of my research in very specific ways. My very physical presence in the Lower Congo evoked cultural memories of a religious movement that challenged the authority of the Belgians during the colonial period and offered hope for a future free from European colonialism. In this way, I encountered the prophet Simon Kimbangu over and over again as he was invoked as an explanation for the presence of African Americans in the Lower Congo nearly six decades after his physical death. The constant association of my embodied presence with Kimbangu's prophecy sparked my own interest in understanding the history and evolution of the religious movement that Kimbangu created and its continued salience in everyday life in modern-day Lower Congo. By privileging the *body as center*, my own body as a researcher is also implicated in the research process and interactions that inform this study. For some my presence was evidence of the truth of the prophecy; for others I was just an American student researcher. From my own perspective, I had come to the Congo as part of a circuitous journey that seemed to always have the continent of Africa at its center.

From the Bronx to Bas-Congo: Journeys and Methods

April, 1, 2005. I have been in the Congo for only a few days and am now living with a Luba host family in Kinshasa. I meet another African American working for the American embassy that then introduces me to a small group of African diasporans living in Kinshasa as employees of various state departments, governments, and nongovernmental organizations. I am invited to meet everyone at a friendly card game of spades, and as my new acquaintance introduces me to about eight people all seated around a large table with multiple decks of cards on display, someone asks where I was from.

"The Bronx," I reply as I sit down and accept a soft drink from the host of the party.

"What part of the Bronx? I am from the Bronx too."

Surprised to find not just another New Yorker but a Bronx native in the Congo with me, I tell him my street intersection, and he says, "Oh, you from the projects. What is the name of those houses again?"

I pause for a moment. I am shocked that he knows my neighborhood, but even more unprepared to have my background revealed for everyone to see. I must admit, for a moment, as I sip my drink in the midst of all these middle- and upper-middle-class Black folks with great jobs, I feel inferior and a bit ashamed of my background. I clear my throat and reply, "Morrisania Houses."

"Oh yeah, Morrisania. So what's up? Are you going to play or what?"

The momentary shame that I experienced at this friendly card game was directly linked to the negative stereotypes associated with both the South Bronx and with public housing projects more generally. The Congo as an imagined space suffers from similar problems of negative associations—from Joseph Conrad's *Heart of Darkness* to present-day pessimistic international news coverage emphasizing death, mayhem, and despair. The Bronx and the Congo are two very different geographical spaces; one is an urban borough in the largest city in the United States while the other is a vast country—the second largest in Africa and the eleventh largest in the world in terms of geographic area. However, what they have in common are bad reputations. The Bronx, and especially the South Bronx, became the poster child for urban decay, concentrated poverty, crime, and drug epidemics during the 1970s and 1980s while the Congo conjures up images of war, violence, disease, rape, and political and economic instability after two civil wars (1996–97 and 1998–2003) and continued civil unrest, especially along the eastern border with Rwanda (Rose 1994; Nzongola-Ntalaja 2002; Gondola 2002). When I told friends and colleagues that I was going to conduct research in the Congo, their reactions were similar:

"You are going to the Congo? Is it safe?"

"Isn't there a war going on there?

"I heard that a lot of women are being raped there. Aren't you scared?"

I tried to assuage their worries and fears by pointing out that my research would be conducted on the western side of the country, far from the instability of the east. Professor Mbala Nkanga, associate professor of theater at the University of Michigan and my dissertation committee member and mentor, was instrumental not only in giving me contacts and bolstering my applications for funding, but also in assuring me that Bas-Congo was a very different space than the larger Congo that gripped the world's imagination. I owe my entire decision to eventually study in Bas-Congo to him. In regards to my family, I was at least comforted because they knew next to nothing about the Congo and thus didn't really object to my going there. By then, they were used to my frequent travels across the country and around the world. For most of my relatives in the Bronx, I was just going to an undifferentiated "Africa" and their good-byes to me were combined with jokes such as "watch out for them lions and tigers out there!" In short, the images of both the Bronx and the Congo that permeate most people's imaginations tend to focus on and exaggerate negative aspects while ignoring the positive. It is true that growing up in the Bronx I saw violence and drug use, but I also saw community togetherness and support; it is true that rape and political instability occur frequently in the Congo, but it is also true that people go to work, love their families, attend church, and try to strengthen their communities. The truth and everyday realities of living in either place, then, are much more nuanced and complex.

My interest in Africa did not start with my family, but rather with my fifth-grade teacher. Ms. Jackson, a young, dynamic African American teacher told my class of Afro-Caribbean, African American, Puerto Rican and Dominican students that the first people on earth, the oldest human skeletons, were found in Africa. Like my classmates, I scoffed at the idea that Africans were first in anything. As she told us that we were all descended from Africans, I found it hard to believe, for I harbored many negative stereotypes of Africans like other Americans, Black and White alike. That life-altering year in Ms. Jackson's fifth-grade class planted within me the first seeds of interest and pride in having African heritage. Several years later, when I left the Bronx to attend a wealthy, majority-White high school in Pennsylvania as a student through the A Better Chance program, this interest in Africa came with me. Later, I went on to attend Brown University on a full academic scholarship as a student in the Program in Liberal Medical Education (PLME). I was the first in my family to go to college, and I decided to major in Afro-American studies and to study abroad in Ghana. I learned about a Spelman College summer program that I could use to develop a senior honors thesis topic while talking with another American student in Ghana. I participated in the summer program in Portobelo, Panama, and studied Congo dances as performed as part of the carnival tradition in this small town on the Atlantic coast of Panama. This experience piqued my interest in examining whether the dances themselves could in fact have been brought with enslaved Africans from the Congo region to Panama.

When I decided to forego medical school for graduate school in anthropology, I focused on studying transformations in dance performance culture and initially envisioned a multisited project incorporating both Panama and the Democratic Republic of Congo. Eventually, for my dissertation, I decided to focus exclusively on the Congo, and my project evolved from a focus on dance to incorporating the multiple ways that people intentionally use their bodies for political purposes in performances in everyday life.

My interest in the politics of the body is rooted in my love of dance. My experience as a dancer gave me a different perspective on my research topic. Although dance was all around me in my family and neighborhood growing up (from hip-hop to Jamaican dancehall), I started dancing publicly in Ms. Jackson's class (which included a "West African" dance performance in front of my entire middle school). I continued to dance throughout middle and high school and college (both at Brown with Fusion Dance Company and in Ghana through courses), focusing especially on dances of Africa and its diasporas. This continued in graduate school and gave me unique preparation for my research in Congo based on the special perspective that I gained through training as a performer of Congolese dance. I am African American, and my grandparents on both sides are originally from North Carolina. However, I had learned how to roll my hips as a young child from my Antiguan godmother and the larger Caribbean community that surrounded me in New York City. These everyday informal lessons helped when I took a Congolese dance class at the University of Michigan. The instructor then invited me to join his company.[5] I danced professionally with Bichini bia Congo, a small Ann Arbor–based company with a MuKongo company choreographer (Biza Sompa) for two years. I performed throughout Michigan, and in places like Atlanta and Kansas City as well. This background aided me in many performance events in the Congo, in that I was able to participate along with others, rather than remaining a distant observer. Because my dance teacher in Ann Arbor is from a nearby area geographically (southern Congo-Brazzaville) and the same Kongo ethnic group, I was already familiar with some of the drum rhythms and knew many of the movements, allowing me to participate at a different level than a true novice. My Congolese (and specifically Kongo) dance background, then, allowed me to have more engaged experiences with performance while in the Congo. For some people there, my familiarity with the music and dance culture was additional proof of Congolese ancestors, no matter how much I tried to explain. My body then, became a tool of my research approach. The next several sections of the chapter describe the Democratic Republic of Congo as a country overall and try to capture the everyday realities of life in both urban and rural Congo, by describing my two research sites: Kinshasa and Luozi.

The Ethnographic Present of Political and Economic Disarray: Introducing Kinshasa

The Democratic Republic of Congo (also known as Congo-Kinshasa, to distinguish it from its smaller northern neighbor the Republic of Congo) is large in many ways—land mass, population, and even regarding the large number of political and social challenges that it faces. Located in West Central Africa with just 37 kilometers of coastline along the Atlantic Ocean, the Congo has a total area of 2,344,858 square kilometers, making it roughly one-quarter the size of the United States. It has an estimated population of over seventy-seven million people, and with a median age of just 17.9 years, it is one of many Sub-Saharan African countries experiencing great population growth. Bordered by nine other countries, the Congo is literally at the heart of the African continent and has both influenced and been impacted by violence and civil strife in neighboring countries, from Angola to the south to Rwanda in the east. About 34 percent of Congo's population lives in urban areas, and its largest city, Kinshasa, has an estimated population of 8.798 million people, a number that rivals even New York City in the United States.[6] Kinshasa is a city of contrasts, with sprawling slums and modern high-rises, congested roadways and street vendors on foot and at makeshift stalls, selling beignets, *eau pure*, grilled Thomson, and other goods and foodstuffs to passersby.[7] The following vignette demonstrates some of the economic conditions and political tensions that marked my stay in Kinshasa:

May 11, 2005. This morning, the electricity went out around 10:00 AM. My friend Didier and I have plans to go to the National Library and the monument to former president Laurent Kabila. We take the taxi around 1:30 PM over to the library, a small building located right behind the national bank and near the presidential residence (the white house of the Congo) in front of which stands the mausoleum of Laurent Kabila. Didier wants to take me to see the mausoleum, and after he eats at a small restaurant located in the back of a truck, we walk over there. Four soldiers are sitting there guarding the wide walkway. Three are sitting elevated on sandbags and one on a chair. They are wearing navy blue uniforms with matching berets, black boots, and serious faces. One has dark shades on. They talk to Didier in Lingala, and I hardly say anything, letting him to the talking. One hefty guy on the sand bags asks me for my identity card. I dig in my bag and hand him the STA travel student identification card I have, which is printed in English. He peers at me and asks Didier if I am "Rwandaise" (Rwandan) then "Ougandaise" (Ugandan), immediately taking on a hostile tone and posture. Didier quickly replies, "No, she is American." They say collectively, "Oh." Then another soldier asks me to come closer so that he can inspect my bag. I approach him and open the bag, and he looks briefly inside. He gestures that it is ok, and I step back. "Careful!" Didier says, pointing downward, and when I follow his gaze I see that I had almost kicked over an AK-47 that is sitting on the ground. I step cautiously away. After some more conversation, Didier gives one of them (the hefty one) one hundred Congolese francs, and they allow us to pass and give us back our identification cards. As we are leaving, they ask if I have a camera, and I say no, and Didier tells me that they are permitting me to take photos. I ask him about the Rwandan/Ugandan question as we walk, and he explains that they are not welcome here (*ils sont persona non grata*) because of all the trouble in the east of the country. The grounds are beautiful and well kept overall, and we walk toward the mausoleum, which consists of four bronze-colored hands holding up a white roof with a star at the top, and a recurring lion motif. As we walk around the decorated coffin under glass, and read the inscriptions, I notice four soldiers there as well, sitting in chairs, and yet another slumped against a wall sleeping. Then, I see a line of soldiers march by single file in front of the presidential palace, across from the mausoleum. When we leave the grounds, I immediately notice the contrast between the well-manicured lawns and immaculate mausoleum on the inside of the guarded compound, and the overgrown shrubbery, crumbling sidewalks, cracked and potholed roads, and trash lining the gutters on the outside, punctuated by an overcrowded, rusty taxi squealing by.

This ethnographic excerpt poignantly captures the political, economic, and overall social conditions of the Democratic Republic of Congo as I experienced them, especially during my extended field research there from March of 2005 to March of 2006. Moreover, my own "misidentification" as Rwandan and resulting hostility from the government soldiers indexes a lingering legacy of antagonism toward Uganda and Rwanda as many Congolese blame these two countries in particular for the continued civil unrest and violence in the eastern part of the country. While some might read the soldiers' reactions as xenophobic, they index nationwide anxiety about the stability of the Congo and the perceived constant instigation of Rwanda and Uganda, neighboring countries that were directly involved in both recent civil wars in the Congo. On the other hand, such an encounter suggests that everyday life for migrants or workers living in Kinshasa—who actually are from Rwanda and Uganda—must be difficult, following from this mistrust.

The two aforementioned Congolese civil wars (1996–97 and 1998–2003) came to involve at least five of the countries surrounding the Congo, and exacerbated the deteriorating social infrastructure and struggling economy caused by years of mismanagement and corruption under the thirty-two-year dictatorship of Mobutu Sese Seko. After taking over the country in 1965 through a military coup, Joseph-Désiré Mobutu (later known as Mobutu Sese Seko) ruled the Congo until 1997, when he was overthrown by Laurent Kabila, the leader of a rebel army from the eastern Congo backed by Rwanda and Uganda. After he took power, Kabila fell out with his former allies, which resulted in fighting in the eastern Congo against troops from these two countries, with Kabila backed by Angola, Zimbabwe, Namibia, and even Chad (Nzongola-Ntalaja 2002, 238–40). After his own bodyguard assassinated Laurent Kabila in 2001 (Nzongola-Ntalaja 2002, 246), his son Joseph Kabila took over. He continued as the president of a transitional government (one president and four vice presidents, or *une plus quatre*) established after the cease-fire of 2003, and garnered the majority vote in 2006 in the first democratic elections since the country gained independence from Belgium on June 30, 1960. The impact of this political stability is reflected in civil society and everyday conditions across the country and is especially visible in Kinshasa.

As the capital and largest city in the Congo, Kinshasa remains the heart and center of the country. Before the arrival of Europeans, Kinshasa was a trading center in an area originally inhabited by both the Humbu and Teke ethnic groups (La Fontaine 1970, 8). Because it was strategically located at the point where the Congo River became navigable and at the end of the overland route from Matadi, Henry Morton Stanley founded a trading station there in 1881. After King Leopold II gained control over the vast area that became the Congo Free State in 1885, increasing numbers of Europeans moved to Kinshasa because of trade. The population of both European and Congolese inhabitants increased even further after the completion of the railroad in 1898, which started in Matadi and ended in Kinshasa (then known as Leopoldville) (La Fontaine 1970, 10–11). Leopoldville became the colony's capital in 1930, which again led to a demographic increase, and the African population increased exponentially during WWII as the Congo became a source for sorely needed materials abroad. The demographic growth and population shifts of Leopoldville are clearly shown by looking at census and survey data. In 1923, the total population of Leopoldville was only 17,825, with Europeans outnumbering Africans by 15 to 1. By 1955, more than 300,000 people lived in Leopoldville, with 290,377 Congolese and 15,221 Europeans (La Fontaine

1970, 29–30). In 1967, Kinshasa (postindependence name for Leopoldville) had an estimated 901,520 inhabitants, in the national census of 1984, 2.6 million people, and today, an estimated 8.798 million people (De Saint Moulin and Ducreux 1969, 121; Institut National de la Statistique 1984; CIA World Factbook). Historically, race played a huge role in the arrangement of the city as spaces were marked as explicitly European or African; European residential and commercial quarters were separated from the peripheral *cité indigenes* (De Boeck and Plissart 2004, 30). Presently, Kinshasa is now the third-largest city in Africa (after Lagos and Cairo), sprawling and ever growing across and beyond its current twenty-four communes (city municipalities).

And what about everyday life in Kin?[8] Although the fighting that continues to this day in the eastern part of the country is what people outside of the country hear about most often in the news media, it was not the main focus or even the most relevant force shaping the everyday lives of people as I saw it in Kinshasa and Luozi. People seemed rather desensitized by it in fact. Rather, the economic depression and dysfunctional infrastructure were the most pressing, especially in the bustling city of Kinshasa. One phrase that people often used to capture the dramatic transformation that has taken place in the country over time in this regard is to say that Kinshasa has gone from "Kinshasa la belle" to "Kinshasa la poubelle" (from Kinshasa the beautiful to Kinshasa the garbage can) (De Boeck and Plissart 2004, 35). This references the pristine, well-kept, and modern city Kinshasa was in decades past in comparison to what it looks like today, which is almost at the complete opposite end of the spectrum. The physical state of Kinshasa is like the material embodiment of the nation at the time I did my field research; scarred, unkempt, falling apart, a vestige of its former self. In Kinshasa in 2005–6, five hundred Congolese francs were equal to US$1; by the time I returned in 2010, the value of Congolese francs had depreciated even further to nine hundred Congolese francs to US$1. The state of civil society was not much better; civil employees were often unpaid, a military presence was in the streets, there were large numbers of homeless street kids (*sheges*), prostitution was rife, state-sponsored public transportation was nearly nonexistent, and urban communities were often crisscrossed with open sewers and dotted with piles of garbage. These were the conditions that I encountered on an everyday basis while living in Kinshasa. However, what was and remains the most amazing, is how people dealt with these issues every day and keep on going with their lives. People would get dressed in their business attire in the darkness because of the frequent loss of electricity, spend several hours waiting for transportation, and go to a civil service or teaching job where they may not have been paid for months.[9] One common conceptualization of just doing

FIGURE 1.1. Intersection near Palais de Peuple, seat of the Congolese Parliament, Kinshasa, 2010. Photo by Yolanda Covington-Ward.

what is necessary to survive is the phrase, "il faut se débrouiller." Researcher Emma Wild-Wood explains it best: "In the Democratic Republic of Congo the phrase 'se débrouiller' has entered the realm of myth, joke, and national identity. . . . The Congolese know that they must learn how to manage on their own, to sort things out by themselves, to cope somehow, to get by" (Wild-Wood 2007, 367). By the end of my time in the Congo, I, like Wild-Wood, had come to appreciate the need for flexibility and creativity in dealing with unfortunate circumstances. My upbringing in the Bronx also helped me in my approach to living in Kinshasa; keep your phone and purse close, always be aware of your surroundings, avoid large crowds, don't flash money. So, I didn't have any major problems while living there. Overall, people were very welcoming and gracious to me, extending all efforts to help me to further my research. Kinshasa, however, as a bustling city was very different in size, temperament, and feel than the small town of Luozi (see figure 1.1).

Crocodiles and Rolling Hills: Introducing Luozi

"You're going to Luozi? There are crocodiles there." "Have you heard about the big crocodile in Luozi?" Each time I mentioned to friends or inquisitive strangers in Kinshasa the fact that I was going to Luozi to possibly pursue ethnographic research, the first word that they associated with Luozi was *crocodile*. Popularized by *Un croco à Luozi*, a short novel dealing with *kindoki* (witchcraft) and the ability of some people with supernatural powers to take on animal forms and harm others (Zamenga 1979), the image of the crocodile in the national imagination is probably the claim to fame of both the town and territory of Luozi. Below, I describe my first trip to Luozi:

May 21, 2005. This will be my first exploratory trip to Luozi. I am going as a guest of Dr. Kimpianga Mahaniah, a MuKongo historian who is returning to the town for the first time in several years. He arrives to collect me a little after eight in the morning on May 21, and we, including his driver, Paul, and his friend Papa Léon, set off in his late-model white Land Cruiser toward Bas-Congo. To reach Luozi by car from Kinshasa, you have to drive southwest on the only main road that connects Kinshasa with the port city of Matadi. This road is paved for the most part, and although we stop several times when we encounter groups of men repairing the road, the trip from Kinshasa to Kimpese (the city where we take another road to Luozi) takes about four hours. We pass through Kasangulu, Kisantu, and Mbanza-Ngungu along the way, with the monotony of the drive being punctuated with huge trucks and lorries speeding by with supplemental passengers perched precariously atop the vehicle's cargo. After passing through Kimpese, we turn right onto a dirt road that runs alongside a range of hills made of red dirt and stone. Here, the going is more treacherous, as the road is often uneven, and we pass over several rivers and ravines using small bridges that lack any kind of guard railing to prevent the vehicle from falling.

I am struck by the beautiful scenery—clear blue skies with drifting white clouds that seemed to brush the tops of the mountain range in the distance, and open lands of tall grasses and brush that, although broken up by some farms, plots, and intermittent villages, seem to go on and on for as far as the eye could see. We often encounter small groups of people walking along the road that would move quickly to the side into the brush as we pass, murmuring greeting of "mbote" and covering their mouths and noses against the dust cloud that follows in our wake.[10]

After about two hours, we arrive at the edge of the mighty Congo River (*Nzadi* in Kikongo), the second-largest river in Africa (after the Nile), whose mispronunciation by the Portuguese led to the misnomer by which the country was known under Mobutu's regime: Zaire. We have to wait for the ferry to return from the other side. An old, dilapidated-looking vessel, it slowly creeps back across the waters to finally arrive, its bottom scraping the shore on our side. Throngs of people wait anxiously to board, but priority goes to the paying passengers—the vehicles. Each vehicle is charged US$15 to cross, and after the cars are loaded onto the ferry, the people can then board for free. The driver of our SUV lines up the vehicle's tires with the rusted planks, and we begin to move forward, on an upward angle over the water. Suddenly, the vehicle stalls, and several of the workers from the ferry began to fuss around the car. I glance down anxiously at the water: were there crocodiles? I hear, "American! American!" Bewildered, I begin to look around outside the car. How could they tell I was American? Then, I realize that one of the ferry workers was responding to the call. His name, or nickname rather, was American! I laugh at this coincidence, and the car finally lurches forward onto the ferry. We park, with both ropes and rocks being used to secure the vehicle. One of the hands gives the signal, and the people waiting on the shore rush to get on, holding shoes and sandals in their hands as they walk through the water, up the planks, and onto the ferry, filling all the available space in the seats upstairs and on the floors on the main level.

After the final preparations, the ferry begins to move. I carefully open the car door, being careful not to hit several passengers seated on the deck, and stand outside to stretch my legs, which are cramped from hours of travel. I look up at the upper deck of the ferry and spot several life preservers, which make me feel better about my trip across the river as I cannot swim. However, I then note the large number of people around me, some standing, some sitting, mothers removing babies from their backs, one man selling oranges, and many people relaxing and talking, and realize that those few life preservers wouldn't do anything in the event of an accident. I silently pray that we would make it to the other side, and try not to focus on the churning waters that had transitioned from a reddish brown near the shore to a dark grayish blue in the deeper part of the river that we traversed.

After about twenty minutes we finally reach the other side. After all the people debark, we descend down the planks into the shallow water and then up onto the riverbank. We continue onto the main road into town, creating dust clouds in the red dirt as we speed up. I take in the sights as they are pointed out to me by the professor: small homemade stands where people sell miscellaneous items, a monument to those who died on a sunken ferry a number of years ago, a bridge built during the colonial period that crosses over the Luozi River, some buildings belonging to the Protestant mission, a small market, the Catholic church and mission, a number of crumbling whitewashed buildings that housed European merchants during the colonial period, a small bar with "Skol" emblazoned in yellow and red on its wall,[11] and many homes and shops lining the main road into town. Finally, the professor points out the dusty soccer field to our right that sits next to another wide road that doubles as Luozi's "airport." We then pass a statue of a crocodile

FIGURE 1.2. The Luozi Crocodile, Luozi, 2005. Photo by Yolanda Covington-Ward.

holding a hoe, a monument erected in Batukezanga Zamenga's honor at the first Festival of Culture and Arts in Luozi (FESCAL), held in 2002 (see figure 1.2). As we turn left to enter the professor's compound, I breathe a sigh of relief. Finally, we had arrived. Welcome to Luozi.

The town of Luozi is located in Luozi Territory, which itself lies in the westernmost province of Bas-Congo, known in the past as Bas-Zaire and in English as the Lower Congo, and soon to be renamed Kongo Central. The province has been further subdivided into two cities (Matadi, Boma) and three districts (Cataractes, Lukaya, and Bas-Fleuve). Luozi is one of three territories in the district of Cataractes (Mahaniah 1989, 18), lying in between the Congo River to the south and part of the southern border of the Republic of Congo to the north (see map 1.1). During the colonial period, this area was referred to as Manianga, based on the name of a major marketplace that existed there during the precolonial era (Janzen 1978, 12). In regards to demographics, the territory of Luozi is sparsely populated in comparison to the rest of the province of Lower Congo. While the entire province had an estimated 1,971,520 inhabitants in 1984 (54,804 square kilometers in area) or around 36 inhabitants per square kilometer, the territory of Luozi had a total population of 143,998 inhabitants (7,502 square kilometers in area), or about 19 inhabitants per square kilometer (Mahaniah 1989, 20–22). Henri Nicholaï's assertion that Luozi was one of the least favored territories in the Lower Congo, primarily owing to its isolated location on the other side of the Congo River, rings true even today, when one looks at the higher population densities in other parts of the province (1960, 53).

Luozi territory is further subdivided into ten collectivities. The town of Luozi is located in the collectivity of Mbanza-Ngoyo and is the political and administrative capital of the territory (Mahaniah 1989, 37). A small town that in the most recent census had about 6,927 people (Institut National de la Statistique 1984, 41),[12] Luozi consists of five neighborhoods and has a number of churches (the three largest of which are the Kimbanguist church, the Catholic church founded by the Belgian Redemptorists, and the Protestant church founded by the Swedish Covenant Mission), one major hospital and several small clinics affiliated with religious institutions, a few small stores selling general goods, several small open-air markets where people from the surrounding area often come to sell their produce, and a number of schools (both religious affiliated and secular) (see figure 1.3).

Life in Luozi revolves around crops as the town, and the surrounding regions are heavily agricultural, with people planting crops both for their own use and for profit. Even those inhabitants with jobs in other sectors (teachers, pastors, and so on) still have their plots of land that they farm, which can be a distance of even a number of hours away by foot. Many of the homes have been constructed with red or brown bricks locally produced in open ovens that dot the landscape of the town. Most of the roofs of homes are covered by metal, but some are covered by thatch. Goats and chickens openly roam the town, and most people get around by foot, as only a minority own cars. One of the defining characteristics of the town at the time was that it lacked electricity. So, this often affected my research as I would have to find a place with a generator running to charge my laptop and other equipment during the day, especially if I knew that there would be an event at night. Overall, the feel in the town was much more relaxed and slower paced than the bustling city of Kinshasa, and the people there were very hospitable and gracious. Also, because of the small size of the town and the fact that everyone seemed

FIGURE 1.3. Open-air market in the town of Luozi, 2005. Photo by Yolanda Covington-Ward.

to know one another, I felt much safer (as a woman) attending events day and night and carrying out my research than I did in Kinshasa. From weddings to funerals, I participated in myriad community events in Luozi (see figure 1.4).

The experiences that I had in Kinshasa, Luozi, and other places where I traveled during my time in Congo were not only defined by infrastructural problems or economic and political crises; they were also defined by who, in fact, I was, as a researcher. Kimbangu's prophecy about African Americans is just one aspect of the web of meanings and perspectives that shaped my everyday experiences in the Congo. Reflecting on her experiences as an African American anthropologist conducting research in both Alabama and Guyana, Brackette Williams highlights the importance of local perceptions for delimiting the ethnographer's role and place. "It is doubtful that anthropologists, even those in exotic lands, had the power to . . . construct an identity for participant-observation that was autonomous of the range of role identities that constituted the social order of power relations into which they entered" (1996, 92). The various ways that people made sense of my body and my presence taught me a great deal about how people in the Congo understand and shape their everyday worlds. By embracing an approach where I felt, moved, and learned through my *body as center* of the research process, I was able to critically analyze how my race, skin complexion, gender, class,

FIGURE 1.4. Funeral procession to a gravesite, Luozi, 2006. Photo by Yolanda Covington-Ward.

education, marital status, and even my hair placed me in different identity roles depending on the context.

The Anthropologist . . . or Just Another Black Woman

June 1, 2005. "Mama Faustine, a tout a l'heure!" (See you later!) I call out to my host mother so that she knows I am leaving. I walk briskly to the blue metal gate and step outside, closing the gate securely. I hear the footsteps of Papa Joseph, the night watchman, as he locks the gate behind me. I stand there, adjusting the hem on my tailored shirt and glancing back to make sure that the zippers of both my shirt and skirt were still lined up in the middle of my back. Clutching my wide black handbag to my side, I begin to walk down the road. I nod at the off-duty soldier/policeman sitting in front of my neighbor's home and look up at the sky. Dusk is just settling, and people in the neighborhood are out and about, with some already sitting drinking Skol, Primus, and soda at the makeshift bar across the street. I keep walking and suck my teeth in annoyance as gritty sand once again enters my open-toed sandals. Why didn't any one warn me that Kinshasa's streets are like a dirty beach! I stop to kick the sand out and continue on my way, passing a cobbler who once fixed the heel on one of my shoes, and a disabled man to whom I sometimes give money and/or food. My friend Charles, dressed in a button-down shirt and khaki pants, joins me at this point, as he had agreed to show me the building that I was looking for as it was on the way to another engagement that he was attending. After another two blocks or so, we arrive at a well-maintained, light-colored two-story building, with yet another night watchman seated behind a wrought-iron gate. Dressed in a blue uniform, he stands and walks leisurely to the gate to address us in Lingala.

"Ozuluka nini?" (What are you looking for?)

I reply in French. "I don't speak Lingala. My name is Ma Yolanda. I am here for the French conversation group."

He responds in French. "There is no group here for you."

"There is a conversation group meeting here tonight. I was invited."

"There are no Congolese inside here."

"I am not Congolese. I am American."

Charles interjects, explaining the situation in Lingala, but the guard just looks at me skeptically and refuses to let me in. Just then, a dark Mercedes Benz pulls up to the gate, and the guard leaps to open the gate, all the while with his eyes still on us. The car pulls in, but I cannot see who is inside because of the tinted windows. He closes the gate securely behind the car, opens the passenger door for a White woman who I do not know, and chats briefly with her driver after she enters the building. He then turns his attention back to us. At this point, Charles has to leave for his meeting, and I am on my own. I realize that if I am to get pass the guard, I would have to act like an American. I did not drive up in a nice car with a chauffeur; I am not White, and I am dressed in a tailored Congolese-style outfit. I straighten my back, and address him in clear English, assuming the same entitled tone that I had heard some White and even some Black Americans use in their interactions with Congolese employees.

"I was invited here. The meeting has already started, so I must be let in."

He smiles, as if amused by my ability to speak English, but his response is the same:

"Tu peux pas entrer." (You can't come in.)

My shoulders slump at the failure of my performance of American and, really, White privilege. I then smile gently, batting my eyelashes and leaning in closer to the gate. I try another tactic.

"Mon frère, vraiment, c'est la vérité. Je ne blagues pas." (My brother, really, it's the truth. I am not lying.)

He continues to shake his head in refusal.

I sigh in frustration. What could I do? I am already about ten minutes late. Just as I am about to give up and leave, I realize that the Portuguese woman who had invited me to the group had given me her phone number. I dig in my bag for the card and call her with my cell phone. She answers:

"Hello?"

"Hello? Marie? This is Yolanda."

"Yolanda! Where are you?"

"I am downstairs at the gate."

"Well come up then!"

"I can't. The guard won't let me in. Can you please come down and get me?"

"Sure. I will be there in a second."

After I hear the click of her hanging up, I stand there, arms crossed until I see Marie coming outside. She says a few words to the guard, who then quickly runs to the gate and opens it, apologizing profusely.

"You are American?" he says, as if I hadn't told him this already.

"Yes," I respond. Stone-faced, I walk past him, trying to ignore the sting of humiliation that is burning my face and neck. As Marie chatters excitedly about the other women taking part in the group, I try to swallow the lump in my throat. After ascending the stairs, we enter an air-conditioned room tastefully decorated with African sculptures with about six women (all White) seated around an expensive wooden boardroom table. I introduce myself to the women and thank the host for allowing me to attend. She smiles and replies, "Oh, that's no problem. What a lovely outfit you're wearing!"

I open with this story of my failed performance of privilege to highlight two major points: First, privilege and class status are repeatedly performed in everyday life in postcolonial Congo in ways that sharply demarcate the boundaries between the haves and the have-nots. As a researcher, I was also implicated in these performances, regardless of whether I wanted to be or not. Second, this story of the denial of access demonstrates how the perceived characteristics of the researcher (race, gender, class, and so on) affect his or her movement throughout research sites. My everyday experiences as a woman of African descent in the Congo on taxi buses, in markets and Internet cafes, in bureaucratic offices, and in nightclubs allowed me to gain a better understanding of the daily lives of Congolese because I was not as clearly marked as a foreigner. I experienced the same daily indignities, such as being told to leave my handbag at a clerk's desk when I entered a grocery store while White women walked blithely by the clerk, swinging their handbags, oblivious to their racial privilege. Conversely, I was able to avoid

FIGURE 1.5. Author (*far right*) with friends at a Catholic church, Paroisse Sacre-Coeur, Gombe, Kinshasa, 2005. Unknown photographer.

some common challenges for White researchers, such as being charged the local taxi rate in Kinshasa while the rate would have been doubled or tripled if the driver saw that I was White. Like other Black female anthropologists conducting research in Africa and its diasporas (Hurston 1938; Daughtry 1997; Jules-Rosette 1975a; Harrison 1991; Ulysse 2007; Slocum 2001; Simmons 2009; Pierre 2012), my perceived identity shaped my experiences and interactions in myriad ways (see figure 1.5).

On Positionality and Being an African American Woman Conducting Ethnographic Research in the Congo

Writing in 1942, Zora Neale Hurston used a common colloquial phrase to summarize the troubled relations between African Americans, often divided among themselves by class, skin color, and other characteristics. "My skinfolks, but not my kinfolks; my race but not my taste" ([1942] 1991, 168). Such a phrase captures the tensions that exist between relatedness and distance; between understanding a degree of connectedness based on shared African ancestry, but simultaneously disavowing too much of a connection. This same concept can be applied to try to understand the importance of race and perceptions of race in the field for anthropologists of African descent working with people who may in fact look like them. In much of what has been writ-ten on conducting anthropological field research, the main categories that have been used are those of "outsider" and "insider." *Outsider* often denotes people foreign to the culture of study who are usually easily visually distin-guished from the community of study. In "insider" or "native" anthropology, the anthropologist is from the community of study. Although the writings of scholars such as Kirin Narayan (1993) have problematized these designations, I'd like to turn our attention to yet another positioning that warrants addi-tional analysis. This positioning is that of a person who was not born in the community of study, yet looks like the relatives of his or her informants; one who isn't fluent in the indigenous language, yet intuitively understands many elements of the cultural body language.[13] In particular, I am referring to the situation of being a brown-skinned African American woman doing research in Kinshasa and Bas-Congo in the Democratic Republic of Congo. Like Karla Slocum's experience of being both close and distant to the Black female trad-ers she studied in St. Vincent (2001, 141) and Irma McLaurin's experience of studying women in Belize (1996), the position that I occupied, not by any choice of my own, hovered in between "native" and "stranger." Because of my skin color and features, I was often seen as one of the "skinfolk." However, local understandings and perceptions of my identity impacted my research in multiple ways, as previously explained through the connections people made with my presence and the prophecy of Simon Kimbangu. My experiences in Congo contrasted vividly with a semester abroad that I spent in Ghana as an undergraduate, during which people would quickly pick me out as a for-eigner, possibly because I was lighter than most Ghanaians, and I was once even called a half-caste. In the Congo, I was able to blend in more readily as there was a broader range of brown skin tones. Often, before people spoke to me, they assumed that I was Congolese, and when I explained that I was not, they continued to assume that my parents were Congolese. If I explained that my ancestors had been taken from Africa and enslaved in the United States, and that I was not sure of where I was from, people would smile, and say assuredly, "Oh, they must be from Congo." If I was not specific about telling them that I was African American, people would make a number of guesses and try and make sense of who I was and what I was doing in the Congo. My "misidentifications" were specific to the region and Francophone nature of the Congo, as I was often asked if I was Ivorian, Togolese, South African, Haitian, Jamaican (because of my locked hair), and finally American.[14] Ini-tially, the identity guessing game was entertaining, but eventually, it became burdensome as I felt as though I had to explain myself to someone every day, at least at first. But later, as I reflected on the value that these cases of misidentification have for indexing relationships, histories, and migrations to and from the Congo, I took it all in stride. The characteristics shaping people's opportunities, interactions, networks, and social status in Kinshasa and Luozi were multifold: race, gender, class, age, education, religion, ethnicity, marital status, language, residence, experience living abroad, and parental status all played a part, depending on the context. Because of how I was perceived, I was able to experience many of the vagaries of everyday life as many Congolese do, in ways that broadly enhanced my perspective on social life in the Congo. I will examine a few of those characteristics here, focusing especially on those that impacted my own research experiences.

"YOU CAN'T COME IN": RACIALIZED BODIES

Blackness, as a concept, identity, and even political perspective, does not have the same meaning everywhere. Every country has its own history and social conditions, and people of African descent may understand and define themselves differently in different spaces. Thus, although sharing a history of enslavement and discrimination, people descended from African enslaved populations in Nicaragua can claim and primarily identify with European ancestors (Gordon 1998) while a broader range of racial categories and everyday understandings of race based on skin tone, hair texture, and racial admixture exists in other places such as Brazil (E. Williams 2013). What, then, does Blackness mean in the Congo? How is it lived and embodied, and how is it understood by everyday Congolese?

Like most other African countries, the Congo has a recent history of European colonization. From 1884 to 1908, as the personal colony of King Leopold II of Belgium (Congo Free State), and then from 1908 to 1960 under the country of Belgium itself, the Congolese were treated as inferiors, at best as children to be treated paternalistically, at worst as a scourge to be eradicated. While other works provide a better account of the atrocities committed against the Congolese population by European soldiers, traders, and explorers during the early years of colonization (Hochschild 1998; Roberts 2013), what the later, more structured colonial administration established was a social structure in which Whiteness and Blackness were often diametrically juxtaposed in everyday practice. Laws restricting movement, forced labor policies, corporal punishment, segregated housing by law, and de facto segregation in public accommodations all defined and restricted the everyday lives of Congolese under Belgian rule (Nzongola-Ntalaja 2002, 39). What the everyday workings of colonial Belgian Congo reinforced was an ideology of white superiority, one that persists until the present day. A short anecdote will suffice:

Walking along a path toward the Protestant mission area in Luozi (*ku missioni*, which is how people referred to it in everyday speech), Pierre and I passed a number of mango trees with dozens of ripe mangos on the ground. Pierre stopped and picked up a huge, plump mango and turned to me.

"You know what we call these?"

"What?" I respond.

"Manga zi Mputu." (European mango.) "Because they are the biggest, juicy and tasty. They are the best."

He turned, and scanning the ground, picks up a small, firm, green mango. Holding it high, he continues:

"Manga ba Ndombe or Manga zi Kongo." (Black or Kongo mango.) "It is small, no good." He tosses it back on the ground with disdain.

"But they are from the same tree. All of these mangos grew here," I say, gesturing to the many mango trees and all the mangos on the ground.

He shrugs his shoulders. "That's just how people call them."

This short exchange is just one example of how Blackness and Whiteness are imagined and understood within the Congo, where Whiteness is associated with power and positive attributes, while Blackness is associated with inferior characteristics and lack of desirability. It is telling that such an ideology is present in the most mundane of items—fruit, yet still reinforces a way of thinking that supports White privilege and Black and African denigration. In her groundbreaking book on processes of racialization in postcolonial Ghana, anthropologist and African diaspora studies scholar Jemima Pierre argues that in Ghana, intelligence, status, wealth, technical know-how, and other positive characteristics are automatically attributed to Whites. Status must be performed for those racialized as Black in Ghana; whereas for Whites in Ghana, it is assumed (2012, 86). This "normative power" of Whiteness (2012, 98) seemed to also be the case in everyday life in the Congo, especially in situations regarding access.

Bodies racialized as Black and/or African in the Congo are policed and monitored in, and often excluded from, certain spaces. My lack of a car, skin color, and propensity for wearing tailored "African" clothes often made it difficult for me to enter certain foreign-owned or foreign-affiliated compounds and buildings in Kinshasa. Once I went to the house of an African American friend for dinner, and the security guard on the ground floor of the apartment building refused to let me in and had to call her to verify and physically come down to get me. In 2010, when I returned to the Congo, I went to the U.S. compound in Kinshasa that houses the Public Affairs section of the embassy. I approached the door and was brusquely ordered by a guard to step to the side and join the line of Congolese waiting in the hot sun while White employees and citizens were let inside without a problem. I had to show my passport before they even let me approach the door to go through security. I have already recounted my experiences with what I perceived to be racial discrimination in grocery stores in Kinshasa, especially in Gombe. Interestingly enough, on all these occasions the guards (and clerks) were Congolese working for foreign-owned or foreign-operated establishments, whose jobs apparently included keeping out any errant Africans. These experiences and others (such as being served after White customers in restaurants although my Congolese friends and I had arrived and ordered at least twenty minutes before the White customers did) exposed me to the everyday indignities that Congolese suffer in their own country, often at the hands of other Congolese. Other researchers of African descent have also written about similar experiences in regards to race in other African countries (see Pierre 2012). Indeed, the unquestioned valorization of Whiteness, seen in general attitudes and specific practices such as skin bleaching (done by both women and men in Congo),[15] is a mindset that is explicitly challenged by movements such as Bundu dia Kongo.

Race, however, was not the only factor that impacted people's everyday lives. Ethnicity was also a key attribute that people used to relate with others. A number of general stereotypes were repeated quite often in daily conversations, especially in Kinshasa: BaKongo as meek and docile; BaNgala as loud and aggressive; BaLuba as educated, business minded and yet selfish and insular. While ethnicity did not affect me directly, it was of great importance for others in certain situations, particularly leading up to elections. I do not address ethnic identification in great detail here, but chapters 2, 3, and 6 provide in-depth explorations of the salience of ethnic identity for BisiKongo people during the colonial and postcolonial eras. The next section uses the case of public transportation to address yet another set of social factors key to organizing everyday experience in the Congo: class and wealth.

MANQUE DE TRANSPORT: VULNERABLE BODIES

Throughout my research, and especially in Kinshasa, I experienced many of the same indignities and inconveniences that the average Kinois faced on an everyday basis.[16] One of the major problems in Kinshasa was the lack of reliable public transportation. The fact that I did not own a car like the other foreigners and more well-off Congolese allowed me to experience the daily struggles of everyday low-income Kinois. Within a few days of my arrival, I was debriefed at embassy-associated facilities and was advised to buy a car, but because I didn't plan on staying in Kinshasa for very long, I did not consider it since all I could afford was a small sedan, which would prove futile in navigating the treacherous roads of rural Bas-Congo, where suvs, pickup trucks, and big trucks reigned. I decided to make do with the public transportation. Now, public transportation in 2005–6 did not mean shiny, spacious buses with air-conditioning, or rapid subway lines. Rather, there are taxis, and taxi buses. Taxis are old, unmarked, barely running personal cars that have been transformed into taxis (three people in the front, and three, sometimes four people in the back). The other option is the taxi buses, which are decidedly less comfortable, with the worse (and more common) ones being converted cargo vans, and the best ones being old school buses from the United States. In addition, groups of youth and men often hang onto the back of the moving taxi bus. As for the train, I'd initially considered taking the train down into Bas-Congo until I saw it passing one day and noticed that there were as many people on the roof of the moving train as there were inside of it!

By the end of my time in the Congo, I'd learned to understand all the hand signals indicating the direction of the approaching taxis, gotten accustomed to grabbing the door handle of an approaching moving taxi and running with it as it slowed down to ensure that I was the first inside, and was prepared to stand for several hours waiting for transportation on crowded corners. I also became adjusted to the random flat tires, holes in car floors, and vendors and beggars approaching the windows. Once, as I was waiting with a friend for a taxi or taxi bus, a bus pulled up loaded with people, and just as we were running to board, people began shouting and jumping out of the doors and windows. The engine had caught fire, and the fire was coming through the floor! I watched in horror and backed away from the flames. Fortunately, no one was seriously injured. Unfortunately, we then had to compete with about fifty more people for a taxi!

One memory from my field notes details the everyday struggle that Kinois face when trying to get from one place to another. My friend Didier and I were taking a trip to a library of the Jesuit mission located at Kimwenza. To get there, we took a taxi and two taxi buses. The trip there was uneventful, and the buses were not too crowded because of the time of day that we departed. However, the trip home was another matter entirely.

May 6, 2005. After several hours at Kimwnza we walk a bit down the road to wait for transportation back to Kinshasa. However, this is when things really become bad. A taxi bus (this one a converted cargo van) arrives, and we run to get in, as other people are running trying to beat us to it. There is space for everyone though. As I try to ascend, I crack my right knee against the edge of a wooden bench. Then, I have to climb over two more benches to get to the seats (a wooden plank) in the last row. I have my back to the trunk door, and hope it will not fly open. However, things deteriorate the next time we stop. A bunch of people come to get in, and several of them get in from the back door! One man kicks me in the side trying to get in, and although there is limited space, he squeezes himself between me and another woman. Oh my God, it is terrible! I am squashed against the right side of the cargo van, with only a round circle to look out of that had been cut out by a blowtorch. To make things worse, the wall is rattling, and bulging outward, and every time we go over a big bump I swear the screws will give and I will tumble out the side of the van. I also think that I am going to get a splinter right in my behind as I involuntarily slide along the wooden plank when we lurch forward. When I try to hold on to the holes in the ceiling, the metal is brown and rusted, and I hope that I don't cut myself and get tetanus. We finally arrive at the next round point.

This tale of treacherous transportation in Kinshasa reveals how unpredictable and even dangerous getting around in Kinshasa could be. I had another Congolese friend named Patricia who was riding a taxi bus to work when the vehicle stopped suddenly, and she banged her mouth against the metal bar behind the driver's seat. She chipped her tooth and had to see a dentist to have the tooth repaired. Sadder tales abound, involving robbery, rape, and even death in countless car and bus crashes. My experiences helped me to understand the vulnerability of the many bodies that crowded Kinshasa's public transportation. The breakdown of the transportation infrastructure made daily life in Kinshasa dangerous in many ways.[17]

FROM "YOU CAN'T COME IN" TO "COME HERE": GENDER, MARITAL STATUS, AND DESIRED BODIES

Another experience that I shared, specifically with Congolese women, was that of being approached by White men. While Congolese men expressed their interest as well, the difference was that White, usually Middle Eastern men (who the average Kinois grouped all together as Lebanese, regardless of their actual origins), thought my interest (and body) were for sale. During the night, le Boulevard du 30 Juin (the main street going through downtown Kinshasa and Gombe) is decorated by many young Congolese women in their finest and most revealing attire, trying to attract the attention of male drivers so that there can be an exchange of cash for sexual services.[18] Moreover, in the dance clubs most frequented by the foreign and wealthy, crowds of beautiful young Congolese women could be found, who I later realized were prostitutes. Some of these White men approached me as they would a Congolese or other African woman who was a prostitute. Several times I had been walking along the boulevard during the day, and White men pulled over their cars to "offer" me a ride. I always refused. Once, a Middle Eastern man followed me out of an Internet café and pulled his car up next to the taxi stop where I was waiting. I tried to ignore him but he kept calling and gesturing to me until I went up to the window and in no uncertain terms refused his company. When I came back to join the crowd waiting at the taxi stop, one elderly man said something to the effect of, "Good for you. They think all of our women are prostitutes."

Yet another incident, involving a taxi, demonstrates some of the possible perils of being a Black woman doing fieldwork in an African country. I was at a corner with many others around rush hour, trying to get a taxi. A small, beat-up gray sedan slowed down but seemed full, so I kept looking. A man got out of the car, came up to me, and asked if I was going to Magasin,[19] and I said *Oui*, and another girl asked "Magasin?" and he said "No, only one person." He led me to the gray car. But when I got in the car and it pulled off, I saw there was extra room. Two people were in the front, and I and the guy were in the back. He began to make polite conversation, and I slowly realized the vehicle was not a taxi as it kept passing people trying to flag down taxis going our way. I became scared and wondered if I was about to be robbed raped, or killed. I noticed the locks weren't automatic, and so had some hope of jumping out and running for safety. The woman (who he introduced as his aunt) asked where I was going, and I told her, hoping and praying they would actually take me there. They stopped at my corner, and as I tried to run out, the guy asked for my number. I politely declined, claiming not to have a cell phone (and hoping it wouldn't ring, revealing my lie) and then took his number, all the while with my right foot out of the door. They pulled off, and I never saw them again, but this incident reveals the everyday dangers that women face in Kinshasa, just trying to get a taxi.

Another aspect of my identity that affected my research was my marital status. At the time that I conducted research in the Congo, I was married. My husband, Lincoln, who I met in Rhode Island as an undergraduate, is originally from Liberia. He came to visit me for a month while I was in the Congo. His presence helped me in many ways, as I was able to introduce him to people in my neighborhood in Kinshasa (especially to men who had been pursuing me romantically) and to friends and neighbors in Luozi as well. My status as a married woman, did, however, limit some of the activities that I engaged in. For example, there was a small performance group formed by some local teenagers (all unmarried) in Luozi performing popular Congolese dance music. I began to attend and participate as a dancer in the rehearsals, just based on my love of *soukouss*. During one rehearsal conducted outdoors I noticed a few disconcerting and even disapproving looks of passersby and one male onlooker who kept staring at me lasciviously as I danced. Afterward, I talked to a few female friends about it. I was told that it didn't look very well for a married woman to dance publicly in that way. I decided then to just attend the rehearsals and to save my dancing for weddings and other public occasions where it would be considered more appropriate. So while opportunities for me to perform existed, preserving my reputation and local standing were much more important to me to assure continued access in regards to my research and the respect of people in the community.

INSIGHTS AND PERSPECTIVES

Being mistaken for Congolese allowed me to experience the vagaries of daily life in the Congo on a much more intimate level, regardless of the number of inconveniences or slights to which I was subjected. First and foremost was my ability to be "unmarked" in the sense that because people did not automatically see me as a foreigner they were less likely to change their behavior just because I was there. My ability to blend in also allowed me a bit more ease in getting around on foot, because, for example, when the street kids (*sheges*) came begging, I was not automatically targeted as a rich foreigner (although they did ask me for money often, as they did every other Congolese that passed). They were much more aggressive and persistent with White people and others driving fancy cars. My skin also provided a form of a pass in situations such as when I paid the Congolese rather than the foreigner entrance fee, which was twice as costly, to the bonobo sanctuary outside of Kinshasa. And had I been a White person walking the streets, I most likely would have had to endure being called *mundele* or even *mundele zoba* (stupid White person), which I witnessed when walking with a German acquaintance in Magasin in Kinshasa.[20] Being unmarked allowed me to listen to and participate in conversations about a wide array of topics in multiple contexts, from taxis, to beauty salons, to churches, without people automatically changing their behavior because of seeing me as a foreigner or visible stranger. Being of African descent was the key to my gaining access to a branch of Bundu dia Kongo in Luozi, when leaders refused to allow a curious young White woman to participate or even see the ceremony, whereas I was allowed to attend and even videotape certain parts of it, as I was "their sister." My African ancestry was also my saving grace when during an interview, a leader of Bundu dia Kongo asked me what field I was studying. When I replied, "anthropology," he sucked his teeth and looked at me with disdain. "If I'd known you were an anthropologist, I wouldn't even have talked to you." A bit flabbergasted, I made my case by explaining that I knew the distasteful history of anthropology, and if we were to change how anthropology is done, more Black people need to become anthropologists. As I continued to discuss being the only African American in my cohort and in my classes, he began to loosen up, and we had a frank conversation about the potential and need for transforming the discipline and how it could be used to promote studies of Kongo culture.

My common Blackness did not, however, erase my own privilege of being a U.S. citizen. My friends who I came to know really well sometimes reminded me of this fact. While walking in Luozi, one friend said, "If anything were to happen out here, your government will come and save you. But we, we would suffer and die." At first I disagreed, based on the history of racial discrimination against African Americans in the United States. But, as I reflected on it, I realized my friend was right. Once people did realize I was American, I had access in many ways that everyday Congolese would not. One example was my experiences accessing the African Archives in Brussels. After being forewarned by a Congolese scholar that Congolese researchers were often treated in a disrespectful manner, I told him about my largely uneventful and positive experience. "They were nice because you are American," I was told. Like with Jafari Allen's experiences in Cuba (2011), I sometimes had a choice of whether or not to use my American privilege in certain situations, and benefitting from that privilege.

Coming back to shared experiences that shaped my time in the Congo, another common incidence for me (and people I encountered) was a heightened sense of familiarity based on physical characteristics. In brief, I met people who looked like African Americans I knew back home. Similarly, for a few people, I reminded them of someone they knew. During my early time in Luozi, I was playing basketball occasionally with a group of youth from the town.[21] In August 2005, my husband, Lincoln, and I went with a friend from Luozi to play basketball at an outdoor gym in the commune of Masina in Kinshasa. Lincoln ended up playing a pickup game with a team, and I watched, shouting words of encouragement. Suddenly, I saw a familiar face. A teenage girl was playing basketball on a neighboring court in the compound. I stared because she looked just like one of my younger sisters from a distance. How could I be seeing my sister in the Congo! I stood up and walked toward her, gazing in disbelief. She had the same eyes, same light brown skin tone, same height and build as my sister. It didn't make rational sense, and when I got even closer, I saw that they were not exactly identical in their characteristics, but even so, she resembled my sister more than I did. Other times

I saw someone who resembled my grandmother, my uncle, and other family members. I also had several experiences when people told me I resembled someone they knew. One young man told me I resembled his ex-girlfriend, and another person likened me to his daughter.

Experiences such as these demonstrate that common African ancestry does create opportunities for more intimate understandings and connections, that however contrived, can still affect relationships between researchers and those they study. However, these perceived links are not without problems, as many negative interactions and perceived stereotypes exist on both sides (Wamba 1999). These bonds between continental Africans and those in the diaspora are not only based on shared physical characteristics or common oppression. As Philippe Wamba writes, "history reveals that far more often than they have clashed, Africans and African Americans have reached out to one another with fascination, purpose, and a spirit of hopeful kinship. And this preoccupation with one another has inspired many significant artistic, political, and religious explorations of the relationship between Africa and the descendants of Africans in America" (1999, 35). My identity as an African American doing research in the Congo was very important both because it affected my daily experiences as a researcher, and also because it had even greater significance tied directly to the history of the Lower Congo.

While I discussed race, gender, ethnicity, and other social factors separately, for my respondents in Congo,[22] identity was intersectional, and in different contexts, certain factors might be highlighted over others. In Luozi, for instance, religious affiliation is a key method for forming social networks and circles and socializing in everyday life, while one's Kongo ethnicity became paramount when Bundu dia Kongo rallied people in Luozi to vote for the group's spiritual leader in the campaign leading to the 2006 elections. In their quest to unite BisiKongo people to vote along ethnic lines and specifically for BDK candidates, one of the key cultural and historical figures that animated Bundu dia Kongo's songs, prayers, rallies, and speeches was the prophet Simon Kimbangu. Just who was Simon Kimbangu, and why was he seen as so important to Bundu dia Kongo? How did he use his body to challenge Belgian colonial authority? And how did he come to lead what Robert H. C. Graham, a British Baptist missionary called "the most remarkable movement the country has ever had" (1921, 192)?

Part II

SPIRITS, BODIES,
AND PERFORMANCE IN
BELGIAN CONGO

CHAPTER 2

"A War between Soldiers and Prophets"

Embodied Resistance in Colonial Belgian Congo, 1921

"Take That Which Your Ancestors Used in Their Battle"

July 23, 2010. Ma Makanda sits in a small chair next to the wall of a ranch-style house shading her from the blazing sun. My research assistant Kilanda and I greet her as we enter the compound. She pulls me down into a hug, looking closely at my face. Cataracts affect her vision, but she smiles in recognition and sings a short song in greeting, as we had last seen each other four years ago. Her daughter, whom we also greet, sets up several chairs on the porch of the house for the interview. At seventy-three years of age, Ma Makanda moves gingerly, wrapping her pagne more securely around her waist as she takes faltering steps, her legs racked with arthritis.[1] After exchanging pleasantries, her hands, wizened and hardened from years of agricultural work, grip the photos of my family that I have brought for her. As the interview gets under way, she speaks in a low, controlled voice, punctuating her responses with songs as she reflects on her experiences growing up as a participant in the colonial-era kingunza or prophetic movements. She remembers hiding in the forest to worship: "It was a war between soldiers and bangunza (prophets). During that time we couldn't play the drum or shakers; we only tapped our legs and sang in low voices. If you sang in high voices you would be arrested" (July 23, 2010). She sang several of the songs that she remembered including the following, accompanied by vigorous hand clapping:

Buabu Tata muana Nzambi telama wabonga
Bio bianuanina Bambuta Tata wutunungisa
Now Child of God, stand up and take
That which your ancestors used in their battle[2]

Ma Makanda explained that the music they made during their clandestine meetings in the forest would bring on the descent of the Holy Spirit, whose presence would be evidenced through the trembling of the prophets' bodies. If, however, they were caught singing or trembling, colonial authorities would arrest the bangunza. Clearly, the Belgians saw the kingunza movement as a threat to their hegemony in the Belgian Congo.

Ma Makanda's story captures the critical uses and meanings of Kongo embodied practices in the context of the colonial period. In European colonies in Africa, embodied practices often became a point of contention between the indigenous population and colonial authorities. While Europeans targeted economic systems, political and social structures, and language for change, they also sought to alter embodied practices such as forms of dress, funerary rituals, hygiene, secular dances and other forms of recreation, and even spiritual worship. With the start of a prophetic movement in the Lower Congo in 1921, certain activities of the Kongo population such as singing, drumming, and more important, trembling, became cause for arrest and punishment. For those involved in the kingunza movement, "it was a war" being fought—not by guns—but with music, prayer, and bodies. Why was controlling the bodies of their colonial subjects so critical for the Belgians, and why did they and other Western occupants of the Congo see these embodied practices as such a threat? More important, how did Kongo people themselves interpret the same embodied practices and use their bodies to resist Belgian colonial authority?

This chapter examines trembling in the Lower Congo as an everyday cultural performance of the BisiKongo that was also a site of religious and political contestation between the church, the colonial state, and the indigenous population. In this chapter, I focus on one year—1921, as this year laid the foundation for both nationalist aspects of the kingunza movement, as well as provided a template for later colonial policies for suppressing the movement. The movement began in March 1921 with a Christian MuKongo prophet named Simon Kimbangu. Thousands of people flocked to him, alarming Belgian colonial authorities and leading to the severe repression of the movement in the following months, followed by the prophet Simon Kimbangu's arrest in September and his trial and sentencing in October 1921. Kongo religious performances in the context of the movement—including practices such as trembling, jumping, prophesying, singing Protestant hymns, and using traditional instruments—were seen as subversive actions menacing the smooth running of the colony and the hegemony of the European-led missions.

Through performative encounters, the kingunza movement used a type of spiritual legitimacy gained from the spiritual realm to subvert Belgian colonial authority, using Kongo bodies as the key weapons of resistance. Embodied cultural performances played a crucial role in the making and unmaking of political and religious authority in Belgian Congo. This was particularly evident when missionaries and colonial agents were placed in positions of having to fight off challenges to their authority. These challenges, in fact, were often mustered through embodied cultural performances on the part of the Kongo people, as shown by the trembling, jumping, singing, dancing, and revelatory visions that characterized the Kongo prophetic movements, which established a powerful, competing religious authority through their prophets. Thus, the desire of European missionaries and colonial agents to maintain their religious and political authority then necessitated numerous efforts to control the embodied cultural performances of colonial subjects, efforts that often failed.

A Note on Methods

Although Simon Kimbangu was the impetus for the movement, the kingunza movement did not end with his arrest and imprisonment; in fact other prophets continually emerged from 1921 (both with and without Kimbangu's recognition) up until independence in 1960.[3] While the terms *Kimbanguism* and *Ngunzism* were often used interchangeably to describe them as well, the movements overall can be called kingunza, or prophetism. Later expressions of prophetism such as Salutism (Salvation Army) and Mpadism/Khakism, while not emerging until the 1930s and later, can also be included under the larger umbrella of Kongo prophetic movements.[4] Many of the same embodied practices described above prevailed in all these groups and movements, and some still exist today in churches of bangunza, such as the DMNA church that I visited quite frequently during my time in the Congo.[5]

Most of my material for this chapter came from archival documents, especially the records of different missionary societies and the colonial administration. I use correspondence and letters from the African Archive of the

Belgian Ministry of Foreign Affairs in Brussels and materials from the archive of the American Baptist Historical Society in Atlanta, Georgia, which houses the correspondence and personal papers of missionaries of the American Baptist Foreign Missionary Society who were posted in the Lower Congo. I also incorporate documents from the Archives of the Baptist Missionary Society in Oxford, UK, and published compilations of firsthand accounts (including those of both missionaries and Congolese) printed by the Royal Academy of Over Seas Sciences in Brussels (Vellut 2005, 2010). In addition to my archival research, I also conducted ethnographic research in Kongo independent *ngunza* churches and interviews with Congolese people in and around Luozi in 2005–6 and 2010. However, virtually no firsthand witnesses are still living who would have experienced the kingunza movement in the early 1920s. Several interviewees, however, were able to discuss their experiences as participants in later waves of the movement occurring several decades after Kimbangu's movement began. As a result, while this chapter is based largely on archival material, the next chapter includes both archival and some interview material.

Using missionary and colonial administration records as the primary sources for this chapter presents both benefits and challenges. On one hand, the observations of missionaries and colonial authorities were often written down and included in letters and other correspondence to their headquarters, home societies, or to other missionaries/agents. These records are usually well preserved in multiple archives and often provide details that colonial administration records lack because the missionaries usually lived in close proximity to the indigenous population. On the other hand, these written reports and letters also reflect the biases of the missionaries and colonial administrators themselves, who generally saw these religious movements as a threat to their own authority and security. As a result, I tried to remain vigilant to the intentions behind the use of terms such as *heathen* or *demented* that different Europeans and/or Americans used to describe the movement. Moreover, these documents do not usually reflect the voices of the Congolese themselves, although there are some written accounts of the movement and letters authored by Congolese participants and some records of interrogations of suspected bangunza written by both colonial administrators and missionaries. Wherever possible, I have tried to draw from these sources as well to provide multiple perspectives on events of interest. What is gained through the use of such a wide variety of sources on the movement is a more complex and nuanced description and analysis of the kingunza movement and its impact on the Congo, both for Congolese and Europeans alike. Missionaries were not an undifferentiated whole; a few even supported the movements.

Likewise, not all Kongo people supported the bangunza. The kingunza movement of 1921 remains, however, a watershed moment in Congolese history, not only for its relation to an emergent nationalism, but also for its use of spiritual power to combat and challenge both religious and secular authority.

Brief History of Christian Missions in the Lower Congo

The history of Christian evangelization on the Lower Congo began with the baptism of Nzinga-Nkuwu (Joao I, the sovereign of the Kongo Kingdom) by Portuguese missionaries in May of 1491. The Kongo Kingdom established contact with Portugal and Rome and received European Catholic missionaries of different nationalities until the late 1700s.[6] Several of these Catholic missionaries (in this case Capuchins from Italy) witnessed a religious revival in the Kongo Kingdom, now known to scholars as the Antonian movement. Dona Beatrice Kimpa Vita was a young woman who in 1704 fell gravely ill and became possessed by the spirit of Saint Anthony. She told others that she had been charged with the mission of restoring the Kongo Kingdom, which at the time was fractured by competing claimants to the throne. She preached about the Kongolese origins of Jesus and certain saints (challenging the European Catholic hegemony established by the Italian missionaries), implored people to return to the abandoned capital city, and said that she alone would choose the next ruler of the kingdom, as revealed by God. Thousands of people came to follow her, and her success threatened both religious and political players in the kingdom, and she was burned alive as a heretic in 1706 (Mbemba 2002; Thornton 1998). Dona Beatrice looms large in the larger Kongo imagination today as a type of cultural and nationalist hero. Thus in many discussions of Simon Kimbangu and kingunza, Dona Beatrice's name is often mentioned as a precolonial example of Kongo nationalist and religious movements. While both were Christian movements where BisiKongo people were seeking autonomy from European dominance of the Christian narrative and ritual practice, in the era of Kimpa Vita, Kongo people were the political rulers while for Kimbangu's era, European dominance extended to political, economic, and social arenas. Moreover, in comparing the movements, Kimbangu's movement drew much more on the body as a weapon of resistance, while such inferences cannot be as clearly drawn about Kimpa Vita's movement, largely owing to the lack of extensive historical documentation.

The BisiKongo were soon to see major transformations in their lives with the arrival of colonialism and the second wave of Christian evangelization, which began in 1865 when the area of Lower Congo was transferred from the Capuchin missionaries of the seventeenth century to the Holy Ghost Fathers, French Catholic missionaries based in Gabon. In 1878 British Protestant missionaries of the LIM (Livingstone Inland Mission) established a station at Mpalabala, near the coast, signaling the start of Protestant evangelization in the Lower Congo. The Lower Congo was opened to colonial exploitation beginning with H. M. Stanley's travels there starting in 1877, leading to the designation of the entire Congo Free State as the personal fiefdom of King Leopold II of Belgium at the Berlin conferences of 1884–85. From 1885 to 1908, the Congo was under the rule of the Belgian king, and his desire to expand Belgian influence in the colony affected Christian evangelization. While the Holy Ghost Fathers had been in the area since 1865, establishing posts at Landana, Boma, and Banana, they withdrew to the French Congo after 1888, when Belgian Catholic missionaries replaced them through an agreement made between King Leopold II and Rome (Koren 1958, 189–90, 223; Slade 1958, 23–24, 142).

King Leopold II never set foot in the Congo Free State himself; instead he used a concession system where private companies made agreements with him for operating in the Congo. The lack of oversight and accountability led to numerous scandals involving forced labor (for example, the red rubber scandal), human rights abuses, and large-scale death and destruction caused by these companies.[7] As a result, the Congo was then removed from the king's supervision and became a colony of the Belgian government from 1908 to 1960. Along with European soldiers, merchants, and colonial officials, missionaries entered a field now opened for evangelization. Protestant missionaries of the LIM established a station at Mpalabala in 1878 and continued to establish stations along the caravan route between Matadi and Stanley Pool. In 1879, the BMS (Baptist Missionary Society of England) founded a post at San Salvador (the former capital of the Kongo Kingdom), and then Ndandanga. In 1881 the first Swedish missionary of the SMF (Svenska Missions Förbundet, or Swedish Mission Covenant Church) arrived. In 1884, after encountering financial difficulties, the LIM divided its stations between the ABFMS (American Baptist Foreign Missionary Society) and the SMF. The first Belgian Catholic missions were established in 1888 by the Scheutists, followed by Peres of Gand (1891), Sisters of the Gand Charity (1892), Jesuits (1893), Sisters of Notre Dame of Namur and the Trappistes (1894), Priests of the Sacred Heart (1897), and the Redemptorists (1899).[8] The Lower Congo during the colonial period had a very substantial Protestant presence (in a country that would become majority Catholic) as most of the Protestant missionaries first established stations in the Lower Congo before spreading to other parts of the colony. By 1921, the major Protestant mission organizations in the Lower Congo were the BMS, ABFMS, SMF, and the CMA (Christian and Missionary Alliance) (see map 2.1).[9]

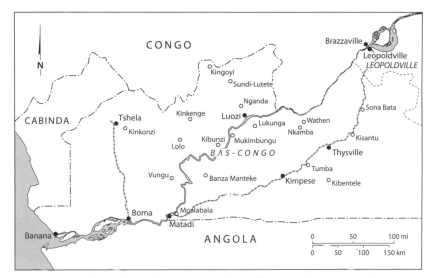

MAP 2.1. Map of colonial-era Bas-Congo province with major cities, towns, and mission stations, circa 1896, prepared by Bill Nelson.

When the Congo Free State was under his authority, King Leopold, as a Catholic himself, lobbied Belgian Catholic missionaries to come and evangelize the Congo. This commitment was first officially recognized in 1906 through a concordat signed between the Congo Free State and the Holy See in Rome (Markowitz 1973, 7). Initially, Catholic missions were given large tracts of land and were often shown state favor in comparison to the Protestant missions, which were not Belgian (Reardon 1968, 86–87). Overall, however, the missions (both Catholic and Protestant) and colonial authorities tended to work together. "The Belgian colonial system operated on the basis of an interdependent triumvirate of missionary, administration, and commercial interests. The missions provided the government with a measure of social and territorial control, and they educated and trained Africans for work on the plantations and in the mines. In return they received subsidies, protection, and land. The collaboration . . . was mutually satisfactory" (Markowitz 1973, 17–18).

The generally good working relationship between missionaries and colonial authorities for much of the early period of the Congo Free State perhaps explains why it took a person unassociated with a mission to publicly condemn the numerous atrocities committed against the native population. In his 1890 public document "An Open Letter to his Serene Majesty Leopold II," based on his own travels in the Congo Free State, George Washington Williams, an African American pastor, civil leader, historian, and journalist brought attention to numerous abuses of the indigenous population (Franklin 1985, 264–79). In 1894 Prosper Phillipe Augouard, a French missionary of the Holy Ghost Fathers, became the first missionary to publicly express discontent with the policies and actions of the state (Lagergren 1970, 147). Numerous public writings and speeches by Protestant missionaries condemning the atrocities followed from 1895 to the annexation of the Congo Independent State by Belgium in 1908. The overall reprehensible treatment of the indigenous population was one among several key factors contributing to the emergence of the prophetic movement in the Lower Congo.

Conditions Leading to the Prophetic Movement

The Kongo cosmological system includes a belief in the continual influence of the dead, of ancestral spirits, on the world of the living. In numerous historic instances, paralleling these ideas, when disastrous situations and general social discord existed in Kongo communities, religious leaders had to reconcile with the ancestral and spiritual world so that a sense of balance and harmony could prevail (Mahaniah 1975, 285). According to MuKongo historian Kimpianga Mahaniah, as Kongo traditional systems of political leadership, healing and therapy, and overall livelihood and health were dramatically transformed as Kongo people were incorporated as colonial subjects, healing movements led by prophets emerged to address the many social and political conflicts (Mahaniah 1975). Like Tshidi ritual practices in South Africa, where the spiritual healing of individual bodies functioned as an attempt to heal the social body (Comaroff 1985), the prophetic movements of the Lower Congo sought to right a world turned on its ear by European colonialism. What sorts of conditions were the Kongo people dealing with?

The Lower Congo suffered a period of depopulation directly caused by many of the brutal policies enacted as the nascent colonial state sought to control the indigenous population. The devastating conditions the BisiKongo faced were multifold, including forced labor (especially portage), violence, the corrosion of traditional forms of chiefship and spiritual leadership, famines, and health epidemics, among other negative social transformations. The Lower Congo became a launch pad for European exploration and navigation into the interior of the vast colony. Boma, a port city in the Lower Congo, was the colonial capital of both the Congo Free State and the Belgian Congo from 1886 to 1926 (Gondola 2002, 75). The Congo River was unnavigable inland after a certain point owing to intermittent waterfalls; thus most goods and supplies were carried on the heads and backs of Congolese porters, as pack animals could not survive in the area and the railroad was not yet constructed.[10] The portage system was sanctioned in an 1889 decree, and later in 1891, another decree established a labor tax system compelling Africans to work for their colonizers. Portage affected so many men in the Lukunga district of Lower Congo that ABFMS missionary Peter Frederickson reported in 1898 that "the carrying of heavy loads to Stanley Pool is the cause of death to many of the men."[11] Many Kongo people reacted to these changing conditions by moving away from the caravan routes, and later, the railroad, depopulating certain areas of the Lower Congo.[12] However, by 1920 the trend was reversing, as men and boys left villages and small towns in the countryside to seek work along the railroad and in large cities. This led American missionary John E. Geil to complain in his 1920 annual report about the impact of labor migration on church membership. "A revision of the church roll," he wrote, "has shown a much smaller membership than that which was reported formerly. . . . In our quest for young men and boys for the schools we were told repeatedly that they were nearly all away to Matadi and places along the railway in quest of money."[13] Geil's report clearly indicates the Lower Congo was undergoing a major demographic shift that was to have a major impact on both the city and the countryside alike.

Between 1872 and 1921, military expeditions into villages, a lack of rain, and a growing "immigrant non-producing population" all impacted disastrous incidences of famine across the Lower Congo (Mahaniah 1975, 187; see also Axelson 1970, 256–63). An American medical missionary writing in 1895 noted a lack of food owing to both state demands and a drought in 1894.[14] Because of such conditions, the Lower Congo was deeply impacted by unexpected food shortages.

Yet another factor increasing the general stress of the indigenous population was the large number of health epidemics that devastated the area. Between 1890 and 1913, sleeping sickness caused many deaths and population movements from plateaus to valleys. In the annual report for the American Baptist mission station at Banza Manteke (Mbanza Manteke) in 1891, the mission was noted as having been "severely afflicted by the mysterious 'sleeping sickness.'"[15] Over a decade later in 1904, the Baptist community mourned the loss of two female British missionaries in the Congo who died of sleeping sickness caused by the bite of the tsetse fly.[16]

Part of a worldwide medical crisis that lasted until 1920, Spanish influenza added to the destruction starting in 1918 (W. MacGaffey 1986a, 271; Mahaniah 1975, 189). An entry from the Kinshasa station logbook of the Baptist Missionary Society dated November 10, 1918, reveals the extent of the devastation caused by Spanish influenza: "During November and December a terrible epidemic of 'flu.' Thousands sick, hundreds died, and 3000 Congos fled to their homes. Many died on the way. Business all upset and much hunger in the town. Mr. Hynes did good work in dispensary and helped many a poor creature."[17] Likewise, in the Sona Bata (Nsona Mbata) medical report for 1919, American Missionary Mattie Frederickson reflected on the impact of Spanish influenza on the area, as well as other epidemics. "This time last year the Spanish influenza had about finished. We reopened schools and services. The death toll had been great, and the people called it the foreign disease, as they call Infantile Paralysis and a couple of other dreaded diseases."[18] Infantile paralysis (also known as polio), smallpox, influenza, and sleeping sickness all had a devastating effect on the population of the Lower Congo in the decade leading up to 1921.[19] Many in the local population referred to these scourges as "foreign diseases" and even "colonial diseases," revealing that the Congolese made negative associations between the presence of Europeans and their impact on the health of local communities.[20]

For all these reasons, the indigenous population in the Lower Congo declined dramatically; one scholar estimates that the population dropped by as much as 75 percent between 1885 and 1921 (W. MacGaffey 1986a, 271). All these factors contributed to an enormous sense of crisis for the Kongo. To add to this, traditional forms of chiefship were also destroyed by colonial imperatives. To administer the colony, the Congo was divided into four provinces, with each province divided into districts, which were themselves subdivided into territories, and then sectors, and then chefferies. Each chefferie (composed of five to twenty villages) was headed by a chief who supervised the heads of each village. The chiefs that were in this system were by and large chosen by the colonial administration, ignoring traditional systems of legitimizing chiefship (Feci 1972, 6; Mahaniah 1975, 176–78). Moreover, banganga, traditional healers, diviners, and priests, were specifically targeted by the colonial staté for arrest and execution (Axelson 1970, 266–73). This led to additional social conflict. As a result of all these social transformations, by 1921 the ground was fertile for a spiritual means of addressing the growing discord in Kongo society. The means of doing so, however, would not come from the mission churches. Indeed, as American Baptist missionary John E. Geil reported on the overall declining church membership at the Banza Manteke and Mpalabala churches in his annual report for 1920, he also made a declaration: "We need missionaries, land, buildings, and equipment but above all a great spiritual awakening in the church."[21] Little did he know that the spiritual awakening that he sought would emerge the next year, through the teachings, prophecies, and very body of a MuKongo man named Simon Kimbangu, especially through one particular form of embodiment—zakama, spirit-induced trembling.

Trembling Embodied Blessings

August 4, 2010. It is my last full day in Luozi, as I am leaving for Kinshasa the next morning. I am finishing a month of follow-up research in the Congo and was invited to dinner at the home of Pastor Kasambi, whose family I had become quite close with since 2005. Their youngest son brings a bowl of water with a small bar of soap and each of us washes our hands in preparation for dinner. I eat at the simple wooden table with the pastor and his wife, while their four children sit in the small seating area of the room. After a wonderful meal of *mfumbwa* with peanut sauce and *kwanga*, along with a small bowl of oranges for dessert, I am stuffed.[22] I compliment Ma Luzola on her cooking and relax in a woven chair in the small room lit by several lanterns as night falls. We chat about our families, Ma Luzola's health, and my pending trip back to Kinshasa and then the United States. Finally, as my departure for the evening draws near, Papa Kasambi stops our conversation.

"Mama and I want to give you a spiritual blessing to make sure that you travel safely."

"I would like that," I respond.

I didn't want to be rude to my adopted family. Moreover, I didn't see any harm in a spiritual blessing, although I am not a member of the DMNA church. He tells me to stand and move my chair to the center of the room. As I sit there, he leaves the room to change and returns wearing his white *soutan* and cap, with his white towel over his arm.[23] He stands in front of me with both of his arms bent at the elbows and perpendicular to the front of his body, with the white towel hanging from one forearm. He begins to lead a song, which all the family joins in singing, shaking several *nsakala* to accompany the song.[24] As the singing gets louder, he then begins to pray in Kikongo, and I sit watching, hands folded in my lap. Suddenly, his body begins to vigorously tremble. His upper body is quaking, his shoulders are jerking up and down, his fingers gesticulating, and his head intermittently making sudden shaking gestures. I had experienced the trembling before in numerous visits to the worship services of the DMNA church, but never had I experienced it up close. I can feel the energy pouring off his body. My hands relax to my sides at first, but then I grip the arms of the chair. I can hear his teeth actually chattering as each tremble wracks his frame. He uses his white towel to vigorously whip/beat the air around me as he continues to tremble. On the other side of me, Mama Luzola begins to speak in tongues as she prays, the children continue to sing, and the air around me is filled with sound and energy. Pastor Kasambi circles me and completes the blessing.

"Mfiaukidi" (Thank you), I whisper.

"Next time you return," he says, folding his towel across his bent arm, "I will perform the ritual to give you the spirit, *dikisa mpeve*."

I smile in response, but inside I am scared. What if I was overtaken by trembling? What would it feel like? My senses are still reeling from the blessing, and I think about the experience over and over again as the entire family escorts me to the main road that leads back to the house where I am staying. As I walk back through the dark, my path lit by the beam of a single flashlight, I wonder, how can trembling be so powerful?

Pastor Kasambi's embodiment of spiritual power through trembling in the present echoed the trembling that became the most notable ritual practice of Simon Kimbangu's colonial-era religious movement. During the precolonial era, trembling was used by banganga in the healing of sick patients and for divination purposes, representing the physical possession of the body by spiritual beings and forces. For example, Catholic missionary Laurent du Lucques, who was stationed in the province of Soyo in the Kongo Kingdom in the early eighteenth century, described a ceremony in which an *nganga* reveals to his apprentices their specializations through divination. "The teacher . . . makes the drums to beat and assembles his disciples. . . . He begins to invoke the demon, clapping the hands, turning, always turning the head, making a thousand unrestrained movements of the body, such as crazy people could do no worse" (Cuvelier 1953b, 135). Similarly, the embodiment of trembling of some sort seems to also have taken place in a seventeenth-century travel description published by Olfert Dapper, which describes an nganga seeking to heal an illness in the Kingdom of Loango, located to the immediate north of the Kingdom of Kongo. "The Ganga [*sic*] . . . paints the eyelids, the face and all the body in red and white figures. . . . He makes violent contortions of the body, raising the lowering the voice from one extreme to the other . . . the Ganga [*sic*] begins to roll the eyes and enter into a fury" (1686, 336–37). Both of these accounts suggest that some sort of trembling was likely taking place, although these European observers did not use that exact term. Trembling as a sign of possession and contact with the spiritual realm—with territorial spirits for example—played a crucial role in healing, divination, and initiation during the precolonial period.

In his analysis of trends in Kongo religious thought before, during, and after European colonialism, anthropologist John Janzen associates trembling with the concept of mpeve and its relevance for spiritual belief and action: "*Mpeve* specified the vital principle or attribute of every individual. Its verbal root, *veeva*, meant to blow, to breathe, or implied the breeze responsible for the fluttering of a cloth or flag. . . . But the interior manifestation of *mpeve* in Kongo thought is trembling, ecstatic manifestation accompanied usually by glossolalia and exorbited eyes" (Janzen 1977, 107). Kimbangu incorporated this cultural tradition into his worship and healing practices so that, as a professed adherent of the Protestant church, his trembling was caused not by territorial spirits but by the Holy Spirit (*mpeve ya nlongo*).

"I Would Be an Apostle": The Prophet Simon Kimbangu

Simon Kimbangu was born in 1889 to his mother Lwezi and his father Kuyela in the village of Nkamba in the Lower Congo. While both of his parents died while he was young, first his mother, and then his father, Kimbangu witnessed his father working as an *nganga-ngombo*, or diviner before his death (Mahaniah 1993). He was raised by his mother's youngest sister, Kinzembo, and Kimbangu became a Christian and a baptized member of the BMS Wathen church in 1915.[25] "Judging by his record," wrote Robert Lanyon Jennings, a BMS missionary stationed at Wathen, "he [Kimbangu] was a good Christian man."[26] Kimbangu apparently had a vision in 1917 or 1918 that evidenced his calling to preach. Other documents suggest that afterward Kimbangu went to study with Kimbangudi, a deacon and traveling pastor, who saw Kimbangu as having a true understanding of religion but lacking sufficient reading skills. Thus, when Kimbangu asked to be appointed the BMS evangelist for Nkamba, the missionaries refused based on his poor reading ability (Mackay 1987, 124). He was clearly a committed member of the mission while at the same time limited in the roles that he could take. He left Nkamba for Kinshasa, against the wishes of local church elders, trying to escape the visions that he continued to have. In Kinshasa he worked for three months at the Huileries du Congo Belge, an oil refinery. Many researchers believe that there Black Americans and other African employees exposed him to Garveyist ideas and readings.[27] Kimbangu was not, however, paid for his work at the refinery and eventually returned to Nkamba, continuing to have visions. In 1920, Nkamba was made into an official substation of the BMS Wathen mission station, and Kimbangu asked the local church elders if he could be the evangelist for Nkamba. While they agreed, other people at Nkamba did not support him, and the position was given to his step-brother instead.[28] After this devastating setback Kimbangu went home to pray. Kongo chroniclers of the movement describe what Kimbangu himself explained happened next: "Then I had a dream and God said to me, 'I have heard your prayer; people think you need the spirit to do my work but I will give you something even greater.' I took no notice of this. But from day to day I heard a voice that told me I would do the work of Peter and of John. I would be an apostle" (Pemberton 1993, 204).[29]

Sometime in mid-March 1921,[30] Kimbangu heard that a woman named Kintondo was sick in the neighboring village of Ngombe-Kinsuka and was compelled to go and heal her. He laid his hands on her in the name of Jesus Christ. He began to pray, and his body began to tremble. Astoundingly, she recovered.[31] Writing in his diary on April 4, 1921, Robert Lanyon Jennings was "informed by Tezo [his cook] that a man was present at communion yesterday who had done miracles."[32] Clearly, news of Kimbangu's healing of Kintondo was spreading. This first healing was followed by other healings, and soon people began to come in droves to Nkamba to be healed by the prophet Simon Kimbangu, so many that "it became impossible to move through the vast crowds" (Pemberton 1993, 212). In a handwritten letter dated May 1, 1921, from Sona Bata, an ABFMS mission station also located in the Southern Cataracts, Thomas Moody describes the impact of Simon Kimbangu: "There has been a great revival of interest the past month at Wathen the English Baptist station next to us. There is a man who is reported to be healing a large number of the people, the blind, half lame, sickness of all kinds. . . . At Thysville the English Baptist Mission has sold out all their hymn books and N.T. [New Testament]. . . . The people are coming to Church in greater numbers. We believe that the man is of God and we are praying that it will lead to a great revival among the people."[33]

The religious movement that was emerging around the figure of Kimbangu was rooted in Protestant Christianity. At the same time, particular practices that came to define the kingunza movement had their origins in precolonial Kongo forms of embodiment. Simon Kimbangu prayed, healed in the name of Jesus Christ, used the Bible faithfully, and upheld the doctrine and moral rules of the Protestant church; he also incorporated many ritual practices that came from his Kongo cultural background, with the most important of these being trembling (zakama). For BisiKongo people living in Luozi decades later, many different terms describe trembling including *tuntuka*, epileptic trembling and shaking; *sunsumuka*, jolting or shuddering after being startled; *tita*, a manifestation of cold conditions; *mayembo*, trembling caused by spirits entering banganga, and *zakama*, trembling caused by the Holy Spirit.[34] Many respondents in 2010 as well as bangunza during the colonial period emphasized that their own trembling came from the Holy Spirit rather than non-Christian spirits. Nevertheless, it is in fact this embodied practice (and its potential connection to pre-Christian practices) that caused concern and anxiety on the part of both missionaries and colonial administrators.

Numerous accounts describe trembling during Kimbangu's movement, both from the point of view of Belgian colonial administrators and European missionaries, as well as from the perspective of the Congolese themselves. For example, a Swedish missionary used the testimony of eyewitnesses to describe Kimbangu's actions as "somewhat violent, and greatly resembling those of the heathen *banganga*. He tossed his head, rolled his eyes, and jumped into the air, while his body often twitched all over" (Andersson 1958, 58). William Brown Frame, a BMS missionary stationed at Kibentele, reported going to investigate several prophets nearby and finding them "in a ringed off compound with our Christians singing for all they were worth while the prophets kept up a shaking of the head or body."[35] Robert Lanyon Jennings, a BMS missionary at Wathen station, the home mission of the prophet Kimbangu, circulated a letter to other Protestant missionaries describing what he and a colleague witnessed at Nkamba: "We witnessed five or six 'prophets' who by their shakings and grimaces seemed demented."[36] Andreas Walder, an SMF missionary at Kibunzi, wrote, "The state of ecstasy was characterized by violent trembling and strong muscle contractions. A young man from Kibunzi had received the spirit, and his body trembled for three days and three nights." Walder and another missionary tried to hold his hands, but the shaking increased in intensity. When they released him, "our hands and arms were burning" (Vellut 2005, 103).

For the indigenous Kongo population during the prophetic movements of the colonial period, falling sick and trembling could be taken as a sign from the spiritual world that a person should become an ngunza, a prophet, and go and heal others. Such an interpretation of illness is part of a larger belief system where the dead or those in the spirit world can influence the lives of the living, such as when *bisimbi* (territorial spirits) "indicated their desire to confer their powers upon particular individuals by afflicting them with certain diseases. . . . Such individuals could only be cured by being initiated into the cult of the appropriate spirit."[37] The importance of trembling as a sign of being called to be an ngunza was also evident in popular songs of the kingunza movement, such as the following song recorded in the mid-1930s in the town of Kingoyi in the Manianga region (present-day Luozi territory).

Song No. 17
Nzambi wakusola,
Wenda zakama
Mfumu Nzambi wansola,
yandi wampana salu
Kamba lendo yena yaku,
Vo Nzambi wakusola mu kedika
Vo masumu maku meni

God has chosen you.
Go and shake.
The Lord God has chosen me,
He gave me the work
If you have received power,
If God has really chosen you,
If your sins are wiped out.[38]

This song illuminates the importance of shaking and trembling in the worship of bangunza in general, and specifically, what the embodiment of the Holy Spirit signifies in regards to a person's relationship with God. If a person receives the Holy Spirit in their body and begins to tremble, it is a sign that they have been forgiven for their sins and chosen by God to become ngunza (Simbandumwe 1992, 167). This embodied indicator was recognized by the Kongo people and colonial administrators alike, who then arrested and questioned anyone suspected of trembling. Trembling thus became a primary way of identifying troublesome bangunza for colonial authorities, but also a means for BisiKongo people themselves to evidence a calling to become bangunza. On August 19, 1921, in a set of interviews in the administrative region of Northern Cataracts in the Lower Congo, the following exchanges took place between Léon Cartiaux, the territorial administrator, and several suspected bangunza from the subdistrict of Kinkenge:[39]

D: How many days have you been ngunza?
R: For only a day. Today I am cured.
D: How did you become ngunza?
R: I don't know anything, one morning I was trembling.
D: You haven't tried to heal people?
R: No, I trembled one day only.

He sent this first interviewee, a woman by the name of Sombe, back home and told her to be wise. Then, he questioned a man named Mahambu:

D: Since when have you been ngunza?
R: For a day; I had a headache; I trembled several hours only. I did nothing but pray.

After the native head of the village confirmed his story, Mahambu was sent back home with a warning. Then, Cartiaux interrogated another man by the name of Bombe Maloba.

D: How many days have you been ngunza?
R: I think that I had a fever, I trembled during a day; the people of

Pembo took me by the hand [and] I was healed. Today I am healed, I haven't done anything.[40]

The sentinels of the chief of Pembo said they hadn't seen the three bangunza in question trying to heal people. Thus, none of them were prosecuted for being ngunza. What is noteworthy is that they were arrested and accused of being bangunza precisely because they had trembled. However, according to these respondents, the trembling was not self-induced or even sought after but was brought on by experiences of sickness.[41] This clearly relates to what John Janzen calls cults of affliction and incidents that were seen as signs that people should be initiated as prophets or healers—whether banganga or prophets possessed by the spirit of Saint Anthony, such as Dona Beatrice Vita Kimpa (Thornton 1998). In yet another earlier document dated July 30, 1921, and addressed to the district commissioner, Léon Cartiaux provided a short list summarizing the statements of six bangunza who had been arrested in the subdistricts of Kibunzi and Bamba:

Inspired by the Holy Spirit in vision[s] and daydreams or dreams
Having wanted to heal sick people through prayers, songs, and the laying
    of hands on the head of people
Not having said nor did evil
Having trembled like the ngunza do.[42]

Although he doesn't specifically say what the list is for, this list of characteristics collected from the bangunza who were questioned most likely entails the experiences and qualities that lead one to become an *ngunza*. Again, trembling is an important element of this list. Moreover, visions and dreams are also seen as important as evidence of having contact with the spiritual world. Overall then, trembling played an important role in the kingunza movements, both for calling people to become prophets or adherents of the movement, as well as providing an embodied sign that attracted the attention of colonial authorities for immediate suppression.

An additional point concerns the role of women in the kingunza movement. As several of the above documents indicate, women, as well as men, were overtaken by the Holy Spirit and called to be bangunza. Positions of spiritual authority and expertise were held by people of both sexes during the precolonial era, and this continued with the kingunza movement. I examine women in the Kongo prophetic movements in greater detail in other work (Covington-Ward 2014), but here it is enough to say that women acted as healers, diviners, singers, and helpers, in addition to being prophets in their own right exhibiting the same embodied trembling (zakama) as the men in the movement.

Battling the Prophets: Colonial Administrators and Missionaries Respond to the Movement, May–September 1921

Initially, the Belgian colonial administration regarded Kimbangu's movement as a purely religious matter in which they had no reason to intervene. Until the end of May in 1921, they saw it as an issue for churches and priests. However, their assessment of the situation changed as businesses were affected by absent workers who joined the crowds leaving to visit Nkamba and witness the miracles of the prophet Kimbangu.[43] Business owners began to pressure the administration for action. Léon-Georges Morel, the territorial administrator for the Southern Cataracts, filed a report on May 17 that is worth quoting at length to demonstrate his ideas about Kimbangu and his practices:

> I learned after from the mouths of the Protestant missionaries of
> Gombe-Matadi, that these expressions . . . are the exact reproduction
> of the manner of behaving of native witch-doctors of the past. . . . I
> have noticed that the current that reigns at Kamba [*sic*] isn't sympa-
> thetic to us: the natives know very well that we can never approve of
> these grotesque and insane manifestations that accompany the reli-
> gion of Kimbangu. . . . The goal of the latter is to create a religion that
> corresponds with the mentality of the natives, a religion that contains
> the elements of Protestantism, which adds to itself external practices
> bordering on fetishism. . . . Everyone can readily see that our religions of
> Europe are all filled with abstractions, not responding to the mentality of
> the African, who longs for concrete facts and protection. The teachings
> of Kimbangu please the natives because they are allegedly accompanied
> by palpable facts: healings, protection against sickness. . . . It is therefore
> necessary to oppose Kimbangu because the tendency of his movement
> is pan-African. . . . The natives will say that they've found the God of the
> Blacks.[44]

Kimbangu's embodied practices (trembling, jumping, and so on) that Morel witnessed at Nkamba and categorized as "fetishist" are what led Morel to distinguish the movement as different from Protestantism. He thus concluded that its goal of founding an African religion was in fact pan-Africanist and therefore a threat to the colonial regime. Indeed, Morel assessed the movement of Kimbangu, enacted through its practices and representing an indigenous Kongo understanding of an alternative religious authority, as a direct challenge to the hegemony of European religious and political authority.

The majority of both Protestant and Catholic missionaries expressed the same hostility that Morel showed in regards to Kongo traditional culture, with some exceptions. In the constant competition between various missionary societies for Congolese converts, Kimbangu's movement provided an advantage for the Protestants in comparison to the Catholics, as Catholic missions emptied in response to the movement. Writing about the impact of the movement at Nsona Mbata in the *Congo News Letter*, Mrs. M. Frederickson notes, "The attendance at our Sunday services are much larger. Backsliders are begging to be restored into the church" (July 1921, 27). However, many more missionaries weren't as pleased with the movement and doubted Kimbangu's abilities. Robert Lanyon Jennings, the district head of the BMS Wathen mission under which Nkamba fell, wrote to the missionary staff of American Baptist and Swedish missions that he and his colleague Albert William Hillard had visited Nkamba and "we did not see one miracle. . . . We have heard of hundreds of miraculous healings, but as far as we can judge we have not been convinced of one. . . . Use every influence . . . to induce your people to keep away from there."[45] In a letter to the governor-general in July of 1921, James H. Starte, the legal representative of the Baptist Missionary Society, reassured the colonial government that "our missionaries at Wathen, Thysville, and Kibentele have publicly and privately discouraged 'Les affaires des Prophets'"(the prophet affairs).[46]

In regards to the embodied practices of the movement, many Protestant missionaries saw them as a revival of traditional Kongo religion. Georg Palmaer, a Swedish medical missionary, believed that Kimbangu's practices resembled those of "heathen banganga." Similarly, Protestant missionaries in Ngombe-Lutete convinced the administrator Morel that Kimbangu's practices were an exact replication of that of "witch-doctors."[47] Mrs. M. Frederickson, an ABFMS missionary stationed with her husband at Nsona Mbata, wrote in the July 1921 issue of *Congo News Letter*, "Thousands of people flocked to the little village of Nkamba where Simon Kimbangu, the original prophet, was doing his work. . . . We realize . . . that the prophets may naturally use the witch doctors old ways in their forms and ceremonies and acts of healing etc. For instance . . . the shaking of his body" (26–28). Missionary and administrator use of problematic terms such as "witch-doctor" implies that the Kongo prophets are deceitful, dealing in trickery. Such an association denies recognition of kingunza as a valid, Christian movement. These reactions of different Protestant missionaries in the Lower Congo make sense because of the threat that the bangunza movement posed to the religious authority of the missionaries. If the Kongo people can receive visions and the Holy Spirit in their bodies, and hear the voice of God themselves, what need do they have for European missionaries to interpret for them? By focusing on condemning embodied practices such as trembling as evil, pagan mannerisms, these missionaries sought to discredit any associations that the prophet movement had with Christianity and a Christian God.

The Catholic missionaries were more unified in their discontent with the movement. For example, territorial administrator Léon-Georges Morel received letters from the Tumba Catholic mission demanding that the "agitation of the prophets" be brought to an end.[48] Jean-Constant Van Cleemput, the vice-provincial of the Redemptorists and the superior father at the Tumba Mission, was likely the author of these letters, as he wrote in another commentary on the movement, "the immediate goal, if one can say: that of founding a religion of a prophet, a Negro religion, must lead to a goal . . . to get rid of the whites, to expel them, to become independent, in a word 'Africa to the blacks.'"[49] Monsignor Van Rosle demonstrated similar animosity to the movement when, in the August 1921 issue of *La Voix du Rédempteur*, the journal of the Catholic Redemptorist Fathers, he threatened excommunication of all Christians who affiliated themselves with Simon Kimbangu's church. In the same issue of the journal, other missionaries agreed that the movement was a political problem, as "these individuals could provoke an insurrection" (Chomé 1959, 22–24). In all these examples, the connection is made between the growing religious authority of the bangunza movement, and what that meant for possibly ending European domination in the Belgian colony.

Missionaries, colonial agents, and European business owners began to work together as they jointly saw the kingunza movement as a threat to European religious hegemony, business interests, and colonial authority. On June 1, 1921, Léon-Georges Morel arranged a meeting with head missionaries of both the Catholic and Protestant churches in the area. During this meeting, according to Morel, Father Van Cleemput, representing the Catholic missions "energetically demanded, and I support his view, that there must be an immediate end everywhere to the unrest of prophets," while on the other hand, Reverend Jennings, representing the Protestants, was inclined toward a more "prudent" solution. Ultimately, the Belgian administrators chose the plan of the Catholics since "they were afraid that Kimbanguism could turn into a political movement" (M. Martin 1975, 58). The district commissioner ordered Kimbangu's immediate arrest. On June 6, Morel returned to Nkamba with soldiers to carry out this order; however, Kimbangu escaped and his followers hid him for several months.

During this time, railroad company officials and other European businessmen were threatened by worker strikes and thus insisted that the government show the native populations that it was "their master," while the movement continued to spread all throughout the Lower Congo.[50] On June 14, martial law was imposed on the subdistrict of Zundu, where Nkamba was located.

On June 20, Morel ordered that all native people owning guns hand them in to the local administration, prohibited "the usage of gongs, drums, or other means of communicating by signals of all kinds," restricted people's movement, and forbade all gatherings.[51] On September 12, 1921, Simon Kimbangu willingly gave himself up to the colonial authorities and was arrested, along with some of his disciples. I have identified a number of incidents from the start of his movement until his trial as key performative encounters that redefined the relationship between Europeans and their colonial subjects in the Lower Congo.

Performative Encounters and the Making of a Movement

For the remainder of the chapter, I will focus on this trembling, zakama, in four specific performative encounters during the year 1921. I see zakama as a type of everyday cultural performance with larger social and political consequences. Each embodied instance of trembling analyzed here meets the criteria of performance: based on restored behavior, consciousness, and intention (as directness and aboutness) owing to the presence of multiple audiences, and having the capacity to transform.

In each specific case that I consider here, the trembling is a form of restored behavior, expressing a manner of embodying spirit possession that dates to the precolonial era. Undergirding this behavior is a belief in the copresence of spirits and their impact on the everyday lives and bodies of humans, which has implications for consciousness and intention. Thus, the Holy Spirit is causing the trembling and other associated acts, such as speaking in tongues. Moreover, bad spirits are also believed to inhabit the body, causing illness or misfortune. They must be chased out with the Holy Spirit (Bockie 1993, 76; Janzen and MacGaffey 1974, 144–45). These insights, along with the work of other scholars researching African spirit possession (Boddy 1989; Engelke 2007; Masquelier 2001) support the assertion that Western conceptions of the willful intentions of an individual person do not apply here. Spirits have a place in many African worldviews as actors using the bodies of individuals to get things done. Matters are further complicated since people have different experiences when possessed by the Holy Spirit. Some claim to lose all awareness, while others experience visions and hear voices while trembling. Thus, Simon Kimbangu's explanation to Léon-Georges Morel that "it's God that ordered him and his apostles to tremble in this way" implies Kimbangu's awareness of his own communication with the Holy Spirit. These varied experiences remind us that consciousness must be understood in a broader way and on multiple levels.

The concept of "audience" also applies in each of these situations, in many ways. In these instances, the person possessed by the spirit, along with their human interlocutor, is also an audience to the mpeve. Each of these incidents is also a public encounter—large groups of people witness the interactions between bangunza and missionaries/colonial authorities. Last and most important, these encounters subvert the existing status quo in regards to relations between colonial subjects and Europeans, showing a larger sociopolitical transformation is taking place. As stated in previous chapters, performative encounters change existing sociopolitical relationships in a manner that did not exist before. These examples of performative encounters demonstrate the important role of individual bodies in processes of social action.

David and Goliath: Léon-Georges Morel and Kimbangu at Nkamba (May 1921)

Kimbangu's exhibition of trembling is most clearly shown in the eyewitness account of territorial administrator Léon-Georges Morel, who went to Nkamba on May 11, 1921, to witness events for himself. Morel's five-page report describes the embodied practices of Kimbangu and his followers. Morel encountered Kimbangu on the road into town as Kimbangu "was shaken by a general trembling of the body, pushed to a fever pitch. Next to him were two native men and two young girls, all shaken by the same trembling and all making bizarre shouts. They began to uncontrollably execute a crazy saraband around me [erratically whirling].[52] I tried in vain to speak with them. Understanding that these grotesque contortions and literally madness was obviously for the goal of trying to impress me, I took the part of calmly contemplating these exhibitions, which themselves slowed down after ten minutes, the dancers being visibly exhausted by fatigue."[53]

Kimbangu and his disciples met Morel on the road while trembling and then surrounded him. This suggests that they wanted him to unequivocally see and recognize the spiritual authority they were imbued with, as Kimbangu attributes his particular reception of Morel to the will of God. Morel enters Nkamba to set up his tent, after failing to communicate with Kimbangu and his small group. Morel described the home of the prophet as being in a barricaded enclosure at the entrance to the village, facing the road, with a huge crowd of people gathered in the enclosure vigorously singing Protestant hymns. Although some of the people suggested another area further away from the prophet's home, Morel stubbornly chose a spot 20 meters from the prophet's home to have a better view of the activities taking place. "In the meantime, Kimbangu came closer with his associates and had resumed his contortions around me and my porters who erected the tent" (page 1).

According to Morel, Kimbangu then read in a loud voice the story from the Bible of David and Goliath, and one of the young girls came to show him a picture of Goliath killed by David. Then, some of the people told him that they wait to see fire fall on him from the sky like in the story of Sodom and Gomorra. Morel then spoke with the native chief of the local administrative subdistrict of Zundu, telling him that he didn't come with hostile intentions (page 2). A little after the commotion had calmed down, Kimbangu came to shake Morel's hand: "I notice that his hand is icy, a reaction following the period of nervous shaking. I took advantage of this period of calm to ask Kimbangu the reason for this not very suitable and grotesque manner of receiving me. He responded that: 'It's God that ordered him to come to meet me in that way and that the bizarre shouts are nothing but his conversation with God. It's God that orders him and his apostles to tremble in this way'" (page 2).

This exchange between the prophet and Morel reveals two things. First, Morel's observation that Kimbangu's hand is really cold suggests physical ramifications for the trembling that Kimbangu is exhibiting. Second and more important, Kimbangu's response that God spoke to him and ordered him and his apostles to tremble subverts Morel's attempts to control their behavior. Later, when Morel asked to question Kimbangu in private, Kimbangu said that he needed to confer with God first. A catechist soon thereafter told Morel that God had ordered Kimbangu not to talk and that the spirit alone would talk and make the necessary responses. "At this juncture, the singers resumed their tunes stressed by the dances, while the five tremblers resumed their manifestations. . . . I tried to interrogate Kimbangu, but in vain; the séance of epileptic craziness resumed. After a quarter of an hour of trembling the visionary began to read suggestive sentences taken from the Bible. . . . It is certain that Kimbangu is not in possession of all his faculties but he is not completely without them. The two native men that are his associates are pretenders, and the two women seem to have a touch of hysteria" (pages 2–3).

The above passages demonstrate the second component of trembling as performance—heightened awareness. While all these interactions are taking place between Morel and Kimbangu, the assembled crowd is watching them. Thus, those in the crowd can view Kimbangu's refusal to stop trembling and his unwillingness to talk as an open protest against Morel's secular authority.

Morel's account reveals conflicting definitions of trembling in this colonial context. For the prophet Simon Kimbangu, while in the past trembling was understood as symbolic of the political authority of the king or the ability of the banganga to communicate with a particular deity or nature spirit (Covington-Ward 2008), Kimbangu provides a rationale for his embodied actions that is based on orders from God, a Christian God, and the trembling is an embodied manifestation of that spiritual relationship, and more specifically, the Holy Spirit. This encounter between Morel and Kimbangu, taken as a whole, shows that Kimbangu is establishing his own authority to exhibit behavior that supersedes the wishes and commands of the colonial administrator. Herein lies the transformative and performative aspect of this encounter. Kimbangu's authority is a religious authority, based on the voice of God. Since he is receiving his instructions and spiritual inspiration directly from God, it is God's wishes as relayed by Kimbangu that prevail in shaping this encounter with Morel, who is himself the physical representative of colonial power. Such an encounter is incredibly performative because, through his trembling and interactions with Morel, which are being observed and witnessed by the assembled crowd at Nkamba, Kimbangu is reshaping the normalized structures of power that would typically guide interactions between a common native MuKongo and a Belgian colonial administrator. As the crowd watches Kimbangu and his apostles openly defy Morel's orders and blatantly challenge Morel's presence in Nkamba, they are able to envision an alternate social order able to be realized by and through the prophetic movement.

Léon-Georges Morel, however, is threatened by the overall encounter. His own reactions and choices, from setting up his tent in an area near Kimbangu although he had been directed to another area, and trying to control the singing occurring around him, can also be interpreted as Morel's own performance of his power as a colonial administrator. His attempts at reasserting his own authority in Nkamba were undermined many times, especially with the trembling. Morel describes the ecstatic trembling with many negative terms, including *crazy*, *uncontrolled*, and *inappropriate*, and even using medical terminology such as *epileptic* and *hysterical*. Trembling, then, was an embodied cultural performance that physically helped to establish the religious authority of Kimbangu and other Kongo prophets, an authority that colonial subjects were not supposed to exercise. Thus, Morel's derogatory attitude in regards to trembling would color how colonial authorities overall would come to view and then suppress trembling in the Lower Congo.

Leading the Faithful: Geil and Anonymous Ngunza (April–July 1921)

The next encounter that I examine occurred between John E. Geil, a missionary of the American Baptist Foreign Missionary Society, and an unnamed ngunza, sometime between April and July of 1921. Geil was stationed at Mbanza Manteke in the Lower Congo and the prophet movement also affected the area where he worked. The following account comes from a report on the movement penned by P. H. J. Lerrigo, the foreign secretary for the ABFMS, who summarized his correspondence with Mr. Geil.

A prophet emerged near Mbanza Manteke, and John Geil sent word to the prophet asking to meet and speak with him. The prophet came after a few days accompanied by others, and they stood outside Mr. Geil's home. The prophet:

> foamed at the mouth and shook violently, but said nothing for a time. Then he suddenly broke out: "You sent for me. What do you want?"
>
> Mr. Geil said, "I would like to talk with you about the work you are doing."
>
> "It is the work of God. Don't you believe it is God's work?" This he ejaculated in a very truculent manner.
>
> Mr. Geil replied, "I do not want to quarrel with you. I should like to talk it over quietly." (Lerrigo 1922, 96–97)

I see this encounter as performative for a number of reasons. First, during the colonial era, Congolese were supposed to address missionaries and other Europeans in the Congo with deference and respect. Numerous everyday interactions, such as missionaries being physically carried in hammocks by Congolese porters, reinforced ideas of African inferiority and European superiority. They often had a paternalistic attitude toward the Congolese and expected them to respect their authority, especially in religious matters for missionaries in particular. In this instance, however, this anonymous ngunza showed from the start that the typical relationship between missionaries and the Kongo population was to change. When summoned by Geil, he did not come immediately; he came a few days later, on his own schedule. Second, in addressing Geil while trembling, he did not show deference. He said, "What do you want?" a phrase that would be used to address someone lower in status rather than higher in status. He also directly challenged Geil, by asking if he believed that the work he was doing was God's work. This was a tricky question, because others were present witnessing their encounter, many of whom already believed or had some idea that the rapidly spreading movement was the work of God. If Geil denied the veracity of the prophet's claim, he would have to convincingly explain the physical manifestations of the prophetism (trembling) as well as explain why only his interpretation of the movement was valid. This would be held up against the Bible itself, which many of the prophets and adherents of the kingunza movement were using to justify the presence of prophets among them.

The prophet had in fact chosen to visit Geil on a Sunday morning. Geil and his church members were heading to a pool of water at the foot of the hill for a baptismal service.[54] "The prophet seemed anxious to assume charge of the assembled crowd, and Mr. Geil feared a disturbance. Placing his hand upon the prophet's arm he warned him not to cause any trouble. Meanwhile the prophet was working himself into a frenzy, shaking, leaping, and rolling his eyes. Mr. Geil led the way to the baptism, but the prophet and his followers came also, shouting and making a noise" (Lerrigo 1922, 96–7). In continuing the analysis of this encounter as performative, this anonymous ngunza also challenged Geil by attempting to take over one of the most importance ritual functions of missionaries in the Congo—baptism. The assembled crowd of people waiting to undergo baptism and their families were all witnesses to this outright challenge to Geil's authority. The way that Geil tries to stop this ngunza is also notable; he "placed his hand" on his arm. Bangunza, especially in the midst of trembling, were not to be touched. Whether Geil knew this or not, his actions could be seen as undermining the power of the prophet. Unfortunately, we do not know the response of the prophet: did he jump higher? Tremble more vigorously? And how did the crowd interpret this? In all, this highly charged encounter diminished the power of missionaries and disrupted their hegemonic hold on religious instruction and interpretation, and on the performance of rituals such as baptism. This anonymous ngunza's open, public challenge to Geil's missionary authority is a performative encounter in that it reconfigured everyday relations and interactions between Congolese and White missionaries and created the possibility of an alternate Kongo spiritual authority willing and able to perform the same functions as a Christian missionary. This encounter disrupted and undermined the status quo by and through the actions of this prophet, especially the trembling, which represented his being chosen by the Holy Spirit.

"We Do Not Want Chiefs Anymore, We Do Not Want Anyone but Jesus Christ" (June 1921)

The third performative encounter considered here involves a more violent interaction between Kongo prophets and the colonial state. Léon Cartiaux had entered into Belgian colonial service in 1909, and by the summer of 1921 he had been territorial administrator for the Northern Cataracts since 1920 (Vellut 2005, 168). As the prophetic movement spread throughout the Lower Congo, he left Luozi, the administrative center for the district, to conduct an investigation of prophets in the area, between June 13 and 16, 1921. After assembling fourteen porters in the Lemba chefferie, he arrived at Dembo village in Bu chefferie. He interrogated the medal chief there and asked him what he has heard at meetings of bangunza that he had attended. Chief Libasa, the medal-chief responded, "They said send us all of your sick, we will heal them. . . . The Whites demand too much money from us for taxes. . . . You don't have to pay. . . . Those were the words of the *ngunza* of the chefferie of Chief Kau, village Kiesa, Southern Cataractes."[55]

Cartiaux continued his investigation in the village of Pangu, also in Bu chefferie. There, when Cartiaux asked whether he had heard ngunza tell people not to pay taxes, a chief named Fielo told him that while he had not heard it spoken directly by an ngunza, a local catechist named Kunku had told him, "*Ngunza* told us that this year we should not pay taxes. . . . It is Kimbangu, *ngunza* from the village of Kamba [*sic*] . . . who said that." Upon further questioning, Fielo also revealed that the catechist said "people shouldn't work anymore because there would no longer be anyone to pray."[56] Cartiaux continued his investigation, arriving the same day at Kimbanza village under Chief Muntanda. The chief tells him that people are going to see prophets in the village Mayombe-Yanga where a man named Timosi leads a group of bangunza. Timosi was the brother of the head catechist on the American mission, and Chief Muntanda reported him as saying, "Now, we should not pay taxes any more. They said: there is one God and we do not obey anyone else but him."

Cartiaux then asked, "You all don't want to pay?"

Chief Muntanda replied, "The people are waiting to see what the *ngunza* will do."

Cartiaux, hot on the trail of the bangunza, leaves Kimbanza at 5:30 in the morning, arriving at Yanga where he questioned Chief Bemba, who then accompanied Cartiaux so that they finally arrive at Mayombé village at 9:00 in the morning. There they saw a large crowd of people singing very loudly. After Chief Bemba pointed out the three bangunza leading the crowd, Cartiaux tried to approach them. "In spite of the songs and howls shouted by the entire crowd, I approach the three N'Gunza and ask them to calm down. . . . So the crowd yelled saying we want nothing else but Jesus Christ, no more chiefs, no more obeying the Whites of the state, nothing."[57]

The reaction of the crowd suggests that they were openly opposed to Cartiaux's presence. Using the language of religion, "we want nothing else but Jesus Christ," their discourse prioritizes religion over everything else. Their opposition to "chiefs," who are themselves Kongo as well, is also telling, because as the previous exchanges reveal, these chiefs were working for and with the colonial administration; most of them had been appointed as chiefs as opposed to inheriting the position. Moreover, Chief Bemba had led Cartiaux to this bangunza gathering. That the crowd not only refused to quiet down but also shouted that they no longer wanted to obey representatives of the colonial state reveals that they are challenging the status quo in the

Belgian colony. Cartiaux continued in his report: "The chief of the N'Gunza, named Timosi, saw that I was opposite him, wanted to take the stick that he had within reach and tried to hit me. At the same time, I gave the order to my twelve soldiers who accompanied me to apprehend them. The soldiers obeyed immediately. The three N'gunza, but the named Timosi above all, mounted a very strong resistance, continuing while all the crowd shouted, 'We do not want chiefs anymore, we don't want anyone but Jesus Christ.' I gave everyone the order to stop the noise and I achieved nothing."[58]

Cartiaux's description of these events clearly shows that the normal order of things was being challenged in this interaction. While it was common to see Belgians and other Europeans inflicting harm and punishment on Congolese bodies during the colonial period, whether with a *chicotte*, rod, or other implement, the reverse was not true.[59] Clearly, the ngunza Timosi was breaking everyday protocol and stepping out of his place as a colonial subject by trying to hit Cartiaux. Moreover, if he succeeded in hitting the territorial administrator, it could embolden the rest of the crowd to attack as well. Cartiaux did not give an estimate of the size of the crowd. However, his frustration at trying to control the crowd suggests the number of people at the bangunza meeting (along with others in the community who may have come to see what would take place in the encounter between the state administrator and the bangunza) outnumbered Cartiaux and his porters and soldiers. Even after his soldiers grabbed the three bangunza, they continued to display resistance and the crowd persisted in ignoring Cartiaux's calls for quiet: "I ordered all my soldiers to tightly tie up the three n'Gunza. They finally did it, but Timosi did not calm down, and all three of them continue the shouts being repeated by the crowd. They [the three ngunza] were making movements with the arms, the head, the body, the eyes rolling up to the sky. All the crowd was singing really loudly so that the three n'Gunza may fly off into the sky."[60]

Here, the movements that Cartiaux is attempting to describe are likely zakama that physically indicated one's possession by the Holy Spirit. It is not clear how Cartiaux came to the conclusion that the crowd wanted the bangunza to fly up into the sky; did he hear this in the songs? Did a porter or soldier, or even Chief Bemba himself, explain this to him? We do know that in the context of the kingunza movement, the loud singing was needed to help bring on the vigorous trembling of the bangunza. If members of the crowd indicated that they believed the bangunza had the power to raise themselves from the ground and fly, they would in fact echo similar beliefs that people had about the prophet Simon Kimbangu himself.[61] Whether or not the prophets could perform such incredible feats is not really what is most important; instead, what the ability to fly represents is the ability to escape and literally rise above the everyday indignities to which the indigenous population were often subjected. Flying away from Cartiaux would also suggest that the prophets were in fact above the reaches of his authority, and closer to God as well.

Cartiaux then ordered his soldiers to tie ropes around the necks of those present, starting with the catechists who were at the front of the crowd. "The catechists against my will continued to sing, but without offering any resistance." Cartiaux then called for silence for the third time. "No one obeyed me. A native of Madimba, chefferie Kimpaka, named Fataki Petro, finding himself across from me, took me by the arm with the intention of hitting me. I quickly freed myself and armed myself with a soldier's gun—in that moment all the noise stopped, and I achieved perfect calm, except for the three N'Gunza, on the ground, who tried to resume the songs."

Once again, Cartiaux's authority is being directly challenged. Here he was actually grabbed by Fataki Petro, and it was only through the very visible threat of his gun that he was able to quiet the crowd. The soldiers tied up Fataki Petro, and he and the three N'Gunza, who all refused to walk, were carried by the crowd in improvised hammocks away from the village. It is not clear whether the catechists were also arrested, or even if other people in the crowd were apprehended as well. This entire encounter, including the obstinate singing of the crowd, trembling of the bangunza, suggestion of the ability to fly away, multiple attempts to physically attack the territorial administrator, and even the refusal to walk of those who were tied up and arrested all signal a performative shift in social relations. The authority of the state was being openly challenged, and Léon Cartiaux himself was physically attacked. The naturalness of the colonial social order was undermined, and while the resistant bangunza were arrested, their bravery and actions remained an inspiring example for all those BisiKongo who witnessed the encounter.

Trembling in the Courtroom (October 1921)

The last performative encounter focuses on trembling in the court trial of the prophet Simon Kimbangu. Kimbangu's trial began almost immediately after his arrest and lasted only eighteen days; from September 15 to October 3, 1921 (Chomé 1959, 55). The sources for the description of his trial are problematic, because they were written by parties who were definitely against the movement; one a Belgian Catholic priest and the other a reporter for a daily newspaper which deeply criticized the movement. What we can take from their accounts of the trial, however, are the multiple ways that the Congolese prophets were challenging colonial authority.

During the trial, Kimbangu and his disciples were not given any legal counsel; they had to mount their defense themselves (Chomé 1959, 56). M. de Rossi, the presiding judge, questioned them about the movement, and their responses demonstrate how spiritual beliefs were being used to challenge the authority of the Belgian colonial state. For example, the first prophet who was questioned, coolly and calmly sought to establish the spiritual authority of the kingunza movement by saying, "The judgment of God will come punish those who do not believe."

The magistrate responded, "The state, and all the whites who are here, if they don't believe?" "Yes" said the man, "the state and all you whites will go to hell if you don't believe in our doctrine" (Chomé 1959, 62).

While the judge and his assistants laughed at this prophecy, the statement of another prophet led to a different response. "He dared to question the judge in the middle of the court and asked him the reason why it was forbidden for Africans to have their god, their prophet, and their Bible, while the whites have their own" (Chomé 1959, 62). Judge de Rossi stopped the proceedings. Yet another significant encounter occurred with Kimbangu himself. Kimbangu's embodied practices during a manifestation of possession brought into stark relief the anxiety and fear that such practices provoked for the colonial administration. Mandombe, a young female disciple of Kimbangu, was being questioned, when suddenly, Kimbangu, who was loaded with chains and under guard, turned toward the other defendants and began to tremble. M. de Rossi, threatened Kimbangu: "If you don't stop, you will get the chicotte." When he didn't stop, de Rossi called a recess and sent for a doctor. The doctor called to the scene to examine Kimbangu found nothing abnormal and prescribed a treatment of a cold shower and "twelve blows of the whip" (Chomé 1959, 63). These were promptly administered, and there is no other mention of trembling during the trial after this point.

Kimbangu's trembling directly defied de Rossi, who unsuccessfully ordered Kimbangu to stop and had to take a recess and make everyone leave in order to find another means of trying to control Kimbangu's embodied behavior. One can imagine de Rossi repeatedly banging his gavel in vain as Kimbangu continued to shake and tremble. Kimbangu's public trembling, in a court of Belgian law no less, is a performative encounter that placed the spiritual authority of the Holy Spirit in direct conflict with the secular authority of the Belgian colonial state. Like Morel in Nkamba, de Rossi sought a medical explanation for Kimbangu's actions. By doing this, he was trying to take away any grounds for legitimacy that Kimbangu may have by reducing his actions to a condition that can be cured as opposed to a revolutionary ideology.

On October 3, 1921, Kimbangu was accused of sedition and hostility toward the White population, along with other crimes. The text of the sentencing reveals a host of fears that gripped the colonial administration:

> Whereas Kibangu [sic] was recognized by the doctors as sound of body and spirit and by consequence responsible for all his acts, that his fits of nerves are nothing but shamming . . . that the accused profited by deceiving the good faith of the masses destined to serve as an unconscious instrument to his ends, that the goal pursued was that of destroying the authority of the state. Whereas it remain established that by his acts, remarks, schemes, writings, songs, and his history dictated by himself, Simon Kibangu [sic] has set himself up as a redemptor and savior of the black race in indicating the White [race] as the enemy . . . the sect of prophets must be considered organized in order to bear attacks on the security of the state, [a] sect hidden under the veil of a new religion. . . . It is true that the hostility against the established powers was manifested up until the present by seditious songs, insults, outrages, and some isolated rebellions, yet it is true that the march of events could have fatally led to a big revolt.[62]

This selection from the sentencing text reveals that, by the conclusion of the trial, the colonial administration saw the prophetic movement as more of a political rather than a religious threat. In the words of the presiding judge, Kimbangu's movement, a "sect hidden under the veil of a new religion" sought to destroy "the authority of the state." In this regard, Kimbangu's religious movement and sudden status as a prophet imbued him with a particular religious authority that the colonial administration found menacing to their own political authority, and in fact construed as a political movement. Moreover, Kimbangu's bodily practices of trembling, while understood in the context of Kongo traditional religion, had no place in the Belgian cultural ethos, and thus the colonizers saw them as fake, stopping his trembling with force as demonstrated in the account of the trial.

Kimbangu was initially sentenced to 120 strokes of the whip and then death. However, several Baptist missionaries (including Ross Phillips of the BMS and Joseph Clark of the ABFMS), along with the substitute public prosecutor appealed to the governor-general in Boma and King Albert in Belgium to commute the sentence (M. Martin 1975, 62). On November 15, 1921, King Albert changed the sentence to life imprisonment. Simon Kimbangu, like many other prophets and followers of the movement, was sent into exile into a penal labor colony far away on the other side of the Belgian Congo. Marie-Louise Martin, who likens these penal colonies to colonial concentration camps, estimates that approximately 100,000 people were sent into exile, when both heads of family and the family members who accompanied them are accounted for (1975, 69).[63] Kimbangu himself died in a camp in Katanga province, in October 1951, thirty years after his initial imprisonment.

Overall, this section demonstrates the critical importance of zakama as a form of resistance by Kongo people against European missionaries and the Belgian colonial state in 1921. Each of these performative encounters was public with a significant audience of onlookers, and in each instance normalized relations of interaction where Europeans are superior and Congolese inferior were upended. One similarity between all the encounters is the inability of the Europeans to control the bodies of the prophets, from Kimbangu's trembling in front of Morel and the judge de Rossi, to the refusal to walk of those arrested by Cartiaux, even to the loud singing of the followers of these prophets. Moreover, European attempts to medicalize the trembling as a "condition" of an illness was a common thread as well. The Holy Spirit, a supernatural powerful entity that supersedes any earthly laws, customs, or rules, and was recognized as real by most European Christians, supposedly caused the trembling that marked these performative encounters. Accordingly, the Holy Spirit buttressed the prophets' blatant disregard for the orders and questions of both state officials and missionaries, as the words and actions of the prophets were not supposed to be of man, but of God. Through access to the Christian spiritual realm expressed through their bodies, these bangunza disputed the unquestioned power of Europeans to decide and control the "natural order" of social life in the Belgian Congo. The reactions of the missionaries and administrators challenged in these encounters were also similar—they often responded with violence or the threat of violence. With this, they participated in their own public performances of colonial power, with the goal of thwarting and discouraging the movement, its leaders, and its followers.

Kingunza and Early Seeds of Nationalism

While thus far we have examined individuals using their bodies to advocate for social and political change, did this religious movement create or coalesce around shared ideals, goals, or identities—in essence, was it a nationalist movement? As stated previously, nationalism is "an ideological movement for the attainment and maintenance of autonomy, unity, and identity on behalf of a population some of whose members deem it to constitute an actual or potential 'nation'" (A. Smith 2006, 175). And what elements are necessary for nationalism to exist? In an earlier study, Anthony Smith writes that "to achieve their common goals—autonomy, unity, identity—there need to be some core networks of association and culture, around which and on which nations can be 'built,'" and language, religion, and historic territories have often provided this common basis for constructing nations (1996, 108). The kingunza movement that started with the prophet Simon Kimbangu shows that in 1921 the inhabitants of the Lower Congo were starting to think, act, and behave in ways that suggested a burgeoning nationalist sentiment, growing out of and alongside the prophetic movement itself.

The most explicit evidence of nationalism in the prophetic movement is the many efforts to seek autonomy through establishing independent churches, separate from the missionaries. This is reflected in the Mbanza Manteke annual report for 1921, where John E. Geil noted, "like all work on the lower Congo our work has been affected by the 'prophet' movement. . . . The Bangu section which joins on the Wathen (BMS) district where the 'prophet' movement had its origin . . . has followed the example of the natives in the Wathen district and separated themselves from the mission and are proposing to establish a church and work of their own."[64] He then added that in the last six months there have been no financial contributions/collections from this particular section, while the contributions of the larger Lukunga field had increased in relation to previous years. From what I can tell, Bangu was one church included in the larger Lukunga area and was closely located to Kimbangu's home village of Nkamba.[65] While it is unclear who the leaders of this exodus from the church are, they sought to establish their own church and had stopped contributing financially to the home mission. This reveals that they are seeking to become an autonomous religious institution, away from European and American missionaries. Many other examples of similar aspirations for religious independence abound. Joseph Bowskill, a BMS missionary reflecting on the prophet movement, writes, "When Mbandila, Kuyowa & Co. found the prophet would not be recognized by the BMS they worked hard to separate the whole native church from the BMS. The flood of money pouring in, began to make them feel independent. Kimbangu, for some time, protested against separation, but in the end he agreed."[66] Mbandila and Antoine Kuyowa were part of the first group to convert to Christianity at the Wathen station. While their actions were surely seen as an affront by Bowskill, their desire to establish their own independent church reveals early seeds of nationalist sentiment, vis-à-vis their urge to redefine their relationship to Europeans in such a colonial context. There are many other examples of the quest for autonomy all across the Lower Congo; from SMF missionary Sven A. Floden's confrontations with Malia and Yambula, a woman and man in Kibunzi (Cataractes Nord) who both trembled, claimed to be prophets, and held mass meetings against Floden's wishes (Vellut 2005, 117–22), to

Robert Kirkland, a BMS missionary in Kinshasa, who testified about men on their mission who "wanted to have private meetings" and "met and plotted in secret" (Vellut 2010, 71) to Peter MacDiarmid, an ABFMS missionary in the Nsona Mbata district of the Southern Cataracts, who wrote about "one church of several hundred, quite independent of the Mission, [that] sprang up with mushroom growth" (*Congo News Letter*, September 1922, 21). Moreover, the leaders of these new religious communities took on many of the powers that until then had been reserved for missionaries; baptisms, marriages, and even removing and restoring people to church membership based on their sins were now responsibilities being enacted by bangunza across the Lower Congo (*Congo News Letter*, September 1922; Vellut 2010, 102).

The second major component of a nationalist movement is creating a sentiment of unity for the group in question. During the kingunza movement in 1921, there was a coalescing of a growing racial identity, such that Africanness and Blackness were defined in diametric opposition to Whiteness—whether Belgian, British, or American. In her hand-corrected typescript of an annual report for 1921, ABFMS missionary Catherine Mabie wrote that "the prophet movement has been an interesting phenomena in race consciousness and closely akin to the world wide developing sense of race solidarity among negroes. . . . Its chief peril lay in the wonderful solidarity it effected in so brief a period among a hitherto disassociated population; also in its undoubted anti-white attitude."[67] Here, Mabie notes a growing sentiment of commonality and racial identity amongst Congolese who in the past did not seem to see themselves as similar. Likewise, in his testimony at the Protestant Mission Conference about his experiences during the outbreak of the prophetic movement in villages on the Bangu, ABFMS missionary Thomas Hill recounted "I held two services on Bangu in one village. In another the leader refused me a chance to speak saying, "We have nothing to do with white men" (Vellut 2010, 206). The anti-White sentiment expressed in this village on the southern bank of the Congo River reflects similar sentiments expressed by the assembled crowd in Léon Cartiaux's encounter with Timosi and the other bangunza in Luozi territory on the other side of the river. Anti-White sentiment in connection with the movement even spread outside of the Lower Congo. In his 1921 report for the Tshumbiri station, located further up the Congo River, ABFMS missionary Paul Metzger writes about the impact of a temporary docking of a ship carrying arrested bangunza. "Though our people knew of the arrests in the Bas Congo they began singing the prophet songs . . . parading through the town. . . . It is claimed by some that the movement is not political. This . . . is an error for it is decidedly anti-white, every means being used to breed race hatred. God's back is turned against the white man and the last shall be first. All white men will be compelled to walk home in the dried ocean bed. Black men from America will come to fight for us" (Vellut 2010, 219). Pronouncements of racial solidarity with Black Americans are echoed in other accounts, such as Léon Cartiaux's letter to the district commissioner where he reports the claims of two BisiKongo who went to Nkamba and said they heard Kimbangu say publicly that, "for so many years the Belgians are our rulers and haven't done anything for us till this day, but before long Americans will arrive here in order to make war with the Belgians and become our rulers."[68] All of this suggests a burgeoning racial conscious-ness emerging in direct response to white domination, a consciousness that was extending beyond clan, language, and geography, to embrace a solidarity of people of African descent both within the Congo and across the Atlantic.

The last component of a growing nationalist movement, according to Anthony Smith, is identity. What defines the kingunza movement as unique, different? This is probably the least developed aspect of the kingunza move-ment as it emerged in 1921. One potential defining factor for the movement is that of ethnicity or ethnic identity. While the movement started in the Lower Congo with a MuKongo prophet, ethnic identity does not seem to be a very important part of the movement in 1921. Cries for freedom from whites and autonomy for newly established native churches are much more common. In fact, in the documents that I examined, there are very few explicit signs of a significant ethnic identity. One possible example is Robert H. C. Gra-ham's recounting of the prophet movement where he writes, "it seems that the original 'prophets' said there would be twelve real prophets in all, and that the very greatest of them would appear here in San Salvador" (*Missionary Herald*, October 1921, 192). This passage is significant because San Salvador (also known as Mbanza Kongo in Kikongo and located geographically in modern-day Angola) was the capital of the former Kongo Kingdom. The rumor of the greatest prophet emerging in San Salvador points to attempts to recreate shared connections with the former Kongo Kingdom. While eth-nicity will become more and more important in later variations and waves of the kingunza movement, in 1921, however, the movement is focused much more on autonomy and racial solidarity based on opposition to whites and white oppression.

Conclusion

By focusing on the Kimbanguist/kingunza movement as it emerged and developed in 1921, I have tried to show that placing the body at the center of analysis can reveal a lot about struggles for power and control in everyday contexts in the Belgian Congo. The kingunza movement in the Lower Congo presents a number of examples of performative encounters that show the ways that Kongo people used their bodies to challenge the hegemony of both the Belgian colonial state and Western missionaries. Embodied trembling allowed multiple prophets to publicly defy European rule in both civil and religious matters and posit an alternate reality where the Congolese ran their own affairs. Moreover, the movement encouraged the development of a nascent nationalism by bringing disparate people together who coalesced around similar circumstances, shared embodiment, and some common goals and ideals for the future. In the next chapter, we will examine how the kingunza movement became even more nationalist and political in the decades leading up to independence from Belgian colonial rule and the multiple ways that both colonial administrators and missionaries sought to use embodied movement to combat the bangunza.

CHAPTER 3

Threatening Gestures, Immoral Bodies

Kingunza after Kimbangu

Nsinsa wa ngoma wusobele, soba makinu maku.
[When the rhythm of the ngoma changes, change your dance.]
—Kongo proverb

May 22, 2005. Today I am going with my host Professor Mahaniah and several other people to one of the independent ngunza churches for service, specifically the DMNA church (Dibundu dia Mpeve Nlongo mu Afelika, or Church of the Holy Spirit in Africa) in Luozi. When we arrive, we can hear the music from outside. The church itself is a small, one-room, white-washed building with a cement floor. We walk to the open door, with the music having stopped by then, and one of the pastors comes to welcome us and invite us in. We remove our shoes at the door, and the pastor motions for the women to enter through one door and the men through another. He then leads us to what seems like "honored guests" seats at the front of the small church, facing everyone else and next to the raised platform of the pastor. I notice one thing immediately as I look at the congregation. The women and men are separated. All the women and girls are seated to the right of the pastor on low benches, while the men and boys are seated to the left on benches or at desks, on the same side where the drums are located.

The pastors and other church leaders are wearing all white soutans, with white hats (*kepis*).[1] I am able to count about seven men who are not only dressed in all white, but who also take major roles in the service. Most of the women have their heads covered in white scarves, and if the scarves are not white, their heads are still covered. Several women are dressed in all-white dresses, and white scarves, and they seem to lead the other women. I count at one time around sixty-five people, including children, in the church. Without a doubt however, women outnumber the men. The pastors and main spiritual leaders were all men.

The entire church dances quite a lot, in accompaniment to the inspired hymns sung by the congregation.[2] The music and singing are so loud that they overwhelm the senses, making it difficult to hear the words. After the sermon, there is an offering, and then a healing session. Four men in white robes line up in front of the sick. The music begins, coming from three small, double-faced drums (*bibandi*) hit with batons, along with two long, thin bamboo trunks (*bikualakala*) hit with sticks and hand-held rattles (*nsakala*) vigorously shaken by the women. Loud call-and-response singing from the men and women accompanies the music. Each healer has a white towel they wave over their patients in order to facilitate the healing process. The healers begin to shake and tremble vigorously, laying their hands on the sick, shouting, massaging, and touching different parts of their bodies; first their heads, then their abdomens and backs simultaneously, then their legs and arms. The healers keep on trembling, and simultaneously the drums are playing loudly and everyone is singing and dancing again (see figure 3.1).

This description from my field notes reveals my impressions of my first encounter with the DMNA church in Luozi. The prophet Masamba Esaie founded this church. He was one of many bangunza who emerged in the Lower Congo (specifically in Luozi territory) after Simon Kimbangu was tried and incarcerated. Esaie was first arrested in 1933, and he was arrested for the third time in 1952, when he was sent to a penal labor camp in Belingo, Bandundu province (Mahaniah 1988, 77). Esaie founded the DMNA church in 1961, after he was released from prison. Many of the gestures used in the context of worship in this church, such as spiritual trembling (zakama), cupped clapping (bula makonko), and others have reappeared over and over again in our discussion of embodied cultural performances both before and during the prophetic movements of the colonial period. The DMNA church is one of many independent churches emerging directly from the Kongo prophetic movements, endeavoring to forge a different path from the mission-led churches. What form then, did Kongo prophetism (kingunza) take after Kimbangu? What relationship did kingunza have to nationalist movements

FIGURE 3.1. Lines of men and women singing and dancing in worship, DMNA church, Luozi, 2006. Photo by Yolanda Covington-Ward.

and sentiments? What particular politics of the body emerged after Kimbangu's arrest?

The Kikongo proverb that opened this chapter is often used in Kongo culture to remind people that when they find themselves in a different situation or place, they should also change their comportment to match their circumstances. This proverb captures the focus of this chapter: examining the shifting nature of the uses and meanings of Kongo embodied practices in the context of the many sociocultural transformations that defined the colonial era. In writing this chapter I am not trying to give a complete ethnohistorical account of the kingunza movement. Other texts provide much more of the history than I am giving here (Andersson 1958; W. MacGaffey 1983, 1986b; Sinda 1972). Rather, I will explore several key historical moments when religion, nationalism, and body politics collide in relation to the kingunza movement during the colonial period. Geographically, much of my focus in this chapter is on events and happenings in Luozi territory specifically (from 1913 to 1949 known as Manianga territory, Mahaniah 1989, 17), although there were other prophetic activities in other parts of Bas-Congo, the country, and even in neighboring French Congo. Limiting my geographic scope in this way helps to provide a baseline for understanding other types of performative encounters in Luozi that I examine in later chapters of the book. This chapter investigates the politics of performative encounters in Luozi in two time periods: 1934–36, and in the mid to late 1950s, just before independence. This chapter demonstrates the importance of the body not just as a tool of resistance, but also as a method of oppression. While chapter 2 highlighted the performative encounters associated with spirit-induced trembling, this chapter helps to make the case that performative encounters are not just "weapons of the weak."[3] Examining the role of secular dances and the redefinition of bodily practices associated with kingunza elucidates the interplay between secular and sacred embodiment and larger political struggles to control prophetism.

The Politics of Dance in the Belgian Congo

To understand the function of secular dances in the Congo state's attempts to control prophetism, I first examine Belgian colonial approaches to indigenous dances. In colonial contexts, the dominating power altered embodied practices such as dance in much the same way that the economy, social and political structures, language, and ways of dress of indigenous populations were subject to change. As Susan Reed notes: "The suppression, prohibition and regulation of indigenous dances under colonial rule is an index of the significance of dance as a site of considerable political and moral anxiety. Colonial administrations often perceived indigenous dance practices as both a political and moral threat to colonial regimes. Local dances were often viewed as excessively erotic, and colonial agents and missionaries encouraged and sometimes enforced the ban or reform of dance practices" (1998, 506).

This section of the chapter considers Kongo makinu, or dances, as embodied cultural performances that had varied meanings and uses by colonial agents, missionaries, and Kongo people themselves throughout the colonial period. Efforts by Europeans to control these dances as practiced by the indigenous population, often couched in terms of policing immorality, revealed the role that influence over the conduct of others played in the ongoing confirmation of European political and religious authority in the Belgian Congo. Moreover, in the context of the prophetic movements in the Lower Congo, some colonial administrators eventually saw a political use for makinu, using them in the service of combating kingunza. The control of mundane bodily practices such as secular dances became a means of undermining the threat sustained from embodiment in the sacred realm.

Following sociologist Christian Smith, I am using the term *morality* to describe shared social understandings about what is good or bad, right or wrong, worthy or unworthy, just or unjust, based not on our own desires or preferences but rather on understandings believed to exist apart from them, providing standards by which our own decisions, actions, and desires can be judged (2003, 8–10). Rules of conduct, expectations, and obligations that make up the shared morals in various groups may differ from society to society, across time and space. In colonial-era Belgian Congo, many moral orders came into conflict as European administrators, traders, and missionaries interacted with local populations, who also had their own ways of understanding right and wrong in their world. Many forms of Kongo dance and other types of embodiment were targeted as violations of particular European understanding of proper conduct and behavior. Specifically, Belgian administrators and Western missionaries generally associated many of the dances with sexuality.

Before European colonization in the nineteenth century, the BisiKongo themselves did not automatically associate nudity or partial nudity with sexuality, as often only the bottom half of the body was covered with cloth (Thornton 1983, 35). They also had more lenient rules for sexual relations, including trial marriages (with sexual contact) before official marriage ceremonies (Laman 1957, 24; Thornton 1983, 31) and fewer restrictions on the sexual lives of unmarried men and women (Laman 1957, 33). Thus, sexual conduct that Belgians and other Westerners might have defined from their own perspective as immoral may not have been perceived in the same way for Kongo people themselves.

To understand what many of the secular makinu in question looked like, I present the following ethnographic memory from my own experiences in the field: August 16, 2005. After a bumpy ride on the uneven, unpaved roads that can only be conquered by motorcycles and vehicles with four-wheel drive, we arrive in the small village of Saka, in Luozi territory. The light of the full moon illuminates the path as we walk toward the large crowd of people haphazardly standing in a circle, laughing, singing, drinking, and dancing. People look at me quizzically as I politely wiggle my way to the front of the circle of onlookers to get a closer look. There are three long, thick drums being played, and the *ngoma ngudi* (lead or mother drum) has a tar circle (*ndimbu*) in the middle of its drum head, giving it the deepest sound as it leads the other two drums (*ntambu*). In the center of the circle of spectators, there are two lines, one of men, and another of women. Two men or boys leave their line and walk with the rhythm across the center of the circle to the other line, and stop in front of two women or girls, thus choosing them as partners. The women then follow them to the center of the circle and begin to dance with them, rotating and shaking their hips and behinds, while the tops of their bodies barely move. The men follow another cross rhythm, shifting from one foot to the other, their own hip movements emphasized by long lengths of cloth hanging vertically from their waists to the ground, making a type of skirt.[4]

FIGURE 3.2. Secular makinu (ndosa dance specifically) in village of Saka, Luozi territory, 2005. Photo by Yolanda Covington-Ward.

The men dance around and jump toward their partners, while the women stay in place, calm and collected, hips moving continuously, with their feet shuffling slightly. At a particular drum signal, the couples stop dancing, genuflect toward each other, and exit the circle, and are replaced by another set of men coming in to start the cycle once again (see figure 3.2).

This ethnographic description provides an image of the most common type of secular dance, which people in Luozi referred to *makinu ya nsi*, *makinu ma luketo*, or *ndosa* (traditional dance), at the time of my research.[5] The skillful rotation of the hips that characterizes dances that accompany *soukouss* or Congolese popular dance music (White 2008) draws on dance traditions such as those described above in Saka. These "dances of the hips" are not unique to Kongo people but exist throughout much of Central Africa, from the Congo to Uganda. And it is these types of dances that became the focus of much anxiety on the part of European colonial agents and missionaries. The following sections consider the question of clashing moralities, reactions of the colonial administration to indigenous secular dancing, and the opinions and efforts of both Catholic and Protestant missionaries to suppress dancing as an activity or pastime. In all these instances, the political and religious authority of the government officials and missionaries respectively is enhanced and confirmed by their ability to prohibit their Congolese subjects from dancing. However, later in the chapter we look at a territorial administrator from Luozi territory who sought to use makinu to combat kingunza, establishing a policy of forced dancing to distract people from participation in activities associated with the prophetic movements.

Moral Legislation and Ambivalent Action

On July 17, 1900, the colonial administration released its first official legislation regarding what they called "indigenous dances." The act basically regulated public indigenous dance events, limiting them to certain days and locations, at specific times, and under conditions determined by the administrative authority. People who broke these rules were subject to arrest and seven days of penal servitude, and/or a fine of two hundred francs. In the following decades, a debate over indigenous dances emerged in the pages of *The Receuil Mensuel*, a circular of laws, ordinances, and general concerns distributed for the "exclusive use of functionaries and agents of the colony" (Congo Belge, Gouvernement Local 1913). These circulars were couched in general terms without discussing particular cultural or ethnic groups. However, from 1886 to 1929 the capital of the Congo Free State and then the Belgian Congo was Boma (in the Lower Congo), making it likely that some of these laws also referenced the activities of BisiKongo people. Within this context, we can better examine how Belgian colonial administrators viewed indigenous dances.

On January 16, 1912, vice governor-general Louis F. Ghislain wrote an interpretive circular commenting on the above law of indigenous dances of 1900, and focusing on his main issue of concern:[6] "It was brought to my knowledge, that in our posts, customary dances take place of a clearly lascivious or obscene character. On the part of the territorial authorities, charged with being the agents of civilization to the indigenous populations, to tolerate these practices and not to suppress them, could be with just cause considered by them as a sign of approval."[7] Thus, in this first circular, Ghislain evinces a concern for the morality of the public, by wanting to prohibit traditional dances that he saw as obscene. He also sees the suppression of such dances as a part of the civilizing mission of the colonial agents. However, Ghislain did not forbid all traditional dances wholesale—he left room for traditional dances that were not a threat to public morale, excluding them from being regulated by the 1900 decree (Congo Belge, Gouvernement Local 1912).

The next year, Eugene Henry, another vice governor-general, wrote a circular showing that "obscene" dances were still a problem: "In a number of posts of the colony and in proximity to them dances of a clearly obscene character take place. I remind territorial functionaries of circular no. 14, of

January 16, 1912, prescribing the prohibiting of dances of this type in all the stations of the colony. The first of their duties is combating energetically the practices that constitute a permanent obstacle to all the civilizing efforts and that oppose themselves to the attainment of indigenous populations to an intellectual and moral level to which we have undertaken to raise them."[8]

In this circular, a similar pattern can be seen. Colonial administrators saw dances they identified as obscene as threats to the civilization that Europeans believed they were bringing to their African colonial subjects. In Henry's view, such dances undermined the intellectual growth and moral standards to which patronizing colonizers, once again, sought to elevate the colonized. Indigenous dances once again menaced the morality of the public. Eugene Henry continued by writing that if obscene dances were taking place, the functionaries must immediately end them, and "write a report to the chief of moral violations and to defer the guilty to court." Thus, he demands the persecution of transgressors of the 1900 decree.

In January of 1915, two years later, yet another circular about indigenous dances appeared in the *Receuil Mensuel*. In it, the governor-general Félix Fuchs takes a more tentative approach to the control of indigenous dances, yet at the same time upholds ideas of European superiority and ethnocentrism that were part and parcel of the colonial endeavor:

> I have the honor to attract the very serious attention of the territorial authorities on the precise interpretation that it is important to give to the circular of the first of October 1913, relating to native dances and to warn them against a too severe application of the prescriptions that this circular contains. If it is urgently incumbent on us to prohibit practices of a clearly obscene tendency, it is also our duty to respect the traditional dances of the populations, when these demonstrations aren't at all in opposition to our conceptions of morality. The usual dances constitute for the blacks a recreation, I will say almost the unique recreation that their primitive mentality and the environmental conditions that surround them, allow them to appreciate. They are to them also a beneficial exercise, the only effort of physical limbering up. . . . It would not be a question of forbidding them excessively; one would thus risk provoking very legitimate discontent.[9]

Here Fuchs argues that the purpose of native dances is to provide a necessary form of recreation and exercise for the indigenous population. He warns that excessively prohibiting these dances will lead to legitimate complaints and discontent among the Congolese. Like Ghislain in the circular of 1912, he also believes nonobscene dances should be excluded from regulation. He justifies a more lax approach to dance regulation by implying that innate Black inferiority leaves dance as the only true African recreational pastime. Moreover, the theme of morality emerges once again, as Fuchs encourages the prohibition of dances that violate "our conceptions of morality," where "our" can be understood as early twentieth-century Belgian Catholic colonials. In sum, each of these administrators took varied approaches to regulating indigenous secular dances. While none of these circulars discuss specific dances, nor links them to particular ethnic groups, it is clear that the regulation of dancing bodies was a primary concern for the Belgian colonial administration in the Congo.

Protestant and Catholic Reactions to Kongo Makinu

The colonial administration's overall hostility and general disdain toward indigenous dances was even more pronounced in the European-led missions. Moral debates concerning dance have a very long history in Christianity. From opposition to dancing in medieval summas to the use of liturgical dances in some modern day churches,[10] there has not been a fixed consensus of opinion over time in Christian churches in regards to dance. Many of the arguments that European missionaries and some colonial administrators in the Congo used against dancing have their antecedents in discussions and debates that took place in Europe, especially during the sixteenth century in the age of the Reformation and Counter-Reformation, when the culture of the post–Middle Ages Renaissance period emphasized dance in court culture and comportment (Arcangeli 1994, 127).The different branches of Christianity were varied in their conceptions of the value or danger of dance.[11] Within Protestantism, Calvinists prohibited dance while the Lutherans were more tolerant. Similarly, some Catholic churches were more open to dance (for example, Society of Jesus) while others were more proscriptive.[12] However, in the debates that occurred about dance, some common themes emerged for both sides, revealing the frame of assessment that many Western Christians had toward dance. These included seeing dance as an amusement, an expression of joy, a physical exercise, an occasion for encounters (often with the opposite sex), a traditional habit or custom, a pagan rite in worship of the devil, and associated with the sexual act, madness, and/or drunkenness (Arcangeli 1994, 138–47). European missionaries and colonial administrators applied many of the same ideas in their evaluation of Kongo dances.

In Protestant churches in colonial-era Belgian Congo, dancing in general was discouraged. For instance, since the early establishment of SMF (Swedish Mission Covenant Church) missions, dancing was strictly forbidden. At an SMF missionary conference in 1894, a resolution was passed that "old customs, habits and conceptions, such as dance, all forms of idolater feasts, hair cut-ting feasts, funeral feasts, gun-salutes and wailing for the deceased, together with the drinking of palm-wine at such feasts, and at palavers, should be vigorously opposed and exterminated" (Axelson 1970, 285). This policy and intolerance for dance persisted in later years as well, as influential Swedish missionaries such as Karl Laman articulated a policy for conversion where individuals had to stop drinking alcohol and dancing, and should have only one wife, or else risk expulsion from the church (Mahaniah 1975, 162–63).

In 1907, the prohibition of "dance . . . [and] drumming at palm wine feasts" was added to the SMF constitution (Axelson 1970, 288). In 1941 eight Congo-lese teachers from the SMF mission at Kingoyi wrote a letter to the colonial administration protesting the physical abuses inflicted by Swedish mission-ary Reverend Karl Aldén, which included whipping a group of young school girls for dancing.[13] This incident demonstrates the hard line that Swedish missionaries took against dancing. While the SMF missionaries dominated the Protestant presence in Luozi territory, other missions, both Catholic and Protestant, enacted similar rules of conduct throughout the Lower Congo and the rest of the colony.

Several detailed studies of "BaKongo dances" written in 1937, 1938, and 1939 by three Belgian priests reveal BisiKongo dances had become a major point of concern for Catholic missions in the Lower Congo. These studies detail the dances that were alluded to in the administrative circulars and demonstrate that certain dances were also a concern for the clergy, who saw the dances as immoral practices unfit for true Christians, and sought methods to actively combat them.

In 1937 Jesuit Catholic priest Joseph Van Wing published the article "Les Danses Bakongo," in *Congo*, an academic review of the Belgian colony. He begins the article with a stereotypical assessment of the genetic ability of people of African descent in regards to dance: "If there is an art in which blacks excel, it is the dance. . . . It is innate to them" (1937, 121). Later in the article, he describes the most common form of BaKongo dances:

> When the drums are ready they are put in the middle of the space, and the dancers come to arrange themselves in front of them: one side of men, the chest bare, . . . the other side of women, covered in a small cloth of dance. The main drum gives the first measures. . . . The *mvudi-toko* (dance master) places himself at the head of the two lines and strikes up the song. . . . The choir picks up the song, and the dance begins. It consists of a shaking, to make wriggle in a certain way the *luketo* [hips], that is to say the lower stomach, in the same rhythmical movement; the

speed and the intensity of movement is regulated by the rhythm of the drums. . . . Two male dancers move themselves forward in front of two female dancers . . . and the two couples dance, watched by the crowd, who mark the tempo of hands and feet. At the signal of the *mvudi-toko*, the two couples withdraw themselves, and two others come forward and do the same, and so on for all the couples. Then . . . [the female dancers] move forward near the men, and each of them grabs hold of a partner, and the two embrace chest to chest, and remain like this, stuck [together], all while shaking the hips, until the *mvudi-ntoko* gives the signal of separation. . . . There is the ordinary dance of eastern BaKongo. (Van Wing 1937, 127–28)

Similar descriptions of Kongo dances can be found for almost all parts of the Lower Congo, some dating to even before the colonial period.[14] Moreover, another dance called *maringa* had become popular by the 1930s. The maringa dance was a partnered dance performed to the accompaniment of European instruments, which displayed a lot of hip movement and was said to imitate certain dances of Europe and the Caribbean (P. Martin 1995, 131). Van Wing wrote of the maringa: "Since some time the *maringa* has spread itself, imitating the whites, and takes place not in the public space but in the interior of huts of palm branches to the sound of an accordion. The couples embrace and wriggle in so disorderly a fashion that nothing remains in regards to the aesthetic. It all turns into shamelessness and obscenity" (1937, 128).

After his descriptions of popular Kongo dances, Van Wing laments, "There is the brutal fact . . . our people have lost the sense of honest dancing" (1937, 128). He then explores various reactions to Kongo dances, from traditional chiefs who have both regulated and allowed dances, to the colonial administration, which in Van Wing's view "hardly has intervened. Faced with certain excesses of public obscenities, it applies sanctions" (1937, 129). He sees similarities between the reactions of the Christian missions, both Catholic and Protestant, and those of the leader of the kingunza movement, Simon Kimbangu: "At the Protestant missions the dancer of ngoma was excluded from the Holy Communion. At the Catholic missions he was deprived of the sacraments and must do a required penance, if he wanted to return to the Christian practice. Kibangu [*sic*] came in 1921. With one word, he did away with the ngoma. Throughout all the country they were broken and burned" (1937, 129).

Finally, Van Wing's opinion and disdain for Kongo dances clearly emerges toward the end of the article: "It is evident that the people need distractions and diversions. . . . But it is also evident that no people need stupid diversions. Now the dance of the *ngoma* is only a direct preparation, public and collective, for the sexual act. . . . It destroys the physical vigor, and the sense of morality" (1937, 130). He suggests that the BaKongo either return to performing other moral traditional dances, or adopt appropriate dances from other Bantu groups around them. Notably, he even conjectures that ngoma dances can become fertile ground for other "kibanguisms" [*sic*] or prophetic movements. Overall, he does not see Kongo dances as diversions, strictly traditional, or vital, and thus asserts that the BaKongo are not being deprived if the dances are prohibited. He closes the article with the following: "If someone wants to participate in the life of Christ, he must refrain from immoral dances. And thus it is no longer a question of indigenous politics. . . . It is an essential principle of Christian morality that coincides with morality and nothing else" (1937, 131).

Thus, in his article, Van Wing pleads for the prohibition of modern dances of the BaKongo, almost all of which he views as immoral. His targeted audience is likely colonial administrators in particular based on his statements about the dances destroying the physical vigor of the people and also being a possible threat to the security of the colony. In endeavoring to police the conduct of all BisiKongo in the colony, Van Wing seeks to exercise more than his religious authority as a Catholic missionary by entering the realm of political authority, legislation, and enforcement. Once again, the question of morality drives the prevailing justification for the prohibition of these dances. Van Wing sees them as violating a sense of Christian morality—really, as overtly sexual dances.

The next year, at a seminar for Catholic priests held in Louvain, Belgium, the dances of the BaKongo once again became the primary focus of discussion. P. DeCapmaker, a priest in the Matadi area of Bas-Congo, gave a presentation on the topic. He starts by explaining the position of the Congregation for the Propagation of the Faith in Rome—that it was not recommended to alter practices that were not positively against religion or morality. Moreover, he explains that the missionaries were not condemning all dances indiscriminately, since to do so would cause many problems (1938, 40). He goes on to say that theological morals make it possible to distinguish three types of dances:

1. The honest dances, inspired by absolutely honest motives. . . . In this category we can place all the BaKongo dances that are not mixed.[15] They are rather games of dexterity. . . . 2. The dangerous dances: that in themselves are not improper, but often end up in licentiousness, as a result of the circumstances that ordinarily accompany them: songs, excessive

drinking, unhealthy exaltation produced by the frenetic repetition of the same rhythm, perverse tendencies of dancers, drums, darkness. . . . These dangerous dances are condemned by morality because they constitute occasions close to sin. . . . 3. The obscene dances: are those in which the gestures, the movements, the touching are shameless, licentious, and against morality. (DeCapmaker 1938, 41–44)

He then discusses these so-called dangerous and obscene dances in Matadi among the BaKongo, quoting the descriptions and opinions of missionaries from the seventeenth century to the 1930s, as well as descriptions of colonial agents, many of which correspond to those already given by Van Wing. Discouraging acts of violence in the suppression of native dances (forcibly breaking drums, and so on), he instead suggests the use of missionary influence to pressure native chiefs to prevent obscene dances, as well as the intentional creation of "honest" diversions such as sports or drama. He ends his presentation with the following conviction: "We are convinced that it is above all by—and at—the occasions of dances that Satan takes his revenge on our savior Jesus Christ and his missionaries" (DeCapmaker 1938, 58). This comment is noteworthy because it reveals that in his opinion, many BaKongo dances were the work of the devil himself, and can thus be seen, by extension, as the enemy of the Christian civilizing mission. Again, sexuality is lurking here, as he describes the dances as "licentious" and "close to sin."

After DeCapmaker's presentation, the Catholic priests present at the seminar had a vigorous debate on the topic. The discussion considered whether Europeans introduced corrupting dances, if games and scout groups should be promoted instead to combat immoral dances, if all dances should be the target of surveillance, and if encouraging a return to more ancient dances would invite a return of other traditional customs. Then, a remarkable exchange took place when one priest, Father Van Hoof, was asked his point of view:

The conclusions of the missionaries of the vicariate of Kisantu are in complete agreement with that of the missionaries of Matadi presented by P. DeCapmaker. In fact, at the present time all the dances of the BaKongo are bad in [their] nature, or indifferent in themselves degenerating into bad in fact.
Father Secretary: Then all the dances are bad?
Father Van Hoof: Certainly all those with the "ngoma," and all those with whatever instrument which are mixed [in sex]. (DeCapmaker 1938, 61)

Here, these Catholic missionaries saw Kongo dances as a direct threat to not only a Belgian conception of morality, but also the ideology of Christianity in particular. Tellingly, Catholic missionaries presuppose immoral sexual activities in any dances including both men and women. The focus on the ngoma as the main instrument associated with immoral dances has an effect to this day on the types of instruments allowed in different churches (Catholic, Protestant, and others) in the Lower Congo.

Kongo dances bothered Catholic priests so much that Monsignor Jean Cuvelier, Redemptorist missionary and bishop of Matadi, conducted an investigation of all Kongo dances throughout the Lower Congo. He sent a list of questions to all the Catholic mission stations in the area and compiled and analyzed the responses.[16] He also used some of the material that he collected to write the last article of interest, "Les Missions Catholiques en face des danses des Bakongo," published in Rome in 1939. In this article, Cuvelier presents historical and current descriptions of dances, distinguishes between different types of dances, and even discusses the dances of banganga, which he describes as dances where "all the devils of hell dance alongside them" (1939, 155). He sees these dances of the banganga, along with funerary dances and dances of mixed sex with hip movements, as essentially bad dances that should be prohibited. He ends the article by highlighting concerns for morality: "There's a lot left to do. The improvement of moral and civil life will allow the hope of better and lasting results" (Cuvelier 1939, 170).

Interviews and written texts illuminate some of the actual actions undertaken by Catholic missionaries in regards to Kongo dances. For example, in a document explaining the conduct and regulations necessary for the operation of a Redemptorist mission in the Congo, Catholic catechists are told they must be "model Christians," and some of their principal functions include "to prudently prevent evil, above all fetishism and obscene dances" (Kratz 1970, 351). In an interview near Mayidi in Lower Congo, Tata Tuzolana, a traditional drummer, recounted an incident when Father Masamba, a Congolese Jesuit priest, broke the skin of his drum to prevent him from playing (July 22, 2005).[17] Similarly, Tata Mbumba, a MuKongo Catholic, recalled that as a student he was threatened with expulsion from a Catholic mission school when he was caught dancing a secular dance (July 21, 2005). These are just a few of many examples of Catholic intolerance toward dancing during the colonial era.

Overall, there was a fundamental conflict of cultural beliefs between European colonizers and missionaries and BisiKongo dancers in the Belgian Congo. The use of overt hip movements in dance, the touching of pelvises in a thrusting gesture that occasioned dancing in a couple, the playing of the ngoma, and many other elements common in Kongo secular performances were not a part of the cultural milieu of Europeans. As a result, many colonial administrators and missionaries were overtly opposed to the majority of the makinu of the BisiKongo, seeking to reform them, replace them with other pastimes, or to outright eliminate them altogether. Their efforts to control the conduct of Kongo people demonstrate the prohibition of dances was one way that their political and religious authority was reestablished and confirmed on a very intimate level for the average Kongo person.

Kongo Reactions to Dance Prohibitions

While European efforts to regulate dances are one side of the story, how did Kongo people react to rules prohibiting dance? To start, we must understand that before widespread European colonization, dance was a part of everyday life for BisiKongo people, used on a variety of occasions, from games, to funerals, to the capture of prisoners of war, to successful hunts (Laman 1968, 72). Thus, dancing, whether in secular or nonsecular contexts, was morally acceptable and appropriate. This moral order shifted dramatically with the arrival of large numbers of missionaries in the late nineteenth and early twentieth centuries. One source that provides insight on this shift is *Au Pays des Palmiers*, a compilation of the recollections of Kongo instructors in the Protestant churches of SMF mission, originally published in 1928. In some cases, BisiKongo who were loyal members of the Protestant church upheld the rules and may have internalized the point of view of the missionaries. For instance, Yoane Nlamba, a teacher at Mukimbungu mission, describes some of the older traditions of the area when he writes, "dance was extremely appreciated by the ancestors. One would dance in all the villages, each village had their own drums. The dance took place during the evening and the night . . . and it was accompanied by immoral orgies" (Ahman [1928] 2003, 59). Similarly, Lebeka Kiniongono, a teacher at Kingoyi mission writes, "The women of long ago really loved dancing. But certain dances were very much shameful" (Ahman [1928] 2003, 92). In both of these descriptions of Kongo dances, the moral interpretation of these embodied practices is very negative.[18]

Similarly, more than seven decades later, in several interviews during my research, people stated that they considered some Kongo dances to be immoral.[19] When pressed for specific reasons, one interviewee, Mama Nsafu, a prominent leader in the CEC Protestant church in Luozi, explained: "There is perhaps a dance of the man and the woman where they approach each other very, very, closely, or there is perhaps excitement. . . . One can qualify that directly, that it is immoral, that, it is not for the church. . . . If it is a dance that shows an odd manner, one where the people can be described as bad, one must not continue, and . . . we don't permit that" (September 20, 2005).

However, not all Kongo people saw Kongo dances as immoral. Ne Nkamu Luyindula,[20] recounting the story of his grandmother's appreciation for Kongo dances, explained that someone asked her, "Ma Batikita, were you baptized? She said, 'Baptized? Why become baptized? To whom will I leave the dancing? That's to say, me, I don't accept to be baptized at the Protestant mission. If I do, I will leave behind my dancing,' and she was baptized really very late [in life], very late" (September 20, 2005). Ma Batikita's story demonstrates that despite the power and influence of Christian missions, some people resisted the rules and policies by continuing to dance. For her, to stop dancing was a public sign of the embracing of a Protestant identity and the acceptance of the religious authority of the Protestant missions. The fact that she became baptized only when she was too old to dance testifies to the importance of makinu as embodied practice to some BisiKongo. Yet another interviewee presented a positive assessment of makinu when he said, "dances of the BaKongo are a part of the process of education. . . . Dance is also for correcting behavior. . . . I don't think that they [dances] were immoral. . . . The adults, the people dance without a lot of negative ideas" (Tata Malanda, October 28, 2005). The next sections of the chapter examine the fate of kingunza after Kimbangu more generally and consider two specific time periods when secular and sacred embodiment (makinu and zakama) clashed in the context of religion and nationalism in the Belgian Congo.

Post-Kimbangu Kingunza in the 1920s

After Kimbangu's imprisonment in late 1921, the movement continued without him as other prophets continued to emerge, and tragically, were prosecuted. Membership dropped in both Catholic and Protestant missions. As the following 1924 interrogation of a woman being accused of being an ngunza in Kunda-Tumba, Bas-Congo demonstrates, many of Kimbangu's followers felt betrayed by these churches, and sought more independence:

> D: Since the missionaries are the agents of the God to whom you pray, why are you fleeing them?[21]
> R: We are not fleeing, we pray to the same God since there is only one. . . . When the affairs of gunza [sic] occurred, all of us, children of God, we went to visit them because they said that they teach the things of God. The missionaries and the state said that these kunza [sic] were crazy. They sent them to Upper Congo, and now it is finished.
> D: And it is for that that you flee the missionaries?
> R: Listen, white man. If your child has grown big, must you always serve

him food? Can't he get it himself? . . . Now the missionaries want that we return to them to sing and pray. . . . We don't want to go anymore, but we want to pray and sing [to] God without their intervention.[22]

This exchange reveals a burgeoning desire for independence in Christian worship, away from the guidance and eyes of European missionaries, who clearly saw the threat the prophetic movements posed to their religious domination and hegemony. In this regard, the meetings and groups that were formed by Kongo people seeking to take control of their own Christian worship, defining it on their own terms, reflected a growing adherence to a religious authority that came not from European missionaries, but rather from a number of Kongo prophets who were inspired by God through visions, dreams, and possession. This desire for religious independence reflects and in many ways drives growing nationalist sentiment in the Lower Congo.

In the decade following Kimbangu's imprisonment, the Belgian colonial government vacillated in its treatment of kingunza when it saw imprisonment and exile were not sufficient deterrents. On January 1, 1924, two hundred Congolese gathered outside of the Catholic mission in Tumba, singing banned songs and demanding religious freedom. The district commissioner told the crowd that he agreed to allow them to freely practice their religion, and they dispersed. As a result, the Congolese quickly began to build some kingunza/Kimbanguist churches and schools. The district commissioner sent a letter to the governor of the entire province, saying he didn't see the kingunza movement as seditious (Geuns 1974, 201; Joset 1968, 107). However, the territorial administrator of the Southern Cataracts disagreed and, in his own letter, urged the governor to repress the movement (Geuns 1974, 202; Joset 1968, 108). The matter was complicated further by reports and newspaper articles released by Catholic priests speaking against the movement, such as a 1924 report by Father Dufonteny claiming that the movement was inspired by Protestant missions and sought to unseat the white colonial administration. After further investigation,[23] the Belgian colonial government switched course and sent military troops throughout Bas-Congo, officially forbidding any involvement with the movement on February 6, 1925. All Kimbanguist institutions were closed, people were arrested, and all religious meetings outside of those directed by missionaries "of the white race" were prohibited (Centre de Recherche et d'Information Socio-politiques 1960, 7; Joset 1968, 108). In a circular that same year, the governor asked the Catholic and Protestant missions to help suppress the movement (M. Martin 1975, 81). The last battalion of troops didn't leave until June 1925 (Joset 1968, 108). After such severe repression of the movement, from 1925 to 1930 there were only sporadic public manifestations of kingunza (Centre de Recherche et d'Information Socio-politiques 1960, 8) although undoubtedly, people continued to worship in secret. This was to change, however, in the 1930s, especially in what is now Luozi territory in the Lower Congo.

Makinu and Kingunza as Performative Encounters in 1930s Luozi

The kingunza movement reappeared openly in January 1931 with public meetings of bangunza in the Boko area of French Congo. This demonstrates the porous borders between Kongo people in either colony, as their religious activities were mutually influential. Additional evidence of their connections across borders can be seen in confiscated letters written from Yoane Mvubi (John the Baptist) in the Belgian Congo to bangunza in Boko, French Congo. One of the letters spoke of "'vita dia ntotila ye makesa,' the war that Ntotila and *makesa* (the heroes) are to wage in order to liberate the Kongo" (Andersson 1958, 98). Andersson interprets "Ntotila" as referring to Simon Kimbangu. Moreover, the letters prohibited contact with colonial officials or missionaries and proclaimed a pending great battle in which the kingdom of the Whites would be overthrown (Andersson 1958, 98–99). All of this leads Andersson to conclude that "the movement had undergone a considerable change. From a movement in which spiritual revival was the central feature . . . it has developed into a movement almost entirely hostile to foreigners and with obviously national or even revolutionary aims" (Andersson 1958, 100). The homes of suspected bangunza Samuel Matuba and Philippe Nkunku in Boko were raided in January 1931, and many people were deported, bringing an end to public manifestations of the movement in Boko for some time.

Just across the border in the Belgian Congo, there was a resurgence of kingunza several years later in 1934–35 in Kingoyi, the northernmost Swedish mission outpost. Secret meetings in the forest became common, as evangelists commissioned by the mission and others (some unaffiliated with the mission) came together to worship away from the eyes of the missionaries. A prophet named Sebuloni Nsonde led this particular movement. Reverend Karl Aldén, a Swedish missionary at Kingoyi, wrote about this particular time period in a diary and described sneaking up on a secret forest meeting in November of 1934. "The partakers in this *fête nocturne*, men, women, children . . . performed the most grotesque motions: running in and out of the crowd . . . jumping high in the air . . . shaking the head and the body as a dog jumping out of the water. This wild 'witch-dance'—same as the old dances in the time of sorcery—was accompanied by two rattles with an intensely exciting sound (Aldén 1936, 350). Aldén even describes an ordeal by fire where man after man jumped into the fire. This array of ecstatic embodiment that Aldén witnessed in the *pendele*, including seeing the entire crowd speaking in tongues, demonstrates that the manifestation of the Holy Spirit was becoming more and more important, especially in comparison to the use of the Bible in worship services, which was becoming less significant in kingunza practices. Bangunza then, whether prophets or followers, were drawing on their bodies to become closer to God, through means that negated the need for the guidance or interpretation of White missionaries. This independent sentiment led to severe reprisals on behalf of the colonial government, including military patrols of the territory and the arrest and exile of at least one hundred people in 1934 (Joset 1968, 109).

As the kingunza movement in Manianga territory continued even after the massive arrests, resurging again in 1935, the colonial administration began to seek other solutions for the prophetism "problem," resulting in a change in attitude toward secular makinu. Foreshadowing this later shift in policy, in 1924, an administrator wrote a letter to the governor concerning the prophetic movements and the possibility of secular dances as a distraction: "The natives who practice the Protestant religion can't drink palm wine, or dance. It is true that dances are also prohibited by the Catholic missionaries. Why prohibit to man the distractions that entertain the spirit and the senses?"[24] This type of thinking reappeared in response to the kingunza movement in Manianga territory. In 1936, J. Maillet, the territorial administrator of Luozi, called many of the chiefs of the area together for a meeting in the village of Kimbulu:

> He [Maillet] made it known that the villagers must begin again to dance and must make an *ngoma*. The chiefs had noticed that the pastors and the priests were opposed to dance with the ngoma and had prohibited it to their followers. The administrator told them that the priest and he each had their own activities but that he, chief of the region, wanted that this order be executed. The chiefs didn't hide their repugnance and said that many of the dances were frankly immoral. The administrator invited the chiefs to come and celebrate at Luozi the national celebration with a group of young men and women. (Gotink 1995, 156)

Moreover, Maillet wanted to make dancing obligatory in the villages between four and five o'clock. He also ordered that when he stopped in a village for the night, he should be welcomed by people dancing. What motivated this shift in policy from a largely negative view and an ambivalent approach of earlier colonial policies regarding traditional dances, to policies forcing performances on the Kongo people? During the annual meeting of the territorial administrators of Lower Congo in February of 1936, the administrators had discussed the aforementioned incidents of prophetism requiring military occupation in Luozi territory, along with other outbreaks of prophetism. In the minutes of this meeting, there were several suggested means of preventing outbreaks of prophetic movements, including the reorganization of villages, creation of more mission schools, and the creation of organized distractions such as dance: "In the regions contaminated by prophetism the native doesn't drink palm wine anymore; dances are abolished. . . . Dances constitute a public repudiation of the doctrine of prophetism. A propaganda for the encouragement of dances must be made by the members of the territorial service."[25]

J. Maillet in particular asked for the state to provide funding for organized dances in Luozi, and two hundred francs were allocated to him for this purpose. Thus, Maillet thought to use secular, traditional makinu to distract people from prophetism.[26] The opinion of missionaries to this implemented policy was very disapproving, as shown in a letter written in 1936 from Belgian Catholic missionary Father Joseph Dosogne to Monseigneur Jean Cuvelier: "Prophetism is a political-religious movement, which . . . interests and profoundly agitates the indigenous soul. It would be the most naïve illusion and the most dangerous one to think that one will impede it seriously and that one will stop it, by this attempt of returning to paganism that is the official introduction of *ngoma* and of dances" (quoted in Gotink 1995, 157).

In this situation, although they had the same goal of eliminating the movement, the colonial administrator and the Protestant and Catholic missionaries disagreed about this particular method of suppressing prophetism. This case of using traditional secular dances to combat prophetism is clearly one where the ostensible collaboration between the missions, both Catholic and Protestant, and the Belgian colonial administration was disrupted. Because of the supposedly "immoral" influence ngoma dances would have on Christian villagers, the missionaries saw the return to this particular form of traditional practice as a step backward in their civilizing mission. However, Maillet, the colonial administrator, prioritizes the issue of state security over concerns about the proliferation of "immoral" dances. Thus, the case of Luozi territory in 1936 can be seen as one where missionaries and colonial authorities bumped heads in the face of the competing authority that the prophetic movements represented, where Maillet prioritized preserving the political authority of the state over maintaining the religious authority of the missionaries. Van Wing's article noted this approach of the administration as well, when he wrote that the administration had reversed its position so that "the highest authority in the province encourages and makes his subordinates encourage the dances of the *ngoma*; because they say, the people need relaxation, and the ngoma is an excellent means of combating Kibanguism [*sic*]" (Van Wing 1937, 130).

But how did Kongo people themselves interpret this intentional use of their secular dances to combat kingunza? Born in 1934, Tata Mukiese described his experiences of colonial-era regulation of secular dances: "The colonizer never prohibited dancing. On the other hand, they wished that people continue to take a lot of leisure time. Because that gave them the possibility moreover of keeping them [the colonized] in a state where they didn't want to bother them [colonizers]. . . . It wasn't with the popular dances that the people were having revelations but rather with the kingunza. . . . The colonizers weren't against the dances; they encouraged them; he [the colonized] could dance like he wanted without a problem. That doesn't bother him [the colonizer]. The thing that bothers him is the kingunza" (January 30, 2006).

Tata Mukiese clearly articulates the knowledge that Kongo people were aware of how much kingunza threatened the colonial government and also saw the strategic manipulations of secular dances for what they were—distractions and deterrents. While I am not focusing here on one specific incident, I see Maillet's makinu intervention in 1936 as a performative encounter that sought to transform the relationship between Congolese subjects and their Belgian colonizers. By forcing people in areas affected by the prophet movement to stop their work and activities to dance at designated times in a manner prohibited by Kongo prophets, Maillet was using people's bodies, against their will, as a tool to combat prophetism. Perhaps Maillet hoped that people in the area would regain an appreciation for makinu, one that had been largely repressed owing to kingunza prohibitions. The music, the dancing, the palm wine that usually accompanied the festivities—makinu as community events were surely enjoyable under normal circumstances. By capturing their bodies, his goal was to capture their minds, encouraging them to reject the prophetic movement for denying them such embodied pleasure. Yet, there is another layer to this performative encounter. Each time these forced dances were held at the designated time, the dancers and musicians, whether overtly or not, were forced to recognize the power of the colonial government. This was even more evident when Maillet or another administrator was present and the dances were to be performed in his honor. Through embodied performance then, Kongo colonial subjects experienced an intrudingly intimate relationship with the colonial state, one that reinforced their domination in an embodied manner.

Kingunza and Nsikumusu in the 1950s

The prophetic movements continued unabated in many different forms from the arrest of Kimbangu until independence, regardless of the violence, arrests, and punishments meted out by the colonial authorities. Some major movements included the arrival of Salvation Army missionaries in 1936, which led to the development of an independent, *ngunzist* salvation army. This was followed by the establishment of Mpadism, or the Black Mission/Khaki Church. Simon Mpadi was a former lieutenant in the Salvation Army and formed his own autonomous church and movement in 1939 in the territory of Thysville in Bas-Congo. After escaping prison four separate times, he was eventually caught again and sent into exile (Geuns 1974; Ryckmans 1970, 14). His Khaki Church continued on, privileging many kingunza embodied practices such as spirit-induced trembling (Andersson 1958, 154). Other important religious movements grouped under prophetic activity in colonial Bas-Congo include Tonsi, the Matswa movement, and Tokoism in the 1940s, and Dieudonné and organized Kimbanguism in the 1950s, among others (Geuns 1974).[27] Through the colonial period, Belgian administrators continued to call a number of diverse religious activities kingunza or Kimbanguist. For example, in 1944 in Manianga territory in the Mbanza Mona sector, a local chief imprisoned a sergeant in the Force Publique for organizing a "kibanguist" [*sic*] cell."[28] Similarly, in Mayumbe territory, the 1947 annual report noted "a regain of prophetic activity . . . in the 'Eastern' region of the territory near the frontier of A.E.F. . . . Two catechists . . . (had) the view of carrying out proselytizing in favor of the Mission of the Blacks. This movement was quickly put down."[29] In 1947 in Manianga territory a "cell" of ngunzists was discovered in Mbanza Ngoyo sector, and authorities imprisoned its leader in Luozi. The annual report notes that "this territory was repeatedly the theater of violent prophetic surges of a more or less subversive character."[30] In 1950, authorities uncovered a "cell" of the Salvation Army and imprisoned sixty-five people in Luozi territory.[31] The language used to describe these groups of bangunza, calling them cells, even implies a sense of political terrorism, as they were seen as such a threat to Belgian political authority and order.

During the resurgence of prophetic movements in the Lower Congo, both Catholic and Protestant missions faced declining membership. Many members of their churches were disappointed in what they saw as the collaboration of European-led missions with the colonial administration in the persecution of the prophetic movements and their leaders. Ironically enough, this reaction led to a major transformation of practices in the Protestant church. According to Tata Mukiese, an older, long-standing member of the *kilombo* at the CEC Protestant church in Luozi,[32] traditional instruments were allowed at one time. However, starting in the late 1930s, all traditional instruments were prohibited in Protestant churches owing to their association with worship in the prophetic movements (January 30, 2006). One could sing only in a classical manner, using European instruments. He recounted the story of a conflict in the town of Kingoyi in Luozi territory over the use of traditional Kongo instruments in the SMF mission church. Swedish missionary Reverend Karl Aldén banned the use of traditional instruments in his church in 1934. Kalebi Muzita, a Kongo leader in the church, disagreed and challenged Aldén's policy. Kongo catechists, teachers, and pastors divided into two groups, some siding with Aldén and others with Muzita. As a result of the standoff, Kalebi and his group decided to leave the church. He reportedly told Alden, "Since you have prohibited playing these instruments, you will see what will happen." According to Tata Mukiese, Aldén and his followers became sick after this proclamation and were healed only when Kalebi returned and prayed for them.

Now, Tata Mukiese was born the same year this incident supposedly took place. While it is clear that he was not a direct witness to the events, the narrative that he tells provides an intriguing perspective on Kongo ideas about the role of their own cultural practices in missionary-established churches. Kalebi Muzita's perceived ability to both cause and heal the illness of Aldén and others blends the spiritual powers of banganga and bangunza. Such an ability suggests that the spiritual power of prophets can successfully compete with that of European missionaries. Moreover, more significant in this narrative is both the conflict over embodied practices in the use of traditional instruments, and the importance for certain Kongo people of including such practices in worship, even to the point of revoking one's membership in a particular church. Karl Aldén's fervent attacks on bangunza in his own mission church have been chronicled in several bangunza songs from Kingoyi that disparage his actions and his negative attitude toward the prophetic movements (Andersson 1958, 279–80, 283).[33] Muzita himself, according to a colonial document, was a member of the prophet movement and by 1941 had been sent into exile to Sankuru in the eastern district of Congo-Kasai.[34] The use of traditional Kongo instruments in worship was clearly part of a larger battle between Kongo-centered and European-centered Christianity and thus was important to large segments of the population in Kingoyi as well as other parts of the Lower Congo.

As more and more people left their churches for the various prophetic movements, Swedish missionaries in the territory of Luozi finally decided on a plan of action. This plan was addressed in the 1956 annual governmental report for Luozi territory: "Since the month of June a new wave of mysticism colored by ngunzism has again swept a big part of the territory. This movement was provoked by a circular sent by the Protestant missionaries of Sundi-Lutete and Kinkenge, inviting their adepts to a moral and spiritual reawakening. Unfortunately, the text of this circular was ambiguous for the natives and was misinterpreted by them. The old ngunzist leaders took up again their subversive activity justifying it by the context of the circular. At a given moment the rumor spread that ngunzism was no longer prohibited by the government. Four big ngunzist manifestations took place in the territory."[35]

The Protestant SMF churches used the Kikongo term *nsikumusu* (revival or awakening) to describe the spiritual movement they were trying to create. In this effort to bring people back to the SMF missions, church leaders appropriated many of the practices of the prophetic movements. For example, traditional instruments could be played in the church once again, and trembling and speaking in tongues were no longer strictly prohibited. While the SMF missions sponsored this spiritual revival, they did not in fact have a monopoly on the discourse that surrounded nsikumusu. First, there had been yet another outbreak of kingunza in Luozi territory in the early months of 1956, before the announcement of the SMF church revival.[36] Second, in and around Matadi and in the areas north of the Congo River (Luozi and adjoining territories), rumors circulated about the possible return of the prophet Simon Kimbangu (long since deceased in 1951) that were explicitly tied to this spiritual reawakening. Monseigneur Van den Bosch, a Belgian Catholic missionary, warned the colonial administration of two Protestant catechists spreading such rumors: "They repeated in the villages that Simon [Kimbangu] was on his way and that he would be preceded by many prophets, who must 'awaken' the country" (Etambala 2004, 118). The great spiritual revival sweeping Luozi territory and other parts of the Lower Congo in the mid 1950s then, for Kongo people, was more related to millennialism and a desire for the return of the prophet Simon Kimbangu than to the efforts of the SMF churches.[37] Indeed, the language and activities of the SMF churches were used to reinforce the idea of Kimbangu's impending return.

This resurgence of prophetism had a great impact in other areas of the Lower Congo as well, including Thysville. In his 1957 annual report, BMS missionary Charles Couldridge reported: "Our church membership figures are down, our followers classes are also down . . . and our annual income in church gifts have fallen. . . . Here at Thysville we are compelled to take the resurgence of the prophet movement seriously. We have been hit hard in some districts where up to 75% of our church members have gone out 'en bloc.' . . . The drop . . . can only be accounted for by the large number of our people who have gone over to 'Kimbanguisme.'"[38]

The colonial administration wrote a disapproving report of the nsikumusu movement the following year, capturing the embodiment they viewed as the greatest threat—trembling: "The movement *nsikumusu* or spiritual awakening, launched by the Svenska Missions Förbundet of Sundi-Lutete in 1956 didn't have much success at the beginning. The propaganda of opposition made by the territory against trembling made the Reverend Missionaries think, who finished by admitting that in the territory of Luozi these phenomena are a characteristic expression of *ngunzism*."[39]

Therefore, the spiritual awakening of nsikumusu presents another case where missionaries (this time Protestant SMF missionaries in particular), and colonial administrators, disagreed on the meaning and usefulness of Kongo embodied practices. Both groups had the same interest of curbing the kingunza movement; however, colonial administrators did not approve of the SMF churches' method of tolerating some of the same practices, such as trembling, which typified the prophetic movement and were persecuted by the state. Although the motive of the SMF churches was to attract people back into their churches, the colonial administration saw the appropriation of such practices as encouraging the prophetic movements and thus increasing the threat to state security.

The performative encounters taking place in this instance are both within and outside of SMF churches. By appropriating the embodied practices of the prophetic movement, the missionaries of the SMF were trying to stage a performative encounter of their own. Incorporating the instruments, speaking in tongues, and especially the trembling (before state intervention) would lead to a redefinition of these practices as "Christian" instead of pagan in the eyes of the missionaries and their staunch supporters. The end result would be a reclaiming of spiritual authority by the missionaries in face of the opposition from the bangunza. The nsikumusu revival in the 1950s and its incorporation of certain traditional instruments and creation and collection of revival songs was in fact the origins of the large kilombo choirs found today in Protestant churches throughout the Lower Congo and even in Congo-Brazzaville (Tata Mukiese, January 30, 2006) (see figure 3.3).

The kingunza movement expanded during this time, outside of the SMF churches, taking even more members away from mission oversight. Bangunza privileged embodied practices such as trembling, thus continuing to demonstrate their calling to become spiritual leaders in a manner that

FIGURE 3.3. Kilombo of CEC Protestant church performing at funeral, with bibandi, Luozi, 2006. Photo by Yolanda Covington-Ward.

missionaries were not. This in fact augmented their spiritual authority and earned them a greater following, especially when coupled with the rumors of Kimbangu's return.

Kingunza and Kimbanguism

From 1921 to 1956, the terms *kingunza* and *Kimbanguism* were often used interchangeably to describe Kongo prophetic phenomena. In 1956, however, Simon Kimbangu's middle son, Joseph Diangienda, led the founding of the Église de Jésus-Christ sur la terre par le prophète Simon Kimbangu (The Church of Jesus-Christ on Earth through the Prophet Simon Kimbangu) (Martin 1975, 104). Kimbanguism went from being a movement to becoming an organized denomination, initially based largely in urban areas like Kinshasa and appealing to the more educated classes of Congolese. The Kimbanguist Church was neither Catholic nor Protestant, eschewed politics, and minimized trembling caused by the Holy Spirit. They also sought to distinguish themselves from "Ngunza" groups who also prayed in the name of Simon Kimbangu but continued to privilege zakama. After a rash of arrests of Kimbanguists in June of 1957 in Leopoldville, the Kimbanguist congregation staged a protest and released several documents to explain their religion, advocate for religious freedom, and increase their profile internationally. In December of 1957, Léon Pétillon, the governor-general of the colony, released a letter allowing for tolerance of the Kimbanguist religion (Geuns 1974, 215; M. Martin 1976, 105–6). Eventually, in December of 1959, the Kimbanguist church was officially recognized by the colonial government, with full rights to exercise their religion.

In these last two chapters most of the discussion of nationalism in regards to Kongo prophetism has focused on calls for autonomy and freedom of worship away from European supervision. However, the question that must be asked is what role did Kongo prophetism play, if any, in the movement for political independence from Belgian colonialism? Joseph Kasa-Vubu, a MuKongo from the Mayombe area in Bas-Congo, led ABAKO (Association des BaKongo), the organization turned political party that drove the movement for political independence in the Congo in the 1950s (Covington-Ward 2012). There is not enough evidence to firmly conclude that ABAKO leaders worked extensively with Kimbanguist or leaders of other prophetic move ments. Indeed, in 1956 Kasa-Vubu pronounced that ABAKO members were "neither Kimbanguists, nor xenophobes" (Etambala 2004, 134). While there are few proven connections between ABAKO and prophetism, in the heady days of the late 1950s, especially after ABAKO's call for immediate independence and the January 1959 uprising (called riots by the Belgians) in Leopoldville, the desire for immediate social change was present in multiple arenas of social life, both religious and secular. This is why scores of people left mission churches once again for the prophet movement in 1959 and 1960,[40] hoping for the spiritual guidance to prepare them for the changes to come. Like during the time of Simon Kimbangu, many people had millennial hopes that deceased ancestors would return and the world and the existing structures of power would be completely transformed. Following anthropologist Wyatt MacGaffey, I agree that Kongo prophetism, "though never organized in the coordinated political form that the Belgians feared, nevertheless prepared the ground for ABAKO" (1992, 339).

Conclusion

An examination of bodily practices in both religious and secular contexts in colonial-era Belgian Congo reveals the shifting meanings and uses of embodied practices so aptly captured in the proverb *Nsinsa wa ngoma wusobele, soba makinu maku*. This chapter explored the complicated uses of Kongo embodied cultural performances in the Belgian Congo in the establishment and maintenance of religious and political authority. The performative encounters examined here demonstrate that the politics of the body is multidirectional—the bodies of Kongo people could be placed at the service of insurgent Kongo prophets as well as crafty colonial administrators, desperate Swedish missionaries, or even disparate individuals trying to define their embodiment on their own terms. All of this reinforces the notion that performances of the body and their meanings are effective means of impacting individual and group consciousness. Moreover, the debates about sexuality and morality in regards to secular Kongo dances demonstrate the clash of cultural perceptions about moving bodies and their potential impact on individuals and society more broadly. The next chapter explores the connection between everyday performances and nationalism in postcolonial Congo under the dictator Mobutu Sese Seko.

Part III

CIVIL RELIGION AND
PERFORMED POLITICS IN
POSTCOLONIAL CONGO

CHAPTER 4
_____

Dancing with the Invisible

Everyday Performances under Mobutu Sese Seko

Happy are the people who sing and dance.
—Mobutu Sese Seko

In the MPR, one surrenders both the body and the soul.
—MPR party motto

Performance and Politics

Excitement and anticipation filled the air in the capital city of Kinshasa on the night of October 30, 1974.[1] Along with television networks and reporters from all over the world, an estimated seventy thousand people packed the 20 Mai Stadium when events began at 3:00 AM local time. The West Central African country newly renamed Zaire was at the center of the international spotlight, hosting the sports event of the decade and performing their nation for all to see.[2] The main event was the famed "Rumble in the Jungle" boxing match between Muhammad Ali and George Foreman. However, the prelude and backdrop for the event was that of hundreds of dancers covering the grassy field of the stadium wearing printed pagnes and raffia, and executing different choreographed sequences inspired by "traditional" dances. As one group of dancers rolled their hips in synchrony, they began to sing in Kikongo as they pointed up toward the top of the stadium, where a large billboard of the face of President Mobutu Sese Seko was placed high above the dancing crowds.[3]

E e e Mobutu wayi wayi wa
E e e Sese Seko e wayi wayi wa
Yambula tata meno yikina kwani
Yati diatila mu nzol'e wayi wayi we

E e e Mobutu wayi wayi wa
E e e Sese Seko e wayi wayi wa
Leave me to dance
This is done with love[4]

This simple song and embodied performance simultaneously venerated President Mobutu Sese Seko while also referencing the united movements of a unified nation through the synchronized gestures. However, what was the purpose of such a crafted, public performance? This performance of *animation politique*—choreographed and scripted dancing, singing, and other types of artistic expression with nationalist themes drawing on performance traditions from different ethnic groups—was not an exceptional occurrence tied only to the famed boxing event. Political and cultural animation (also referred to as animation politique or simply animation) was widespread and reached into all aspects of everyday life in Zaire, formally emerging in the early 1970s and gradually fading in the late 1980s (White 2008, 73). Such dances, along with marches, rallies, salutes, and other public demonstrations were part and parcel of quotidian nationalist activities in postcolonial Zaire under President Mobutu. Why were such performances so important? What can an examination of animation politique tell us about the relationship between the body, performance, and state power, especially in a state relying on coercion and violence? Moreover, how are such performances related to another realm—that of civil religion?

This chapter emerges from interviews with people who participated in animation politique at different levels of engagement, documents retrieved at the National Archives in Kinshasa, speeches, newspaper articles, pamphlets, and other written propaganda of Mobutu's regime, along with limited analysis of videos of political animation. I use animation politique to explore the everyday embodied dimensions of performed nationalism in postcolonial Zaire by examining multiple types of everyday performances and how they are used in defining Zaire, Mobutu, and one's place as a citizen and relationship to the state.[5] From daily performances at schools and businesses to performances for visiting foreign dignitaries, animation politique became enmeshed in everyday life (see figure 4.1). I also expose the coercion, both implicit and explicit, lying beneath performances of animation politique during Mobutu's era, paying closer attention to the role of force

FIGURE 4.1. Political animation performance with Jacques Chirac (*center, in white jacket*) and Mobutu (*to his left*) watching at International Assembly of French Mayors, ©Jacques Langevin/Sigma/Corbis (Kinshasa, 1985).

and punishment in certain instances of "performing the nation." My focus on the varied experiences of men and women who experienced animation while living in rural Luozi territory allows me to posit coerced performance as an often overlooked but quite potent governmental technique. As a type of performative encounter which the state imposed on individuals, coerced performances not only sought to shape individual and group subjectivities but also disrupted the socioeconomic and moral order of local communities, belying state discourses promoting order, hard work, and proper conduct in everyday life. Focusing on Luozi territory in Bas-Congo (former Bas-Zaire) also enables me to examine how performed nationalism was realized in even the more rural and marginalized corners of the nation-state. Moreover, post-colonial Congo serves as a case study to interrogate the relationship between civil religion, nationalism, and citizens' bodies.

Nations, Nationalism, and Performance

Benedict Anderson defines a nation as an "imagined political community . . . both inherently limited and sovereign" (1991, 6). In his study of the emergence of nationalism in Europe, Anderson emphasizes print media and assumed homogeneity in creating nationalism. Such an approach is not as relevant in Zaire or even most of Africa, where illiteracy and many disparate ethnic groups (Zaire was estimated to have about 250, Meditz and Merrill

1994, 79) prove a challenge to ideas of a unified "nation." Moreover, in Anderson's discussion of the development of nationalism in postcolonial countries specifically, he pinpoints mechanisms that clearly privilege the perspective of colonizers (censuses, maps, and museums) that may be seldom used or even neglected by postcolonial governments in Africa. How then are sentiments of nationalism developed in African countries, especially in instances of weak or limited infrastructure? For further insight, I turn to Michel Foucault's oft-cited treatise on governmentality, where he writes that government focuses on men and things, including "men in their relation to . . . *customs, habits, ways of acting and thinking*, etc." (1991, 93, emphasis mine). In Foucault's analysis, the population is the primary target of government; the government will act either directly or indirectly through particular techniques to affect individual and group consciousness (1991, 100). Similarly, studies of colonial-era Congo have shown that clothing, hygiene, childbearing, and even schools were government techniques of controlling populations (Hunt 1999). Embodied performances are another way that many postcolonial African governments, such as Guinea, Malawi, and Zaire (Gilman 2009; Straker 2009; White 2008), have tried to transform consciousness through transforming bodies and bodily activities.

A number of studies have examined how, in a wide variety of postcolonial African nations, emerging national identities and ideologies were often expressed through the embodied performances of their citizens, whether by force, a sense of loyalty, or other means. Research on animation in former Zaire fits in with contemporary scholarship on what Straker calls "state scripted nationalism" (2007, 209). Anthropologists, historians, and other scholars have examined the role of musical performance in Tanzania (Askew 2002), ballets in Senegal (Castaldi 2006), dancing women at political rallies in Malawi (Gilman 2009), popular musicians in former Zaire (White 2008), theater troupes in Tanzania (Edmondson 2007), and "militant theater" in revolutionary Guinea (Straker 2009). While most of these works examine public performances in spaces often set apart from everyday life, my work adds to this literature by exploring the larger implications of animation in local, marginalized communities and examining how state-scripted nationalism in everyday life settings is just as important for creating nationalism and a sense of belonging.

For a relevant study of nationalism in everyday life settings, I turn to Achille Mbembe, who in analyzing state power in postcolonial Cameroon and Togo describes what he calls the "banality of power." By this he means the repeated actions and gestures, including the obscene and vulgar, that come to define everyday life in relation to the state (1992, 1). Mbembe explains further, "to account for postcolonial relations is thus to pay attention to the working of power in its minute details. . . . That is, one must examine the orderings of the world it produces; the types of institutions, knowledges, norms, and practices that issue from it; the manner in which these institutions, knowledges, norms and practices structure the *quotidien*" (1992, 4). Mbembe focuses on visual imagery and discourse, such as mischievous wordplay with the words of songs and political slogans and rude jokes, for example. He demonstrates that, in considering subject-state relations in postcolonial Africa, scholars must move away from a strict binary of resistance and domination, and instead investigate the complexity of everyday negotiations that lead to "a promiscuous relationship" such that subjects of a state can publicly enact their loyalty to their leaders and perform rituals that reinforce state authority, while simultaneously making fun of them in covert ways (1992, 5).[6] Similarly, theater scholar Mbala Nkanga's work on the power of "radio-trottoir" or sidewalk news offers an alternate space in everyday life for challenging the hegemony of the Mobutu-led state in Zaire (1992).

Mbembe's concept of the banality of power is highly applicable to postcolonial Zaire under President Mobutu. While during the colonial era, the Belgian colonial state operated through "impersonal, institutionalized, and unchallengeable force" (Young and Turner 1985, 397) as its basis, in postcolonial Zaire a system evolved merging bureaucracy with a highly personalized state. Under Mobutu, the state had a dual nature: "formally institutionalized, in party and administration, but informally patrimonial and personal. Mobutu from the outset used the analogy of chief and followers, joined in a quite personal bond of rulership" (Young and Turner 1985, 397). As a result, the nature of the relationship between citizen and state changed dramatically under Mobutu, and this chapter explores several types of performative encounters in everyday life that enabled this transformation to take place.

Throughout this chapter, I discuss Zaire as a coercive state. I use the term *coercion* in the sense of one person or group of people using physical force, threats, or sanctions to control the behavior of another person/group such that they act in a manner that they would not have without the coercion. Political philosopher Michael Bayles outlines two major types of coercion: "In one type physical force is directly applied to cause behavior in another person. . . . Such "occurrent" coercion takes place infrequently. . . . In a second variety, dispositional coercion, one man (the agent) threatens another (the victim) with a sanction if the latter fails to act as requested. This type of coercion occurs more frequently than the other" ([1972] 2009, 17). Here, one could see both types of coercion as uses of force: "one immediate, one latent. In both cases, the principal effect is to constrain possibilities for action, either immediately or in the future" (S. Anderson 2008, 21). In using this definition of coercion, I depart from more narrow definitions in political theory that define coercion based only on threats and largely focus on rational choice (Gorr 1986; Leiser 2008). Privileging the everyday lived experiences of people in postcolonial Zaire, where soldiers and police arrested, beat, raped, and even murdered citizens of Zaire with impunity, even in small towns and villages (Schatzberg 1988), allows us to take a different perspective. In the eyes of the average citizen of Zaire there was likely not much difference between threats of force and actual use of force; because actual use of force was so common, threats of force were not seen as a different category unto themselves.

Not only am I placing myself in conversation with Africanist scholars of performed nationalisms, but I am also interested in helping to chronicle a very important chapter in Congolese history. While animation was pervasive throughout Zaire under Mobutu, there are only a few past studies of political and cultural animation. The only full monograph and most extensive study is *Les spectacles d'animation politique en Republique du Zaire* by Gazungil Sang'Amin Kapalanga (1989), which provides an overview of the history, goals, and structure of animation politique, and an analysis of both its theatrical and nontheatrical aspects. Bob White's ethnography *Rumba Rules* (2008) considers the impact of animation politique on musicians in Kinshasa in one chapter, while he has further explored Mobutu's ideology of authenticity and its effect on animation politique in an article (2006). While these and other works have aided in recuperating the history of animation politique,[7] very few studies consider the firsthand experiences and sentiments of people who were ordinary citizens forced to perform. Furthermore, an analysis of animation politique also enables an examination of how civil religion and nationalism came together, operating in tandem, in postcolonial Congo.

Postcolonial Congo

After a major uprising (which Belgians called a riot) in January 1959 in the capital of Leopoldville (Covington-Ward 2012), the Belgian Congo was hastily transitioned toward independence with few preparations. The Congo state underwent major sociocultural and political transformations after gaining independence from Belgium in 1960. The first republic was named the Republic of Congo and was under the leadership of President Joseph Kasa-Vubu and Prime Minister Patrice Lumumba.[8] Between 1960 and 1965, a number of crises tore the nascent nation-state apart, including a mutiny of the armed forces, the assassination of Patrice Lumumba in 1961, the attempted succession of two mineral-rich regions (Katanga and Kasai), and the intervention of international peacekeepers. On November 24, 1965, General Joseph-Désiré Mobutu seized power of the country through a mainly bloodless coup d'état. He became the most influential political figure in Congo postindependence, and, over his thirty-two-year reign (1965–97), became a fervent dictator. Between 1965 and 1967 the multiparty system was prohibited, a new constitution was adopted, and a single national party was created, the Mouvement Populaire de la Révolution (the People's Revolutionary Movement, also known as MPR) (Kannyo 1979, 58–60; C. Young 1983, 329).

The MPR was the party of the state, and all Congolese citizens were members of the party automatically according to the national constitution (Kannyo 1979, 60). One's membership was not a matter of choice, which was clearly articulated by one of the slogans popular during the time: "O linga, O linga te, O zali kaka MPR." In Lingala,[9] this basically translates to: "If you want to, or if you don't want to, you are in MPR" (a slogan repeated by many people in interviews and conversations). Over the course of Mobutu's thirty-two-year regime, the ideology of the MPR was rebranded several times but remained essentially the same. Thus, according to political scientist Edward Kannyo:

> The ideological assertions of the Mobutu regime have been termed *nationalism, authentic Zairian nationalism, authenticity*, and *Mobutuism* at various periods. Whatever the terminological variations, the core of the ideology is essentially conservative anti-colonial nationalism. The aims of this orientation involve the "indigenization" of the political and economic structures of Zaire without altering them to provide for a more egalitarian and democratic socioeconomic system. . . . Authenticity has also been invoked to justify the authoritarian political system. . . . Another important dimension [is] . . . cultural nationalism and nativism. In this aspect, authenticity seeks to combat the sense of cultural inferiority that was inculcated by colonial domination. (Kannyo 1979, 61)

These interconnected ideas of authenticity were realized on the ground in many ways. The prime example was in 1971, when, going along with his ideological shift to promote authenticity and reject the influences of Belgian colonialism, Mobutu changed the name of the country, major river system, and currency to Zaire. The national hymn was rewritten, African styles of clothing were privileged, and citizens were prohibited from using their Christian names. Mobutu himself went from Joseph-Désiré Mobutu to Mobutu Sese Seko Nkuku Ngbendu Wa za banga.[10] All these changes demonstrate the importance of a return to an authentic precolonial past through an erasure of practices explicitly tied to colonialism and the reinvention of significant symbols. Moreover, the development of the arts was to aid the shedding of a colonial identity and the embracing of a new national identity privileging African artistic expression, and also demonstrating loyalty to the one-party state and its leader. The Mobutu-led regime enacted a number of policies and propaganda strategies attempting to make the worship of Mobutu and his ideas as a type of religion unto itself—a civil religion.

Civil Religion and Nationalism Embodied, or How Mobutu Became a God

During Mobutu's presidency, a key strategy his administration pursued was to create a type of personality cult around the president. Through strategic propaganda efforts, Mobutu became omnipresent in the lives of average citizens in many ways. These ideological attempts were especially pronounced after his diplomatic visits to China in January 1973, and to both China and North Korea in December 1974 (*Salongo*).[11] Both Mao Zedong and Kim Il-Sung were well known for arranging public performances of nationalism, and for having their citizens perform their worship of their leaders on a quotidian basis (Kim 2010; Leese 2011). Writing about North Korea, Suk-Young Kim observes that, "aiming at social control by forcing people to participate in state ritual is North Korea's most efficient governing strategy" (2010, 17). Thus, it is very likely that Mobutu was influenced by the approaches of these leaders, especially as significant changes in policy were enacted immediately after he returned from these trips (especially the December 1974 trip, which was followed by a shift to an ideology of "radicalization" [see January 1975 issues of *Salongo*]). As Bob White has observed, political dancing and singing in the Congo existed well before Mobutu's trips to Asia (2008, 75). However, the massive mobilization of propaganda that took place in the 1970s with the goal of elevating Mobutu and his ideas was vastly different than anything that had existed in the Congo in the past.

Zaire under Mobutu is just one example of the creation of what can be termed a civil religion. Writing about the particular case of myths, imagery, and even speeches in politics in the United States, sociologist Robert Bellah first defined civil religion as a "public religious dimension [that] is expressed in a set of beliefs, symbols, and rituals" (1967, 4). Since Bellah's groundbreaking article, there have been a number of scholarly approaches to civil religion, which can be grouped into five different definitions of the concept. The first is civil religion as folk religion, where shared ideas and values emerge out of the history of a society. The second is civil religion as transcendent universal religion, where there are shared symbols and ethical principles by which the nation is judged. The third is civil religion as religious nationalism, where the state is legitimized through religion. The fourth is civil religion as democratic faith, based on particular concepts such as equality, freedom, and justice. The fifth is civil religion as Protestant civic piety, which is based on Protestant values of individualism, work ethic, and missionizing (Jones and Richey 1990, 14–18). Most of these studies of civil religion have focused on the United States, examining how songs, speeches, myths of founding fathers, holidays, and concepts such as manifest destiny have played a role in shaping the collective identity of the country and legitimizing certain actions (Angrosino 2002; Bellah 1967; Coleman 1970; Jones and Richey 1990). Studies of civil religion in other nations, however, have revealed a diverse array of forms this phenomenon can take (Agadjanian 2001; Markoff and Regan 1981), supporting Cristi's assertion (2001) that historical circumstances and social contexts play a defining role in the expressions of civil religion in different societies.

To fully contextualize how I am using civil religion here, I take a Durkheimian approach to religion, understanding religion as a social project based on a set of shared representations and rites. "Religious representations are collective representations which express collective realities; the rites are a manner of acting which take rise in the midst of the assembled groups and which are destined to excite, maintain, or recreate certain mental states in these groups" (Durkheim [1915] 1964, 10). From media programming, to forced meetings and marches, to collective dancing, to public adulation of Mobutu (organized by his government), a strong argument can be made for the existence of a civil religion in Zaire. One argument against seeing the case of Zaire as a civil religion is that before colonialism, traditional chiefs and other leaders were often praised through song and dance. Thus, Mobutu was simply continuing precolonial practices. However, there are three major differences between precolonial practices and postcolonial Zaire. First, the level of scale is much different. In the precolonial era, leaders ruled over much smaller, more homogenous groups of people; even kingdoms were not at the same level of scale as a massive country with tens of millions of people. These millions of people come from different ethnic groups and clans, and thus much more must be done to get them to share collective representations and practices. Second, coercion and the threat of violence became key motivators in the aspect of Mobutu's civil religion devoted to political animation. On the contrary, ritual adoration of chiefs in the precolonial era was more often based on will and obligation rather than force, with some exceptions. Third, civil religion under Mobutu was based on a reimagining and recreating of a number of different cultural practices from all around the country, all changed in some way to accommodate the Mobutu narrative, while precolonial ritual was more limited and particular to the region or ethnic group where it was based. In addition, some scholars even see precolonial Congo as having evidence of civil religion in many ways, based on many leaders exhibiting interwoven dimensions of religious and political power (Booth 1976). What, then, can a case study of postcolonial Congo (renamed Zaire) add to the ongoing discussion about civil religion?

An analysis of civil religion in Zaire provides a better understanding of the relationship between civil religion, nationalism, and bodies/embodied action. One underexamined area of focus is the relationship between civil religion and nationalism. "The link between civil religion and nationalism," writes Marcela Cristi, "seems to me not a 'tangential issue' . . . but rather a question of utmost importance—one that seems not to have attracted the attention it deserves" (2001, 200). She rightly points out that both civil religion and nationalism operate in similar ways, promoting a sense of collective identity and greater meaning for people within a country (2001, 198). But how do we define the relationship between them? Are they mutually exclusive? Does one lead to the other? Or do they exist in continual dialogue with one another?

This and the next chapter allow us to use the case of postcolonial Zaire to bring another perspective to the study of civil religion. First, in Zaire civil religion and nationalism were interrelated and interacting. Mobutu was heralded both as a sacred and as a political figure: savior and president of the nation. The relationship that all citizens were supposed to have with him was one of the common threads bringing the nation together. However, this shift to creating a cult of personality happened several years after he took over the country, after he was already trying to create a sense of nationalism in the fragmented polity. This suggests that nationalism can in fact precede civil religion. Second, much of the literature on civil religion in the United States examines common myths, symbols, and values that have been developed over the course of two hundred years, since the American Revolutionary War. The case of Congo, however, is another matter. What symbols are shared when people in a country don't have much in common besides the experience of Belgian colonization? The particular form that civil religion takes in a society is informed by its history; this suggests that a lack of shared symbols shaped the form of civil religion that came to predominate in Zaire—that of religious nationalism. Markoff and Regan suggest that in a context of pluralism "when the gap that separates local and national is most acute," civil religion can serve to bring these separate identities together (1981, 343). Third, an examination of postcolonial Zaire reveals the importance of embodied action for both civil religion and nationalism in the country. Much of the research on civil religion in general has focused on texts and concepts, and much less so on the role of the body in everyday experiences of civil religion. The focus on political animation in this and the following chapter suggest that coerced performances were at the center of a state strategy to inculcate both nationalist sentiment and the embodiment of civil religion in Zaire.

The leadership in Mobutu's government actively promoted Mobutu, the MPR, and Mobutu's ideas in ways that encouraged worship and adoration, creating a civil religion with Mobutu at the top. Analysis of speeches and state owned newspapers during Mobutu's era demonstrates multiple ways in which this was achieved. For example, in a 1974 speech at the Institute Makanda Kabobi, the ideological institute of the MPR, Mobutu used the language of religion to describe the role of the MPR's leaders in spreading his ideas to the masses:

> When one speaks of Christianity, one understands by it the thought, the teachings, and the action of its founder Jesus of Nazareth. . . . An idea such as thus could not endure and be developed if it wasn't conceived within an organization and a solid structure. This structure, for Christianity, is the church, and for "Mobutuism" it is the Mouvement Populaire de la Révolution. . . . In the church, the leaders are the transmission relays of the thoughts of Christ to all the faithful. In the same way, the leaders of the Mouvement Populaire de la Révolution relay the thoughts of the President-Founder to the popular masses. . . . The role of political commissioners, in the context of "Mobutuism" can be compared to that of theologians. (Mobutu 1975, 527)

Here, Mobutu uses the language, institutions, and roles associated with organized Christianity to define and explain similar structures within the MPR. He also likens the relationship that Christians have with the church and its leaders to the relationship they should have with the MPR and Mobutu. This shows that Mobutu and his administration were very explicitly trying to get people to think about the MPR and the nation's president in a religious manner.

References to Mobutu in the state newspaper *Salongo* also reveal attempts to elevate Mobutu to the status of a God in many ways. While in previous issues of the paper in 1972 and early 1973, Mobutu is referred to as the "Head of State," "Founder-President," "Citoyen Mobutu," or "General de corps d'Armée" (March 6, 1972; April 26, 1972; October 14, 1972; November 23–26, 1972, among others), after his January 1973 visit to China, there is a shift in language such that he is referenced as "The Guide," throughout the 1970s (*Salongo* January 24, 1973; January 30, 1973; February 2, 1973; October 14, 1975, among others). He is also often called the "Father of the Nation" (*Salongo* November 5, 1973; November 12, 1973; December 1 and 2, 1973; November 9, 1976, among others). There are more explicit religious references as well. In multiple issues of *Salongo*, President Mobutu was called "the savior" of the people of Zaire (November 27, 1972; November 27, 1973; January 1, 1975; May 20, 1976, and others) and was even called a prophet or prophetic (November 23, 24, 25, 1973; December 6, 1973 and others). The editors of the newspaper freely used religious language and metaphors to describe the place of Mobutu and the MPR in the lives of the citizens of Zaire. For example, in a special issue, November 24 (the date of Mobutu's takeover of the government) was heralded as "the day of our miraculous resurrection" (*Salongo* November 24, 1974, page 3). In another article entitled, "MPR Applies the Message of the Gospel," Mobutu is quoted as saying in the context of a speech, "All that God demands, we do it in the MPR. We preach respect and love. . . . We put an end to the boy and monsieur relationship, we made pygmies full Zairian citizens and ended feudalism in Kivu, both situations that missionaries knew about and left as is" (*Salongo*, November 5, 1973). Here, the MPR is being presented as not only a surrogate for Christianity, but also as a better and more moral option, as the essay highlights the mistakes of Christian missionaries in ignoring societal injustices. This suggests that the author of the article is attempting to actively undermine the power and authority of institutionalized religions (especially the Catholic Church).

In 1975 Mobutu's interior minister, Léon Engulu Baanga Mpongo, captured the idea of the worship of Mobutu as a religion when he wrote, "In all religions, and at all times, there are prophets. Why not today? God has sent a great prophet, our prestigious Guide Mobutu—this prophet is our liberator, our Messiah. Our Church is the MPR. Its chief is Mobutu, we respect him like one respects a Pope. Our gospel is Mobutism. This is why the crucifixes must be replaced by the image of our Messiah" (quoted in Young and Turner 1985, 169). All these speeches, articles, and essays show that the national government of Zaire had the goal of deifying Mobutu.

However, the civil religion revolving around Mobutu was not just in text; it was also presented visually and made real physically through animation and other everyday performances of nationalism. One visual manner was through television. Before every news broadcast, there was a short video of Mobutu's face emerging from drifting clouds (Ne Tatu, October 10, 2005). Clad in his trademark leopard-print hat and dark-rimmed glasses, his stern face hovers in the heavens as drums beat in the background and a group sings his praises.[12] This propaganda symbolically demonstrates how Mobutu was visually presented as god-like,[13] above the rest of the population and nation. Similarly, in movie houses/theaters, before every film there was a ten-minute movie reel about Mobutu's activities the previous week (Callaghy 1984, 450). Loyalty and adherence to Mobutu were part and parcel of the MPR ideology, placing him at the head of this national party as not only its guide, but also its "prophet" (Adelman 1975, 103). Reflecting on their everyday experiences during Mobutu's regime, several interviewees in Luozi suggested that Mobutu was presented and viewed by some a type of god: "The era of Mobutu, it is then that we had songs that invoked Mobutu like a king, invoked Mobutu like a god. . . . It is especially during the era of Mobutu, they elevated Mobutu like a god. They were blind. . . . Many came to think that Mobutu wasn't going to die. He did whatever he wanted. . . . People no longer knew the living God, they only knew the god that was Mobutu" (Pastor Kasambi, November 12, 2005).

Here, the interviewee expresses sentiments shared across the nation about Mobutu as not just a man or a politician, but as a deity in many ways. Nationalism in Zaire then was not just about an abstract nation and sense of belonging; nationalism was also defined by the worship of Mobutu as the nation's president and leader. Glorifying Mobutu is a concrete way of displaying nationalism, and indeed Mobutu himself is a symbol of the nation. In this instance, nationalism and civil religion are interrelated and intertwined.

The civil religion that came to define Zaire was also reflected in everyday performances of animation. Mobutu saw animation as a way of using performance to promote national unity and the adulation of the nation's leader. According to Adelman (1975), the difficulty in Zaire was that while Mobutu wanted to encourage unity and respect for Congolese cultures through the concept of authenticity, most people's alliances were local (for example, clan affiliation) and ethnic. "An ingenious solution to this contradiction was found in animation, described by the state press as 'the national consecration of our vital force and our arrival at the national spirit'" (1975, 135). Animation would be the actual means of arriving at a national identity, one that did not exist before. Through moving bodies and shared daily performances, a new, shared national consciousness was created, uniting a fragmented nation under a common leader and a supposedly shared philosophy of authenticity. Mobutu's ideologies, policies, and coercive authority then had a significant effect on the meanings and uses of citizens' bodies under his regime. The new national identity was enacted and embodied through the scripted performances of animation politique, performed not only at political events but also in mundane settings such as businesses and schools, all with the purpose of spreading the ideas of the Mobutu-led government.

Politics of Performance: Dancing a New Nation

Mobutu himself, in an interview with French journalist Jean-Louis Remilleux, defined *animation* as: "At the same time a dance performance, a procession, a choreographed parade and a lesson in political education. Practically, we don't have an anniversary, congress, or popular assembly without animation, and each region, each village even, distinguishes itself competing in presenting its own animation" (Remilleux and Sese Seko 1989, 155–56). Animation drew on many different genres of performance, from dance, to poetry, to theater and song, all with the intent of spreading the message and ideology of the party and its leader to the masses. It was also present in many areas of everyday life, from nationalist songs intoned by everyone from earnest school children to private business owners early in the morning in front of the Zairian flag, to average people, regardless of status, who were compelled to clap and cheer lining the streets as Mobutu's motorcade passed by, to annual animation festivals and frequent rallies, to nationalist songs on the radio and television. While conducting research in the National Archives in Kinshasa in 2005, I accessed several cartons of government deposited material about political animation. Several documents detailed the songs and slogans used by groups from each region of Zaire during the national animation festival in 1973. Among them was the following song included in the "shock repertoire" of the region of "Bas-Zaire."

Tulanda Tata Mobutu (Kikongo)
Eh landa ah a landa ah a
Ta Mobutu ikuenda landa
Kina ye wonga ko eh e e
Eh landa ah a landa landa eh
Ulembi landa Mobutu, ngeyi nani?
Uzoba, dianene
Eh muana eh eee muana eh e[14]

Suivons le Guide Mobutu (French)
Suivez à jamais le Guide
C'est Tata Mobutu, le guide qui je suis [sic]
Je n'ai pas peur
Suivez, suivez le Guide
Si vous cessez de suivre le Guide Mobutu, qui êtes-vous?
Vous êtes un idiot, un grand imbécile
Une pauvre enfant qui pleure

We follow the Guide Mobutu
Follow the guide forever
It's Father Mobutu the guide who I follow
I am not scared
Follow, follow the guide
If you stop following the guide Mobutu, who are you?
You are an idiot, a big imbecile
A poor infant that cries
—National Archives, Kinshasa 1973

This song is the quintessential example of *animation* as civil religion, demonstrating dedication and loyalty to Mobutu. It berates those who do not follow Mobutu by insulting their intelligence, and overall stands as a performed praise of "Mobutu the Guide." The last line (Eh muana eh eee, or a poor enfant that cries), interestingly enough, is often used in a call-and-response pattern during the performance of traditional Kongo dances (makinu) that I witnessed in Luozi and Kinshasa. Such a practice was very common during Mobutu's rule; traditional songs, dances, and even gestures were often appropriated for the purpose of MPR and given new meaning, in line with the ideology of the party and its leader.[15]

While song texts and government documents were important for my study of animation, the most important sources for this chapter are open-ended interviews with ordinary people of the Kongo ethnic group who experienced animation in all its mundane forms. For the research on animation I used personal contacts and references from friends and colleagues in Kinshasa and Luozi and interviewed numerous people in their midthirties or older who would have personally experienced animation politique at its height in the 1970s and 1980s. My interviews with teachers, civil servants, and business owners about their experiences with animation highlighted its omnipresence in people's lives during Mobutu's regime. According to George Matadi, a MuKongo promoter of cultural arts in Kinshasa who is hailed as one of the founding fathers of animation politique, it became so popular that "even in the house the children sang it. Animation politique. It was in the streets, in the market. They became the songs of everyday. Everyday songs. Animation had, they say, intoxicated the streets. . . . At the end, we had become like robots of song. Your servant, for example, he can, while working, whistle a party song because they were beautiful songs . . . even if you didn't like Mobutu but [liked] the melody" (July 16, 2005).

This statement demonstrates the effectiveness of political performances such as patriotic and reverential songs for inculcating the ideologies of Mobutu's state into the minds and bodies of its citizens. In a number of instances during my interviews in both Kinshasa and Luozi, people would break into song (with others who were present joining in), sometimes spontaneously and other times because I asked about them—songs that heralded Mobutu, his policies, and ideologies, songs that performed the nation that was Mobutu's Zaire even after it has ceased to exist. These and other examples demonstrate the songs had become second nature, with words spilling from people's mouths almost involuntarily even as some of them had roundly criticized animation politique. Like elementary school songs in the United States that act as mnemonic tools for remembering the date of Columbus's transatlantic voyage, the songs of political animation in Zaire referenced and continue to reference the political authority and dictatorial power of Mobutu Sese Seko.

If political animation had such an impact and presence in people's lives, where did the idea for such a practice originate? Different opinions have been given for the origins of political animation. Kapalanga sees the practice as evolving from the establishment of the first political parties in the Congo, between 1958 and 1959, when these parties (whose membership was usually based on ethnic groupings) established youth groups to excite the general population and ridicule rival parties (1989, 122–24). He also suggests the secondary influence of other African countries, specifically Guinea and Ghana, which had similar practices of political dancing and singing (1989, 128). George Matadi believed the origin of the practice of political animation lay with a group of dynamic young singers of the Red Cross Church and movement in Kintambo, a neighborhood in Kinshasa, who sang for Mobutu repeatedly on official occasions (July 16, 2005). Regardless of their differing opinions on the antecedents of political animation, Kapalanga, Matadi, and anthropologist Bob White (2008, 74–75) agree that the first consistent presentations of political animation associated with Mobutu's regime were through the Corps de Volontaires de la République (CVR) (Voluntary Corps of the Republic). The groups within CVR that performed at rallies and other public functions were known as "Groupes Choc d'Animation" (shock animation groups) (George Matadi, July 16, 2005). The CVR disappeared with the birth of the MPR (which was created in 1967) which continued the traditions of the CVR. Political animation became much more organized, involved dance choreography and rehearsals, and expanded even further, particularly in 1970 (Kapalanga 1989, 134–36).

According to an MPR ideological glossary, within MPR there were two types of animators, or people who animate: political animators, who transmit the party's ideas through conferences, popular meetings, and other sessions, and cultural animators, who transmit the same messages through slogans and songs, and uphold the cultural values of the nation through dance and choreography, and the general movements of the ensemble (FORCAD 1986, 79). Animation ballets (*ballets d'animation*) were groups of people who danced and sang for MPR meetings and events. Both of these types of animation (political and cultural) seemed to have worked hand in hand in practice in Zaire, hence the common phrase bringing the two together as one. What political and cultural animation had in common as their foundation was that both were ways of transmitting the ideas of the MPR party and its founder, Mobutu. In fact, the ultimate goal of animation in general, as stated in a party document from the 1980s, was "to reach and to win all the masses, their soul, their conscience and their participatory actions thanks to a sophisticated process of songs, dances, gestures, speeches, and movement with the intention of their massive adhesion to the message of Mobutisme and of the Zairian revolution (National Archives, Kinshasa, n.d.).

Through various types of performance (music, dance, song, theater, speeches, and so on) party leaders wanted to impress on the citizens of the country its ideology and its leader, who in fact hadn't been voted in democratically. Thus, political and cultural animation played a very important role in legitimizing both the new leadership in postindependence Congo, and its associated ideologies and agendas. Politics were clearly implicated in the performances that people took part in, and were in fact the main cause for the performances taking place.

The Organization of Political and Cultural Animation
TYPES OF PERFORMERS

Kapalanga discusses four types of performers who danced and sang in animation troupes: animators by vocation, meaning artists, dancers, and others who already were professional performers; animators by obligation, or people who were forced by local leaders or officials to become members of a troupe; animators for profit, people who became active in animation only with the intention of gaining social mobility or wealth; and animators by conviction, or people who sincerely wanted to thank and honor Mobutu and his government through performance (1989, 141–43). Outside of performing troupes, ordinary citizens were also obligated to "perform" in many different ways that shall be addressed later on in the chapter. These categories that Kapalanga proposes were thus not mutually exclusive.

In the interview quotation cited previously, where Mobutu defined animation, he also intimated the types of occasions where one could see political and cultural animation. In her dissertation, Huckstep provided even more detail:

> Official professional and semi-professional (those who danced but had other professions) performers were called *animateurs* and *animatrices*. According to all the interviewees, *animateurs* and *animatrices* performed at every official public gathering large or small, and before every public social/entertainment event. Additionally, people could observe political animation on television; animation occurred at the beginning of the broadcast day and before news and newsreel-type broadcasts. Moreover, every day, almost everyone danced animating the political vision of the nation promoted by the Mobutu government each morning while the flag was being raised at schools and universities, institutions, government buildings, businesses, or in villages. (Huckstep 2005, 130)

There were also huge annual festivals of political animation, bringing together many different groups from all the different regions, subregions, and so on to perform in a huge stadium for Mobutu. The first such festival was held on November 24 and 25, 1973. Political animation also played a huge role at events in which citizens "performed the nation" not only for themselves and Mobutu, but for the benefit of others watching outside of Zaire. A case in point is the Muhammad Ali–George Foreman fight, the infamous "Rumble in the Jungle," where a number of political animation troupes were required to perform (George Matadi, July 16, 2005; Group members of Groupe Traditionelle Manianga, December 17, 2005). The wide variety of venues and media for political animation and its omnipresence in the quotidian lives of average citizens of Zaire illuminate its strategic importance to the authenticity project of Mobutu. Thus, during his regime, there was a particular administrative structure created and put in place specifically for the organization of political animation.

The administrative structure Mobutu's government established to oversee the spread of its propaganda was called MOPAP (Mobilisation Propaganda et Animation Politique) (Mobilization Propaganda and Political Animation). According to Huckstep, "its central office was in the capital, Kinshasa, and official offices were maintained within each provincial government. MOPAP also had an extensive network of 'unofficial' offices that allowed a presence in almost all aspects of Zairian life" (Huckstep 2005, 133). Kapalanga adds that offices were maintained on a national level and on each step of the scale descending down to towns (1989, 141).

In the following section of the chapter, by including information from interviews with people representing all categories of performers, from those who were already professional artists and dancers, to ordinary people who were forced to participate, women and men, from farmers to teachers, I hope to provide a more location-specific, detailed account by focusing on the impact of political and cultural animation on Kongo people, especially in Luozi territory. Animation had salience for every citizen of the nation, in multiple areas of their daily lives.

All Citizens, to the Streets!

Political animation was not limited to performance stages in huge stadiums and festivals, or animation groups brought into towns and cities to sing and dance for visiting authorities. It was a part of the everyday lives of Zairois and impacted almost all sectors of society, as the following exchange from an interview in Luozi demonstrates:

> Y.C.-W: How was political animation visible in daily life for the average citizen?
>
> K: Here in Luozi, for example, when you learn that there is a leader who is going to come, then, they mobilize everyone. Then, rather than going to work, everyone must stay in order to wait for the leader . . . all along the route, from the beach all the way to the market here, from the market to the air strip.
>
> Y.C.-W: And the people must do what?
>
> K: The people must remain there in order to sing a little and to watch a group of dancers, so, there are men and women who come into the sector, who come to meet the superior authority figure. . . . When the group [of the authority figure] arrives, group after group passes in front of them to show what they have prepared.
>
> (Tata Kimfumu, September 29, 2005)

This description creates a surreal visual image; people lining the route from the beach where the ferry lands all the way to the unofficial airport runway, a distance of several miles, leaving jobs and other obligations just to sing and welcome the arrival of one or another dignitary of Mobutu's government. Apparently, this happened all over the country, as other interviewees have talked about having to stand on the side of the road in Kinshasa and clap and sing as Mobutu's motorcade sped by. Moreover, in this particular Luozi example cited above, citizens were also expected to actively watch groups of political animation that were performing. This adds a twist to the phrase "captive audience," as citizens of Luozi were expected not only to perform their own nationalism through singing and lining the road, but also to watch others perform their nationalism in groups of political animation dancing for the pleasure of the visiting authority figure(s). The remainder of this section explores how political animation was experienced and lived in three types of local spaces: schools, businesses, and churches.

Schools

The political authority of the Mobutu state was imposed in other ways on the everyday lives of citizens not in performing political animation troupes. One such area was the primary and secondary schools of the nation, including Luozi territory. Although secondary level students were expected to play a more active role in MPR activities than primary school students, all students had to participate in morning animation sessions, and all students were automatically members of JMPR (Jeunesse de Mouvement Populaire de la Révolution, or Youth of the People's Revolutionary Movement).[16] It was the youth wing of MPR,[17] "designed to integrate and control all youth political groups and act as the vigilance committee for the party" (Callaghy 1984, 172). Tata Nkuku, a retired primary school teacher who'd worked in both Mbanza-Mona and Mbanza-Mwembe sectors in Luozi territory, summarized the way animation worked in people's everyday lives at schools: "It was an obligation. Before beginning work, it is necessary to go to salute the flag. When you go to salute the flag one must sing, one must dance . . . before going to work or else before entering the classroom. It was first of all, the first task" (September 29, 2005). Tata Kimfumu, the director of a primary school, provided more detail about political animation in the schools:

> In the Mobutu era, the objectives [of political animation] were to honor, to recognize, the chief. . . . At the school specifically, it was saluting the flag, each morning, we must first sing the national hymn, after which we follow political animation, singing political songs . . . and dances also. . . . We began from seven o'clock. . . . To seven thirty, it is animation. At eight o'clock we begin the courses. . . . The arrival of a territorial head, the arrival of an inspector, the arrival of a head of state, the arrival of a governor, thus, all the authorities, when they arrive at the school, we must greet them with animation, for some minutes. (September 29, 2005)

Teachers and school administrators were expected both to take part in political animation, and to lead it. Schatzberg discusses the role of primary school teachers in political animation when he writes, "at the primary level, the students themselves are involved in the organization of the JMPR only in the most cursory and passive way. . . . Each class is a JMPR cell, and the teacher is the cell chief. . . . At the primary level then . . . party activities are generally confined to learning chants and slogans by rote" (1978, 421).

Here, one sees how the party ideology was actively taught to young children, who had to memorize, repeat, and perform the songs and slogans. The important role of teachers as leaders of animation was also confirmed in interviews: "Each teacher must train their children then, each teacher must also show how they [the children] must dance" (Tata Kimfumu, September 29, 2005). Tata Kimfumu also added that the teachers themselves composed the songs the children sang.

Like other interviewees who expressed their opinions about political animation in other parts of this chapter, teachers I interviewed had two major issues with animation in the schools: first, it was coerced, and second, the students could be exposed to potentially immoral situations. When asked whether he felt pressure to participate in political animation, Tata Kimfumu frankly explained, "Well, as it was an order, one couldn't refuse." Moreover, when asked his opinion about political animation in the schools, he had this to say: "It was not good because we must not habituate the children to dancing. It was not good. . . . They could misbehave. It is that which one invited" (interview, September 29, 2005).

Animation in schools transformed the relationship between students and the postcolonial state. Throughout the vast majority of the colonial history of Congo, both under King Leopold (1885–1908) and Belgium (1908–60), Christian missionaries, especially Catholics, ran the colony's education system and institutions. "Except for military institutions run by the Forces Publique," writes political scientist Patrick Boyle, "secular education was practically inaccessible to the Congolese before 1954" (1995, 459). Even postindependence, the majority of the nation's schools were religious in nature. Mobutu saw the need to change this system to match the goals of his revolution. Speaking to the National Legislative Council on November 30, 1973, he stressed the importance of moving away from a colonial system: "We must also conquer certain prejudices inculcated in us by colonization. The educational system, that which was created by our colonizers, does not hold the monopoly on training or on education. . . . We must train ourselves and educate ourselves in the context of our authentically Zairian society" (1975, 403). Mobutu wanted to reform the educational system in a way that was anticolonial and amenable to his ideology of authenticity and African pride. Many changes occurred during his regime that highlight increasing conflict between the state and the church (especially the Catholic Church) in regards to education and the growing influence of the state in the daily lives of students at all educational levels. In 1971, Catholic and Protestant universities in Kinshasa and Kisangani were nationalized (Callaghy 1984, 304). Sections of the JMPR were to be placed in all Catholic seminaries starting in 1972, or they would be closed (*Salongo*, March 8, 1972); all schools were to be operated by the state starting in 1974 (Boyle 1995, 467), and in 1975, Mobutu's government decreed that religious education in the nation's schools was to be replaced by civic education; moreover, local sections of the JMPR were to be placed in all the nation's schools (Gondola 2002, 143; Schatzberg 1978, 420). All the schools, from primary to university level, were nationalized.

Animation came to be performed at the start of each school day, and school children became intimately involved in performing the nation. Each session of animation was a performative encounter redefining students' relationship to the state. While Mobutu was not physically present in each classroom, the flag, images of the president, and other people representing the government to whom performances were directed made the president seem omnipresent in many ways. These all serve as the audience to whom the performances were aimed. The slogans and songs were intended to inculcate the ideology of Mobutu in the minds of the students and the dancing served to physically remind them of their role in performing the nation. Animation in schools served as a daily performative encounter transforming social relationships by elevating Mobutu further in relation to the average citizen of Zaire, and by creating a seemingly more intimate bond between each citizen and their president for whom they sang praises each day. Herein also lies the importance of civil religion, as singing the praises of the president was how the student population understood and embodied nationalism.

Although the intended purpose of animation in schools is clear, how effective were such tactics of inculcating students with party ideology? In his assessment of animation and the JMPR in primary and secondary schools in Lisala, Zaire in 1974–75, Michael Schatzberg notes that "the J.M.P.R. has been largely unsuccessful both in implanting Mobutisme and in mobilising the student population of Lisala. . . . On a superficial level, one can see that the students have learned the party chants, songs, and slogans, but their enthusiasm . . . is strictly limited. . . . Were there not elements of coercion involved, participation in such manifestations would be minimal" (1978, 429–30). Schatzberg's observations suggest that animation was only superficially successful in shaping the minds, sentiments, and consciousness of the students. Nevertheless, the purposeful intent of the government in using everyday performance to shape young, impressionable minds shows that they believed it was an effective tool for garnering support for their policies, ideologies, and practices.

Businesses

Like the schools, political animation affected all businesses in Luozi territory, even those privately owned. Ne Mosi remembers the routine he took part in as a worker on a cattle farm: "Each morning before beginning work they made the workers dance. . . . Each morning . . . for thirty minutes, one must dance, to glorify the Guide." He also noted that the owners of the businesses had to take the lead in these performances. "You the head, you must make your workers sing also, they must dance. . . . You are first of all the animator. . . . It is you that calls out the animation shouts." In the case of an official of the state or party visiting the business "it was necessary to mobilize the workers. When they gave the schedule that they were coming to your business, if you didn't do it, you have problems" (October 10, 2005).

On a larger scale, enterprises played major roles in political animation, especially after Zairianization began in 1973, during which the businesses of foreigners were confiscated and given to citizens of Zaire. While on the surface the removal of foreigners from the economic sector was a bid for economic independence, those who received the confiscated enterprises (called *acquéreurs* by the general population) most often were friends and allies of Mobutu (Dr. Mbala Nkanga, July 19, 2007). For example, the interior minister, Léon Engulu Baanga Mpongo, reportedly received thirty-five plantations while a regional commissioner in Shaba grossed $100,000 per month from his businesses (Young and Turner 1985, 338). The CEOs of the major companies thus had great self-interest in seeing that they kept their newly acquired businesses, which the state reserved the right to take back if they were not run properly. As a result, many of these companies that were nationalized sponsored animation ballet groups to sing the praises of Mobutu, using the groups' performances as "an expression of loyalty" and gratitude to Mobutu, who had appointed them to their positions. Major companies sponsoring animation groups included SNEL (Société Nationale d'Electricité, or National Electrical Company), OZACAF (Office Zairoise du Café or Zairian Coffee Bureau), and Regideso (Régie de Distribution d'Eau, or State Water Distribution Company), among others, who not only had their groups perform at major festivals but also paid the national television station to air performances of their groups (informal, Dr. Mbala Nkanga, July 19, 2007). All in all, political animation was not only an obligation, but also how the heads of major nationalized companies ensured they would be able to keep their jobs and standard of living, and remain in good favor with Mobutu. According to Bob White, by the mid- to late eighties and in the midst of a growing financial crisis, the state was gradually shifting the responsibility and financial burden for propaganda supporting the state (including animation) to the private sector (2008, 77).

Animation in businesses (both private and nationalized) also served as a daily performative encounter with President Mobutu Sese Seko. Through daily animation performances and the sponsoring of animation troupes, business owners reaffirmed their allegiance to Mobutu while simultaneously venerating him and his ideas. The relationship between the business sector and the state was also greatly transformed as the state, like in schools, came to have a more intimate role in the daily lives of workers in many types of industries through *animation*.

Oh, That Mobutu May Be with You! Churches and Mobutu's Religious Authority

During Mobutu's regime, especially after his turn to an ideology of authenticity, a tension developed concerning the role of religion and churches in Zaire, and the expansion of the power and ideology of the one party state. As mentioned previously, in many ways the MPR had become a sort of civil religion seeking to replace other religions in people's lives, taking on many of the roles that churches served. As American diplomat Kenneth Adelman writes: "In addition to presenting authenticity as a secular theology, the party attempts to fulfill functions and meet needs ordinarily accomplished by religion. It prescribes social conduct; . . . instills identity by stressing that every Zairean is a party militant; . . . uses symbols; . . . celebrates its own holidays; . . . provides its own rituals in the form of party chants, dances, and songs; emphasizes its historical heritage; . . . and places itself as the guiding light or unifying force in the life of its members. . . . The party thus serves as a religious surrogate, an attempt to satisfy the personal need for meaning, identity, and values which are normally filled by a religion" (1975, 103).

Moreover, Christian language was appropriated in everyday settings as, according to Adelman, party halls were called "temples," Catholic hymns were converted into party chants, and even common religious phrases were transformed, so that "May God be with you" became "Oh, that Mobutu may be with you!" (1975, 103; 1976, 54). All the measures discussed earlier in the chapter demonstrate that MPR sought to impose itself not only as a political authority, but also as a religious authority. This usurpation of the power and ideology of the church by the Mobutu-led state resulted in a number of conflicts in the struggle for religious authority.

In a law released in December 1971, the Zairian state formally recognized and sanctioned only three religious groups: the Catholic Church, the Kimbanguist Church and the Eglise du Christ au Zaire (a group of Protestant churches) (Callaghy 1984, 310). All other churches were considered illegal and had to apply or affiliate with one of the sanctioned denominations to remain open. Because the Catholic Church was the largest religious organization in the country, it also became a threat to Mobutu and his government. According to Adelman, the following statement by Mobutu encapsulated the conflict between church and state during this time: "In Zaire, it is the MPR and not the Church that will lead the way" (Adelman 1975, 113). With this statement, Mobutu places himself and MPR as the highest authorities in the nation. A number of conflicts occurred between churches and their leaders (especially the Catholic Church), and Mobutu and his government, which point to Mobutu's regime's goals of suppressing the power of churches, quelling opposition, and attempting to supplant religious ideologies and institutions with the MPR. After Cardinal Joseph Albert Malula made several public critiques of Mobutu, he was forced into exile in January of 1972, and his home was turned into a JMPR headquarters building (Callaghy 1984, 304–5). Other issues of conflict both before and after the expulsion included the installation of the JMPR in religious seminaries, the mandatory dropping of Christian and other non-African names to be replaced by authentic African names, and the government ban of religious youth groups, religious television and radio broadcasts, and religious pamphlets and publications (Adelman 1975). Moreover, in 1973 people were prohibited from attending any regional and national religious meetings and were allowed to meet only locally. Large regional and national meetings were reserved for MPR events (Adelman 1975, 110). In late 1974 the government announced that all crucifixes and images of the pope were to be removed from religious institutions and replaced by images of Mobutu (Callaghy 1984, 305). However, one of the ways that religious leaders felt their submission to the political and religious authority of Mobutu most intimately was through forced dancing and singing.

As chapters 2 and 3 demonstrate, in Catholic and Protestant churches in the Lower Congo, secular dances have often been associated with licentiousness and immorality. Thus, one role these churches play is that of policing conduct in regards to dancing, and prohibiting the participation of church members in any dances deemed immoral. Many churches, such as the DMNA church, prohibit any form of dance outside of the church, while others frown on dancing in any context. Under Mobutu's regime however, neither ordinary congregation members nor church leadership were excluded from performing their adoration of the president. "According to the President, Zairean priests are required by the Constitution to be militants in the MPR. Even the Bishops are supposed to participate in party chants and dances praising the party and President" (Adelman 1975, 104). Imagine the lasting impression of seeing a man or woman of God dancing basically in praise and worship of Mobutu. This policy, in seeking to reinforce the ideologies and authority of Mobutu through the body, had an impact on not only the people dancing, but also everyone else who witnessed priests and other religious leaders dancing. In these instances, the dancing and singing physically enact the idea that Mobutu and his government are higher in spiritual authority than local church rules, national clerical leaders, or even the pope himself.

Although there was a lot of pressure and threats of arrest, fines, and even death if one didn't comply with the demands of the government, for some religious communities it was exactly on the question of dance that they sought to take a stand against Mobutu's regime. The example that I consider is the refusal of members of the DMNA church in Luozi to participate in dancing for Mobutu. Pastor Kasambi explains the history of this protest in the following exchange about political animation:

> K: The authorities, when they present themselves in your village, you must search for a beautiful girl that you must give them. That is the MPR, and then people had become very, very, very profane. Religion went away more and more. Even the people who didn't have a strong faith, [but also] the religious; there were certain pastors and priests who danced in the era of Mobutu.
>
> Y.C.-W: But, do they have a choice? They didn't have a choice.
>
> K: They didn't, well, because if you didn't dance, they are going to kill you. But, among the bangunza in our denomination, there were a large number of arrests, the time from 1970 to 1975. Because they rejected this. Thus, they were against the movement.
>
> Y.C.-W: Against the movement of—
>
> K: Against the movement of MPR. . . . They didn't want to dance. And so, they forcefully arrested us. Here, in 1970 . . . they arrested people who didn't want to dance.
>
> Y.C.-W: Here in Luozi?
>
> K: Here in Luozi. And they were freed in 1975. . . . They took pastors and deacons . . . arrested us over two months, three months, four months, put in the prison. . . . You weren't in the dungeon but you couldn't pray. . . . There were arrests where you were tied up like a sausage. . . . They couldn't function spiritually. It was hard. (November 12, 2005)

With this recollection, Pastor Kasambi singles out the DMNA church as having the courage to stand up to the moral turpitude that was represented by dancing for MPR and Mobutu. He distinguishes his church members as having a stronger sense of faith than other religious leaders who complied with the demands to dance and sing and discusses the persecution of these church members who refused to dance over a number of years. This harkens back to bangunza during the colonial period that persisted in practicing their form of praise and worship including ecstatic trance and trembling although they were arrested and exiled to labor camps for several decades. Callaghy (1984) notes the persecution that the DMNA church in Luozi suffered in the 1970s at the hands of local government officials: "The zone commissioner arrested members of the sect living in the town of Luozi . . . and put them in jail without following proper legal procedures. . . . The zone commissioner then ordered all his collectivity chiefs to arrest members of the church in their jurisdictions. . . . The chief of Kimbanza collectivity imprisoned some church members indefinitely. . . . The chief of Mbanza-Mona Collectivity assembled church members and publicly humiliated one by making him dance nude before the gathering" (312–13).

Dance is used in this instance to publicly shame and humiliate DMNA church members. In both the colonial case (persecution by the Belgians) and the postcolonial case (persecution by Mobutu's government), the bangunza maintained a sense of a higher spiritual authority guiding their principles and conduct, one that challenged European missionaries who condemned their embodied forms of worship, and upheld their belief in secular dancing as contrary to the wishes of a higher God. In the telling of the story of one particular member of the church in Luozi who was arrested, Pastor Kasambi reiterates the courage bangunza showed by sticking to their religious beliefs in the face of arrests and punishment: "If you refused, they arrested you, took you to Mbanza-Ngungu. And if you were taken to Mbanza-Ngungu, where you met hardened people, they kill you. It wasn't anything. It was like that. But fortunately we didn't have any people that they killed. But it was hard. . . . I know an ngunza that they arrested here, on the road to Mbanza-Ngungu. His son who had some means, went to release him. . . . They said to him [the arrested ngunza], you can't pray! He [said], I will pray to my God. Come and dance! I won't dance" (Pastor Kasambi, November 12, 2005).

In this story of bravery, the arrested ngunza explicitly refuses to accept the imposition of the religious and political authority of the state on his body. By seeking to pray even when prohibited to do so, and refusing to dance even when required to do so, he challenges the impingement of Mobutu's religious and political authority on the religious authority of the DMNA church, whose tenets, principles, and practices are believed to have been received from God. His and the protests of other bangunza forcefully pushed back against the ability of Mobutu and his government to control their conduct, thus undermining the total political and burgeoning religious authority that Mobutu sought to have over the citizens of Zaire. With his statements and actions, he is also rejecting the idea of Mobutuism as a civil religion for the nation.

Animation in churches and for church leaders in particular was at the crux of a power struggle between the state and numerous religious groups. The state-scripted dancing and singing had multiple purposes in the context of churches: to venerate Mobutu rather than God or the pope, to spread the message of the regime, but also to show the churches that the government had more power and also to diminish the power and social standing of church leaders, especially in the eyes of their congregations. Politics and religion clearly intertwined in the state's engagements and conflicts with churches throughout the country.

Conclusion

In short, political and cultural animation was not limited to animation ballet troupes but was evident in most areas of daily life for citizens of Luozi territory and the nation during Mobutu's reign. The presence of coerced dancing and singing in schools, businesses, churches, and on streets when national leaders and representatives visited local areas demonstrates a form of political and even growing religious authority that Mobutu exercised over the population. Exercising such authority, he also used political and cultural animation to legitimate his rule over and over again on a daily basis. Whether or not people recognized him as the nation's leader, when they were compelled to perform for him and his government, the very actions of singing and dancing demonstrated his authority over them—his ability to influence and control their actions. These embodied cultural performances were crucial to spreading Mobutu's ideology across the nation and consolidating his power and influence in everyday life. Animation politique thus serves as a critical site to examine the intersection of civil religion, nationalism, and bodies.

CHAPTER 5

Dancing Disorder in Mobutu's Zaire

Animation Politique and Gendered Nationalisms

Three Women

Ma Ntima sits with her hands gently clasped in her lap, wearing a simple tailored top and matching pagne, with a piece of fabric tied to cover her head. Her teenage son sits next to her on the sofa, on her left side. She understands my questions in French but is more comfortable responding and clarifying in Kikongo, and so her son acts as the translator. We sit on opposite sides of a coffee table, sipping red Vitalo soft drinks.[1] Our interview takes place in Luozi, in the home of the professor with whom I am staying. Ma Ntima was born in Luozi territory in 1959 and continues to reside there. She is married, the mother of six children, and the wife of a pastor of an African Independent church. She has a reserved demeanor, with a calm, serene air about her. In the middle of our interview, it begins to rain heavily, and the sound of raindrops pelting the window provides the ambient backdrop as she recounts her own experiences. After our interview, she continues on to a meeting with other local women of the Protestant churches in Luozi, lifting her pagne slightly as she navigates the puddles created by the rain.

Ma Bangoma greets me with the hearty handshake and genuflection (*dekama*) used by many of the women in town, and when I respond in kind, she laughs with delight. Our interview also takes place in Luozi, and we chat briefly and snack on peanuts and soda before Tata Nkolele, a middle-aged man who helped to arrange our meeting, arrives to take part in the conversation with us. A married mother of eight children, she was born in 1953 in Luozi territory and currently resides in the town of Luozi. She works as a functionary of the state. She often responds to my questions with laughter and eagerly demonstrates several songs and dances over the course of the interview, showcasing her expertise as a performer.

Ma Mayazola spent a significant part of her youth back in Luozi territory, where her family is from, but now lives in the Mont-Ngafula neighborhood in Kinshasa. After several rides in crowded taxi buses and a long twisting walk through sand-covered paths, my friend Laurent and I arrive at her small, one-level home. It is situated near some of the urban gardens giving the neighborhood a sense of being a village inside a big city. Born in 1953, she is married, the mother of eight children, and farms for a living. She is also a member of Bundu dia Kongo, a religious-sociopolitical organization (non-Christian) with the goal of rebuilding the precolonial Kongo Kingdom (see chapter 6). She interrupts our interview several times to sharply call out orders to her children as she chops greens over a large pot simmering on an outdoor fire, preparing the evening meal for her family.

While they all have different personalities and life trajectories, these three women have much in common; they are from the same ethnic group (Kongo/BaManianga), all have ties to Luozi territory, all are married, and all have children. However, another tie that binds them is a common experience—in their youth, primarily during the 1970s, they were all dancers in local performance troupes of animation politique during Mobutu Sese Seko's rule. I examine the gendered dynamics of the interrelationship of power and performance in Zaire through their stories. Using their experiences I specifically ask, what can we learn about the ways that citizenship is gendered by looking at coerced embodied performances? How is the civil religion of Zaire—the worship of Mobutu and his ideas—made real by and through women's physical bodies?

In this chapter, I seek to recover the voices of women and their experiences as performers in many different settings as subjects of an oppressive nation-state. The sexual exploitation of female dancers emerges as a prominent theme in my interviews. By focusing on the experiences of young Kongo women recruited into local animation troupes in rural Luozi territory, I examine the ways their participation as citizens in Zaire was a form of gendered embodied citizenship that differed from the experiences and expectations of male dancers, and more specifically, was subject to the intimate violence of the state.[2] I build on Achille Mbembe's work on the banality of power by examining the experiences of women in their engagement with a coercive state—one demanding specific performances from them, both on and off the stage. I argue that the penetrative forms of gendered embodied citizenship that young women experienced in Zaire clearly differed from the experiences of their male counterparts and fostered negative sentiments among local communities, thus undermining the nationalist project. Thus, my investigation of women's experiences of animation politique in Luozi will illuminate the gendered dimensions of performed nationalisms in everyday life.

Gendered Nationalisms and Coercive States

While Achille Mbembe's work on the banality of power has transformed approaches to subject-state relations in Africa, one critique of his analysis of power in postcolonial Africa has been the lack of attention to gender (Butler 1992, 70), specifically the role of women under an oppressive state. Studies of state power and nationalism more generally, like Eley and Suny's edited volume, have also called for more attention to the "gendered dimensions and meanings of nationalist discourse" (1996, 27). This can be done by examining the place of women in nationalist movements (such as McClintock's [1991] study of the role of white women in Afrikaner nationalism) and by looking at how women are socially constructed as citizens in different nation-states (Nira Yuval-Davis 1997, 1999; Olesky, Hearn, and Golanska 2011; Seungsook Moon 2005; Veena Das 2008).[3] Citizenship can be most simply defined as "a form of membership in a political and geographic community [that] can be disaggregated into four dimensions: legal status, rights, political and other forms of participation in society, and a sense of belonging" (Bloemraad, Korteweg, and Yurdakul 2008, 154). The idea of citizenship has always been gendered, ever since its origins in ancient Greece, where citizenship was based on the exclusion of women (McEwan 2000, 630). Thus, to understand the full complexities of how citizenship is realized in daily life, studies of gendered citizenship explore how men and women live and experience citizenship differently.

There is a need for further analysis in existing discussions of gendered citizenship of the varied ways the bodies of male and female citizens are used to further nationalist aims. The concept of embodied citizenship deals with the interaction between bodies and citizenship, the private and the public, examining subjectivities both political and material, and thoroughly social in nature (Bacchi and Beasley 2000, 350; 2002, 325). In this chapter, I put forward a conception of "gendered embodied citizenship" to capture the everyday imposition of coercive states on women's bodies in ways that differ from the expected activities of male citizens. This concept also tries to describe how within a discourse of inclusive citizenship, women's individual choices and obligations to self, family, and local communities are superseded by the needs and wants of the coercive state. This differs from other studies of gendered citizenship that tend to focus on ideologies of women as reproducing mothers within families (Moon 2005) rather than examining at the micro level how women actually perform with their bodies in everyday life in the service of the state. Gilman's study of the role of performing women at political rallies in Malawi is one of the few to examine gender, politics, nationalism, and embodied performance (2009). Through my analysis of animation politique and other required performances as manifestations of gendered embodied citizenship, I hope to do the same for Kongo women in Zaire. Moreover, although both men and women were performers in Zaire, the voices of women remain marginalized in the few existing studies of animation that exist presently (Huckstep 2005; Kapalanga 1989; Thassinda 1992; White 2008). To fully understand how citizenship was both gendered and embodied in Zaire, I center women's experiences in this chapter.

O Linga, O Linga Te: How They Came to Perform

Returning to the stories and experiences of the three women introduced at the start of the chapter, one aspect of animation politique illuminated by interviews with women ex-performers in Luozi is the different opinions that exist between people who were part of the animation machine, and others who felt as though the performances had been forced on them. In my interview with George Matadi in Kinshasa, who as I previously stated played a founding role in animation politique, I inquired about the nature of participation in animation groups. The exchange follows:

Y.C.-W.: Were people paid for animation?
G.M.: NOOO! (insistently)
Y.C.-W.: But, was it by force?
G.M.: No, it wasn't by force. Not forced. . . . We say because of spontaneity, enthusiasm.
Y.C.-W.: It was a voluntary choice?
G.M.: Voluntary! Voluntary! Free! . . . It was free. They came in droves. They sang! They sang! They sang! Everyone was having a good time. From young mothers, to young girls, to young men. No, everyone was having a good time. When Mobutu had power, everyone was having a good time. (July 16, 2005)

While Matadi's response paints a picture of happiness and choice, the portrait that emerges in recollections of women performers in animation troupes in Luozi territory presents a direct contradiction. When each woman was asked about the objectives of political animation, their responses were very similar. Ma Mayazola said people danced for the glory of Mobutu, and Ma Ntima reiterated the same notion with her response of "during the time of Mobutu, it was obligatory to dance for Mobutu whether you wanted to or not" (Ma Ntima, October 10, 2005, and Ma Mayazola, October 5, 2005). Ma Bangoma responded with, "You were obligated . . . to go and sing political songs. . . . It was animation" (Ma Bangoma, October 14, 2005).

In discussing how they came to perform in these troupes, all three women mentioned the importance of coercion, although some described this in greater detail than others. When asked how she came to be a dancer in a group of political animators, Ma Mayazola explained she was chosen from her village in the sector of Kivunda by virtue of her age and marital status: "They took the young men and women from the village to go; it was obligatory, to go and sing and dance for the head of the sector. . . . They took the youth that were single and who were not students in school, women who had one or two kids but were not married, and young men who were not married, people who were unemployed. If you refused to go, they would send soldiers to get you and take you by force, and they would take you to the sector town, and you would pay a fine" (Ma Mayazola, October 5, 2005).

Ma Mayazola explained this group of selected youth formed the JMPR for the village. The state's focus was largely on youth who could be thought of as unproductive and idle—unemployed, unmarried, and not enrolled in school. Ma Mayazola was about eighteen years old when she began to dance with the troupe. What is clear here is the importance of coercion in recruitment, such that one's refusal to participate would lead to intervention and force by soldiers.

For Ma Ntima, who was chosen to dance while living in her village in the sector of Mbanza-Mona, the story is similar: "They would choose single people, those whose marriages were not recognized by the state, girls who left school. I left the school because my mother was sick, and for this, I was chosen. . . . The chief of the village helped to choose people because he knew whether they were married, studying, or not" (Ma Ntima, October 10, 2005). Ma Ntima's account reiterates the state's focus on pursuing "idle" youth for the dance troupe. Her response also demonstrates the complicity of village chiefs in selecting youth for recruitment.[4] Similar to Ma Mayazola, Ma Ntima was eighteen years old when she was recruited to dance.

Although Mama Bangoma did not go into detail about how she specifically was initially chosen to join the animation troupe, coercion still emerges as a general theme. "Because I sung very well, and I danced very well, I was chosen as an *animatrice*. . . . Whether male or female, it was obligatory [to dance]. *O linga, o linga te*" (Ma Bangoma, October 14, 2005). Rather than being a completely voluntary activity, as Matadi suggested, a person's age and educational and marital status determined whether he or she would be conscripted to dance in local animation troupes in Luozi territory. The expectation that both male and female "idle" youth place their bodies at the service of the state for performances as a matter of public policy and service reveals the ways that their citizenship was in fact embodied. These women were chosen by others and did not join the troupes of their own volition. The fact that they felt coerced to dance against their will and saw it as an "obligation" reveals the ways Mobutu's political authority was enacted in the lives of these women, and moreover, was in fact legitimized by their coerced performances. Moreover, gender also seems to impact the likelihood of being recruited into an animation troupe, especially in rural settings. During the 1970s and even today, girls are disproportionately more likely than boys to not be enrolled in either primary or secondary school or to be disenrolled in the case of financial exigencies, for example.[5] They are also less likely to find employment in the formal sector. Thus, girls and young women were structurally disadvantaged and very likely to be targeted as an "idle" subset of the population.

Conditions of Dancers and Rehearsals

One theme emerging from the interviews was that the conditions in which the dancers were obligated to perform for visiting officials and public functions were not ideal and often downright exploitative. For example, I asked a question about compensation for dancing and singing, since these women had been pulled away from their other duties to perform for the state. All three of the women said they were not paid. Yet, differences in their points of view began to emerge when they gave details on other types of conditions such as the transportation to performance sites. Ma Mayazola relayed the following story about transportation from her home village when her group had been told they had to perform: "You leave the village in the morning around 7:00 AM to arrive around 5:00 in the evening, on foot. You yourself had to prepare and bring your own food. . . . To sleep, the people slept on the floor in the compound of the head of the sector. . . . Because the head of the sector was from my home village . . . my group could have the advantage of sleeping inside his home on the floor or in front of his home" (Ma Mayazola, October 5, 2005).

Mama Ntima depicts similar circumstances in her story of the typical, deplorable transportation conditions she endured while a member of her troupe: "When an authority came to our village to tell us we had to perform in another place, for example if we had to go to Nkundi, we would go from the village to Luozi, and from there to Nkundi. . . . They would take the car of a man that they saw as having a lot of money and use it to transport us. . . . We walked from the village [six hours of walking] to Luozi, and from there the truck would take us to Nkundi. . . . Even if you were in the fields . . . you must stop work and leave. . . . There were no words to say. . . . When we came to Luozi we slept on the floor in the compound of Hotel Madou" (Ma Ntima, October 10, 2005).

Both Ma Ntima's and Ma Mayazola's narratives reveal that animation was a disruptive force in their lives. They had to stop whatever work they were doing and heed the call to dance in faraway parts of the territory. While they were expected to fulfill their duties as citizens performing in these local animation troupes, the state did not consistently uphold its part of the bargain to transport, feed, or lodge the performers.

While Ma Ntima's story was similar to Ma Mayazola's, the situation was rather different for Mama Bangoma, since she was an animatrice for the entire territory and was called to travel often to other cities and towns in the district to learn new songs and dances that she in turn would teach to the animation groups of each sector in the territory of Luozi upon her return. The state took care of her needs: "They gave transportation. There were state vehicles. . . . There was food brought by the state itself . . . housing also by the state . . . clothes also" (Ma Bangoma, October 14, 2005). Clearly, while Ma Bangoma was not paid, she received many other benefits for her services to the state.

Thus, the position one held in the overall hierarchy of political animation affected the performance conditions, accommodations, and the types of gifts (if any) that the person received. Some women clearly benefited more than others from their participation as performers in local animation groups in Luozi territory. These multiple perspectives and experiences of animation politique relate directly to Achille Mbembe's notion of conviviality in subject-state relations in postcolonial Africa, as everyday relations cannot be simply defined as collusion or resistance. The fact that individuals were able to benefit socially, politically, and even economically from animation while others saw their participation as negatively impacting their lives complicates a simple black-white perspective on animation.[6]

The rehearsal schedules each woman reported also reveal great differences in the time allocated in their lives to these animation troupes as well as their opportunities to travel to perform. For Ma Mayazola, practices were done based on an upcoming event; besides that there was no set schedule. Ma Ntima explained that all the members of the animation groups in the sector of Mbanza-Mona practiced for one or two weeks, learning the dances together in the sector capital of Kinsemi. Ma Bangoma, as an animatrice for the entire territory, confirmed these weeklong or lengthier practices when she said she would teach the new dances and songs to the groups in each sector, and these practices could last a day, two days, or even a week. Moreover, Ma Bangoma also remembers traveling to many places to perform outside of Luozi territory (but still in Bas-Congo), including places like Inkisi, Mbanza-Ngungu, Kimpese, and Matadi. On the other hand, Ma Ntima recalls performing only in Luozi territory. This difference in performance venues suggests that higher-level performers had greater opportunities for travel sponsored by the state. This would also affect their perspective on the benefits and detriments of animation in their lives.[7]

Performing the Nation in the Bedroom

While coerced dancing in animation politique groups was the main way that loyalty and support for the Mobutu led government was expected to be performed, one of the more unsavory details about the era of animation politique deals with performances that were required in yet another area: the bedroom. A theme that emerged over and over again in regards to the conditions of performing in these animation troupes was the potential sexual exploitation of the female members of the groups. Ma Mayazola recounts the following: "There are [were] sisters that were called for example to go and drop off paperwork or food or dossiers or whatever, and there they [the male authority figures] did tricks in order to take them, and then there were sisters who became pregnant" (Ma Mayazola, October 5, 2005). Ma Mayazola's recounting seems to suggest many women did not expect or understand that the errands they were sent on, delivering various items to visiting authorities, were in fact a ruse to get them to engage in sexual activities.

Mama Ntima reports seeing similar occurrences in her experience as a dancer for JMPR: "When you arrived where you were going, they chose the beautiful girls to sleep with the people who came from MPR, the superiors. It was stupidness, really. The authorities, the chiefs, the leaders would choose. . . . When we came to Luozi we slept on the floor in the compound of Hotel Madou, and they chose beautiful girls to sleep with the authorities in the rooms" (October 10, 2005). During my time in Luozi, I walked past Hotel Madou numerous times, unaware that the crumbling and dilapidated building had once been a site for both vibrant performances of animation politique and the sexual exploitation of young women during Mobutu's era. Both of the women volunteered this information about the sexual exploitation of female dancers (one very early on in the interview), which leads me to believe that it was very important for them to clearly state that such a practice existed and was commonplace. However, neither woman went into a lot of detail about their experiences in this regard. It makes one wonder about the personal impact of such policies on these women and others that they knew and danced with during the time in question. Perhaps they wanted to avoid memories of past experiences, or just didn't feel comfortable sharing further information with me at that time. In both cases, at least one other person was present at the time of the interview, and that likely also influenced the depth of their responses. Seeking to respect their privacy, I did not delve any further, intuitively feeling that it was not appropriate to pry. Such an approach, where researchers simply "point toward silences" out of respect for interview participants is also characteristic of a feminist approach to social research (DeVault and Gross 2007, 184). The sexual exploitation of young women during Mobutu's era was, however, an "open secret." Bob White mentions people talking about the common practice of "offering the sexual services of female singers and dancers to visiting politicians and dignitaries" (2008, 78), while Georges Nzongola-Ntalaja refers to women who could better their fortunes and careers if they surrendered body and soul to the MPR (2002, 167). This practice was also confirmed by Dr. Mbala Nkanga, who directed theater productions during Mobutu's regime and observed similar practices (July 19, 2007, Michigan).[8] The state's expectation that female performers should have sexual encounters with politicians and other powerful male figures (regardless of the women's consent) makes their engagement with the state unique and different from the duties required of male performers. This is the gendered embodied citizenship defining how these female performers thought about their relationship to the state. Similar expectations of sexual performances were also held for girls and women attending secondary schools and universities (Mianda 1995; Schoepf 2002). While the three women I interviewed did not give extensive details at the time, other people in the community (specifically men) had explicit opinions about such practices and their impact on local communities. Before exploring their perspectives, however, I would like to examine the types of social and political discourse that were used to justify this sexual exploitation that, while not openly discussed, was endemic during Mobutu's regime.

Intimate Tyranny and Sacrificed Bodies:
Nation, Family, and Moral Disorder

When the MPR was created as the sole national party in 1967, all inhabitants of the country were automatically made members. Along with this political transformation, Mobutu and leaders in his government began to shape political ideology as well, metaphorically using the language of family to describe Mobutu's relationship to average Zairian citizens. This became especially prevalent during the economic deterioration of the 1970s. Georges Nzongola-Ntalaja captures this sentiment when he writes, "He [President Mobutu] was given titles such as 'father of the nation,' 'father of the revolution.' . . . Compared to a household head and a village chief, he and his wife were presumably father and mother to all citizens" (2002, 166). In his book exploring political authority and the relationship between the state and civil society in former Zaire, Michael Schatzberg quotes a government official in Zaire who says, "The MPR presents itself as a large family to which all Zairians without exception belong. All Zairians are born equal members of the MPR. . . . This characteristic of familial organization distinguishes the MPR from classical political parties" (1988, 71). Mobutu himself also used the metaphor of family in his speeches, such as in a May 1983 speech marking the sixteenth anniversary of the MPR: "Sixteen years ago, we created the People's Revolutionary Movement. We defined it before as being just a big family within which everything in national life had to be achieved. . . . During sixteen years, the party mobilized, spread awareness, persuaded, and succeeded in reconciling and uniting ethnic groups, tribes, regions. . . . The large family of the People's Revolutionary Movement today numbers close to thirty million souls" (Mobutu Sese Seko 1983, 60–61).

This selection from Mobutu's speech demonstrates that the metaphor of family was supposed to unite a fractured nation—giving the inhabitants of Zaire a common sense of belonging existing across ethnic, geographical, and linguistic lines, shaping their subjectivities as citizens. In his analysis of political imagery under Mobutu, Schatzberg further explains that the family metaphor in Zaire had a larger cultural significance that was part of what Schatzberg called a "moral matrix" of legitimate governance: "The imagery of father and family and the moral matrix on which it is based provide, first of all, an implicit promise of nurturance and paternal care. . . . Second, the metaphors create an intimacy between rulers and ruled and thus succeed in representing complex political realities in a simplified form. . . . Third, the images are 'natural.' . . . Furthermore, such symbols and imagery mask an exploitatively unequal flow of resources with authoritarian overtones" (1988, 89–90).

In sum, when Mobutu invoked "family" (from the point of view of a citizen of Zaire) it created a more natural and personal relationship. Achille Mbembe echoes Schatzberg's findings when he writes that "an intimate tyranny links the ruler with the ruled" in postcolonial Africa (Mbembe 1992, 22), suggesting that citizens in Zaire expected President Mobutu to take care of them and guide them as a father would. However, he was a father on two levels; father of the nation, and father of each citizen. This led to a treacherous ambiguity that allowed Mobutu and his government officials to manipulate this relationship at their convenience: "Since all he does is, by definition, for the benefit of the corporate family, he can assert his actions always place the good of the whole uppermost. . . . If then, an unlucky or disadvantaged citizen should invoke his personal relationship with the father and request or expect nurturance, Mobutu can claim he has acted for the good of the entire clan" (Schatzberg 1988, 91). Thus, ideas of "family" as applied to nation also served to ideologically justify behaviors and actions that often negatively impacted the individual citizens.

The numerous propaganda outlets that promoted Mobutu as a "Father" to the nation also presented a discourse of feminine liberation and equality to the masses. However, the state's larger discourse on women and their role in society had many contradictions. Speaking at the conclusion of a symposium on women in Zaire on May 20, 1975, President Mobutu proclaimed that his takeover of the government in 1965 had liberated the women of Zaire: "November 24, 1965, was not only the date that marked the beginning of our total independence . . . but equally the start of the liberation of women in all forms" (1975, 587). The concept of liberation was given short shrift, however, just seven years later in another speech given at the third regular conference of the MPR: "We want to recognize in the Zairian mother the rights that give her the quality of equal partner to men. But it remains understood that . . . there will always be in each family one boss. . . . The boss . . . is he who wears the pants. Our female citizens must also understand that, accepting it with a smile and a revolutionary submission" (Mobutu 1983, 693). These two quotes reveal a stark contradiction; while the buzzwords of liberation and equality are used in state discourse, the president himself sees limits in the authority and decision-making power of women in their own households and families. He is clearly promoting a patriarchal system in which women (who he largely refers to as mothers and wives) are to remain subservient to their husbands.

The president's personal ideas about the limited role of women explain why throughout his presidency, there was much more political rhetoric and discourse rather than significant transformative gestures in regards to the status of women (Mianda 1995, 59). There were three major phases of government action in relation to women in Zaire: propaganda starting in the 1960s promoting the idea of "new" men and women emancipated from the inferiority complexes of colonialism; the creation of a department dedicated to women and family in 1980; and the family code of 1988 (Mianda 1995). However, the discourse promoting women's equality belied the reality.

A 1988 World Bank report revealed that 63.6 percent of girls in Zaire attended primary school versus 88.3 percent of boys, while at the university level, women made up only 13 percent of the student population. Further, women were a small minority in public sector jobs, making up only 3.82 percent of public service personnel in 1982, 17 percent of national bank employees, and only 21 percent of the personnel in the department of primary and secondary education in 1985 (Mianda 1995). Within secondary schools, like in animation troupes, there was widespread sexual abuse of girls by teachers and a common practice of older men having secondary school girls as mistresses outside of school. Legislation like the family code of 1988, among others, also set women's rights backward considerably. While the legal age of marriage for males was eighteen, the age of marriage consent for girls was lowered to fifteen. This further facilitated the exploitation of teenage girls by older men. The code also legislated that wives had to get their husbands' permission to engage in any legal matters, and their husbands had the right to manage and even take their wives' property, money, and goods, even if the wives had earned the money or purchased the property themselves. Husbands were declared the heads of their families, and wives were legally obligated to obey them. Alimony was eliminated, and limits were placed on bride price payments as well. One woman in Lubumbashi lamented the impact of the family code on her life: "We lost our dignity. We lost our status in society. The code says we have no rights as women or wives and our husbands can do anything with us, even take our property or just abandon us and take up with other wives" (McGreal 1997). Overall then, the everyday realities for women were far from equal in regards to men, both within and outside of their households.

Returning the discussion to the specific case of young women dancing in animation troupes in Luozi, the national "family" metaphor used by the state was explicitly undermined by the negative impacts of national policies on local families, communities, and moral order more broadly. For example, men in Luozi repeatedly spoke of sexual impropriety and the disruption of local communities, a theme that also tied into some of the information provided by the female interviewees. Tata Nkolele, the program director for a local NGO, had this to say:

> There are certain girls for example, who were incorporated into these groups, who weren't old . . . who weren't old enough to be able to be carried in front of the general public. . . . For the population, it wasn't a good thing that all of these girls were exposed to presenting shows. . . . There was a certain exaggeration because the girl who danced . . . it was pleasing for the politico-administrative man. . . . In fact, it distanced the people who sometimes were horrified to watch all these dances, which were considered as obscene. . . . These youth that were recuperated for the needs of the party, sometimes for two weeks to learn songs, slogans, to please . . . the revolution. For two weeks they are absent from their work environment. Look what it does to the economy of their area and to them themselves. It is this that makes it so that many young girls found themselves pregnant as a result of all of these absences. . . . There were young girls who discovered their sexuality too early. (October 14, 2005)

One of the first observations Tata Nkolele makes about girls dancing in JMPR troupes was that some of the girls who performed in public were not old enough for such activities. This indicates that the performative duties of the nation are disregarding local concepts of age-appropriate conduct. He also notes that some of the dances were considered by those watching (the parents and families of the girls) to be obscene, and this led to them distancing themselves from the dances—this sentiment very clearly contradicts with the goals of national animation policies, which seek to use performance to create unity and a sense of national belonging. He also indicates that there was an economic impact from the absence of youth who were recruited to perform—in Luozi territory, a largely agricultural community, the physical labor of large numbers of young men and women who are removed for several weeks would have a detrimental impact on harvesting and other agricultural activities. Removing this population for animation activities also undermined Mobutu's policy of *salongo*—obligatory collective work—which in Bas-Zaire, was largely based on agriculture.[9] Moreover, Tata Nkolele also discusses unintended pregnancies, which can impact local families and communities in a number of ways, such as disrupting prearranged marriages; leaving the girl's family without bride wealth; and leaving the dancer, her family, and larger community responsible for the child, without the benefits of marriage. This is further complicated by the fact that the majority of the Congolese population during Mobutu's era was estimated to be Christian (50–65 percent in 1979 [Kaplan 1979, xiii]), suggesting that there was some social pressure to have children within marriage or at least sanctioned by bride wealth payments.[10] All of this, in addition to the negative emotional and psychological consequences for the girl herself, belied the expected role of Mobutu as a protector of his "children." Rather, sexual access to young women was something that government officials expected as their right, following their leader Mobutu. The second translation of Mobutu's name, "invincible warrior, cock who leaves no chick intact," is quite relevant here as Mobutu was well known for expecting sexual access to many women, including the wives of some of his officials (Schoepf 2002; Zagorin 1993). Such illicit and immoral behavior came to define everyday life under Mobutu's regime, so much so that the "sexualization of politics" in Zaire came to symbolize the corruption of the regime and the authenticity project (White 2008, 78–79). As Mbembe states in his analysis of the state in Cameroon, an "anxious virility" is performed by the state's president and officials, such that "pride in possessing an active penis has to be dramatized, with sexual rights over subordinates, . . . the keeping of concubines, and so forth" (1992, 14). Such an observation also applies well to the case of postcolonial Zaire and relates further to civil religion. If Mobutu was to be seen as powerful and godlike, the sexual consumption of large numbers of women aided to confirm his strength, masculinity, and virility.

Ne Mosi, a farmer in Luozi territory, also discusses concern for the sexual morality of young women and the compromising positions that they were placed in during this era: "Generally, I can say that the dances of the female animators were especially dances that consisted of rotating the hips really well. It is during this dance that, the chief or the animators choose them . . . those who must spend the night with the chief or else with this person, with that person. Animation consisted of a display, if you will, of women or else young girls, for the selection of chiefs and animators. . . . Because you can't say anything, because you are a female animator, they take you; they say there you are, we are going to see the chief" (October 10, 2005). His conceptualization of performances of animation politique as displays of young girls for sexual selection hints at yet another layer of the moral disorder, that their families and loved ones were also watching them be chosen for sexual services. This is further supported by Tata Nkuku, a middle-aged school teacher who considers the impact of political animation on youth and social morality: "I think that it was there in order to deform the youth especially because . . . there are sometimes dances that were very exaggerated, gestures and dances were going too far, that one couldn't even allow in the presence of one's parents" (September 29, 2005). All these interview excerpts express several interrelated themes that recur in people's remembrances and assessments of animation politique: moral corruption, sexual exploitation, and disruption of families and local communities. For unmarried women who were not enrolled in school, animation presented a threat to their very bodies. As another interviewee explains, "it was a danger for girls" (Ne Tatu, October 10, 2005). This danger was not only moral but a physical one as well. What justification can be given for young women expected or even forced to give the most intimate part of themselves to complete strangers? Returning again to the metaphor of father and family, Schatzberg notes that one aspect of acting as a "big-man" and "father-chief" for Mobutu is generously distributing wealth in gifts to his subjects. In return, Zairian citizens are supposed to morally reciprocate his generosity (1988, 80–81). However, in the case of these young women dancing for JMPR, they ARE the gift—one that is being freely "given" to other government officials and even visiting politicians (White 2008, 78). Thus, kinship and sexuality intersect, which, if one accepts the family metaphor, not only allows for "incest" between Mobutu as father and female citizens as children, but justifies it as good for the well-being of the national family.

There seem to be conflicting understandings of morality in this instance. For Mobutu and other government officials in Zaire, the "right" thing for female citizens to do was to willingly comply with requests for sexual services, for the good of the nation. However, in a majority-Christian nation, these acts of sex, outside of marriage, were not seen by most of these women or their families as "right" or "good."

While some women used these sexual liaisons as opportunities for improving their lot through connecting to wealthy politicians and state officials, for others the moral repercussions and potential negative impact on their families and own lives loomed large (for example, pregnancy, diseases such as HIV, and psychological trauma. One scholar, in explaining how AIDS became a huge public health problem in the social context of the large-scale sexual exploitation of girls and women in Zaire, called it "Mobutu's disease" (Schoepf 2002). What cannot be lost in the larger discussion of the situation of female performers is the elimination of choice, whether the coercion was explicit or subtle. The consequences of saying no to Mobutu or his representatives—imprisonment, fines, outright rape, and even death[11]—likely guided the decisions and the actions of these women. Forced sex is rape, even if the women cannot explicitly say no. With the aforementioned examples, the sexual exploitation of women in the service of the "nation" during Mobutu's era is likely the most extreme exercise of political authority and state control over the very bodies of the citizens of former Zaire, and in particular, the bodies of women. These young women served, in the words of Foucault, as both "object[s] and target[s] of power" ([1977] 1995, 136). Thus, Mbembe's concept of intimate tyranny needs to be extended beyond subjects reproducing state behaviors in their everyday lives. The other type of intimate tyranny that needs to be considered is the forceful penetration of the state into the most private parts of one's own body, all in the name of the national family. These performances in the bedroom are performative encounters that dramatically transformed the relationship between the state and individual female dancers. These women were expected to sacrifice their personal bodies for the national body, not just once (as a soldier killed in combat would for example) but over and over again. Moreover, continuing with the comparison of these women with soldiers sacrificing their bodies in war, a soldier's death brings honor to the country and family. A young woman forced to have sex with government officials or visiting dignitaries is not seen as a source of pride; rather, as the previous comments of the other interviewees show, it was a source of community discord, shame, and frustration. A young woman who dies of AIDS-related complications following from numerous sexual encounters is not seen as honorable. Thus, an additional layer of the duties and meanings of gendered citizenship is exposed by placing women's experiences at the center of our analysis of animation politique. The everyday performances these young women were expected to carry out and embrace as a part of their service to the nation had decidedly negative moral, physical, economic, and social consequences for themselves, their families, and their local communities.

Political Animation and Its Impact on the Community:
Women's Perspectives

Discussions of the value of animation politique for the country reveal that many people saw it as undermining core values and morals of society, whether by interrupting holy worship, teaching sexually suggestive dances that offended Christian decorum, or placing young girls in situations where they were taken advantage of sexually by powerful men. However, not all the responses characterized animation as negative; people who clearly benefited from their role in animation politique often saw it as much more positive. In response to a question about what they thought about animation overall, and whether or not they thought it had been good for the community, the responses of the three female interviewees varied once again. Mama Bangoma responds in the following manner: "It was good for the population . . . because in that time . . . the young girls and the young boys . . . if they received word that an authority was coming . . . everyone went down, they attended. . . . It was good for the dancers. . . . It was obligatory" (October 14, 2005). Mama Bangoma's overall assessment of political animation is quite positive, which reflects her past higher status in the animation hierarchy. This is not surprising since she gained social mobility and status and was able to travel and more than likely was able to use her position as an animatrice to get an even better job with the regime. Thus, it is probably not a coincidence that it is she, among the three women, who currently has a civil service job with the government.

On the other hand, Mama Ntima disagrees. Mama Ntima says that "it was bad because . . . like here in Luozi, people wanted to pray, and when they [other people] were dancing stupid dances, it was obligatory, and it wasn't good for the people" (October 10, 2005). For her, dancing and singing for JMPR clearly violated her ideals and values as a Christian woman whose church explicitly bans participation in secular dancing. In fact, Mama Ntima chose to escape by getting married early, since couples in state-recognized marriages were not forcibly recruited into these local JMPR groups to dance for the regime. She was in the group in 1977 and got married in 1978.

Mama Mayazola also seemed to view political animation as a negative social phenomenon: "For me it was torment. I was tormented. . . . To take this long journey . . . to leave your work in the fields and all that you have as an occupation, you must drop it to go and dance for someone, without being paid, without being given food, without being lodged. It was practically a punishment. . . . This movement created disorder . . . in the village, for the fact that there was obligatory traveling. . . . In the songs there was nothing else but the glory of Mobutu" (October 5, 2005). Ma Mayazola's comments highlight the economic consequences of animation. In an area where the vast majority of the population makes its living through agriculture, unexpected rehearsals and performances depleted the area of an important source of labor.

Ma Mayazola's overall assessment of animation as negatively impacting her life was also reflected in the ways she sought to avoid her embodied national service. She ran away when her animation group was traveling out of the sector to the town of Luozi. She also often feigned sickness to evade performing obligations. Others who were caught dodging their dancing duties were taken to the chief of the sector to be punished by paying fines or doing hard physical labor. Ma Mayazola was in the group from 1971 to 1973, until she, like Ma Ntima, was married.

The varied responses from these women support Mbembe's statement that "the postcolonial relationship is not primarily a relationship of resistance or of collaboration, but is rather best characterized as a promiscuous relationship: a convivial tension" (1992, 5). This is clearly shown in the differing assessments of political animation. Under the pressures and threats of a coercive state, all the women felt obligated to perform. However, they did not necessarily all see themselves as having to resist the impositions of the state. In general, one's position in the hierarchy of animation performers affected one's opinion about political animation and its impact on the population. Mama Ntima and Mama Mayazola, the two women who were simply dancers compelled by force, did not see political animation as a good thing for the country or themselves and in fact used different strategies (marriage, fleeing, and so on) to avoid having to perform. This clearly contrasts with Ma Bangoma, for whom political animation seemed a great benefit in comparison to other women lower in the hierarchy of performers. Their responses show each of them evaluated their own gendered embodied citizenship through animation politique in different ways.

Conclusion

State-scripted nationalism through public performances was hugely important as a tool of creating (or attempting to create) nationalist sentiment in many nations in postcolonial Africa. The specific case of animation politique in Zaire reveals the importance of constant and omnipresent public performances for spreading the ideologies of Mobutu's government, whether people agreed with it or not. Moreover, animation politique impacted people in both urban areas and rural and marginalized parts of the country; thus, it can be considered an extreme form of the banality of power in the former Zaire. My interviews with three different Kongo women about their experiences with animation politique, as well as interviews with men in the community in Luozi, suggest that a more complex understanding of engagement with the state at the level of the body needs to be considered in studies of performed state nationalism. Specifically, different citizens engaged with the state through animation politique in different ways. An analysis that privileges gender and embodiment reveals the complex and multifaceted meaning of citizenship through performance in Mobutu's Zaire. Following from overt sexual exploitation of female ex-performers, their experiences of animation reveal a gendered embodied citizenship differing considerably from how male performers engaged with the state. The performative encounters that these women had with government officials in the bedroom made the state a very intimate presence in their lives and in their bodies. The expectation of sexual performances also goes along with the deification of Mobutu as a leader as he was the model par excellence in his own sexual exploitation of women during his regime. While the stated intention of animation was to inculcate the messages of Mobutu into the very bodies of Zaire's citizens, the actual outcome, specifically in regards to the sexual exploitation of young women in rural animation troupes, was quite different. Animation politique led to moral disorder and disengagement from the nationalist project by not only some of the female dancers, but also their families and communities. However, even these negative outcomes were not shared by all—men and women who were able to benefit from animation politique largely saw it as a positive experience. These findings suggest that the banality of power in postcolonial Africa cannot be fully understood until the diverse experiences of all citizens—both men and women—are taken into account. The intimate tyranny Mbembe discussed must be expanded to include the unique experiences of girls and women who were forced to engage, by and through their bodies, with a coercive state seeking to consume them sexually.

Part IV

RE-CREATING THE PAST,
PERFORMING THE FUTURE

CHAPTER 6

Bundu dia Kongo and Embodied Revolutions

Performing Kongo Pride, Transforming Modern Society

Encounters and Embodied Revolutions

Saturday, February 18, 2006. On the way to an interview, I see a large group of people coming down the main road in Luozi. Carrying a five- or six-foot-tall painting of their leader, Ne Muanda Nsemi, they are members of Bundu dia Kongo (the Church of the Kongo, also known as BDK), singing, waving small branches with green leaves, and walking in time to the percussive sound of three bass drums and an *ngongi* being played by several men in the back of the group.[1] Some of the women wear highly recognizable yellow BDK head coverings. Many members of the crowd are carrying backpacks or sacks over their shoulders, on their backs, or on their heads, with food, blankets, and other items needed for an overnight stay for the two-day meeting. Previously, one of the local leaders of the group had told me there would be a general assembly from Friday to Sunday I could attend, and so I run to get my video camera. As I dash back, out of breath and panting, I open the camera to begin to film, assuming the people are members of the Luozi-based BDK group. Almost immediately, people in the crowd begin to protest and wave their arms erratically. I stop the camera, and several people approach me and began to fiercely throw questions my way.

"You have to ask for permission!" a tall man in a red shirt states emphatically.

"OK. OK. I'm sorry. Who do I ask?" I respond quickly, closing the camera and putting it back in my purse.

Another person chimes in, "Who are you and what are you doing filming?"

I anxiously reply, "I am a student working on my dissertation at the University of Michigan. I am a Black American from the United States. I am doing my research on Kongo culture and dance, from the Kongo Kingdom to the present day. I was given permission by the members of Bundu dia Kongo here in Luozi."[2]

It turns out this group is actually from Kinshasa, not Luozi. So, they didn't know me; thus, I am suspect. I explain my research and intentions several times to several different people. I reassure them that I am not a government or foreign spy. When the leader of this group from Kinshasa arrives, I explain everything to him. He gives me and several friends permission to film the group and tells us to come to the meeting area in the evening at 7:00 PM. My friend and assistant David runs ahead and films the group some more. Then, as I am waiting for him to come back, another group appears but something is going on. There is a tall, nonmember of the group in the middle, in dark tan khakis. As people argue and fuss around him, Mama Kudia and others watching near me begin to piece things together. Apparently, he was on a motorcycle and hit one of the people marching when he came through the crowd without beeping or giving advance notice. This person was hurt, and the other members of the group "arrested" him. It does not help that he isn't MuKongo, but rather a Swahili speaker. They take his motorcycle and hold him "hostage" in the center of the group. I don't know what they did with him. A friend said that they said they were going to take him to the authorities.

Later that evening, I arrive with two friends at the meeting site to observe the proceedings. A soccer field–sized clearing is filled with men, women, and children, all facing a small area of ground acting as the stage, located just in front of a thatch covered structure where group leaders and honored guests are seated in chairs. A musical group performs to the left of the stage. The music is infectious and sounds like Congolese popular dance music with lyrics espousing BDK's ideas and politics. If I close my eyes, I could swear I am listening to Werreson![3] I note that curious nonmembers of BDK, attracted by the singing and thronging crowd, walk by leisurely or stand at the fringes of the clearing, observing the goings on. Many BDK security personnel (known as *makesa*), in blue uniforms with red berets and armbands, surround the open space in the middle. I approach a "welcome" desk where dues were collected, and ask for the local leaders with whom I am acquainted, explaining to the security people that we had been given permission to attend.

They said wait, you have to see the chief. Then, a serious escort leads us to a small house, where several men in sunglasses, tight pants, and serious faces guard the door, with arms crossed. They again tell me to wait, and finally, who emerges? Ne Mosi, whom I'd interviewed several months before. We exchange pleasantries, and I explain that I am asking for permission to film.

"How can I give you permission to film, and you still haven't given me the film and pictures you took last time?"

The skeptical look he gives me is not helping matters. I am frustrated and a bit annoyed. By that point, it seemed as though everyone at every event I attended expected that I would print every last one of the pictures I took and give it to them. Most people in the area had nondigital cameras, and a local shop printed those photos. Since I was using a digital camera in an area where facilities for digital printing were scarce, it was hard to fulfill such requests immediately, although I gave VCDs and CDs of events and photos to people, and actual photos when I had the chance to print them out.

"It depends on you," I respond.

"I will give permission, but on the condition that you give us a copy of the pictures and photos that you take, and the other ones you took already."

I said, "If you give me a blank CD, I can do the copy of the photos and other film right now!"

After he responds that he did not have a CD, I explain that I can do this in Kinshasa, as I didn't have any more CDs with me in Luozi. We agree that I will give the copies to his wife. After finally getting his permission to film, my two friends and I walk back to the open area. However, when I open my video camera, yet another leader stops me and tells me that I need his permission to film. This happens several times over and over again, and, after at least an hour and a half, I am finally allowed to film. Looking back on the experience, I realize a few factors were at play: other BDK groups visiting Luozi did not know who I was and were suspicious; BDK members in general knew that the government was persecuting them and feared I was spying on them; moreover, BDK leaders wanted me to take their movement seriously and not approach it as simply an object of study to be filmed, photographed, and analyzed. Thus, my interactions with BDK were some of the most challenging moments that I experienced while doing research. To put it simply, BDK often told me "No!" when other groups did not. However, these interactions also taught me the biggest lessons about the power differentials, politics of conducting research, and expectations of my relationship as a researcher with various community members.

Seated among the honored guests with two friends who accompanied me, I face the crowd, seeing men and women dressed in security uniforms placed at intermittent points not only to maintain order, but also as I have realized from visits to their *zikua*,[4] to warn of possible attacks by government and police forces. The crowd continues to grow, spilling over past the clearing, as members have come from Boma, Matadi, Mbanza-Ngungu, Kinshasa, and other places in the Lower Congo especially.[5] As the meeting gets under way, I stand when everyone else stands, kneel when everyone kneels, and generally act as a silent participant-observer of the events. When I feel more comfortable, I leave the space of the honored guests, begin to record the meeting, and take photos. Several iconic images are strategically placed around the stage area. One is a painting of Mama Vita Kimpa,[6] majestically posed in front of roaring flames that took her life on July 2, 1706, anachronistically depicted wearing one of the female BDK yellow head coverings discussed earlier. Another image is of Ne Muanda Nsemi, three paintings of whom animate the stage, as he was unable to attend the meeting. During a lull in the program, I approach the most elaborate of these paintings for a close-up. At the top are the words "Ne Muanda Nsemi, the Vehicle of Kongo Wisdom, the Kongo Nationalist Movement," and at the bottom is a sketch of a map showing a restored Kongo Kingdom. However, what is even more interesting to me is the image of Ne Muanda Nsemi himself. In the painting, he is depicted in a black suit with a red scarf tied around his forehead, with his right hand slightly cupped and raised over his left hand, which has two scarves (yellow and blue) draped over it. In this and the other three paintings, he is thus shown enacting the bula makonko gesture (see figure 6.1). What does gesture have to do with the politics of Bundu dia Kongo?[7]

This chapter explores ever-evolving relationships between nationalist politics, religion, and everyday performances for Kongo people in the context of a postcolonial and post-Mobutu nation. I examine the use of embodied cultural performances in the politico-religious-nationalist movement of Bundu dia Kongo. Their activism has led to the two-time election of their spiritual leader as a national congressman (in 2006 and 2011), and their political engagement and overall challenge to the status quo has sparked numerous confrontations (often fatal) with local, provincial, and national law enforcement and military, capturing national and even international headlines. The government dissolved and prohibited Bundu dia Kongo as an organization by an official decree in 2008, and the group reorganized itself as a political party Bundu dia Mayala, which was also banned in 2011. This chapter is based on my experiences with the group in 2005–6, before their major conflicts with the state in 2007 and 2008. For Bundu dia Kongo, embodied

FIGURE 6.1. Still video image of painting of Ne Muanda Nsemi doing bula makonko gesture, Luozi, 2006. Image captured by Yolanda Covington-Ward.

gestures have come to play a huge role in the marshaling of popular sentiment and spiritual power toward the social and political goal of creating a sovereign Kongo nation. Changes in the ways the members use their bodies in their interactions with each other, other Kongo people, and the spiritual realm, and the meanings associated with these embodied cultural performances, call our attention to the importance of the body in advancing ideologies and political goals and establishing other forms of authority that subvert the prevailing status quo. Culturally relevant gestures take on multiple meanings and uses as they enable the very embodiment of the overall cultural and political mission of Bundu dia Kongo.

Conflicted Feelings: The Decision to Write about Bundu dia Kongo

Initially, I did not intend to write about Bundu dia Kongo. In fact, when I left my last BDK event in February of 2006, I stated emphatically to my friends, "Je suis fini avec BDK!" (I am finished with BDK!) I was angry at all the accusations that were continuously leveled at me of being a spy although I had done all I could to alleviate their suspicions. I was upset at the almost schizophrenic behavior of being embraced as a sister of the diaspora whose research in Kongo performance culture and history aligned with their goal of revitalizing Kongo culture, to then being ridiculed for not doing more to support the group and for attending other Christian churches, and even being denounced as a spy because I hadn't brought hard copies of pictures I'd taken although I'd given them CDs and VCDs with the photos and video footage. I was threatened that I would be spiritually attacked if my motives were impure, and I avoided their more overtly political activities not only because I didn't want to be explicitly associated with the group during a tension-filled election campaign season, but also because of the potential for violent conflicts with police. I argued with them over what I saw as historical facts they'd creatively rewritten and was told, "You got that from a white man's book. That is not the truth. Read the black man's book!" Coming from a family where strong women reign and females dominate numerically, I bristled at their ideas of inherent male superiority and rolled my eyes in defiance as I was told what my "proper" role as a woman should be.[8] To be candid, their overall aggressive attitude and even militarism frightened me although simultaneously they often reminded me of Black Power groups in the United States like the Black Panthers, whom I respected. When the memory card in my camera failed at the February mass meeting, I came back just as the crowd dispersed. I then asked a leader's permission to take photos of some of the remaining banners and signs, and the general area, and he refused. "Why do you want photos with no people in them? This is not a museum!" Frustrated, I complied and left the area, vowing to never deal with them again. In the moment, I felt they didn't respect my work as a researcher; yet, conversely, they wanted me to see them as a valid movement with aspirations, and not just as objects of scientific study.

In addition, friends and community members made it clear to me that working with BDK could put me at risk of harm. Ever since first talking with BDK leadership in September of 2005, people had warned me about the group, saying things like, "Bundu dia Kongo, they're dangerous," and "You have to be careful—people have been killed." Thus, I was apprehensive and wary about the group, because of the warnings I'd received, the overall aggressive tone of the group, and the hostile response they continued to receive from the local authorities. I didn't want to be in the wrong place at the wrong time.

Owing to my conflicted feelings about writing about the group and concerns for my safety, I did only a few interviews with local group leaders, only one of which was recorded because of their suspicion of recording equipment, while I took notes during the other interviews. Most of the data this chapter is built on is based on those interviews and other informal conversations with BDK members, along with my experiences as an observing participant in several worship sessions in the zikua in Luozi, a multiday mass meeting, and several other organized events. Moreover, I incorporate the numerous published writings of Ne Muanda Nsemi, which guide the ideology and development of the group as a whole. In all, when I look back on my experiences, I realize that although I didn't always like it, the members of Bundu dia Kongo continuously challenged my motives, privilege, and position as a Black American woman ethnographer who until then had not had much trouble gaining access and permissions for events in other settings.[9]

Although I did not agree with some of the points of view and ideology of Bundu dia Kongo, and even their tactics and behavior at times, as a member of the African diaspora, I was unequivocally in agreement with, or at least sympathized with a number of their principles. Their emphasis on a religion that is Kongo focused, their mission to rehabilitate the use of Kikongo, their need for a history written by and for Kongo people, their goal of self-government and the erasure of colonial borders, their belief in Pan-Africanism, their recognition of the ill treatment of people of African descent all over the world by Europeans and their descendants including slavery and colonialism—all these principles struck a chord within me.

Regardless of my reservations, I have decided to include BDK in this book for several reasons. First, there hasn't been much scholarly attention paid to the group, especially in English-language publications, although the group has been in existence for several decades.[10] For this reason I have dedicated a large portion of the chapter to explaining who Bundu dia Kongo is as a movement. Second, BDK members were the target of a fatal state suppression campaign in 2007 and 2008, which impacted many communities in Bas-Congo, including Luozi. Third and most important, as I reflected on their influence in politics, the revitalization of Kongo culture and language, and finally, the redefinition of Kongo cultural performances in terms of gestures in everyday life, I realized I could not write about the relationship between nationalism, religion, and the body in modern Kongo society without talking about Bundu dia Kongo.

Post-Mobutu Congo

After Laurent Kabila's overthrow of Mobutu in 1997 and Kabila's subsequent assassination in 2001, a transitional government was formed, headed by his son, Joseph Kabila. The Democratic Republic of Congo stood poised at the precipice of an uncertain future. For the first time since June 30, 1960, free democratic elections were finally going to be held in 2006.[11] This new environment engendered fear and wariness about the future, but also hope and numerous opportunities for challenging existing political authority structures. This was directly reflected in the large number of registered political parties and independent candidates (there were 267) several months before the presidential elections,[12] parties with numerous agendas and visions for the future, intent on transforming the nation that had become a decrepit shadow of its former self, economically, structurally, politically, and culturally. However, this urge to transform was not limited to politics but also existed in other aspects of Congolese society and manifested itself in myriad ways.

The Bundu dia Kongo movement has appeared in a number of Congolese newspaper headlines over the past decade, especially as their political activity has increased. Some examples include "Ne Muanda Nsemi, Elected Member of the National Assembly from Luozi, Called to Reaffirm Peace in Bas-Congo" (Agence Congolaise de Presse 2008); "Terror at Luozi and Seke-Banza: Bundu dia Kongo Challenges the Authority of the State!" (Uhuru 2008); and "Arrest of Twenty Members of 'Bundu dia Mayala,' the Banned Former Politico-military Group 'Bundu dia Kongo'" (Agence Congolaise de Presse 2012). Notwithstanding the fact that many of the newspapers do not agree with the group's politics and ideology, and often sensationalize the news they report, Bundu dia Kongo has reappeared over and over again in and around political issues in the Lower Congo, with their conflicts with authorities even leading to an expansion of the United Nations military presence in Bas-Congo in 2008.[13] What is Bundu dia Kongo? What are their politics and ideology, and how are they related to embodied cultural performance? The first section of this chapter will examine the goals and ideology of this group. The second section provides a historical and diasporic context for Bundu dia Kongo by exploring the antecedents of the group's political and sociocultural activism (in particular, the importance of ABAKO), and the role of Pan-Africanism in the movement. Finally, the third section of the chapter will discuss how bodies are used to physically enact Bundu dia Kongo's goals through embodied cultural performances, particularly in gestures associated with both everyday interactions and spiritual collective worship.

What Is Bundu dia Kongo?

Bundu dia Kongo is a group and movement that combines religion, politics, and cultural revitalization in furthering the overall goal of restoring the former Kongo Kingdom. Composed of BisiKongo people (which members of BDK refer to as Bena Kongo), it was founded in 1986 in the Democratic Republic of Congo by Ne Muanda Nsemi, who remains the spiritual leader of the group. Born Badiegisa Zakalia in Mongo-Luala,[14] a northern sector in the territory of Luozi, he received a spiritual calling to continue the work of the famous colonial-era Kongo prophet Simon Kimbangu (see chapters 2 and 3). In a newspaper interview, Ne Muanda Nsemi explained he was called to take on a mission in 1969 while in his third year at Lovanium University studying math, physics, and chemistry: "I began to have visions. For someone who, in his youth, saw only math, physics, and chemistry, and who had never prayed, it was a whole other world. I began to see a giant being who measured more or less four meters. And this being came . . . to tell me: 'Vakatukidi nganga, nganga uvingananga vana'" (this means: here where a chief/priest retired, another chief/priest must take the place). And he goes on to add: 'Here is the mission that you are going to take on. It is going to now be your turn. But you, you will be at the same time a mixture of Kimbangu and Kasa-Vubu'" (Kabuayi 2006).[15]

Ne Muanda Nsemi describes denying this call for seventeen years before accepting his mission and founding Bundu dia Kongo in 1986. The visions Ne Muanda Nsemi reports having continue a long tradition of continuous revelation that permeates Kongo culture and history, in both traditional religious beliefs and Christian practices, from the possession of Dona Beatrice Kimpa Vita by Saint Anthony in the eighteenth century, to Simon Kimbangu's own visions in the twentieth century (Thornton 1998). Notably, the otherworldly being in the vision places Ne Muanda Nsemi in the same category as other powerful Kongo leaders and cultural heroes, such as Simon Kimbangu and Joseph Kasa-Vubu. Inspired by the visions, what objectives does Ne Muanda Nsemi and Bundu dia Kongo as a group and movement seek to fulfill?

Mission and Ideology

Bundu dia Kongo's overall mission was described in one of the many pamphlets written by Ne Muanda Nsemi as the following: "the diffusion of the Kongo religion, the promotion of scientific research, and the moral and spiritual education of political leaders of the country practicing the Kongo Religion" (1994a). The overall ideology of Bundu dia Kongo can best be encapsulated through a discussion of trinities,[16] so when I asked about the teachings of Bundu dia Kongo, one interviewee explained that the essential teachings of BDK were threefold: spiritual, scientific, and political. Each aspect of the group's ideology is associated with particular colors, ancestors, and characteristics. A similar type of trinity is reflected in the concept of God in BDK (Ne Mosi, October 10, 2005). God (in Kikongo called *Nzambi Mpungu*) is one but has three principle attributes: power (*Nzambi 'a Mpungu*); love (*Nzambi 'a Kongo*); and intelligence (*Nzambi 'a Mbumba*) (Nsemi 1994b, 2–3; Nsemi 1995, 6). According to the teachings of BDK as espoused in their pamphlets,[17] small books, newspaper interviews, and interviews I myself conducted, these three attributes correspond to the three children of the primordial ancestors who became the Bena Kongo, or Kongo people:

1. The ancestor Nsaku was a prophet, great priest, religion, spirituality, the color blue, divine love, the spiritual church, Kinlongo kia Kongo, Mfumu'a Nlongo. 2. The ancestor Mpanzu was a blacksmith, artisan, sciences and technology, the color yellow, divine intelligence, the academy of sciences, Kinkimba kia Mazayu, Mfumu'a Lusanga. 3. The Ancestor Nzinga was a king, the government, the color red, divine power, the political party, Kabu dia Mayala, Mfumu'a Mayala. The names of these three children became the names of the three clans at the base of the Kongo Nation: the clan Nsaku, the clan Mpanzu, and the clan Nzinga. . . . The ancestor Nsaku is the incarnation of the love and the wisdom of God. The ancestor Mpanzu is the incarnation of the creative intelligence of God. The ancestor Nzinga is the incarnation of the power of God that governs the universe. The Kongo trinity is thus the representative, on the earth, of the trinity of the skies. It is the chosen people made in the image of God. (Ne Muanda Nsemi 1995, 11–13)

According to Ne Muanda Nsemi, the name of the *kanda*, or clan, of each person can be traced back to one of these three founding ancestors, and people's own individual attributes will reflect that association (for example, if they have a propensity for music, this can be traced to their belonging to one of the clans of Mpanzu).[18] All these ideas and associations have been captured in the following phrase in Kikongo: *Makuku Matatu Malamba Kongo*: the three hearthstones on which the Kongo was prepared/cooked.[19] Moreover, two of these trinities (Nzambi 'a Mpungu, Nzambi 'a Kongo, Nzambi 'a Mbumba) and (Nsaku, Mpanzu, Nzinga) are arranged on top of one another to form a six-pointed star that is the emblem of Bundu dia Kongo as a movement (see figure 6.2).[20]

The influence of the trinities of God and the characteristics of the three major ancestors are thus reflected in defining what Bundu dia Kongo is, as shown in Ne Muanda Nsemi's response to a question about the nature of Bundu dia Kongo in a newspaper interview: "Bundu dia Kongo is in effect a crystal with three faces: when you look at Bundu dia Kongo on the face of the ancestor Nsaku, you say that Bundu dia Kongo is a church. But when you look at the face of the ancestor Mpanzu, you find that it is technology, applied science. Bundu dia Kongo is thus an institute of scientific research. And when you go to look at Bundu dia Kongo on the face of the ancestor Nzinga, it becomes politics because the king is political" (Kabuayi 2006).

With this knowledge, the painting of Ne Muanda Nsemi discussed at the beginning of the chapter makes even more sense; he wears the color red on his forehead because he belongs to the Nzinga clan and thus is a leader and

FIGURE 6.2. Still video image of Bundu dia Kongo flag with six-pointed star emblem, Luozi, 2006. Image captured by Yolanda Covington-Ward.

engaged in politics. Yet, he holds the blue and yellow scarves, indicating he is also powerful spiritually as the leader of the movement, and is well regarded intellectually as well, as the author of numerous pamphlets and small books on Kongo culture and history, and the mission and ideology of Bundu dia Kongo. The next section of this chapter shall briefly examine the three major "faces" of Bundu dia Kongo.

Spiritual Teachings

In the spiritual teachings of BDK, an ancestral Kongo religion called BuKongo is privileged. In this religion, a spiritual hierarchy exists where a supreme being rests at the top, who is the same for all races and people, who BDK members call Nzambi or Ne Kongo Kalunga (Nsemi 1994a, 3). Beneath the supreme being is a grouping of beings in a celestial hierarchy who again serve all humanity. Beneath them is the "supervisory genie" of the Kongo people, as each nation or grouping of people has their own. Then, lowest in the spiritual hierarchy are divinized ancestors of the Kongo people (*mvidi bakulu*) (Nsemi 1994a, 2). Thus, the prayers of the Kongo people are believed to go up through each level of the spiritual hierarchy before reaching Nzambi: "En route to God, man passes obligatorily through the first bridge that is made up of his divinized ancestors. The second bridge through which he passes is constituted by the supervisory genie of his nationality, and at last through all the great celestial hierarchies devoted to the service of God" (Nsemi 1994a, 2).

In the religion of BuKongo, Christianity is scorned. This is significant because the vast majority of people in the DRC are Christian, and mostly Catholic. The members of Bundu dia Kongo see Christianity as a religion created by and for *mundele*, or white people. According to another interviewee, when a Kongo person prays, the prayers go first to divinized ancestors, such as Simon Kimbangu or Dona Kimpa Vita. Then, these divinized ancestors carry the message on to Ne Muanda Kongo, the archangel and supervisor of the Kongo people, who then carries it to Tata Nzambi Mpungu, who is the highest God.[21] The important role both Simon Kimbangu and Kimpa Vita play as divinized ancestors can also be seen in the lyrics of many of the songs performed in worship. The following is one such example that I observed in Luozi:

Song in Kikongo
Oh, Mfumu Kimbangu wiza
Oh, Ya Kimpa Vita wiza
Wiza kunguna
Mansangaza mu meso meto
Oh, lu babosono
Mansanga lwiza kumuna
Mu meso meto

Song in English
Oh, Mfumu Kimbangu come
Oh, Ya Kimpa Vita come
Come wipe
The tears from our eyes
Oh, everyone
You all come wipe the tears
From our eyes

This song is an appeal to both Kimbangu and Kimpa Vita, major Kongo prophets who have a huge influence on modern Kongo culture and thought. Another notable fact in explaining BDK's constant use of these two prophets is both of them were connected to nationalist movements: Kimpa Vita in advocating for a Catholicism that privileged the perspectives of the Kongo people and for trying to restore a fractured Kongo Kingdom, and Kimbangu, whose movement was eventually associated with calls for independence from

Belgian colonialism. Thus, in invoking these prophets, BDK is connecting their own nationalist movement to famous nationalist movements of the past.

In all, BDK advocates a return to a traditional Kongo religion based on the Kongo people and their experience. One such example of this is the sacred book of BDK. It is called *MaKongo* or *Makaba* and was written by Ne Muanda Nsemi, who was inspired by visions, communications, and revelations from the ancestors. With this sacred book, Ne Muanda Nsemi seeks to establish written legitimacy of his ideas and BuKongo as a religion. He challenges the hegemony of other sacred books such as the Bible, which many people accept as unquestionable truth, but was also written by people inspired by visions and revelations.

Scientific Mission

The scientific (or cultural) teachings of BDK revolve around a revitalization of Kongo culture and history. The centerpiece of activities in this vein is the privileging of the use of the Kikongo language. For BDK members, Kikongo is the preferred language for everyday conversation, speeches, and community worship. Members drop any European names and privilege their Kikongo names. Men also place the word "Ne" in front of their names as a male honorific term, like the use of "Mr." or "Sir" in English, and women are referred to as "Ma," which is a term already in common use (I was referred to as Ma Londa or Mama Londa by most of the people I came in contact with in Luozi, whether members of BDK or not). The speaking of French or other languages of the Congo, such as Lingala—the dominant language in Kinshasa and in the popular music scene—is discouraged. The women in BDK don't wear pants, makeup, or hair extensions or wigs. Polygamy is authorized as one of many ways to return to traditional, precolonial practices. This stands out because official polygyny is rare in the DRC, perhaps because it was extremely discouraged and actively combated by missionaries during the colonial period, and was taxed and then restricted by the Belgian government. The use of drugs is also not condoned, and periods of sexual abstinence are required for those people who are very spiritually advanced in the group (Ne Mosi, October 10, 2005).[22]

Political Strivings

Bundu dia Kongo is most well known for their political activities. The political teachings of BDK have one central objective: the reunification and rebuilding of the Kongo Kingdom as a separate nation-state. The major goal of BDK is to have sovereignty over the area that during the precolonial period made up the Kongo Kingdom and its surrounding areas, including parts of

Republic of Congo, the Democratic Republic of Congo, Angola (and even Gabon in some BDK writings). Members of BDK call this area Kongo dia Ntotela. The Kongo people were split into these different political entities during the colonial period. The group advocates their reunification based not only on righting past colonial wrongs, but also on satisfying the will of God.

> The politics of Bundu dia Kongo . . . must first be a politics that must be in accordance with the law of nature, the law of God. That is to say, first to do all to accomplish the will of God, this politics must be in accordance with divine law. Thus, we for example, the Kongo people, it is God that created us, so that we are BaKongo. And the colonialists came and divided us. The BaKongo were divided in three countries, Angola, Belgian Congo, French Congo. Whereas . . . God in his will had created one people. Then, it was the colonial politics that go against divine will. And, it is for that reason that Bundu dia Kongo, to rehabilitate, to conform to the will of God, searches to reunify that which God had created united, that is to say, the reunification of the Kongo people. (Ne Mosi, October 10, 2005)

Thus, Bundu dia Kongo's goal of the reunification of the Kongo people is based on erasing arbitrary colonial divisions and also finds authority in the spiritual will of God, who is said to have originally created a unitary Kongo people. In this way, Bundu dia Kongo is able to put forth spiritual backing for their political mission.

Sovereignty is a huge issue for BDK members, who insist that Kongo people rule over their own land. Currently, as Bas-Congo is still a part of the DRC, BDK members protest people from other provinces who are not Bena Kongo having positions of power in Bas-Congo. These cultural foreigners usually don't speak Kikongo and members of BDK see them as ineffective leaders who can't understand how to govern in Bas-Congo, and whose political authority shouldn't be respected or acknowledged because they are not Kongo people. A recent example of this was BDK challenges to the gubernatorial elections in Bas-Congo, when Simon Mbtashi Mbatshia (a candidate who some Kongo people saw as loyal to non-Kongo interests) and Déo Nkusu, his running mate for vice/deputy governor, were declared the winners in an extremely close race with Léonard Fuka Unzola and Ne Muanda Nsemi, who of course had the support of BDK (Mona 2007). Clashes with police forces during BDK protests and marches throughout the Lower Congo led to more than one hundred deaths in late January and early February of 2007, followed by other confrontations (Mabandu 2008). Before this, people were killed on both sides in numerous incidents of violence in confrontations between BDK and police or military forces sent to quell protests and restore order (although the vast majority of the fatalities were BDK members).

The first major victory for Bundu dia Kongo in the political arena was in a competitive election in 2006 when Ne Muanda Nsemi won the sole seat in the National Assembly to represent the territory of Luozi. This became a springboard for his subsequent bid for vice governor in 2007, and then his subsequent reelection to the National Assembly in 2011, this time representing Kinshasa. All of this demonstrates the growing political power of Bundu dia Kongo as a movement, a point we will return to later in this chapter. In all, for members of Bundu dia Kongo, the history of economic exploitation and violence that characterized the colonial period was further exacerbated by the marginalization of Kongo people in a postcolonial society. In a country where politics are still organized around ethnic allegiances, the Kongo people have not been able to garner any major political clout, not since the election of Joseph Kasa-Vubu as the first president of a newly independent Congo in 1960. Moreover, the Lower Congo province is still a mainly rural province (outside of the major towns dotting the railway and main road between Kinshasa and the port city of Matadi), which has not experienced much development since independence. Thus for many Kongo people, Bundu dia Kongo is an effective tool to address these social and political disparities.

Bundu dia Kongo Organization, Membership, and Reception

In his description of an organizational structure that can be used to develop reformulated Pan-African religions across the world, Ne Muanda Nsemi discusses members of religions being organized into "prayer and research groups" rather than churches: "These groups are not churches; they are centers of research charged with gathering, in each nationality (in each tribe), the materials that constitute the doctrine of the Negro African Church, of which the Kongo religion is the principal axis" (1994a, 11). More specifically, these groups are called *zikua* (*mazikua* in plural) (Wamba-dia-Wamba 1999, 217; Nsemi 1994a, unnumbered page). In regards to the membership of the BDK movement, according to Wamba-dia-Wamba, in 1994, there were close to fifty thousand members in around five hundred mazikua (1999, 217). More than a decade later, in 2005–6, although I did not get any estimate of the membership, the numbers at the time were likely growing as the movement gained popularity.

So far, this chapter has discussed the reception (or lack thereof) of the Bundu dia Kongo movement by the government, police, and military forces as evidenced by the numerous conflicts and fatalities. Evidently, BDK's growing calls for sovereignty and political power threaten many groups and institutions. Yet, what do other Kongo people who are not members of Bundu dia Kongo think of the group and movement?

In my conversations with Kongo people in both Kinshasa and Luozi, the overwhelming sense I got was that many Kongo people applauded the call for political power, the revitalization of Kongo culture, and the recognition of important Kongo cultural heroes. The goal of reforming the Kongo Kingdom also was seen as a positive, for the most part. People often said that Bundu dia Kongo was saying publicly the things that many Kongo people thought themselves. However, the point where many Kongo people tended to diverge from the group was on religion. Many BisiKongo who were not members of Bundu dia Kongo berated the group for its derision of Jesus Christ and Christianity. In fact, there have been several instances of physical confrontations between Bundu dia Kongo members and members of Christian churches.[23] However, the possibility of larger political and ethnonational goals overriding religious loyalties can be seen in the results of both elections of Ne Muanda Nsemi to the National Assembly.

Before Slavery, Christianity, and Colonialism: History in BDK Politics

October 9, 2005. Today I am going to the Bundu dia Kongo zikua in Luozi. Ne Zole comes to get me about fifteen minutes after 9:00 AM, and David goes with me. We walk to the church, which is a brown thatch and stick structure, with a thatch roof as well (see figure 6.3). People have their shoes off, and when I finally sit down and remove my shoes, two guys come around to collect everyone's shoes and put them outside.

The seats are elevated wooden slats that form benches, and I notice immediately the men on one side and the women on the other side, like in the DMNA church. I count those in attendance several times throughout the service, and the numbers are something like this: twenty-four adult men, eleven adult women, and fifteen children and teenagers, including six boys, and nine girls. Men are definitely in the majority, contrasting vividly with the congregations I have observed in the DMNA, CEC, and even Kimbanguist churches in Luozi. There is a desk in the front center of the space, with three cups on it, red, blue, and yellow, to represent Nsaku, Mpanzu, Nzinga (religion, science, and politics). Underneath the desk are three baskets, red, green (supposed to be blue), and yellow, and when the offering takes place, people place their money or gift in the basket that corresponds to their ancestral clan.[24] The man leading the session is seated behind the desk, and there are chairs on either side of him, and Ne Zole sits in one of the chairs. I sit on the side in a more gender-neutral space. As an invited guest, Ne Zole asks me to stand

FIGURE 6.3. Bundu dia Kongo zikua, Luozi, 2005. Photo by Yolanda Covington-Ward.

and introduces me to the congregation. A small group of people comes to the front of the church, and as I continue to stand, they sing a song composed in my honor. I include the text below, first in French then in English:

Song in French
I.
En Egypt, ils étaient nos esclaves
Ces Européens qui envient toujours nos richesses
Au point de se réuni et se partagent l'Afrique
Voila la source de notre malheur!
(refrain)
Du partage de l'Afrique commençaient nos souffrances
Notre ancêtre Nzinga fût enterrée vivante,
Yaya Vita-Kimpa notre sœur jetée vivante au feu!
Tandis qu'ils ont condamné à mort notre grand prophète Kimbangu.
Oh! Quel enfer pour toi noir qui se dit (éparse?) de Jésus?
Qu'as-tu fait du mal pour mériter ce sort?
Uniquement parce que Dieu te donne un pays riche!
Et toi albinos qui t'a donné l'Europe?
Rentre chez-toi, je t'en prie
Ramène avec toi les armes et ta bible.

II.

Ils ont amené des fusils pour tuer les noirs

La bible et leur religion nous a été imposée par la force,

A grand prix ils ont vendu les noirs

Nos objets d'art et autres biens prétendus (impie, impie)!

III.

Dans leurs belles maisons, une fortune sale

Fruits de leurs vols et de l'exploitation des noirs

Du fond en comble, ils pillé notre pays,

N'est-ce pas qu'ils disent que voler c'est un péché!

Song in English

I.

In Egypt, they were our slaves

These Europeans who envied all of our riches

To the point of meeting and dividing up Africa

There is the source of our misfortune!

(refrain)

With the dividing up of Africa our suffering began

Our ancestor Nzinga was buried alive

Yaya Vita-Kimpa our sister thrown live into the fire!

While they condemned to death our great prophet Kimbangu

Oh! What hell for you black person who tells himself to hope in Jesus?

What wrong did you do to deserve this fate?

Only because God gives you a rich country!

And you albinos what has Europe given you?

Go back home, would you please

Take back with you the weapons and your Bible

II.

They brought guns in order to kill Black people

The Bible and their religion were imposed upon us by force

At a high price they sold Black people

Our objects of art and other goods laid claim to (ungodly, ungodly)

III.

In their beautiful homes, a dirty fortune

Fruits of their thefts and the exploitation of Black people

From top to bottom, they pillage our country

Isn't it true that they say that stealing is a sin!

This song reveals the importance of understanding and using history for BDK's larger goals. Evidently, while portraying some of the key ideological elements of Bundu dia Kongo, the composer(s) of the song are also trying to connect with my identity as an African American. My positionality is particularly important in that not only was the song composed for me (the hastily scribbled words were handed to me on a piece of paper at the end of the song) but it was also written in French, since my hosts knew my Kikongo was limited. This stands out as members of Bundu dia Kongo make a concerted effort to speak in Kikongo as opposed to other languages. As a "sister" of the African diaspora (and potentially the Kongo diaspora as they explained to me) and student of Kongo culture and history, they clearly expected many of the themes in the song to resonate with my own experiences and sentiments, which they did.

This song directly critiques Christianity and injustices dealt out by European perpetrators. Treachery and hypocrisy on the part of Europeans are contrasted with African suffering at their hands and nostalgia for a great African past before their arrival. The song chronicles the unjust deaths of divinized ancestors such as Simon Kimbangu and Vita Kimpa, the transatlantic trade in enslaved Africans, the parceling of the African continent at the Berlin conference and thefts, violence, and exploitation that defined subsequent European colonization in Africa. These stand in stark relief against Christianity, a religion that supposedly stands for peace and love, and yet, "the Bible and the gun" often worked hand and hand in oppressing native populations during the colonial period.

The opening line, "In Egypt, they were our slaves," references a longing for a past when relative positions of authority were reversed. It also establishes a kinship bond with the great civilization of Egypt, a point expounded on considerably in writings of Ne Muanda Nsemi and in the sacred book *Makongo*, which discusses the migration of the founders of the Kongo Kingdom from Egypt. The suffering of Africans, which continues in the present, is juxtaposed with the riches and relative comfort Europeans have gained through slavery and colonization, and continue to gain through the exploitation of Africa's natural resources. The song ties directly into many of the goals of Bundu dia Kongo: to have Kongo people reject Christianity, which members of BDK see as a white man's religion used to oppress them; to have Kongo people govern not only Kongo people but historically Kongo land so they benefit from its vast resources; and to re-form and re-create the Kongo Kingdom that was so divided by arbitrary colonial boundaries. These political claims to sovereignty and land are not made without justification; in fact, BDK strategically employs a history of a magnificent past to bolster its claims in the present.

In BDK there is a particular narrative of the origins and migration of the Bena Kongo connecting the Kongo people to great civilizations and thus supporting claims for sovereignty in the present. This narrative greatly differs from largely accepted histories of the Bantu Migration from the Cameroon/Nigeria area down into central and southern Africa. According to Ne Muanda Nsemi, the Bena Kongo come from a fascinating union. Beings from space (*bana ba zulu*) came from the planet KaKongo and descended into Ethiopia. There, they intermarried with the *Bana ba Tumi*, people coming from India, and gave birth to the primordial ancestors, and in turn, the Kongo people. According to a passage from the sacred book *Makaba*, Nzambi passed on a powerful message to the Bena Kongo:

> 101. You are my elected people
> Your first ancestors came from space
> But you, you were born in Ethiopia
> 102. I brought you to Egypt
> Now I make you leave Egypt
> And I send you far beyond Ethiopia. . . .
> 104. You will inhabit the Promised Land
> Of a great king, the great Mani Kongo
> Who will come from the sky, from space
> 105. It is here that the prophecies will be fulfilled. . . .
> The light that will rehabilitate the world
> Will come from Kongo dia Ntotela (quoted in Nsemi 1994b, 2–3)

According to BDK, the journey of the Bena Kongo began in Ethiopia and eventually ended in West Central Africa (see figure 6.4). In this story of migration the Kongo people were born in Ethiopia and dispersed into Nubia, Egypt, and even Israel as well. They dispersed further south into Africa, influencing and intermarrying with groups in Namibia, Zimbabwe, and South Africa. The majority of people made it to the Promised Land in West Central Africa and founded Kongo dia Ntotila. From there they spread east and northward into the Manianga area across the Congo River. In the year 690 many people returned to Kongo dia Ntotila, and 691 signaled the end of the construction of Mbanza Kongo. This date differs from the one posited by historians of the Kongo region, who have suggested the fourteenth century rather than the seventh century as the most likely date for the consolidation of the Kongo Kingdom.[25] With the arrival of the Portuguese in 1482, the Kongo Kingdom made contact with Europeans, and the transatlantic trade in enslaved Africans led to the dispersal of Kongo people into the Americas. These people are referred to by BDK as the diaspora. In addition, with the founding of Liberia in 1847 by freeborn and newly freed enslaved Africans, some people of the African diaspora went back to Africa, and some of them were Kongo people.

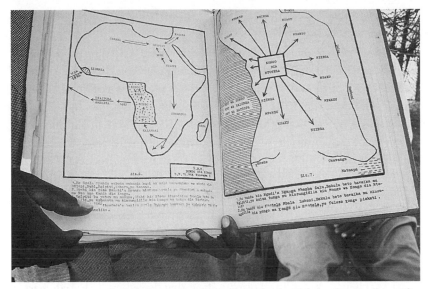

FIGURE 6.4. Portrayal of the migration of Bena Kongo in the *Makaba*, the sacred text of the Bundu dia Kongo movement (published circa 1989, by Ne Muanda Nsemi, the leader of the movement). Photo by author, Luozi, 2006.

BDK bases this idea on the fact that in Monrovia there is a neighborhood called Congo town, and Americo-Liberians are also called Congos.[26]

The BDK narrative of the migration of the Bena Kongo explicitly rejects both the historical time line and origins narrative that historians use. Since the overarching goal of the group is to rebuild the Kongo Kingdom, gain sovereignty for Kongo people and reclaim land divided by colonial powers, reworking the historical narrative to place the Kongo people and the building of the kingdom earlier on the time line strengthens claims for sovereignty and rights to the land. The story of supernatural and extraordinary origins is also useful for demonstrating the unique and special nature of the Kongo people, and the story of the migration and connections to other ethnic groups is useful for gaining the support of other groups and emphasizing Kongo dia Ntotila as the Promised Land, the final destination of a continuously displaced people. In all, the historical claims of BDK, from the narrative of migration from Egypt, to their time line for the establishment of the Kongo Kingdom, to their connections to the wider diaspora, all serve to show that the Kongo people are special and unique with a great history. This then supports their demands for sovereignty and autonomy. Such demands, however, have antecedents from which BDK drew many lessons in designing their own strategies for achieving their larger political goals.

The Continuity of Kongo Nationalism

Bundu dia Kongo is not the first and will likely not be the last group organized around the goal of reuniting the Kongo people under a restored and sovereign Kongo Kingdom, or to deal with issues of the revitalization of Kongo culture. L'Association Musicale BaKongo (AMUBAKO), founded in 1940 by J. Tangala, and Renaissance BaKongo (RENAIBAKO), founded in 1944 in Kinshasa by J. Mavuela, are two examples of early associations formed during the colonial period that dealt with Kongo cultural issues (Centre de Recherche et d'Information Socio-politiques 1962, 10).[27] However, both of these organizations had basically ceased to function when the most memorable, significant, and really most revolutionary organization was founded in 1950 by M. Edward Nzeza-Landu: ABAKO (Association des BaKongo).[28] This organization would eventually play a crucial role in calls for a sovereign Kongo nation and independence from colonial rule for the country as a whole.

ABAKO began as a cultural organization that, based on its initial charter, sought to "unify, conserve, and perfect the Kongo language" (CRISP 1962, 10). Created in Leopoldville as a "scientific, linguistic, cultural and social organization" (CRISP 1962, 14) based on the Kikongo of "Ntotila" or "Mbanza Kongo,"[29] the organization sought primarily to publish a journal in Kikongo and organize cultural activities. This focus on the Kikongo language took place in a context of changing demographics, where although the Kongo ethnic group made up an estimated 60 percent of the African population of Leopoldville (La Fontaine 1970, 40–41), the preferred language of the city was quickly becoming Lingala, a trade language based on the Bobangi language of the Upper Congo River (Verhaegen 2003, 90–91). As a language developed for trade purposes between Europeans and middlemen on the Upper Congo River, Lingala also came to dominate the colonial army, administration, and many missions in Leopoldville as many of the workers in these institutions were also from this area (Verhaegen 2003, 91–92). The people from the Upper River areas are often collectively referred to as Bangala,[30] although Lingala is not the true indigenous language of any one group. Thus, in the growing city of Leopoldville, although the BaKongo dominated numerically, their language was in fact not the primary non-European language being spoken (Covington-Ward 2012, 74). ABAKO's focus on the preservation and proliferation of the Kikongo language was highly significant in the plural society of Leopoldville at the time, and even in the present, as demonstrated by organizations such as Bundu dia Kongo that seek to promote Kikongo.

Although the urge to preserve and advocate the use of Kikongo was an important objective of ABAKO, calls for Kongo nationalism appeared simultaneously. Dialectical variants of Kikongo were to be brought together in the pages of the journal of ABAKO serving as a form of "linguistic nationalism" (Verhaegen 2003, 94) that sought to include not only all the Kongo subgroups in the Belgian Congo (Bantandu, Bandibu, BaManianga, and so on) but also "a page for the BaKongo of the A.E.F.[31] and another, for our dear brothers of Angola" (CRISP Centre de Recherche et d'Information Socio-politiques 1962, 12). Indeed, all Kongo people who defined themselves as "brothers who came from the same founder/roots: Kongo dia Ntotila" were encouraged to join (CRISP 1962, 11). Thus, this founding charter had most of the major ideological components of later manifestations of Kongo nationalism: shared language and history of the Kongo Kingdom serving as the basis of Kongo cultural unity, revitalization of Kongo culture and language, and a reimagining of Kongo areas geographically, across existing borders, revised to include the relevant provinces in the Belgian Congo, people in the French Congo, Portuguese Cabinda, and Angola (Verhaegen 2003, 127). These are all key elements that also define the ideology of Bundu dia Kongo today.

Joseph Kasa-Vubu was elected president of ABAKO in 1954, replacing Edmond Nzeza-Landu. In August of the same year, ABAKO made its first attempt at political action, by presenting some of its leaders to the colonial administration as candidates to administer the Congolese section of the city. Although another non-Kongo person was chosen, this attempt foreshadowed the increased political engagement of ABAKO that would take place in the future (CRISP 1962, 29–30). ABAKO came to lead the call and political action advocating for the independence of the Congo, asserting great influence on the political process and resulting in Joseph Kasa-Vubu becoming president of the country alongside Prime Minister Patrice Lumumba (Covington-Ward 2012).

In all, ABAKO serves as the closest and most relevant predecessor of the mission and ideology of Bundu dia Kongo. At the moment of the critical transition to independence in the late 1950s and early 1960s, Kongo people rallied together and organized in pursuit of the goal of not only political power, but also Kongo sovereignty. Likewise, as the country transitioned to yet another new governmental structure in 2006 (the third republic),[32] political conditions were amicable to fostering the rise of Bundu dia Kongo as a movement that renews dormant sentiments for a restored Kongo Kingdom and seeks to augment the political strength of Kongo people overall.

Bundu dia Kongo and Pan-African Consciousness

Bundu dia Kongo has many similarities with movements and ideas from throughout the African diaspora. Moreover, among the many ideological sentiments of Bundu dia Kongo lay explicit calls for Pan-Africanism and efforts to establish and maintain connections with people of the African diaspora worldwide. This section shall briefly explore some of the Pan-Africanist tendencies and beliefs of BDK. With this, it becomes clear that Bundu dia Kongo, while a locally based organization grounded in Kikongo and histories and cultural ideas relevant to the Kongo people, also has and seeks to have a broader appeal and relevance extending beyond Kongo cultural borders.

Pan-Africanism can be generally defined as "a wide range of ideologies that are committed to common political or cultural projects for Africans and people of African descent" (Appiah and Gates, 1999, 1484). Appearing first in the African diaspora in the nineteenth century, Pan-Africanism involved ideas such as the unity and common destiny of people of African descent around the world, divine providence derived from the Bible, the need for the establishment of an independent nation-state, Black control over African land, and a focus on emigration of the African diaspora, often but not always, back to Africa, among other ideas.

Ne Muanda Nsemi and Bundu dia Kongo as a movement advocate many of the aforementioned theoretical components of Pan-Africanism. For example, Ne Muanda Nsemi prophesizes and encourages the return of Africans in the Kongo diaspora back to Kongo, where the Kongo diaspora as I understand it means people descended from enslaved Africans possibly taken from the Kongo area, and also Kongos in Liberia. In preparation for the moment when there will be a massive migration of the African diaspora to the Lower Congo, BDK has laid out several rules for their integration into society, including: to accept and follow the true religion of the Kongo people, which is BuKongo, including its rules of conduct and rituals of prayer; to learn and speak only the Kikongo language; to register with the minister of the interior of the Kongo government; and to share all their knowledge with their Kongo brethren and work for the well-being of the Kongo people (Ne Zole, February 8, 2006).

Ne Muanda Nsemi's ideas of Pan-Africanism can also be seen in his objectives regarding Kongo sovereignty and how these interact with the larger continent of Africa. Seeking first to establish an independent Kongo nation, he then envisions abolishing all colonial frontiers, forming medium sized autonomous states that can then be grouped into five confederations,[33] which themselves would then form the United States of Africa (1995, unnumbered page). While the United States of Africa is not a new concept, dating back to Kwame Nkrumah's ideas and the debates surrounding the original formation of the Organization of African Unity, the larger objective of uniting all of Africa plays a key role in Ne Muanda Nsemi's writings and the goals of BDK as a whole.[34]

Reformed Bodies, Re-formed Histories:
Bimpampa in Bundu dia Kongo

As we have seen throughout the previous chapters, everyday cultural performances play an important role in creating, confirming, and challenging social
orders, structures, and ideals of authority. The members of Bundu dia Kongo
have made a concerted effort to publicize and popularize their points of view
through printed pamphlets translated into multiple languages, vocal protests
and gatherings, as well as through how they use their bodies. Citing Pierre
Bourdieu's concept of bodily practices as a form of mnemonics, John and
Jean Comaroff emphasize the importance of targeting bodily reform in situations of social transformation for the Tshidi in South Africa: "Scrambling
this code—that is, erasing the messages carried in banal physical practice—is
a prerequisite for retraining the memory, either to deschool the deviant *or to
shape new subjects as the bearers of new worlds*" (1992, 70, emphasis mine).
Along these same lines, Bundu dia Kongo uses Kongo *bimpampa* and modifications to other forms of embodied practice and comportment to remake
its members, and other people (both Kongo and non-Kongo) who come
into contact with them, as the creators of a very particular social world: a
re-formed Kongo Kingdom. Simultaneously, bimpampa are used as a form
of mnemonics to activate particular cultural memories of the glory of, and
everyday practice within, that same kingdom. Bula makonko (cupped hand
clapping), dekama (genuflection), fukama (kneeling), and yinama (bowing)
all play significant roles in the everyday efforts to recreate the former Kongo
Kingdom here on earth in the present day.

Bula Makonko and Fukama

The primary example of the modification and amplification of certain embodied practices to further the goals of Bundu dia Kongo is bula makonko, a
form of bimpampa based on a cupped clapping of the hands that makes a
sound like Bo! Bo! Bo! Bula makonko is a gesture of respect that could often
be seen in the interactions between the Kongo king (*mfumu*) and his court,
and between members of the nobility and people of lower social classes. For
example, a sixteenth-century report of Catholic missionaries in the Kongo
Kingdom revealed that when the Kongo king eats boiled or roasted meat
with his fingers from a large pot in front of him, he then "distributes it to
his servants, giving to each their ration, which they receive with big claps of
the two hands in a sign of thanks" (Cuvelier and Jadin 1954, 132–33). Moreover, twice a year the governors and local leaders throughout the kingdom
come to the capital to pay their tribute to the king. When the king expresses

his approval to a governor, the governor claps his hands many times. "In a sign of contentment, he throws himself to the ground, covering his body in dust. His servants (*baleke*) do the same thing" (Cuvelier and Jadin 1954, 133). Similar behavior is expressed by the winner of a civil dispute who "claps his hands, covers himself in dust, and was conducted throughout the town in triumph" (Cuvelier and Jadin 1954, 135; also see the relation of Father Laurent de Lucques, Cuvelier 1953b, 82).

Further, when the king leaves his home, those around him must demonstrate their respect and ask for his blessing, as illustrated in the report of Giovanni Francesco da Roma, an Italian Capuchin missionary who was stationed in Mbanza Kongo from 1645 to 1646, and in Loanda for several months during 1647: "The courtiers and soldiers who are held in the interior court, get on their knees and, in quickly making two or three claps of the hands, each asks his blessing; the king holds the right hand, lightly moving the fingers as if he is playing the lute. The one to which the king would not stretch the hand in this way, would think himself unfortunate because this would be an evident index that he fell in disgrace. The king takes around half an hour to give everyone his blessing in this way (Bontinck 1964, 125).

This passage suggests a belief on the part of the courtiers in the blessing of the king, demonstrating the intertwining of both political and spiritual authority, and that the position of the Kongo king could be considered to embody divine kingship.[35] Other examples of bimpampa in everyday interactions outside of the court reveal that bula makonko also seems to have been an embodied form of greeting. Respect must be shown by anyone who encounters someone of higher rank on the road for example: "Meeting on the road any person of quality, they get on their knees, greet them with a clapping of the hands and continue on their journey. If they are equals, they simply continue on their way" (Cuvelier 1953b, 81). Capuchin missionary Luc da Caltanisetta's observations, however, suggest bula makonko played a role even in greetings between equals in the town of Ngobila in 1698: "In this mbanza, we could also observe how these people greet each other: they touch each other's right hand, by lightly hitting it, and then having withdrawn the hand, each hits his own hands three times one against the other; finally the person inferior in rank continues to clap his hands in order to ask the blessing of he that is superior, who during this time remains motionless" (Bontinck 1970, 130).

In the precolonial era, bula makonko then, was used in a wide variety of ways; to say thank you, to ask for forgiveness or pardon, as a gesture of respect, or additionally, as a greeting. Many Kongo people do still use this gesture in Luozi and other parts of Lower Congo, but it doesn't seem to be the main form of greeting used in interactions. Rather, one observes men touching heads three times while shaking hands and women kissing on the cheek thrice in Kinshasa, and handshakes by both sexes (often while grasping the right wrist or elbow with the left hand) combined with dekama for women and yinama for men in Luozi. However, in Bundu dia Kongo bula makonko (combined with dekama for women and yinama for men) is used as their way of greeting not only other members of the movement but also almost all people with whom they come into contact. Members of BDK, through their responses and lack of responses in interactions with others, subtly influence the embodied practices of others. In fact, if when people on the road in Luozi or in the streets of Kinshasa greet each other in this particular way (cupped hand clapping rather than touching one another), it is an embodied signifier that they are most likely members of Bundu dia Kongo. In conversations with members, they explained to me that this way of greeting one another was the normal form of greeting in the Kongo Kingdom, and they are bringing it back into present day use. It can thus be seen as an embodied form both of history and of cultural revitalization, a way of moving that represents an ideology and appreciation for Kongo culture and history that is put into practice in everyday gesture for members of Bundu dia Kongo. The moments of awkwardness that arise when a person reaches out to shake hands and is met by empty air, are used as opportunities for educating nonmembers of Bundu dia Kongo about the meaning and history of the gesture. In fact, BisiKongo who are not members of the group are often scolded for not embodying this form of greeting, which Bundu dia Kongo members tout as the most authentic and traditional form, in comparison to the disdained "white man's" handshake.

Bula makonko as the preferred method of greeting is one example of how, through embodied cultural performances, members of Bundu dia Kongo are establishing their own authority in their local settings. As I observed in Luozi, people in the town knew the members of Bundu dia Kongo, and would in fact be sure to use bula makonko as a greeting when interacting with them, even if only to avoid a verbal chastisement (see figure 6.5). Thus, with every cupped hand-clapping greeting of their members and especially the people around them who are not members of the group, Bundu dia Kongo challenges the cultural and political authority of non-Kongo people while simultaneously laying the ground for their own authority in regards to Kongo people.

Bula makonko is also incorporated into the ritual practices of Bundu dia Kongo. In this particular context, it seems to take on meanings more associated with opening and closing prayers, asking for forgiveness, and expressing gratitude rather than being simply a greeting. Fukama or kneeling also plays a major role in that during services that I attended in the local BDK zikua and even more so during the February mass meeting described earlier in the

FIGURE 6.5. Demonstration of the bula makonko gesture, Luozi, 2010. Photo by Yolanda Covington-Ward.

chapter, the vast majority of the worship service was done while kneeling. In this posture, pants are rolled up and skirts pushed out of the way so that the bare skin of the knees actually touches the rocky ground (see figure 6.6).

I was told that being on one's knees causes a person to suffer while in the process of repenting (Ne Zole, February 9, 2006). At the February 2006 BDK mass meeting, the leader of the service faced everyone else in the audience, also on his knees, with a microphone in hand. During the first opening songs of the service during the mass meeting, the crowd sang along as everyone simultaneously clapped. Then, the next part of the service involved a vocal call of "*Yenge*" (peace) issued by the leader to which the crowd responded bodily with three cupped claps, followed by a short prayer that began "*Nzitusu kwa batata bampungu tulendo*" (give thanks to the all-powerful fathers). This sequence was repeated several times. In this instance, bula makonko was used to open the prayer giving thanks to the spiritual beings of the Bukongo religion, including the divinized ancestors, supervisory genie, upper celestial hierarchy, and Nzambi.

One of the most notable and important aspects of the service of Bundu dia Kongo is a long, intense prayer punctuated by bula makonko that is done by the kneeling members of the zikua. The text of the prayer is as follows:

FIGURE 6.6. Bula makonko and fukama in the zikua of Bundu dia Kongo, Luozi, 2005. Photo by Yolanda Covington-Ward.

Prayer in Kikongo
Kembo, Kembo, Kembo,
mu kayengele vava ntoto,
yenge mayangi mingi kiese
mu kumbwa tata mpungu tulendo
tu lombele mlemvo watata mpungu tulendo

Prayer in English
Joy, Joy, Joy
in the sky, Joy here on land
A lot of joy, happiness
In the name of the all-powerful father God,
We ask for forgiveness from the all-powerful father.
(translation provided by Pierre, research assistant)

I witnessed this prayer at the February 2006 mass meeting and in every local zikua service as well. In unison, the church members begin to simultaneously pray out loud and clap quickly with their hands cupped in four-four time. According to interviewee Ne Zole, the clapping is done for purification and to ask for forgiveness from Nzambi Mpungu (God) for sins committed (February 9, 2006). I did, however, note some differences in this particular worship practice in regards to the number of times it was enacted.

At the mass meeting, the leader called out *"Iya, Sambodia, Iya,"* or "Four, Seven, Four" in Kikongo, perhaps as a reminder to the participants of the number of times they were to repeat the prayer for each section. The members present then repeated the prayer four times with clapping,[36] seven times without clapping, and then another four times with the clapping. However, at the services I attended in the local zikua, the prayer was repeated forty, then seventy-two, then forty times (I actually counted them). When I asked about this particular sequence and number of claps, I was told they represent the number of stages of the passage of the prayers to God: from the BisiKongo, to divinized ancestors, to Ne Muanda Kongo the archangel, and finally to Tata Nzambi Mpungu.

As the prayer is repeated over and over again with the clapping, it becomes like a chant intonated in unison by the members of Bundu dia Kongo. In the context of the worship service, the repetitive gesture of bula makonko takes center stage as an embodied cultural performance for Nzambi that is an act of simultaneous repentance and demanding forgiveness. This chanted and clapped prayer thus presents a challenge to the hegemonic Christian "prayer pose" of unmoving palms clasped together, fingers pointing upward, that one finds in all the worship services of Christians churches of Luozi, whether Protestant or Catholic, DMNA or CEC. Moreover, as this prayer and especially the clapping are seen as a means of purification and seeking absolution, bula makonko in this ritual context presents an embodied alternative to global mainstream Christian rituals such as water immersion, confession, and in the past, self-flagellation. The number of claps represents the number of stages that the prayers must pass through to reach Nzambi. Thus, this particular use of the gesture of bula makonko actually embodies the religion of BuKongo and enacts an alternate spiritual realm where divinized ancestors regain their rightful place, an archangel looks out for the Kongo people, and the messages of the BisiKongo ascend a spiritual hierarchy where Jesus Christ has no place. In this sense, bula makonko can be seen as a direct challenge to the religious hegemony of Christianity in the Lower Congo and its relevance to the experience and needs of the Kongo people.

Bula makonko is used in other ways in the spiritual worship service of Bundu dia Kongo. For instance, the three principal attributes of God are also reflected in hand clapping practices to open, close, and punctuate prayers, such as when the leader vocalizes and the congregation responds with three claps:

Mu zola (3 claps) (love)
Mu ngangu (3 claps) (intelligence)
Mu lendo (3 claps) (power)

Bula makonko in a sequence of three cupped claps was also used in other parts of the service, for example in response to a call intoning the names of the three founding ancestors of the Kongo people "*Nsaku, Mpanzu, Nzinga*."[37] Moreover, at times the congregation would respond to calls of "*kunda*" or "*tukunda*" to open or close a prayer with three cupped claps. Kunda in Kikongo (*kukunda* in the infinitive) has several related meanings, including to salute or honor someone by clapping and bowing slightly, to worship, to implore, to invoke, to ask for pardon (Laman [1936] 1964, 335).[38] In this case, prayers and embodied practices are both intertwined in the carrying of the message of the group to the spiritual world. Bula makonko then, is a multivalent embodied cultural performance that can be used to address and interact with both the spiritual realm and beings here on earth. All these examples demonstrate the importance of embodied cultural performances such as bimpampa like bula makonko for manifesting in the body the beliefs and goals of Bundu dia Kongo, both in ritual space and also in interactions in everyday life.

Yinama

Another way of using the body that I consider is *yinama* (bowing), which again is a sign of respect often coupled with bula makonko. For example, Bundu dia Kongo members bowed in unison at the end of several prayers that began with bula makonko during the worship services. However, yinama plays a major role in another part of the service, one which BDK has creatively reimagined. MuKongo scholars such as Tata Fu-Kiau Bunseki and anthropologists such as Wyatt MacGaffey have studied the cosmology of the Kongo people, and one concept they have written about is a cycle of life that follows the counterclockwise path of the sun, and has four major points.[39] Thus, contrary to popular belief, the cross was not introduced to Africans by Christian missionaries but was known in Kongo culture before the arrival of Europeans. Life was seen as a cycle between the two worlds, with the upper half of the cross representing the world of the living, and the lower half that of the dead, with the two worlds thought to be reflections of each other across a large body of water often known as Kalunga, which divides the two worlds (W. MacGaffey 1986b; Thompson 1983; Thompson and Cornet 1981). Thompson and Cornet further explain the four points in the cycle of life between two worlds as four moments of the sun: "the Four Moments of the Sun—that is, dawn, noon, sunset, and midnight. . . . The right hand sphere or corner stands for dawn which, in turn, is the sign of a life beginning. Noon, the uppermost disk or corner, indicated the flourishing of life, the point of most ascendant power. Next . . . come change and flux, the setting of the sun, and

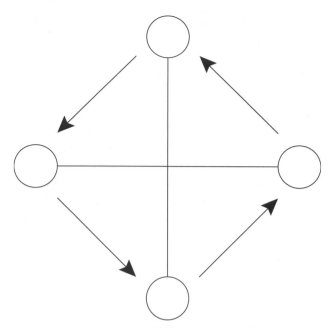

FIGURE 6.7. Adapted image of the Four Moments of the Sun (originally portrayed in A. kia Bunseki-Lumanisa Fu-Kiau, *N'Kongo ye nza yakun'zungidila/Le Mukongo et le monde qui l'entourait*, 1969)

death, marked by the left-hand median point or disk (Thompson and Cornet 1981, 27–28). There are many symbolic drawings of this concept, including a spiral, a diamond, but namely a cross. The cross is symbolic of the meeting of the two worlds, and the crossroads (where four roads meet) thus has significance as a place of extreme spiritual power (see figure 6.7).

In the worship services of Bundu dia Kongo, there is a practice of the entire congregation turning to the four cardinal points while in the midst of song and bowing at each point in unison. The chorus of this song is, "O Kongo Dieto, Tulombele." *Lomba* as a verb (*kulomba* in the infinitive) has a number of related meanings, including: to pray, to beg, to ask forgiveness or permission, to demand (Laman [1936] 1964, 404). Thus, in this particular context, "O Our Kongo, we ask of you/beg of you" and so on, is an impassioned, sung prayer being sent up to the sky as Bundu dia Kongo members sway gently from side to side with their arms stretched upward, rocking back and forth in time to the music. At the end of each verse and chorus, the crowd bows to that side, and turns in unison to face the next cardinal point and continue the song. When I asked what the turning to the four sides represented, I was told: "We are paying homage to four great angels of the Kongo people: Ne Fwani kia Nzambi; Ne Makinda Ngolo; Ne Nganga Buka; Ne kia kwa Nzambi. They are at the door of the people, and we have to honor them by turning to the four cardinal points at each session" (Ne Tatu, October 23, 2005).

Ne Zole, who echoed Ne Mosi's identification of these four great angels, referred to them as "spiritual beings who know the great secrets of the world" (February 9, 2006). The embodied cultural performance of bowing to the four moments of the sun maps the divinized ancestors of Bundu dia Kongo onto a long standing Kongo cosmological tradition while at the same time making irrelevant Christian theology and the cross as a symbol of the crucifixion of Jesus Christ. Thus, yinama serves as an embodied rejection of and challenge to Christianity, supplication to ancestors, and means of establishing the religious authority of Bundu dia Kongo as a spiritual organization.

Bimpampa as Performative Encounters in BDK

As an organization, Bundu dia Kongo strategically uses bodily reform to transform group consciousness and existing social structures. Bula makonko as a greeting is a daily performative encounter that subtly changes social relationships by bringing together Kongo people as a group through their embodied interaction that references the former Kongo Kingdom. The BDK's use of bula makonko as an intentional greeting in mixed ethnic settings, such as Kinshasa, also helps to draw a line of demarcation between themselves and other ethnic groups as well and provides a visual means of identifying other Kongo people in such a setting. Thus, it aids in furthering sentiments of unity as well as visually representing nationalist aspirations.

Turning to bula makonko, fukama, and yinama in the context of prayer and worship in BDK, while these gestures are most often exhibited in the zikua, at the mass meeting I attended in 2006, everything was done outdoors, in full view of curious non-BDK members. In a town and country where Christianity dominates (whether Catholic or Protestant, former mission church or African Independent Church), BDK members are directly challenging the hegemony of Christian forms of prayer and worship and the relevance of Christianity as a belief system for Kongo people. Public performances of these gestures transform social and political relationships by undermining the existing social hierarchy where Catholic priests and Protestant pastors exercise considerable power in everyday life.

In some ways, Bundu dia Kongo's emphasis on changing how people use their bodies, to shape their consciousness, is similar to that of President Mobutu. By this I mean both Mobutu's government and Bundu dia Kongo's leadership recognized how messages could be transmitted through consistent, daily orchestration of bodily practices. Within Bundu dia Kongo, a new member who uses the bula makonko greeting in daily life and multiple gestures in prayer and worship make the former kingdom real in the present. By embodying manners of interaction that existed in the past and worshipping Kongo ancestors, BDK members are using their bodies to create the past in the present and reposition themselves socially and politically not as members of a marginalized ethnic group and economic class, but rather as men and women worthy of respect and admiration. As BDK strategically deploys the past to shape the present, what do they do with bodies that won't behave?

Conflicting Performances: Machine Guns, Karate Chops, and the Subversion of Official Ideologies

February 18, 2006. I am at the general assembly meeting of BDK in Luozi, waiting for permission to film. A group of singers and musicians enthusiastically play music, and as I wait, I survey the scene and take in the music animating the space. Although like everyone else I rock to the familiar rhythms, frankly I am disappointed, for what I am seeing doesn't seem to go along with the "traditional" ideology of Bundu dia Kongo. I am expecting a concert of traditional instruments, the likes of which I hadn't yet seen during my field research. What I see instead are an electric guitar, a synthesizer, European-made conga drums, bass drums such as found in marching bands, a lone ngongi painted blue, red, and yellow, and several nsakala. The group rented the instruments from the Protestant church right up the road! The performers, a small group of enthusiastic BDK members, are basically singing nationalist battle songs to modern rhythms. As long as the listener didn't understand Kikongo, the music could have been that of any number of popular Congolese artists, from Koffi Olomide to Le Marquis de Maison Mere.[40] For example, the lyrics of one song include the following lines:

Song in Kikongo
Wiza, Dumuka Mu Mvita,
Muanda Nsemi Wiza, dumuka mu mvita
Tata Kimbangu, Wiza, Dumuka mu mvita
Etc.

Song in English
Come, Jump into the fight,
Muanda Nsemi, Come, Jump into the fight
Father Kimbangu, Come, Jump into the fight
Etc.

The song implores the great heroes of BDK and the Kongo people in general to join the fight, and the implications of the fight are numerous: the fight for Kongo sovereignty, the fight against police and state suppression of the movement, the fight against the erasure of Kongo culture, the fight against neocolonialism—all fights Bundu dia Kongo wants to win. Later in the evening, after receiving permission to film, it becomes clear to me that words and songs were not the only things being marshaled against enemies of the movement, but actual bodies were "jumping into the fight" as well.

In the midst of filming members singing to a tune reminiscent of Congolese rumba from several decades earlier, I notice a woman crouching on the ground in front of the crowd. Some people beside her move out of her way, and so I turn my camera toward her. I see her arms outstretched as she rises slowly to a deep bend of the knees, quaking slightly. It looks as though she is possessed. I then have a flash of recognition. Earlier in the day, as I gathered my equipment to film arriving Bundu dia Kongo members, Ma Kumi, an acquaintance, had done the same gesture, making sounds like a machine gun and mimicking shooting. She said, "This is what the people in Bundu dia Kongo do. Ka Ka Ka Ka." Astounded and incredulous, I'd left the compound not knowing what to expect.

Now, as I film, the woman (who was a bit heavyset) begins to jump up and down, and, finally, does a tuck and roll right in my direction, and then, crouching again, does another tuck and roll back toward the crowd. Several makesa guards come to loosely encircle her, and she begins making a shooting gesture again, this time with one arm. She punches outward, and then on her knees, continues to shoot, this time using her middle and index fingers on each hand, going all the way down to the ground. By this time, many more guards surround her, and one motions for her to get up. As they close the circle tighter around her, they begin to escort her away from the front of the crowd. I don't see how it ended because one of the organizers of the event comes up to me and indicates that I should not continue filming that incident. I take the hint, and turn my camera elsewhere.

The next day, when I come back to the assembly, I see that toward the back of the crowd, a circle had formed where people manifested their possession. Many of them are doing fighting gestures. They punch straight outward with their arms as if doing karate, lift up their knees, and thrust their leg forward to end with a powerful planting of the foot on the ground. They often hold their fingers or arms so they seem to be imitating a gun, and others even make the sound of a machine gun spitting bullets. As the day goes on, here and there in the crowd, people are jumping, doing fighting gestures, and imitating shooting. Several times, another person comes to put their hand on the possessed person's head and calm them down. The makesa readily step in when people become possessed and start to embody the possession. At one point, when many people start manifesting all at once, the makesa tell them to go to the back of the crowd and to do it back there. It seems as though the BDK leadership are trying to hide it or minimize attention to these "nontraditional" forms of embodied possession.

When I witnessed the aforementioned events, the first thing that came to my mind was that karate and machine guns had nothing to do with Kongo history and traditional culture. How do these embodied possessions fit in with the ideology of Bundu dia Kongo, if at all? Why were the leaders and organizers of the meeting reacting in the way that they did to these instances of possession?

Karate is a martial art from Japan, and machine guns could not be found in the precolonial Kongo Kingdom. Yet both of these things are familiar to Congolese, from the popularity of karate films throughout Africa (Barber 1987, 25; Frederiksen 1991, 143) to the recent history of civil war and present-day prevalence of machine gun–toting soldiers on the streets of most cities and towns in the country. Although these gestures may signal a heightened spiritual warfare, and maybe even actual actions people are willing to take to fight against state suppression, these particular embodied possessions can be seen as going against the Kongo traditionalism that BDK advocates and seeks to return to. The reactions to these types of possessions prove most fruitful for revealing the attitude of leaders of the movement. As people became possessed, security guards were sent to escort them away from the crowd, where they were almost hidden at the back, away from the gaze of the camera. Rather than embracing the spirit possession, and using it as the focus of the service, as in the DMNA church for example, the leaders, organizers, and security personnel present at the event seemed almost embarrassed by it all. It seemed clear that Bundu dia Kongo did not sanction this particular embodied practice.

The BDK members who exhibited karate moves and imitated machine guns in their states of possession are themselves engaged in performative encounters. Their embodied performances, however, can be seen as directed at multiple audiences. First, their embodiment of fighting against an unseen adversary suggests many possible targets: Christianity and Christians, critics of BDK, government leaders, corrupt officials, actual police and government soldiers, and so on. Thus it seems they are engaging in spiritual warfare on multiple levels. In their actual face-to-face encounters with police and soldiers, BDK members did not usually have guns. According to a special report issued by Human Rights Watch after the deadly confrontations between BDK and military forces throughout Bas-Congo in 2008, BDK members were armed with "stones, nuts, sticks, and pieces of wood fashioned into the shape of weapons" (2008, 76). A MONUC special report echoed this finding, adding that BDK members believed their innocuous objects would be supernaturally turned into powerful weapons through singing and chanting (2008, 13). In Luozi, while attending a ceremony at the grave of several BDK members who had been killed in prior conflicts with local police (prior to 2006), BDK members told me that they had used spiritual powers to protect themselves from the bullets of police, but the faith of some members had wavered and that led to people being shot. All of this shows that BDK members primarily sought to engage in battle on a spiritual plane. My point here is spiritual power plays a large role in the ability of BDK members to challenge the authority of the state, especially when they are trying to seek justice for what they see as wrongs committed against them. While I cannot say for certain whether karate or embodied machine guns were used in these confrontations with police/soldiers, I can say that for some BDK members, they play a role in the spiritual preparation for real world battles.

The other side to consider in terms of karate and embodied machine guns as performative encounters is their relationship to the leadership of BDK. As mentioned earlier, in the mass meeting I attended, people who started to show these expressions of possession were moved to the back of the crowd. Their possession had the potential for challenging the hegemonic order of the organization. The karate chops, punches, and machine gun arms were like embodied challenges to the existing authority structures within BDK because not only did they subvert the official narrative of "traditional" with their insertion of foreign modernity, but these gestures occurred while spiritual forces possessed people, which presented a challenge as well. Spirit possession presents possible access to authority sanctioned by the spiritual realm, authority that may confirm or contradict the authority of Ne Muanda Nsemi, who himself was first called through visions and dreams of spiritual beings. For example, what would happen if someone received a revelation while possessed and spoke to the crowd? Would the leaders present recognize their authority to speak? What if they claim to be the true leader of the Kongo people? What if what they say challenges the writings and speeches of Ne Muanda Nsemi? Like the Capuchin missionaries in the Kongo Kingdom in the early 1700s who sought to monopolize the authority to interpret the Bible and teach Christianity, and were thus threatened by the possession and revelations of Dona Beatrice Kimpa Vita, continuous revelation and the challenges it presents are issues that loom ever present in the movement of Bundu dia Kongo as demonstrated by the contentious embodiment of Asian martial arts and automatic assault weapons.

Conclusion

"There was shooting, shooting, and more shooting. I was here alone with my sister and the kids, and we crouched down and waited, scared, until it stopped. It went on and on." July 25, 2010. Ma Kudia is recounting the story of the confrontation between government forces and the local BDK group in Luozi. According to a MONUC special report, on February 28 and 29, 2008, a police force was dispatched to the town of Luozi in a larger mission to reestablish state authority in the area and suppress Bundu dia Kongo specifically (2008, 3).[41] In some areas such as Luozi where the police presence is minimal in daily life, Bundu dia Kongo had reportedly begun to take over state functions and administered their own justice, arresting and punishing people, and even allegedly killing several people in different towns throughout Bas-Congo.[42] While the police reportedly were sent to the area to arrest those responsible for the murders, the February/March 2008 campaign to restore state authority and suppress "organized resistance" (2008, 3) became a wholesale eradication of Bundu dia Kongo, as mazikua were destroyed wherever the police went, hospitals, pharmacies, and homes were looted, and people (usually unarmed or holding stones or sticks) were indiscriminately fired on, both BDK members and some unrelated civilians alike. In the confrontation that occurred in Luozi town between local BDK members and the police force, authorities confirm the deaths of seven BDK members while other witnesses claim many more were killed and their bodies were thrown into the Congo River. The zikua was burned down, along with twenty homes/buildings in the vicinity (2008, 16–17). Besides the death and destruction, sixty people were arrested in Luozi. From here, the police force moved west in search of and confronting BDK groups all along the way. Overall, the government campaign against Bundu dia Kongo lasted from February 28 until about March 16, 2008 (MONUC 2008). While the official count of casualties the Congolese government released is twenty-seven dead, including three police officers, investigations by external organizations (including the discovery of mass graves) led to estimates of one hundred (MONUC 2008) to more than 200 (Human Rights Watch 2008) dead.

When I returned to the Congo and Luozi in 2010, many things had changed. The BDK zikua was gone; in fact, BDK itself appeared to be gone. People seemed frightened to even talk about them, and I was told that any remaining members had gone further into Luozi territory, closer to Congo-

Brazzaville and away from the main roads and government soldiers. And who could blame them? The 2008 mass killings of BDK members were not the first; in the aftermath of Ne Muanda Nsemi's unsuccessful run for vice governor of the province in January and February of 2007, BDK members staged numerous demonstrations against electoral fraud, and 105 people were killed when police forces arrived to quell the protests (MONUC 2008, 7). Bundu dia Kongo was seen as a threat to the existing political system and leaders not just in Bas-Congo, but in Kinshasa as well, and their embodied performances that were used to represent their larger goals and ideas were a significant part of the movement itself.

The ideology and objectives of Bundu dia Kongo, from a Kongo-centered religion to the reformation of the Kongo Kingdom, all run counter to the existing structures of political and religious authority and openly challenge their basis of relevance for the Kongo people. In their pamphlets and publications, marches, speeches, songs, and embodied cultural performances, the members of Bundu dia Kongo espouse a message of redemption and autonomy for a BisiKongo population whose political power and cultural influence has diminished since the country gained independence.

Prayers and songs legitimize the religious authority of Bundu dia Kongo, but one of the most important ways that the spiritual beliefs of the group are shown is through embodied cultural performances in everyday life, such as the gestures of respect and gratitude to the ancestors who carry the messages of the Kongo people to Nzambi Mpungu. Bula makonko is used to open and close prayers and as the key component of a chanting prayer that embodies the number of stages in BDK's spiritual hierarchy that the prayer must travel through to reach Nzambi. Yinama is also used to close prayers, and also to enact the paying of respect to divinized ancestors that can be found in the BuKongo religion. Fukama is used in many different contexts, for repentance and to demonstrate respect or gratitude. In all, embodied cultural performances serve as an excellent medium for the transmission of the values and beliefs of Bundu dia Kongo as a movement.

Moreover, the responses from the spiritual realm in the form of visions, revelations, and even spirit possession at times serve as spiritual legitimacy of Bundu dia Kongo's practice, mission, and ideology. If messages come from the spiritual realm, are they not as valid (if not more so) as those messages received by Christians? How can their mission be challenged if it comes from God? In this way, Bundu dia Kongo offers a compelling alternative to religious traditions such as Christianity: that of a religion with its foundation in the particular history and experiences of the Kongo people. However, contact between the world of the living and the spiritual world not only confers legitimacy on the movement but also presents a potential space to subvert the authority of BDK, an authority that is still being established. This can be seen in the efforts of the meeting organizers and security personnel at the February 2006 general assembly in Luozi to control and curb the manifestations of modern warfare (karate, machine gun gestures) in the spirit possessions of certain members of the group.

By focusing on reforming bodily practice inside and outside of ritual contexts, Bundu dia Kongo effectively re-forms the history of the Kongo people in a contemporary space. New subjects are being shaped, and the social world that they are bearing and attempting to create is that of a considerably reimagined, yet not less real, Kongo Kingdom. Embodied cultural performances such as bula makonko, dekama, fukama, yinama, and participating in makinu outside of the church represent a revitalization of Kongo culture, as well as a reaffirmation of the spiritual, political, and cultural ideology of BDK through the body.

By advocating a religion that places Kongo people at its center and scoffs at Christianity and "white gods," Bundu dia Kongo presents a direct challenge to the religious authority of numerous Protestant and Catholic churches that dot the landscape throughout the Lower Congo. By actively pursuing Kongo sovereignty by supporting candidates such as Ne Muanda Nsemi for member of the National Assembly, and then vice governor of the province, and also protesting the legitimacy of non-Kongo administrators to govern Kongo people (as seen in the bloody confrontations in 2007 and 2008), Bundu dia Kongo openly defies the political authority of the state in the Lower Congo.

In all, the ideology and political mission of Bundu dia Kongo becomes more concrete and real to its members through influencing their embodied practices not only in the zikua, but also in everyday life. These changes in everyday cultural performances play a key role in the transformation of the mindset and vision of possibilities for both participants in the movement and other Kongo people observing their actions. The case of Bundu dia Kongo also shows embodied cultural performances can have multivalent meanings and uses that may be subversive of authority, both within and outside of the Bundu dia Kongo movement. Thus, these embodied cultural performances can even be seen as embodied revolutions, playing a key role in transforming the place and future of not just individuals, but the Kongo people overall in modern society.

Conclusion

Privileging Gesture and Bodies in Studies of Religion and Power

In January 1701, Father Marcellino d'Atri, an Italian Capuchin missionary, made his way to the royal compound of King Pedro IV, sovereign of the Kongo Kingdom. Accompanied by Giovan de Rosa, an Aragonese soldier, Father Marcellino had already planned an audience with the king to introduce de Rosa to the royal court. Before arriving, Father Marcellino told de Rosa that "in no way should you copy any of the people's customs such as smearing your face and eyes with dust because you are white and not black, and besides you are in my company" (Toso 1984, 260–61). The missionary was referring to the greeting practice of common people of lower status falling to their knees (fukama) in front of Kongolese nobility, as they clapped their cupped hands repeatedly (bula makonko) and covered their faces in dust. The iconic gesture of throwing dust on oneself while in a prostrate position demonstrated subservience, submission, and reverence for the power and status of Kongo nobility. After Father Marcellino and de Rosa passed guards posted at several courtyards and waited for some time, King Pedro IV finally emerged from an adjoining room. Father Marcellino entered another room with the king and told him that de Rosa, being White, would have nothing to do with the greeting customs of the Kongo Kingdom. The king's advisors immediately protested, and the king addressed the priest. "This can't be," he said, "for being in my kingdom he has to follow the same customs." The two parties argued for more than two hours until the king said, "I will not be seen with this man, and furthermore I do not want him any longer in my kingdom." Father Marcellino angrily departed the royal quarters without Giovan de Rosa being received by the king, and the disagreement continued for several days thereafter.

This incident is a prime example of a performative encounter, as it illustrates the importance of the micropolitics of gesture in interpersonal relations. Gestures, that is (usually) intentional movements of the body that are meaningful in specific sociocultural contexts, lay at the heart of this dispute over the appropriate etiquette for a lay White visitor to the Kongo Kingdom. Whichever way de Rosa eventually interacted with King Pedro IV would have political consequences—if he greeted the king in the customary Kongolese way, he would undermine the authority of the White missionaries and other Europeans living there; however, if he refused to kneel and cover his eyes with dust, he would publically insult the authority of the king. Indeed, decisions about what we do with our bodies in our encounters with others can have much larger ramifications. Therein lies the usefulness of an analytical approach that privileges performative encounters, where doing something as small as bowing, is doing something more than what seems to be such a simple, inconsequential act.

In choosing to develop my analysis around the concept of performative encounters, several themes emerge and are present to various degrees in each of the chapters in this book. I have chosen to identify these themes as body as center, body as conduit, and body as catalyst, themes I first introduced in the introduction that I will revisit here. The first theme, *the body as center*, refers to the study of the body in encounters as an actual method. I am advocating starting with the body (whether through a focus on gestures, dance, spirit possession, or other areas) to examine social processes both in the past and the present. If we start with the assumption that each person's individual body is their primary means of engaging with the world (Merleau-Ponty [1962] 1981), the means and interpretation of this engagement will always be fraught with possibilities, anxieties, and politics of control. Thus, I support placing the body at the center of analysis rather than seeing it as a marginal tool of inquiry. Like scholars such as Edda Fields-Black who use "non-traditional sources and interdisciplinary methods" such as historical linguistics to explore previously unwritten histories (2008, 21), I challenge other scholars to consider actual physical bodies as sources within themselves that can yield novel insights. A focus on the politics of the body in the performative encounter between King Pedro IV and Father Marcellino d'Atri in the Kongo Kingdom illuminates the process of racialization in eighteenth-century West Central Africa. It also provides a harbinger of the discord and dissatisfaction with ideas of White superiority that the general population expressed several years later with their involvement in the Antonian Movement of Dona Beatrice Kimpa Vita, the female prophet who claimed that Jesus and many saints were in fact Black (Thornton 1998). Focusing on the body also entails examining how the researcher's body engages with the research site, as perceived race, gender, class, nationality, and marital status shape everyday experiences in a number of ways that then affect the direction and possibilities of research itself.

The second major theme, *the body as conduit*, interrogates the relationship between body and ideas, movement and mind. By this I am referring to the many examples we encountered throughout the book of people and groups intentionally using movement to try to shape thought processes. From the colonial administrator who tried to use forced secular dancing to distract people from prophetic movements in the Belgian Congo, to Mobutu's use of political animation to engender nationalist sentiment, to Bundu dia Kongo's use of bimpampa in everyday life and worship to try to recreate the Kongo Kingdom—in all these instances, regularized bodily movement was supposed to affect individual and group consciousness and subjectivity in some way. While we may question the effectiveness of any of these approaches, I would ask the readers to think about some of the ways that they move on a daily basis, and what histories, ideas, or group affiliations that these movements may reveal. I offer as an example the following narrative.

In 1666 an Italian Capuchin missionary named Michael Angelo of Gattina traveled to Pernambuco, Brazil, on the first leg of an evangelizing mission to the Kingdom of Kongo. Upon his arrival, he was struck by the curious behavior of one particular Black woman whom he encountered: "As soon as we landed in the port of Fernambuco [sic], we saw a great crowd of people, as well Blacks as Whites, about us, and among them a Black Woman, who kneel'd, beat her Breast, and clapt her hands upon the Ground. I enquir'd what the good Woman meant by all those motions with her hands; and a Portuguese answer'd me: Father, the meaning of it is, that she is of the kingdom of Congo, and was baptiz'd by a Capuchin; and being inform'd that you are going thither to baptize, she rejoices and expresses her joy by those outward tokens" (Churchill 1704, 616).

This story of the role of everyday cultural performances in a chance encounter on the other side of the Atlantic illustrates the important role that the body plays in chronicling history, in the sense that embodied cultural performances related to past institutions, social structures, and experiences, are reenacted in new contexts, across space and time, largely because they have become second nature, and are "sedimented in the body" (Connerton

1989, 72). Embodied cultural performances, whether consciously learned or unconsciously absorbed, are a crucial means of instilling ideologies, beliefs, and value systems in the bodies of people in all societies. So, while the woman in this story was thousands of miles away from her home in Congo and living in a foreign society based on plantation slavery and the racial subjugation of Africans, she continued to enact Kongo cultural performances such as fukama and bula makonko upon recognizing a Capuchin missionary. Her actions reference her own past experiences in the Kingdom of Kongo, while simultaneously alluding to a history of social hierarchy that went back several centuries in which political and religious authority were constituted, confirmed, and also challenged through embodied cultural performances such as these. How does a focus on bodily movement change what we think we know about what African captives and others of African descent brought with them to the New World? What can a focus on the body add to the grand debates on the development of the New World cultures of people of African descent?

A focus on the body as conduit provides a new area of inquiry that many scholars (with some exceptions in regards to dance and martial arts, for example, Desch-Obi 2008; Thornton 1991) have overlooked, both in studies of Africa and of the African diaspora. It was only after I had done extensive research on Kongo bimpampa in West Central Africa that the gestures of the woman in Brazil made sense to me. In fact, I had read that same passage before but had skipped over it as insignificant for my project. How often have other scholars failed to notice descriptions of embodied practices such as these? Enslaved Africans brought their ideologies and beliefs with them to the New World, carried in their gestures, dances, and general comportment. Recognition of the importance of embodied cultural performances in the constitution of social life and authority in Africa challenges us to look again with fresh eyes at the embodied practices of enslaved Africans in the Americas. Moreover, more attention is needed on the influence of Central African groups on cultures, religions, and practices in the Americas (R. Brown 2012; Heywood 2002; J. Young 2007). While enslaved Kongo people were unable to rebuild the Kongo Kingdom in the New World, the social hierarchy and concepts of spirituality lived on in their embodied cultural performances, which themselves may have been a source of challenging the authority of their owners and oppressors in New World societies. Yet, like their counterparts in Africa, these performances had various meanings and uses over time and in changing contexts. Attention to embodied cultural performances will renew dialogue on the development of New World cultures and bring a new focus on the everyday interactions that referenced larger social structures, institutions, and belief systems that were embedded in the bodies and gestures of enslaved Africans who were taken to the Americas. How might studies of everyday cultural performances provide a fresh take on existing scholarly questions, such as studies of identity formation in the New World or even in colonial Africa?

The last theme is that of the *body as catalyst*. My major point with this book is to argue the importance of performative encounters through embodied cultural performances in the active and ongoing constitution of quotidian social life. Social positions are made and unmade through everyday interactions with others that are defined by and through everyday cultural performances. For example, in the seventeenth century, when a prospective provincial governor kneeled and threw dirt on himself before the Kongo king, the king confirmed the authority of his political appointment by giving the new governor a scepter, after which the governor kissed the king's hand. Or when Simon Kimbangu performed healing miracles through trembling, jumping, and the laying of hands, he was recognized as a powerful prophet during the colonial period. Likewise, when Mobutu Sese Seko organized national festivals of animation that were built on the everyday songs and dances of his subjects, their performances legitimized his position as the president of a one-party state. These examples demonstrate that embodied performances are not about just *meaning-making*, but also *meaning-doing*. My challenge to other scholars is to urge them to consider performances not just on the stage but also in daily situations as critical to processes of social life. The multiple uses and meanings that the same set of gestures may have underscores Margaret Drewal's point that "indeed both subversion and legitimation can emerge in the same utterance or act" (1991, 2). Thus, any discussion of the interrelatedness of performance and power must attend to the role of everyday cultural performances in the making and unmaking of authority and status. Another striking aspect of this study in looking at the body as a catalyst of social transformation is the importance of the spiritual realm for legitimizing political claims enacted through embodied cultural performances. From the colonial era bangunza, who drew on their trembling in their challenges to missionaries and the colonial state, to Mobutu's creation of a civil religion in Zaire, to the religion of BuKongo, which was used to support claims for an independent Kongo state by members of Bundu dia Kongo, one's relationship to the supernatural realm has a critical role to play in staking nationalist and other political claims. What this suggests is that politics and religion cannot be seen as distinct, separate spheres of influence; rather, they are often intertwined and are both crucial elements in the constitution of social life.

In all, my hope is that seeing the body as center, conduit, and catalyst will open up new possibilities of inquiry for scholars in various fields. The concept of performative encounters offers one way of capturing all three of these themes as we seek to understand our larger social world, and the place that we make within it.

GLOSSARY

Note: The terms in this list are in Kikongo unless otherwise indicated.

bakulu: ancestors

bascule: (French) the ceremony where the spirits of the members of the DMNA church are publicly weighed

bikualakuala: long lengths of bamboo laid on or across tables and played with sticks

bimpampa: body gestures

BisiKongo: the term that I am using to describe the ethnic group one finds throughout the Lower Congo, who speak varying dialects of the same language, Kikongo. This group is also known as *BaKongo*, a term frequently used by colonial administrators. The term *Kongo* describes the cultural area of this group, which was the basis of the Kongo Kingdom, and covers parts of present-day Congo-Brazzaville, Congo-Kinshasa, and Angola. *MwissiKongo* is a singular term used to describe an inhabitant of the Kongo Kingdom, while *BisiKongo* is the plural form. *BisiKongo* or *Kongo people* were phrases more often used by interlocutors in describing themselves as members of a larger group, so I am respecting the political choice that some people have made to use *BisiKongo* rather than *BaKongo* to describe themselves, although most of the scholarly literature still uses *BaKongo*.

bula makonko: cupped hand clapping that is used and was used in the past as a gesture of respect; to open and close meetings and prayers; to ask for pardon, forgiveness, and blessings; and also as a form of greeting other people

Bundu dia Kongo: a politico-religious-nationalist movement of Kongo people that seeks to reestablish the Kongo Kingdom, revitalize Kongo culture, and return to certain elements of "tradition" in the face of growing political and economic marginalization in the country

dekama: genuflection

Dibundu dia Mpeve ya Nlongo mu Afelika: Church of the Holy Spirit in Africa

dikisa: to give someone something to ingest. Often used to refer to passing on the

Holy Spirit and the ability to heal to someone else, called *dikisa mpeve*. Also used to describe giving the *nkasa* poison to someone to ingest as a test of his or her innocence

dumuka: to jump

dumuna: ritual jumping for a blessing or other purposes

fukama: to kneel

kibandi (pl. *bibandi*): double-skinned drums that are beaten with batons

kindoki: witchcraft or the use of spiritual powers to harm others

kingunza: word used to describe the prophetic movements throughout the Lower Congo during the colonial period, sparked by the healing of the prophet Simon Kimbangu

koko (pl. *moko*): hand

luketo: hips

makinu: general term for dances, of which there are many types

malembe: peace

malu: legs

mfumu: chief; king

mpeve: vital principle of every individual; spirit or Holy Spirit; breeze

nganga (pl. *banganga*): healers, priests, and diviners in the system of Kongo traditional religious beliefs

ngoma: a tall (waist-high), thick wooden drum with one side covered by an animal skin that is tightened by heating it with fire. In many secular makinu, this is the lead drum. The term *ngoma* is also used to describe the dance event at which ngomas and other drums are being played

ngunza (pl. *bangunza*): prophet

nitu: body

nkasa: a poisonous drink given to accused parties during the precolonial period to test their innocence. If they vomited the drink, they were considered innocent, but if they died, they were considered guilty

nkisi (pl. *minkisi*): material object in Kongo traditional religion that has been given spiritual power by traditional priests. Wyatt MacGaffey has referred to them as "charms" (1986b, 137–45), while John Janzen refers to them as consecrated medicines (1982, 4).

nsakala: shakers or rattles that are often made from small calabashes mounted on sticks. They also can be tied to strings and worn on the wrists of drummers to accentuate the playing.

ntambu: another term for drum

ntwadisi: person in the DMNA church who weighs the spirits of members during the bascule

yinama: to bow

zakama: to tremble (spirit-induced)

zikua (pl. *mazikua*): prayer and research group of Bundu dia Kongo

NOTES

Introduction: Gesture and Power

1. The province that I am referring to as the Lower Congo is currently known as Bas-Congo, and it was also referred to as Bas-Zaire during the presidency of Mobutu Sese Seko.

2. Léon-Georges Morel Report, "Ministère des Affaires Étrangères (Archives Africaines), Brussels, Belgium (AIMO)," 1634/9191B, unnumbered document, pages 2–4.

3. Throughout the book, I am mostly using pseudonyms for my interlocutors. It was very important to protect people's identities, especially when discussing political animation under Mobutu and Bundu dia Kongo. In a few instances I have indicated where a person's real name is being used. Following the customs in the Congo, I use honorific terms such as Mama or Ma for women and Tata for men.

4. In this book, I use the terms *religion* and *spirituality* interchangeably. In academic circles, the term *religion* often connotes more institutionalized organizations with leadership and set rituals, while *spirituality* is more commonly used to describe individual, subjective experiences with the divine (Zinnbauer et al., 1997, 551). In my book, the social movements that I describe often began with individual experiences and became larger movements and institutionalized churches, so the boundary between religion and spirituality is not clearly defined. I thus use both terms to describe human interactions with the supernatural realm.

5. By Holy Spirit, I am referring to the third aspect of the Holy Trinity that comprises the Father, the Son (Jesus), and the Holy Ghost/Holy Spirit. The varied European missions that came to evangelize the Lower Congo at the end of the nineteenth century translated this concept into Kikongo in different ways. The British Baptist Missionary Society missionaries preferred *mwanda a'vedila* (where *mwanda* means pure and *vedila* means breath) while Swedish Svenska Missions-Forbundet missionaries (Mission Covenant Church) preferred *mpeve ya nlongo*

(where *mpeve* means breeze and *nlongo* means sacred) (Janzen and MacGaffey 1974, 15).

6. By social conduct here, I am referring to rules for church members in Protestant mission churches that prohibited ingesting alcohol, participating in secular dances, and having more than one wife (Mahaniah 1975, 162–63).

7. The BisiKongo, also known as BaKongo, is the ethnic group one finds throughout the Lower Congo. The term *Kongo* describes the cultural area of this group, which was the basis of the Kongo Kingdom and covers parts of present-day Congo-Brazzaville, Congo-Kinshasa, and Angola. I have found that *BisiKongo* or *Kongo people* are phrases more often used by informants in describing themselves as members of a larger group and thus have chosen to use that terminology in my book.

8. *Merriam-Webster Online Dictionary*, "Movement," accessed June 30, 2014, http://www.merriam-webster.com/dictionary/movement.

9. Strine, Long, and Hopkins begin their survey article on performance by recognizing it as an essentially contested concept, meaning "its very existence is bound up in disagreement about what it is" (1990, 183). Such an approach to performance fosters constant, often fruitful discussion among scholars as there is no one agreed-on definition.

10. Searle likens the "background" to Pierre Bourdieu's habitus, a set of structured and structuring dispositions discussed later in the chapter.

11. Laman wrote about four parts of man: an inner and an outer person, each in turn consisting of two parts. See [1936] 1964, 1.

12. By "set apart from," I mean performance events that are specially marked or framed as separate from everyday life. This could include staged performances of dance, but also a planned ritual healing in the DMNA church in Luozi with a set program, date, and time, and beginning and end.

13. See Goffman 1961, 1967, and especially 1959. Goffman categorized face-to-face interaction into two separate types: unfocused interaction, which results "solely by persons being in one another's presence," and focused interaction, "when people effectively agree to sustain for some time a single focus of cognitive and visual attention" (1961, 7). Theater and performance studies scholar Richard Schechner (2013) also recognizes performance in everyday life as part of a continuum of types of performance.

14. Thomas Csordas defines "somatic modes of attention" as "culturally elaborated ways of attending to and with one's body in surroundings that include the embodied presence of others" (1993, 138).

15. Although I independently came up with this term, in later research I found that Paulla Ebron (2007) used the term *performative encounter* as part of a heading in her book chapter on the performance of gender. She did not, however, theorize or define the concept in her book chapter.

16. Authority has also been defined in numerous ways in the social sciences more broadly and in anthropology in particular. Weber, for example, discussed it as "legitimate domination" (1968, 215), Bierstedt as "institutionalized power" (1950, 733), and Parsons viewed it as "the right to use power, or negative sanctions . . . or

even compulsion to assert priority of a decision over others" (1986, 112). Swartz, Turner, and Tuden defined authority as "rights to use and acquire power" in a hierarchy of statuses in a group (1966, 17). Begler defined authority as "the legitimate utilization of power exercised within an institutionalized hierarchy of statuses" (1978, 575), and Rushforth considered it in two senses: "the power to inspire justified belief in others (being an authority, having legitimate knowledge) and the power to influence or determine others' conduct (having control over the action of others" (1994, 336).

17. *MuKongo* is the singular word to describe someone of the BaKongo (plural) or BisiKongo ethnic group.

18. Bauman and Briggs consider these critiques in the discussion of performance from a linguistic perspective particularly (1990, 79).

19. In *Le Geste Kongo* (2002), Thompson examined different gestures portrayed in a collection of Kongo art and artifacts at the Dapper Museum in Paris as a form of embodied knowledge of the Kongo people. In *Tango: The Art History of Love* (2005), Thompson concisely describes makinu in the Kongo Kingdom and contemporary Congo-Brazzaville and Congo-Kinshasa in order to examine the Kongo cultural influence on the development of the tango in Argentina. Pastor Esther Luhunu Mahema (2005) has also written on bimpampa, specifically in relation to the expected conduct of Kongo women. Her work, while focusing overall on the place, roles, and issues of morality of women in Christianity, has proven useful for identifying some of the most important recurring gestures in traditional Kongo society.

20. *Bimpampa* is not a perfect translation for *gesture*, but is one among several choices presented by my interlocutors. *Bisinsu* and *bidimbu* are other terms, although they are more clearly associated with inscription and signs in graphic writing (see Martinez-Ruiz 2013). There is no exact term for bodily gestures in general, although there are many specific terms for specific movements such as *yinama* (bowing), *dekama* (genuflection) and *fukama* (kneeling).

21. There is even a linguistics-focused gesture studies book series through John Penjamins Publishing Company. The series editor is anthropologist Adam Kendon.

22. In my experience, *nsi* was not used to mean nobility, but rather land or country. See Laman ([1936] 1964, 764).

23. Coming in third in the total number of votes for the presidential election, Antoine Gizenga was eventually appointed the prime minister of the Democratic Republic of Congo after the national elections in 2006, a position he held until 2008.

24. The Republic of Tanganyika and the People's Republic of Zanzibar joined together under President Julius Nyerere in 1964.

25. Durkheim uses the term *church* to refer to any collective of people sharing religious beliefs ([1912] 1995, 41).

26. The abbreviation AIC is used for African Independent/African Initiated Churches, which are usually categorized separately from churches established by missionaries or Pentecostal churches (although scholars have noted the permeability of these categories) (Meyer 2004).

27. Weber saw these three cases (legal authority, traditional authority, and charismatic authority) as three pure types and actual forms of domination in reality that "constitute combinations, mixtures, adaptations, or modifications of these 'pure types'" (1968, 954).

28. See Thornton 1998.

29. Several anthropological studies have focused on textual authority, the authority that comes from reading, interpreting, and reciting sacred texts (Lambek 1990; Messick 1993). Lambek's study of Islamic *fundis* (scholars) in Mayotte, however, extended beyond textual authority to also consider the authority that comes from social performances: "The ability to read texts is not an automatic source of power; personal authority is constrained by ritual performance and must be continually confirmed in social performance" (1990, 35).

30. In regards to spirits, there are six spirit families in the Songhay pantheon, each representing a period in Songhay history. The Hauka are the spirits of colonization and date to 1925 (Stoller 1995, 33).

31. This idea of remaking of the self through individual conduct can also be found in the earlier work of scholars such as Jean Comaroff (1985).

32. Sociologist Robert Bellah, who used the particular case of myths, imagery, and even speeches in the U.S. government, first defined civil religion as a "public religious dimension [that] is expressed in a set of beliefs, symbols, and rituals" (1967, 4). During Mobutu's era, the worship of President Mobutu and his ideas became a type of civil religion, as marches, rallies, songs, television broadcasts, speeches, images, and monuments, and forced performances of the population were all used in everyday life to show reverence and adulation for Mobutu Sese Seko. This topic is explored further in chapters 4 and 5.

33. My use of the term *audience members* here also recognizes that most of the performances that I witnessed in Congo (both onstage and offstage) lacked a strict boundary between performers and observers. Audience members might go on the stage (as even I did repeatedly), respond in a call-and-response fashion, or in other ways interact such that there is no fourth wall between the performers and the audience.

34. Key cultural consultants are people who "by accident, experience, talent, or training can provide the most complete or useful information about particular aspects of life" (Kottak 2006, 257).

35. This was preferred over DVDs because most people did not have the financial means to own a DVD player but at least might own or know someone with a VCD player or a radio that played VCDs, since these were considerably cheaper and more common.

36. Owing to the lack of a recent census, it is very difficult to accurately estimate the total number of BisiKongo in the Democratic Republic of Congo. The most recent census was released in 1984 and, as far as I can tell, did not count people by ethnic groups (Institut National de la Statistique 1984). However, Kikongo is recognized as one of four national languages along with Tshiluba, Lingala, and Swahili (French is the official language).

Chapter 1: Neither Native nor Stranger

1. For more information about the DMNA (Dibundu dia Mpeve ya Nlongo mu Afelika, or Church of the Holy Spirit in Africa) and its connection to Simon Kimbangu, see Covington-Ward (2008) and (2014) as well as W. MacGaffey (1983).

2. AIMO 1634/9191B Letter from Léon Cartiaux to district commissioner of Bas-Congo, Luozi, June 13, 1921. Although there is another person's brief statement at the bottom of the document affirming that these were indeed the words of the witnesses, it is not clear whether it was written verbatim, or with some liberty that may have led to certain changes. In particular, I am referring to the idea that the Americans would become the new rulers of the Congo rather than partners, or guests of the Congolese.

3. W. MacGaffey (1968, 176).

4. Paul Gilroy's concept of diasporic intimacy, while initially applied to cultural production, also illuminates ties of affiliation across populations of African descent based on common experiences and struggles. See Gilroy (1993, 16).

5. The fact that there was a Congolese dance company based in Ann Arbor offering classes at the University of Michigan was one of the deciding factors that led to my choice of the University of Michigan when deciding between graduate schools.

6. CIA World Factbook, accessed August 1, 2014, https://www.cia.gov/library/publications/the-world-factbook/geos/cg.html.

7. Beignets are balls of fried dough, often served with hot pepper sauce. *Eau pure* (pure water) is a phrase called out by street vendors selling water (though it sounds more like O-P! O-P!), and Thomson is a type of mackerel imported from South Africa and Zimbabwe, which is often sold in the open-air markets in Kinshasa.

8. *Kin* is a shorthand way that people in Congo refer to Kinshasa.

9. See De Boeck and Plissart (2004) for a more extensive discussion of the deteriorating economic and social conditions in Kinshasa and the reactions of individuals and groups, especially youth, to these conditions.

10. *Mbote* in Kikongo is the adjective *good,* which is also used as a shortened greeting to say hello.

11. Skol and Primus are the two most popular beers in Congo. Primus is brewed by Bralima Brewery (owned by Heineken International), and Skol is brewed by Unibra, a Belgian corporation.

12. At the time of writing this chapter, the Democratic Republic of Congo had not had a full census of the entire population since 1984.

13. The intuitive body language that I am referring to are gestures such as rolling eyes, sucking teeth, and other embodied ways of being that people in the African diaspora continue to exhibit, which have largely the same meanings on the continent of Africa. These embodied ways of being have been passed on from African ancestors in the diaspora, although this enculturation was often not explicit.

14. In fact, if my hair was uncovered, it was often the index that I was not a native

Congolese, because at the time, locks were very rare among Congolese women; however because women also sometimes assumed that my hair was in hair extensions (*mesh* in French), this was not always as big an index of foreignness as it could have been. Women sometimes asked me where I bought my hair.

15. While I had seen some skin bleaching in Ghana, there it was mainly practiced by women. The Congo was the first place where I saw skin bleaching practiced by a large number of men along with many women.

16. A colloquial term in French to describe an inhabitant of Kinshasa.

17. When I returned in 2010, I noticed that many of the taxis were now painted in similar, more uniform colors, and that le Boulevard du 30 Juin had been widened. Competition for taxis did not seem as intense as in the past.

18. Widespread prostitution is one of the most heartbreaking symptoms of the bureaucratic and economic crisis in the Congo and the dire and desperate straits of most of the population there. I have seen prostitutes before, but I have never seen the sheer numbers of girls and women who ply their trade along the boulevard and other prominent streets in Kinshasa. For further discussion of this, see Janet MacGaffey (1988, 161–76).

19. Magasin is another neighborhood at the opposite end of le Boulevard du 30 Juin.

20. This female German was the girlfriend of a Congolese friend and a student visiting Kinshasa. She did not have a personal car. She told me that she had been called many names as she walked on the streets, especially by people who were very poor or homeless. My personal interpretation is that everyday Congolese see her as very privileged and are reacting to the lack of opportunities that they themselves have in comparison.

21. Basketball was another embodied way of getting to know people in the community. I played basketball on the varsity team back in high school and played for the women's team at the University of Ghana while studying abroad in college.

22. I adopt the usage of this term from Jafari Allen (2011).

Chapter 2: "A War between Soldiers and Prophets"

1. *Pagne* is a French word for cloth, in this context used to describe yards of printed cloth that women wrap around their waists.

2. Ne Nkamu Luyindula provided the French translation of this Kikongo song, which I then translated into English.

3. In fact, prophets continue to be present in many communities in the Lower Congo, both associated and unassociated with mainstream churches. I met several female prophets both in 2005–6 and in 2010 in and around Luozi.

4. The first corps of the Salvation Army was established in Kinshasa in 1934. The huge "S" on their flags was interpreted by many BisiKongo as a symbol of Simon Kimbangu. People rushed to join Salvation Army churches, eventually blending some *kingunza* practices with Salvation Army rites and starting independent churches. Simon Mpadi, a MuKongo born in the Belgian Congo who had joined the Salvation Army, started Mpadism/Khakism/La Mission de Noirs (Mission of Blacks) in 1939. Adherents of his church wore Khaki uniforms and many of them were former bangunza (Andersson 1958, 126–40).

5. For more information about this church and its connection to Simon Kimbangu, see Covington-Ward (2008, chapter 4).

6. For more detailed information about Kongo Christianity during this historical period, see Thornton (1984).

7. See Hochschild (1998); Morel (1907); Nzongola-Ntalaja (2002, 20–23) for detail and description relating to this period.

8. See Bontinck (1969, 139); Gotink (1995, 7–14); Kavenadiambuko (1999, 33); Mahaniah (1988, 7–20); Slade (1959).

9. In 1921, the American Baptist Foreign Missionary Society stations in the Lower Congo included Banza Manteke, Mpalabala, Lukunga, Sona Bata, Matadi, Kimpese, and Mukimvika (*Congo News Letter*, July 1921). Baptist Missionary Society stations included Thysville, Kibentele, Matadi, Kimpese, and Wathen (Vellut 2010, unnumbered map). Svenska Missions Förbundet missions included Mukimbungu, Kibunzi, Nganda, Londe, Kinkenge, and Kingoyi, mainly on the northern bank of the Congo River (MacGaffey 1986a; Vellut 2005). Christian and Missionary Alliance mission stations were mainly in the Mayombe region of Bas-Congo, including the four main stations of Boma, Vungu, Lolo, and Kinkonzi (*Alliance Weekly*, volume 56, no. 28, September 23, 1922, 438–39; volume 56, no. 29, September 30, 1922, 454).

10. The Matadi-Leopoldville railroad was constructed between 1890 and 1898 (La Fontaine 1970, 10).

11. *Baptist Missionary Magazine* 78 (1898): 223.

12. See Mahaniah (1975, 185–90); also Axelson (1970, 256) and W. MacGaffey (1986a, 266).

13. American Baptist Historical Society archive (ABHS), Banza Manteke annual report, 1920, Geil correspondence.

14. Baptist Missionary Society Archive (BMSA), W. H. Leslie letter to Duncan, July 7, 1895, cited in Mahaniah (1975, 187).

15. ABHS, 77th Annual Report of the American Baptist Foreign Missionary Society, 1891, page 128. American missionaries used "Banza Manteke" in their writings about this town, but the proper spelling in Kikongo would be "Mbanza Manteke."

16. *Baptist Missionary Magazine* 84: 1904, 101.

17. BMSA, A/102.

18. ABHS, 1919 Sona Bata Medical Report, Frederickson correspondence. The proper spelling for this town in Kikongo is Nsona Mbata.

19. See the mention of influenza and infantile paralysis in John E. Geil's letter dated August 20, 1920 (ABHS). See also the letter from Stanley Thompson dated April 12, 1920, which mentions an outbreak of smallpox at Wathen station (BMSA), and the 1918 medical report from San Salvador station, which mentions sleeping sickness (BMSA). British missionaries also noted the impact of influenza; see the 1918 annual report for Thysville and Kibentele stations (A126/Africa/Thysville, BMSA).

20. See Lyons (1992) for more about sleeping sickness in particular as a colonial disease.

21. ABHS, 1920 annual report, Geil correspondence.

22. Mfumbwa is a fibrous type of greens that grows in the Congo. Kwanga is a type of soft bread made from manioc and wrapped in banana leaves.

23. The soutan is a long dress-like garment worn in different styles for men and women.

24. *Nsakala* (sing.) or *binsakala* (plural) are shakers or rattles that are often made from small gourds mounted on sticks. They can also be made from repurposed insecticide cans filled with seeds.

25. William Brown Frame, *Congo Mission News*, October 1921.

26. BMSA A/133, R. L. Jennings, "The Prophet Movement in Congo," page 2. Wathen was also known as Ngombe-Lutete and was the home mission of Kimbangu.

27. Many researchers believe that it was at the refinery in Kinshasa that he was exposed to Garveyist ideas and readings by Black Americans and other Africans working there. Marcus Garvey was a highly influential yet controversial Jamaican nationalist leader who created a back to Africa movement and advocated Black pride and African independence during the early twentieth century. The influence of Garveyist ideas on the Kimbanguist movement has been explored by several authors, and although interesting, is beyond the scope of this chapter. For further information on this subject, see Andersson (1958, 250–57); Kodi (1993, 263–88); W. MacGaffey (1968, 171–81); Mahaniah (1993); and Vellut (1987, 55–66).

28. BMSA, A/133, Jennings 1936, "The Prophet Movement in Congo" (MacKay 1987, 126).

29. The document "The History of Simon Kimbangu, Prophet by the Writers Nfinangani and Nzungu, 1921," was found among the papers of Kimbangu and his followers in Nkamba and was confiscated by colonial officials on June 19, 1921, after Léon-Georges Morel had failed to arrest Kimbangu (Pemberton 1993, 194). It was written in Kikongo and translated by Belgian colonial officials. While the actual original document cannot now be found, the translated typescript (into French) still exists and is located in the AIMO archive (AA portefeuille 1630/9184. II. Q.3.a.1. 1. Dossier: Documentation Générale sur le Kibanguisme. Document 84). I am using Jeremy Pemberton's annotated English translation of this document. The authors of the document are two MuKongo followers of Kimbangu; not much is known about Nzungu while Nfinangani was described as Kimbangu's secretary (Pemberton 1993, 195).

30. The account of Nfinangani and Nzungu dates these events to occurring between March 13 and 19, 1921. This is supported by several missionary accounts, which also indicate that Kimbangu's healing activities started in March 1921; J. S. Bowskill, "Notes on the prophet movement," n.d., in Vellut 2010, 28; BMSA A/133 Kibangism Wathen, Robert Lanyon Jennings, "The Prophet Movement in Congo" (undated document, page 4).

31. Mahaniah (1993, 412); M. Martin (1975, 45); Pemberton (1993). Other accounts indicate that Kimbangu actually healed a child. See Andersson (1958, 51).

32. BMSA, A 38/A R. L. Jennings Diaries.

33. ABHS, Thomas Moody, correspondence, May 1, 1921, letter to Mr. Lipphard.

34. Pastor Kasambi (July 19, 2010), Tata Kizole (July 20, 2010), Tata Vita (July 21, 2010), Ma Kudada (July 26, 2010), and Ma Luzitu (July 27, 2010).

35. BMSA, A/43/2 Frame, letter dated June 25, 1921.

36. BMSA A/38/2, R. L. Jennings, letter dated May 19, 1921.

37. See W. MacGaffey (1977, 186), and Janzen (1982) and (1992) more generally.
38. Anderrson (1958, 285). The Laman Kikongo-French dictionary defined *zakama* as both shaking and trembling. I have chosen to use *trembling* as the term *tremblement* was the term most often used by my interlocutors in Luozi.
39. In the exchanges that follow, D stands for Cartiaux (*demande* or question) while R stands for each respondent (*reponse*) who is being interrogated.
40. AA portefeuille AIMO 1633/9190, II.Q.3.c. 1. Dossier: Incidents en Territoire de Luozi (Manianga) et Cataractes Nord; L. Cartiaux, interviews sent to the district commissioner in Boma.
41. AA portefeuille AIMO 1633/9190, II.Q.3.c. 1. Dossier: Incidents en Territoire de Luozi (Manianga) et Cataractes Nord; L. Cartiaux, interviews sent to the district commissioner in Boma.
42. AA portefeuille AIMO 1633/9190, II.Q.3.c. 1. Dossier: Incidents en Territoire de Luozi (Manianga) et Cataractes Nord; Bamba, July 30, 1921. Document number 226.R, page 1.
43. AA portefeuille AIMO 1630/9183; II.Q.3.a.2. 1. Dossier Kibangu Simon. Document 33; letter to governor-general from vice governor-general, subject: Kimbangu Movement; Leopoldville, October 14, 1921, page 2; Chomé (1959, 27); and Asch (1983, 23).
44. AA portefeuille AIMO 1634/9191B, unnumbered document, 2–4.
45. BMSA, A/38/2, letter dated May 19, 1921.
46. AA portefeuille 1630/9183; II.Q.3.a.2. 7; Dossier Attitude des Missionaires Etrangers; document 44.
47. Andersson (1958, 58); AA portefeuille AIMO 1634/9191B, unnumbered document, 2–4.
48. AA portefeuille AIMO 1630/9184. II.Q.3.a.1. 1. Dossier: Documentation Generale sur le Kibanguisme. Document 84. Leopoldville, September 22, 1921. Letter to the vice governor-general from Léon-Georges Morel, territorial administrator. Page 6.
49. AA portefeuille AIMO 1630/9183, II.Q.3.a.2. 8. Dossier: Articles des journaux. Document 64 (no. 3863) Leopoldville [July or August] 14, 1921. Objet: Mouvement Kimbangu. Included in a letter from Dupuis, the commissaire de district adjoint, to the governor-general.
50. AA portefeuille AIMO 1634/9191B, II.Q.3.c. 12. Dossier: Incidents en Territoire des Cataractes Sud (Thysville). Documents # 17 and unnumbered following; Thysville, July 2, 1921. Letter from Guasco to Geerts, Ingenieur Director, and July 5, 1921, letter from Geerts to the governor-general of Boma.
51. AA portefeuille AIMO 1634/9191B, Decision, Kamba June 20, 1921, Léon-Georges Morel, territorial administrator, Southern Cataracts.
52. A saraband is a type of dance, specifically a European courtly dance from the seventeenth and eighteenth centuries. In this case, I believe he is trying to say that it was like they were dancing around him.
53. AA portefeuille AIMO 1634/9191B, II.Q.3.c. 12. Dossier: Incidents en Territoire des Cataractes Sud (Thysville); unnumbered document; Rapport d'enquête Administrative sur les faits et incidents de Kamba (sub-district de Zundu); Thysville, May

17, 1921; to the district superintendent of Bas-Congo, Boma from the territorial administrator Morel, page 1.

54. Jason Young (2007) examines the history of baptism in the Kongo Kingdom (eating salt), and the transformations that had to take place in the Americas. By the 1880s, water immersion was being used by missionaries in the Lower Congo, although running water was already being used in purification rites by *banganga* (Laman 1957, 6).

55. AA portefeuille AIMO, 1634/9191B, Cartiaux Report to the district commissioner of Boma.

56. AA portefeuille AIMO, 1634/9191B, Cartiaux Report to the district commissioner of Boma, page 2.

57. AA portefeuille AIMO, 1634/9191B, Cartiaux Report to the district commissioner of Boma, page 4.

58. AA portefeuille AIMO, 1634/9191B, Cartiaux Report to the district commissioner of Boma.

59. The chicotte is a whip made of hippopotamus hide that was dried in the sun. It was used frequently in public floggings (Nzongola-Ntalaja 2002, 37); See also images painted by Tshibumba Kanda Matulu in Johannes Fabian (1996).

60. AA portefeuille AIMO 1634/9191B, II.Q.3.c. 12. Dossier: Incidents en Territoire des Cataractes Sud (Thysville); unnumbered document. Rapport sur mon voyage d'enquête vers Yanga du 13 au 16 juin 1921. Luozi, June 17, 1921. Letter to the district superintendent in Boma from L. Cartiaux, the territorial administrator, page 5.

61. In June 1921, Léon-Georges Morel returned to Nkamba with soldiers in order to arrest and detain Simon Kimbangu. Kimbangu mysteriously escaped, and many legends about his powers began to circulate. "It was said that Kimbangu's hand-cuffs snapped as though they had been the strands of a spider's web. . . . When his hut was surrounded by soldiers, Kimbangu was wafted up into the sky and sat there singing" (Walder, page 27, cited in Andersson 1958, 65).

62. AA portefeuille 1630/9183, II.Q.3.a.2. 1. Dossier Kibangu Simon; unnumbered document; Jugement. Conseil de guerre de Thysville, October 3, 1921, pronounced by Judge De Rossi, page 2.

63. During my own research in the African Archives in Brussels, I also saw files containing the names of hundreds of these persecuted and arrested bangunza who were sent to penal labor camps, although I was not allowed to copy the files.

64. ABHS, Individual Missionary Correspondence (John E. Geil).

65. The July 1921 issue of the *Congo News Letter* of the ABFMS missionaries includes a report of special meetings held in the Lukunga field in May 1921, including visits to Kimpaka on the north bank of the Congo River, and to Lukunga station and Paka on the Bangu, both on the southern bank of the river. See also the map of Bas-Congo province (map 2.1).

66. J. S. Bowskill, "Notes on the prophet movement," n.d. in Vellut 2010, 32.

67. ABHS, Box 280, Folder 1921, Annual Report of the Belgian Congo Mission, Catherine Mabie.

68. AA portefeuille AIMO, 1634/9191B, Dossier Incidents en Cataractes Sud; Luozi,

June 13, 1921, Léon Cartiaux to the district commissioner at Boma. Although there is another person's brief statement at the bottom of the document affirming that these were indeed the words of the witnesses, it is not clear whether it was written verbatim, or with some liberty that may have led to certain changes. In particular, I am referring to the words "our rulers" where the "our" could be referring to the Belgians or the Congolese themselves.

Chapter 3: Threatening Gestures, Immoral Bodies

1. The particular clothing church members wear was said to have been received in a vision held by Masamba Esaie. Similarly, in the Cherubim and Seraphim African independent churches in Nigeria, the founders of the church had visions and dreams that helped to constitute their religious authority over others. Distinctive garments seen in these visions were then made and worn to embody the spiritual power of these founders of the church. See Renne 2004.

2. The hymns of the DMNA church are considered holy because they have been received through visions or dreams and are inspired by the Holy Spirit.

3. Here I am referencing James Scott's book *Weapons of the Weak* (1985), which explores everyday forms of resistance for peasants in Malaysia.

4. This male type of dress is called *mbokula* in Kikongo.

5. *Makinu ya nsi* refers to dances of the land or tradition while *ndosa* references the actual gesture the men make when they kick out their cloth skirts as a part of the dance, but people use the term to refer to the dance event itself as well.

6. In the following decades, the post of "vice governor-general" was renamed "provincial governor."

7. Congo Belge, Gouvernement Local 1912.

8. Congo Belge, Gouvernement Local 1913.

9. Congo Belge, Gouvernement Local 1915.

10. Wagner 1997, 6. Summas were books popular in Europe during the medieval period that explained sins, punishments, and restitution for followers of the Christian faith.

11. For example, John Calvin's attitude toward dance is clear when he compares dancers to "mad folk" and writes that "nowadays we see many men seek nothing . . . in so much as they have none other countenance but in seeking to hop and dance like stray beasts. . . . Let us understand that it is not of late beginning, but that the Devil hath reigned at all times" (quoted in Wagner 1997, 27).

12. An example might be churches that adhered to the concept of dance as an invitation to lust, an idea advanced by Catholic priest Juan Vives in 1523 in a manual on proper Christian behavior (Wagner 1997, 13).

13. AA portefeuille AIMO 1634/9191B, letter to Le Juge Président de Tribunal, from Thomas Demvo, Mayaki Daniel, Nkwese Rubin, Nzonzi Solomon, N. Esaie Dicocon, Niembani David, and Kibassa Jeremie.

14. See Richard F. Burton (1876) and Joachim John Monteiro (1875, 136–38).

15. Mixed here refers to dances mixed in sex (both men and women participate).

16. Father Hugo Gotink, in discussion with the author, Mbanza Ngungu, March 11–12, 2006. This material is apparently what DeCapmaker used for his own pre-

sentation at the seminar. Gotink shared with me his copies of the two dossiers on Congo dance deposited at the Archives of the Redemptorist Fathers in Rome.

17. The Kongo priest in question apparently changed his mind about these issues, as he later became one of the first people to reintroduce traditional instruments into the Catholic Church (Father Masamba, June 3, 2005).

18. The passages written by these instructors could have been influenced by the fact that the readership was a Swedish audience, rather than a Kongo one. However, I have also encountered other Kongo Protestants in the present who viewed dancing as inappropriate for members of the church.

19. Tata Kimfumu (September 29, 2005); Tata Nkuku (September 29, 2005); and Tata Yangalala (October 30, 2005).

20. This is his real name, which I have been given permission to use.

21. "D" stands for interrogator and "R" for respondent.

22. AA portefeuille 1630/9184. II.Q.3.a.1. 1. Dossier: Documentation Generale sur le Kibanguisme. Unnumbered document. January 11, 1924. Proces-verbal no. 1 (affaire Kundu-Tumba). Pages 4–5.

23. AA portefeuille 1630/9193, II.Q.3.a.2. 5. Dossier Relations avec le R. P. Dufonteny.

24. AA portefeuille 1630/9184, II.Q.3.a.1. 1. Dossier: Documentation Generale sur le Kibanguisme. Document B. Gungu, January 13, 1924. Objet: Mouvement Kibangiste. Letter to the governor from Noirot.

25. AA portefeuille AIMO 1878/9981. Conference de Administrateurs Territoriaux du Bas-Congo, compte-rendu de la conférence.

26. Policies of forced dancing during the colonial period foreshadowed similar practices to follow in postcolonial Congo under Mobutu Sese Seko. This will be addressed in chapter 4.

27. Munkukusa was another movement that emerged in the 1940s, although it is not classified as a prophetic movement. It was a community eradication of witchcraft through engaging in certain rituals together (see Andersson 1958; Geuns 1974; and Mahaniah 1982).

28. AA portefeuille AIMO. *Territoire de Manianga. Rapport Annuel, 1944.*

29. AA portefeuille AIMO. *Territoire de Mayumbe. Rapport Annuel, 1947.*

30. AA portefeuille AIMO. *Territoire de Manianga. Rapport Annuel, 1947.*

31. AA portefeuille AIMO. *Territoire de Luozi. Rapport Annuel, 1950.*

32. *Kilombo* in Kikongo means a large group (of people, insects, and so on) that is so numerous they cannot be counted. In the past it also referred to the army in the Kongo Kingdom (Mahaniah 1989, 87). In the context of the CEC Protestant church in Luozi, and other churches as well, the name is most commonly used for a choir, often large, that incorporates traditional musical instruments.

33. For example, one verse of one song says, "Father Aldén has accused me before the administrator. A prophet cannot fear anything" (Andersson 1958, 280).

34. AA portefeuille AIMO 1634/9191B, Plainte Contre Reverend Aldén de la Mission de Kingoie.

35. AA portefeuille AIMO. *Territoire de Luozi. Rapport Annuel, 1956.*

36. AA portefeuille AIMO. *Territoire de Luozi. Rapport Annuel, 1956.*

37. The annual report for Thysville in 1956 also complained of Kimbanguist activity

in the northern part of the territory during the later four months of the year. AA portefeuille AIMO. *Territoire de Thysville. Rapport Annuel, 1956.*

38. BMSA, A 126/Africa/Thysville/Folder Thysville, annual report 1957.

39. AA portefeuille AIMO. *Territoire de Luozi. Rapport Annuel, 1957.*

40. See BMSA, Muriel Jennings "Dear Friend" letter, December 1960; 1959 Thysville annual report.

Chapter 4: Dancing with the Invisible

1. This motto in the second epigraph is mentioned in Nzongola-Ntalaja 2002, 170n41.

2. The Democratic Republic of Congo was renamed Zaire in October of 1971, under the presidency of Mobutu Sese Seko (Gondola 2002, 142).

3. This part of the description comes from archival footage used in the documentary film *When We Were Kings*, which chronicles the Ali-Foreman fight in 1974.

4. *Wayi wayi wa* is a term of veneration for Mobutu. The translation of the Kikongo text of the song was provided by Ne Nkamu Luyindula.

5. As stated earlier, I am using Anthony Smith's definition of nationalism as "an ideological movement for attaining and maintaining the autonomy, unity, and identity of an existing or potential 'nation'" (1996, 108). Anthony Smith defines a nation as "a named community possessing a historic territory, shared myths and memories, a common public culture and common laws and customs" (2002, 15).

6. My work is also informed by Lisa Wedeen's work on nationalism in Yemen where she examines everyday practices of nationalism (such as discourse, qat chews, and religious practices), which help people to "constitute the self . . . as an explicitly national person" (2008, 5). Her works also points to the importance of nationalist activities in everyday life settings.

7. Joan Huckstep's dissertation (2005) is based on interviews with members of a Congolese dance company located in Philadelphia (five men, one woman) and provides a general overview of animation politique and its administrative structure, and an analysis of several videotaped performances. Other studies of animation specifically are much more brief such as a few pages dedicated to it in a larger text on cultural policy and infrastructure in Zaire (Botombele 1976), a chapter dedicated to some of the larger and more famous animators (Thassinda 1992, 73–91), and mention of the omnipresent practice in other chapters and books that focus on other topics concerning Zaire under Mobutu (Callaghy 1984, 320–26).

8. For further information on the First Republic specifically, see Catherine Hoskyns 1965.

9. Lingala is a language serving as the lingua franca for people of the Upper Congo River region and is also the vernacular language of Kinshasa (Pype 2007, 254). It became even more popular under Mobutu because he would also give speeches in Lingala. Lingala is also the language of choice for the lyrics of most Congolese popular dance music songs.

10. As Callaghy notes (quoted in Dunn 2003, 192) this name had two meanings in Ngbandi, "the warrior who knows no defeat because of his endurance and inflex-

ible will and is all powerful, leaving fire in his wake as he goes from conquest to conquest," and in Tshiluba, the more concise meaning, "invincible warrior, cock who leaves no chick intact." Both translations of this name point to highly aggressive, sexualized, and hypermasculine features.

11. *Salongo* was a state-sponsored daily newspaper published from 1972 to 2004. It was released daily, while Saturday/Sunday issues were usually combined and published as one issue. During the 1970s, the primary decade of interest for this chapter, it was edited by Nsama Bondo. The name *Salongo* referred to a larger policy of cooperative work, usually on agricultural and public works projects, which citizens were supposed to do for the well-being and betterment of the nation as a whole.

12. A short clip of the opening to news broadcasts in Zaire can be viewed in the film *Mobutu: King of Zaire* (Thierry Michel, director) at 39:50 into the film.

13. The expansion of Mobutu's political power into the religious realm and representations of Mobutu that cast him as divine again bring our attention to the interrelatedness of political and religious authority. In a sense, it could be argued that Mobutu was trying to present himself as a divine king, with his almost absolute power over the citizens fully sanctioned by the spiritual world.

14. I have reproduced the Kikongo and French sections as they were written in the MPR document, and I translated the French to English.

15. There is a song called "Djalelo" that was a traditional Luba song used for the investiture of a new chief. It was appropriated and changed into a song praising Mobutu and became one of the most popular songs of his regime. For more, see Covington-Ward 2008, 253–55.

16. The information in this section is based mainly on primary schools. For further information on the different levels of participation between primary and secondary students, see Schatzberg 1978.

17. Youth here, like in other parts of Sub-Saharan Africa, is usually constructed in opposition to elder (Shepler 2010, 630) and is more of a social category than a biological category.

Chapter 5: Dancing Disorder in Mobutu's Zaire

1. Vitalo is a grenadine soft drink of the Belgian-owned Bralima beverage company.

2. Achille Mbembe coined the term *intimate tyranny* to describe the relationship linking the rulers with the ruled in African postcolonies, such that "the subjects . . . have internalized the authoritarian epistemology to the point where they reproduce it themselves in all the minor circumstances of daily life" (1992, 23). However, while this term captures the close relationship between ruler and ruled, the women involved that I interviewed were not reproducing their negative experiences of animation in other areas of their lives. Intimate violence then attempts to capture the literal and physical intimacy that is a part of unwanted sexual encounters between the young female dancers and male state authority figures.

3. The scholars mentioned here have begun to fill that gap by looking at the roles of women as figurative and reproductive mothers in nationalist discourses, the place

of sexuality, and women in violent conflict between and within nations, among others.

4. In his research in Guinea, Jay Straker (2009) found similar practices of local leaders and residents pointing out youth for recruitment into militant theater troupes.

5. During the 1970s in Zaire, during the height of animation politique, girls were disproportionately excluded from both primary and secondary education. For example, in 1971, only 37 percent of primary school pupils and 21 percent of secondary school pupils were female. Ten years later, gender disparities still remained, as 42 percent of primary school pupils and 27 percent of secondary school pupils were female (World Bank Databank Gender Statistics).

6. One example of the economic benefits of having a high position in the animation hierarchy could be seen when various businesses were nationalized, taken from foreigners, and given to supporters of Mobutu. In a list of acquirers who received businesses in the town of Bumba, one assistant regional animateur received a general commerce business to run (Young and Turner 1985, 342).

7. Ma Mayazola, October 5, 2005; Ma Bangoma, October 14, 2005; and Ma Ntima, October 10, 2005.

8. In her book on women's political dancing in Malawi, Lisa Gilman briefly mentions that some women dancers were expected to offer sexual favors (2009, 67, 78). However, there is no further investigation of this practice in the book.

9. Salongo was a policy of collective work in the national interest that Mobutu instituted in 1973. Citizens had to provide their labor, without pay, for various projects such as road building, construction, agricultural work, repairs of government buildings, and so on. Participation was obligatory, and refusal to comply could lead to imprisonment and/or fines (Callaghy 1984, 299–301).

10. In the 1990s, 86.5 percent of the country's population was conservatively estimated to be Christian (Meditz and Merrill 1994).

11. For some of the gross abuses of citizens of Zaire under Mobutu, see Schatzberg (1988), particularly chapter 4: "The State as Bandit."

Chapter 6: Bundu dia Kongo and Embodied Revolutions

1. The ngongi is a metal double bell that in the past was associated with the aristocracy and the royal court in the Kongo Kingdom.

2. This conversation actually took place in French.

3. Werreson (also known as Le Roi de la forêt, the king of the forest) is a popular musician of Congolese soukouss dance music. In 2005–6, his song "Alerte General" was one of the most popular songs.

4. Zikua (mazikua plural) is how members of BDK refer to their prayer and research groups.

5. See map 2.1 (of the Lower Congo province).

6. Mama Vita Kimpa, also known as Doña Beatrice Kimpa Vita, was a powerful prophet holding a treasured place in the history and collective imagination of the Kongo people. Possessed by the spirit of Saint Anthony, she tried to restore a crumbling Kongo Kingdom and was burned alive at the stake for the threat she posed to not only certain elite rulers, but also to European Catholic mission-

aries stationed there at the time. See chapter 2 for further detail, and also Rudy Mbemba (2002); John Thornton (1998).

7. Owing to the delicate political situation in the Congo in regards to Bundu dia Kongo, I have tried to be extremely careful to protect the identities of those members with whom I came into contact. Besides using pseudonyms, I have chosen to minimize the number of images that I use in this chapter, and in those that I do include, to make sure that any markers of identity (such as faces) are not visible.

8. Most of my interactions with Bundu dia Kongo members were with the men. I did not interview any of the women.

9. I thank Patricia Van Leeuwaarde Moonsammy for helping me to see this through her comments on this chapter.

10. Some of the few English publications that do exist include the following. John Thornton devotes a paragraph to the group in relation to discussions of the origins of the Kongo Kingdom (2004, 36). Wendy Lee Bernhard (1997) focuses primarily on the writings of Ne Muanda Nsemi, writing from the point of view of a Christian missionary seeking to combat BDK's attacks on Christianity. Thus, the partial nature of her master's thesis necessitates an extremely careful reading. A chapter on BDK by Ernest Wamba-dia-Wamba (1999) provides a useful introductory overview to the group and their ideology, from the point of view of a MuKongo scholar able to decipher the nuances of the Kikongo terms and phrases found throughout BDK literature.

11. The presidential elections were held on August 30, 2006.

12. Website of the Independent Electoral Commission of the Democratic Republic of Congo, accessed December 14, 2007, http://www.cei-rdc.cd/parti_politique.php3?page=0.

13. "Calme précaire à Luozi." Le Potential 2008.

14. Ernest Wamba-dia-Wamba 1999, 216.

15. Information about Ne Muanda Nsemi's visions is also provided on the new website of BDK, under the subsection "L'appel," and also in Ernest Wamba-dia-Wamba (1999, 216). For further in-depth discussion of Simon Kimbangu and his religious movement, see chapter 2.

16. Many different sorts of trinities abound in the teachings and philosophy of Bundu dia Kongo.

17. Bundu dia Kongo published numerous pamphlets printed in Kikongo, Lingala, French, and even English. Some of these documents, authored by Ne Muanda Nsemi, are available at select libraries in the United States. They are published on a number of topics, from historical pamphlets about the Kongo Kingdom, to a discussion of the need to dissolve colonial frontiers, to information about the return of African Americans and others of the "Kongo diaspora" to the Congo. A listing of the pamphlets and longer documents can be found on their website at www.bundudiakongo.org. The smaller pamphlets, which can be handed out on streets to passersby, are very important tools of transmitting BDK's message to the larger community.

18. Ne Muanda Nsemi n.d., 3–5.

19. Kabuayi 2006; Ne Mosi, October 10, 2005; Ne Zole, September 19, 2005.

20. The emblem of Bundu dia Kongo is a six-pointed star that I, like many others, first think of as the Star of David and associate with Jews. In the writings of Ne Muanda Nsemi, the six-pointed star is said to symbolize "the alliance between the trinitary God of the sky and his chosen people, the Kongo people, who are also a trinitary people: Nsaku, Mpanzu, Nzinga" (1995, 13). However, the star is also explained as coming from the long history of the Kongo people in the world. "As a result of the marriage of King Solomon of Jerusalem with queen Mankenda Saba, of the clan Bena Kongo, King Solomon married the six-pointed star with the Menorah" (Ne Muanda Nsemi 1995, 15).

21. Ne Zole (February 7, 2006); Ne Muanda Nsemi (1996, 19).

22. This requirement of sexual abstinence is similar to restrictions laid out for bangunza prophets and healers to enable them to amass spiritual power for healing.

23. For examples of some of these conflicts, see the newspaper article citations.

24. As an intellectual, I was told to give to the Mpanzu basket, and at the end, the tallies from each basket were announced to the group members.

25. See John K. Thornton 2001, 1–31.

26. My discussions with BDK led me to explore this particular historical connection with Liberia even further. As it turns out, several thousand African recaptives on slave ships coming from the Congo River area were captured by U.S. naval ships in the nineteenth century. These recaptives were resettled in Liberia and integrated into Americo-Liberian society over time. This is what led to the term *Congo* being used to refer to Americo-Liberians. I am currently researching this story for a book-length historical manuscript.

27. L'Association Musicale BaKongo (AMUBAKO) translates as BaKongo Musical Association. Bakongo Renaissance was a group formed for alumni of the Kisantu Catholic mission schools in Lower Congo.

28. AMUBAKO, RENAIBAKO, and ABAKO are all examples of Kongo cultural organizations that were focused more on Kongo people as an entire group rather than on local or regional differences. Before and after these organizations were founded until the present day, there continue to be many mutual aid societies or organizations focused on members being Kongo people from particular sectors, districts, and even villages. For further information on local and regional ethnic organizations and alumni associations in Kinshasa in general, see Verhaegen (2003, 55–85).

29. Mbanza Kongo was the capital of the former Kongo Kingdom, while *Ntotila*, in this context, is often taken as an alternate way to refer to the Kongo Kingdom, although the word itself refers to the head, leader, or ruler of the Kongo Kingdom. The meaning of *Ntotila* continues to be debated by some Kongo scholars, although the root verb of the word *Ntotila* is "tota," to gather together.

30. Bangala refers to the people, while Lingala refers to their language, just as BaKongo refers to the Kongo people and Kikongo refers to their language.

31. At the time, the AEF was the acronym for the Afrique Équatoriale Française, or French Equatorial Africa. This was a conglomeration of all the French colonies in Middle Africa, including what are today the countries of Gabon, the Republic of Congo, the Central African Republic, and Chad. In the Republic of Congo, in

particular, the majority of the population is people of the Kongo ethnic group (estimated 48 percent of the population), CIA World Factbook, accessed May 29, 2008, https://www.cia.gov/library/publications/the-world-factbook/geos/cf.html #PeopleU.

32. The first republic refers to the first government of the Congo postindependence under Kasa-Vubu and Lumumba. The second republic refers to the country under the rule of Mobutu for nearly three decades. The third republic refers to the new government formed in 2006 in the first free elections since independence.

33. He calls these confederations common markets, and these include North Africa, West Africa, East Africa, Central Africa, and South Africa; unnumbered page.

34. For further discussion of these issues and Ne Muanda Nsemi's articulation of Pan-Africanism, see Nsemi 1994a. The European Union is the modern day articulation of the type of structure that Nkrumah envisioned for the United States of Africa.

35. For an extensive overall review of anthropological literature on divine kingship, see Gillian Feeley-Harnik 1985, 273–313.

36. I counted the number of claps during the first sequence of four prayers, and there were eighteen claps per prayer, seventy-two claps altogether.

37. In other churches in Luozi, I also saw the three hand claps being used, but to reference the Holy Trinity. For example, in the DMNA church, it was used to emphasize "Mu Pere, Mu Fils, Mu Saint Esprit" (the Father, the Son, the Holy Spirit).

38. The "tu" in tukunda is simply the first-person plural (we) form of the verb kunda.

39. The first person to really explicate this cosmology in published form was A. kia Bunseki-Lumanisa Fu-Kiau (1969). This publication is likely the most important overview of Kongo cosmology to have ever been produced. Written in both French and Kikongo by a MuKongo who comes from the Manianga region on which much of my own research is based, it explains many of the symbols and ideas that prevail in Kongo cosmology. Other authors who have also written about Kongo cosmology, based on their own research, include influential studies such as Wyatt MacGaffey (1986b), and Thompson and Cornet (1981).

40. These are both artists of Congolese popular soukouss dance music.

41. According to the MONUC report and the Human Rights Watch report, this police force was not a regular group of police but largely consisted of ex-military soldiers. Relatedly, the weapons used by the police force on the BDK protesters/ groups were automatic weapons such as AK-47 machine guns.

42. The MONUC report says that in Luozi, local BDK members freed inmates from a Luozi prison after allegedly threatening authorities there (2008, 3). Most alarmingly, two men accused of sorcery were burned to death by BDK members in the towns of Kinkenge and Bethelemi on February 24 and 25, 2008, and a member of the DRC military was killed by BDK members on March 1, 2008.

REFERENCES

Primary Sources

MINISTÈRE DES AFFAIRES ÉTRANGÈRES (ARCHIVES AFRICAINES), BRUSSELS, BELGIUM (AA)

AIMO 1630/9190

AIMO 1630/9184

AIMO 1634/9191B

AIMO 1878/9981

Rapport Annuel, Territoires des Mayumbe, Manianga, Thysville, Luozi

AMERICAN BAPTIST HISTORICAL SOCIETY ARCHIVE, ATLANTA, GEORGIA (ABHS)

Assorted Missionary Correspondence

Assorted Annual Reports

Box 280

BAPTIST MISSIONARY SOCIETY ARCHIVE, OXFORD, UK (BMSA)

A/38

A/43

A/102

A/126

A/133

NATIONAL ARCHIVES, KINSHASA, DRC

MPR Documents

1973 Festival d'Animation, November 24, 1973. Répertoire Choc des Chansons et
   Slogans, Révolutionnaires du Bas-Zaire. Carton MPR, Juillet IV.

N.d. Unnumbered document, MPR carton, "Topo et Synthèse de la nouvelle concep
   tion."

PERIODICALS
Alliance Weekly
Baptist Missionary Magazine
Congo Mission News
Congo News Letter
Courrier d'Afrique
Missionary Herald
Salongo

INTERVIEWS CITED IN MANUSCRIPT

Ne Nkamu Luyindula, April 28, 2005, Kinshasa, DRC, September 20 and 23, 2005, Luozi, DRC.

Father Masamba, June 3, 2005, Kinshasa, DRC, interview by author and Alain Nkisi.

Tata George Matadi, July 16, 2005, Kinshasa, DRC.

Tata Mbumba, July 21, 2005, Mayidi, DRC.

Tata Tuzolana, July 22, 2005, Mayidi, Bas-Congo, interview by author, Ndundu Kivwila, and Abbe Hippolyte Ngimbi.

Mama Nsafu, September 20, 2005, Luozi, DRC.

Tata Nkuku, September 29, 2005, Luozi, DRC.

Tata Kimfumu, September 29, 2005, Luozi, DRC.

Ma Mayazola, October 5, 2005, Kinshasa, DRC.

Ma Ntima, October 10, 2005, Luozi, DRC.

Ne Mosi, October 10, 2005, Luozi, DRC.

Ne Tatu, October 10, 2005, and October 23, 2005, Luozi, DRC.

Ma Bangoma, October 14, 2005, Luozi, DRC.

Tata Nkolele, October 14, 2005, Luozi, DRC.

Tata Malanda, October 28, 2005, Luozi, DRC.

Tata Yangalala, October 30, 2005, Luozi, DRC.

Pastor Kasambi, November 12, 2005, and July 19, 2010, Luozi, DRC.

Group Members of Groupe Traditionelle Manianga, December 17, 2005, Kinshasa, DRC.

Tata Mukiese, January 30, 2006, and February 18, 2006, Luozi, DRC.

Ne Zole, February 7 and February 9, 2006, Luozi, DRC.

Dr. Mbala Nkanga, July 19, 2007, Ann Arbor, Michigan (informal interview/conversation).

Tata Kizole, July 20, 2010, Luozi, DRC.

Tata Vita, July 21, 2010, Luozi, DRC.

Ma Makanda, July 23, 2010, Luozi, DRC.

Ma Kudia, July 25, 2010, Luozi, DRC.

Ma Kudada, July 26, 2010, Luozi, DRC.

Ma Luzitu, July 27, 2010, Luozi, DRC.

Secondary Sources

Adelman, Kenneth Lee. 1975. "The Church-State Conflict in Zaire: 1969–1974." *African Studies Review* 18 (1): 102–16.

Adelman, Kenneth Lee. 1976. "The Zairian Political Party as Religious Surrogate." *Africa Today* 23 (4): 47–58.

Adler, Patricia, and Peter Adler. 1987. "Everyday Life Sociology." *Annual Review of Sociology* 13: 217–35.

Agadjanian, Alexander. 2001. "Public Religion and the Quest for National Ideology: Russia's Media Discourse." *Journal for the Scientific Study of Religion* 40 (3): 351–65.

Ahman, Birgitta. [1928] 2003. *Au pays de palmiers: Récits du Congo écrits par des moniteurs Indigènes*. Stockholm: Èditions Svenska Missionskyrkan.

Aldén, Karl. 1936. "The Prophet Movement in Congo." *International Review of Missions* 25: 347–53.

Allen, Jafari. 2011. *Venceremos? The Erotics of Black Self-Making in Cuba*. Durham, NC: Duke University Press.

Anderson, Benedict. 1991. *Imagined Communities: Reflections on the Origin and Spread of Nationalism*. London: Verso.

Anderson, Scott A. 2008. "How Did There Come to Be Two Kinds of Coercion." *Amintaphil: The Philosophical Foundations of Law and Justice* 2 (1): 17–29.

Andersson, Efraim. 1958. *Messianic Popular Movements in the Lower Congo*. Uppsala, Sweden: Almqvist and Wiksells Boktryckeri AB.

Angrosino, Michael. 2002. "Civil Religion Redux." *Anthropological Quarterly* 75 (2): 239–67.

Appadurai, Arjun, ed. 1986. *The Social Life of Things: Commodities in Cultural Perspective*. Cambridge: Cambridge University Press.

Appiah, Kwame Anthony, and Henry Louis Gates Jr. 1999. *Africana: The Encyclopedia of the African and African American Experience*. New York: Basic Civitas Books.

Arcangeli, Alessandro. 1994. "Dance under Trial: The Moral Debate 1200–1600." *Dance Research: The Journal for the Society of Dance Research* 12 (2): 127–55.

Argenti, Nicholas. 2007. *The Intestines of the State: Youth, Violence, and Belated Histories in the Cameroon Grassfields*. Chicago: University of Chicago Press.

Arondekar, Anjali. 2005. "Without a Trace: Sexuality and the Colonial Archive." *Journal of the History of Sexuality* 14 (1/2): 10–27.

"Arrestation d'une vingtaine de members de 'Bundu dia Mayala' l'ex-groupe politico-militaire interdit 'Bundu dia Kongo.'" 2012. *Agence Congolaise de Presse*. February 20. Accessed April 1, 2013. http://www.digitalcongo.net/article/81488.

Asch, Susan. 1983. *L'eglise du prophète Simon Kimbangu: De ses origines à son rôle actuel au Zaïre, 1921–1981*. Paris: Editions Karthala.

Askew, Kelly M. 2002. *Performing the Nation: Swahili Music and Cultural Politics in Tanzania*. Chicago: Chicago University Press.

Austin, J. L. 1962. *How to Do Things with Words*. Oxford: Clarendon Press.

Axelson, Sigbert. 1970. *Culture Confrontation in the Lower Congo: From the Old Congo Kingdom to the Congo Independent State with Special Reference to the Swedish Missionaries in the 1880's and 1890's*. Sweden: Gummessons.

Bacchi, Carol, and Chris Beasley. 2000a. "Citizen Bodies: Embodying Citizens—A Feminist Analysis." *International Feminist Journal of Politics* 2 (3): 337–58.

Bacchi, Carol, and Chris Beasley. 2002. "Citizen Bodies: Is Embodied Citizenship a Contradiction in Terms?" *Critical Social Policy* 22 (2): 324–52.

Barber, Karin. 1987. "Popular Arts in Africa." *African Studies Review* 30 (3): 1–78.

Batsîkama ba Mampuya ma Ndâwla, Raphaël. 1999. *L'Ancien Royaume du Congo (Ndona Béatrice and voici les Jagas): Séquences d'histoire populaire.* Paris: L'Harmattan.

Bauman, Richard. 1989. "Performance." In *International Encyclopedia of Communication*, edited by Eric Barnouw, 262–66. Oxford: Oxford University Press.

Bauman, Richard, and Charles Briggs. 1990. "Poetics and Performance as Critical Perspectives on Language and Social Life." *Annual Review of Anthropology* 19: 59–88.

Bayles, Michael. [1972] 2009. "A Concept of Coercion." In *Nomos XIV: Coercion*, edited by J. Roland Pennock and John W. Chapman, 16–29. Piscataway, NJ: Aldine.

Begler, Elsie B. 1978. "Sex, Status, and Authority in Egalitarian Society." *American Anthropologist* 80 (3): 571–88.

Bellah, Robert. 1967. "Civil Religion in America." *Daedalus* 96 (1): 1–21.

Bernard, H. Russell. 2011. *Research Methods in Anthropology.* 5th ed. Lanham, MD: Altamira.

Bernhard, Wendy Lee. 1997. "Bundu dia Kongo: A New Non-Christian Religious Movement in Zaire." Master's thesis, Fuller Theological Seminary.

Berrey, Stephen. 2006. "Against the Law: Violence, Crime, State Oppression, and Black Resistance in Jim Crow Mississippi." PhD diss., University of Texas at Austin.

Bierstedt, Robert. 1950. "An Analysis of Social Power." *American Sociological Review* 15 (1): 730–38.

Bloemraad, Irene, Anna Korteweg, and Gokce Yurdakul. 2008. "Citizenship and Immigration: Multiculturalism, Assimilation, and Challenges to the Nation-State." *Annual Review of Sociology* 34: 153–79.

Bockie, Simon. 1993. *Death and the Invisible Powers: The World of Kongo Belief.* Bloomington: Indiana University Press.

Boddy, Janice. 1989. *Wombs and Alien Spirits.* Madison: University of Wisconsin Press.

Bontinck, Francois, trans. 1964. *Brève relation de la fondation de la mission des frères mineurs Capucins du Séraphique père Saint François au Royaume de Congo, et des particularités, coutumes, et façons de vivre des habitants de ce Royaume.* Louvain: Editions Nauwelaerts.

Bontinck, Francois. 1969. "Le conditionnement historique de l'implantation de l'église Catholique au Congo." *Revue de Clergé Africain* 24 (2): 132–45.

Bontinck, Francois, trans. 1970. *Daire congolais de Fra Luca da Caltanisetta (1690–1701).* Louvain: Editions Nauwelaerts.

Booth, Newell. 1976. "Civil Religion in Traditional Africa." *Africa Today* 23 (4): 59–66.

Botombele, Bokanga Ekanga. 1976. *Cultural Policy in the Republic of Zaire.* Paris: UNESCO Press.

Bourdieu, Pierre. 1977. *Outline of a Theory of Practice.* Cambridge: Cambridge University Press.

Bourdieu, Pierre. 1990. *The Logic of Practice.* Cambridge: Polity Press.

Boyle, Patrick. 1995. "School Wars: Church, State, and the Death of the Congo." *Journal of Modern African Studies* 33 (3): 451–68.

Braddick, Michael J., ed. 2009. "The Politics of Gesture: Historical Perspectives." Special issue, supplement 4, *Past and Present* 203.

Bremmer, Jan, and Herman Roodenburg, eds. 1992. *A Cultural History of Gesture.* Ithaca, NY: Cornell University Press.

Bronner, S. J. 1988. "Art, Performance, and Praxis: The Rhetoric of Contemporary Folklore Studies." *Western Folklore* 47: 75–102.

Brown, Peter. 1988. *The Body and Society: Men, Women, and Sexual Renunciation in Early Christianity.* New York: Columbia University Press.

Brown, Ras Michael. 2012. *African-Atlantic Cultures and the South Carolina Low Country.* New York: Cambridge University Press.

Burton, Richard F. 1876. *Two Trips to Gorilla Land and the Cataracts of the Congo.* Vol. 2. London: S. Low and Searle.

Butler, Judith. 1992. "Mbembe's Extravagant Power." *Public Culture* 5 (1): 67–74.

Butler, Judith. 2004. "Performative Acts and Gender Constitution." In *The Performance Studies Reader*, edited by Henry Bial, 154–66. New York: Routledge.

Callaghy, Thomas. 1984. *The State-Society Struggle: Zaire in Comparative Perspective.* New York: Columbia University Press.

"Calme précaire à Luozi: La MONUC renforce son dispositif militaire au Bas-Congo." 2008. *Le Potential*, March 4. Accessed March 4, 2008. http://digitalcongo.net /article/50199.

Carlson, Marvin. 1996. *Performance: A Critical Introduction.* New York: Routledge.

Castaldi, Francesca. 2006. *Choreographies of African Identities: Negritude, Dance, and the National Ballet of Senegal.* Urbana: University of Illinois Press.

Cavazzi, Giovanni Antonio. 1687. *Istorica Descrizione de Tre Regni Congo, Matamba, et Angola. sitvati nell'Etiopia inferiore occidentale e delle missioni apostoliche esercitateui da religiosi Capuccini.* Bologna: Giacomo Monti.

Central Intelligence Agency. 2015. "Democratic Republic of the Congo" and "Republic of Congo." The World Factbook. Accessed March 31, 2015. https://www.cia.gov /library/publications/the-world-factbook/geos/cg.html and https://www.cia.gov /library/publications/the-world-factbook/geos/cf.html.

Centre de Recherche et d'Information Socio-politiques (CRISP). 1960. *Le Kibanguisme* 47: 2–20. Courrier Hebdomadaire de CRISP.

Centre de Recherche et d'Information Socio-politiques (CRISP). 1962. *A.B.A.K.O. 1950–1960. Documents.* Brussels: L'Imprimerie D. Van Keerberghen & Fils.

Chomé, Jules. 1959. *La passion de Simon Kimbangu.* Brussels: Les amis de la Présence Africaine.

Churchill, Awnsham, and John Churchill. 1704. *A Collection of Voyages and Travels.* London: Printed by H.C. for A. and J. Churchill.

Coleman, John. 1970. "Civil Religion." *Sociological Analysis* 31 (2): 67–77.

Comaroff, Jean. 1985. *Body of Power, Spirit of Resistance: The Culture and History of a South African People.* Chicago: University of Chicago Press.

Comaroff, Jean, and John Comaroff. 1992. *Ethnography and the Historical Imagination.* Boulder, CO: Westview Press.

Congo Belge, Gouvernement Local. 1912. *Recueil bi-Mensuel des ordonnances, circulaires, instructions et ordres de service*, no. 1 (January), circular #14.

Congo Belge, Gouvernement Local. 1913. *Recueil mensuel des ordonnances, circulaires, instructions et ordres de service*, no. 10 (October), circular #139.

Congo Belge, Gouvernement Local. 1915. *Recueil mensuel des ordonnances, circulaires, instructions et ordres de service*, no. 1 (January), circular #2.

Connerton, Paul. 1989. *How Societies Remember*. New York: Cambridge University Press.

Conrad, Joseph. 1900. "The Heart of Darkness." *Living Age*, June 16–August 4. Accessed May 3, 2012. http://www.conradfirst.net/view/serialisation?id=75.

Covington-Ward, Yolanda. 2008. "Embodied Histories, Danced Religions, Performed Politics: Kongo Cultural Performance and the Production of History and Authority." PhD diss., University of Michigan.

Covington-Ward, Yolanda. 2012. "Joseph Kasa-Vubu, ABAKO, and Performances of Kongo Nationalism in the Independence of Congo." *Journal of Black Studies* 43 (1): 72–94.

Covington-Ward, Yolanda. 2014. "'Your Name Is Written in the Sky': Unearthing the Stories of Kongo Female Prophets in Colonial Belgian Congo, 1921–1960." *Journal of Africana Religions* 2 (3): 317–46.

Cristi, Marcela. 2001. *From Civil to Political Religion: The Intersection of Culture, Religion, and Politics*. Waterloo, Ontario: Wilfrid Laurier University Press.

Csordas, Thomas. 1993. "Somatic Modes of Attention." *Cultural Anthropology* 8 (2): 135–56.

Csordas, Thomas. 1999. "The Body's Career in Anthropology." In *Anthropological Theory Today*, edited by H. Moore, 172–205. Cambridge: Polity.

Csordas, Thomas. 2008. "Intersubjectivity and Intercorporeality." *Subjectivity*, no. 22: 110–21.

Csordas, Thomas. 2011. "Embodiment: Agency, Sexual Difference, and Illness." In *Companion to the Anthropology of the Body/Embodiment*, edited by Frances E. Mascia-Lees, 137–56. Chichester, UK: Wiley-Blackwell.

Cuvelier, Jean. 1939. "Les Missions Catholiques en face des danses des Bakongo." *Africanae Fraternae Ephemerides Romanae* 17: 143–70.

Cuvelier, Jean, ed. and trans. 1953a. "Documents sur une mission Française au KaKongo (1766–1776)." *Académie Royale des Sciences d'Outre-mer Classe des Sciences Morales et Politiques, Mémoires* 30 (1): 1–132. Brussels: Institute Royale Coloniale Belge.

Cuvelier, Jean, ed. and trans. 1953b. "Relations sur le Congo du Père Laurent du Lucques (1700–1717)." *Académie Royale des Sciences d'Outre-mer Classe des Sciences Morales et Politiques, Mémoires* 32 (2): 1–358. Brussels: Institute Royale Coloniale Belge.

Cuvelier, Jean, and O. de Bouveignes. 1951. *Jérôme de Montesarchio: Apôtre du Vieux Congo*. Namur: Grands Lacs.

Cuvelier, Jean, and Louis Jadin, eds. and trans. 1954. "L'ancien Congo d'après les Archives Romaines (1518–1640)." *Académie Royale des Sciences d'Outre-mer Classe des Sciences Morales et Politiques, Mémoires* 36 (2): 1–600. Brussels: Institute Royale Coloniale Belge.

Dapper, Olfert. 1686. *Description de la Afrique, contenant les noms, les situations . . .*

Translation from Flemish. Amsterdam: Wolfgang, Waesberge, Boom, and Van Someren.

Das, Veena. 2008. "Violence, Gender, and Subjectivity." *Annual Review of Anthropology* 37: 283–99.

Daughtry, Carla. 1997. "Greenness in the Field." *Michigan Today* 29 (3): 21–22.

De Boeck, Filip, and Marie-Françoise Plissart. 2004. *Kinshasa: Tales of the Invisible City*. Tervuren, Belgium: Royal Museum of Central Africa.

DeCapmaker, P. 1938. "Danses des BaKongo." In *La Mission et les Joies Populaires: Compte Rendu de la XVIe Semaine de Missiologie de Louvain*, 40. Brussels: L'édition Universelles, S.A.

DeFrantz, Thomas, and Anita Gonzalez, eds. 2014. *Black Performance Theory*. Durham, NC: Duke University Press.

De Jorio, Andrea. 2000. *Gesture in Naples and Gesture in Classical Antiquity*. Translated by Adam Kendon. Bloomington: Indiana University Press.

Denzin, Norman K. 2002. "Much Ado about Goffman." *American Sociologist* 33 (2): 105–17.

Derrida, Jacques. 1996. *Archive Fever*. Chicago: University of Chicago Press.

De Saint Moulin, Léon, and M. Ducreux. 1969. "Le Phénomène Urbain à Kinshasa: Évolution et Perspective." *Études Congolaises* 12 (4): 117–42.

Desch-Obi, T. J. 2002. "Combat and the Crossing of Kalunga." In *Central Africans and Cultural Transformations in the American Diaspora*, edited by Linda Heywood, 353–72. Cambridge: Cambridge University Press.

Desch-Obi, T. J. 2008. *Fighting for Honor: The History of African Martial Arts Traditions in the Atlantic World*. Columbia: University of South Carolina Press.

DeVault, Marjorie, and Glenda Gross. 2007. "Feminist Interviewing: Experience, Talk, and Knowledge." In *Handbook of Feminist Research: Theory and Praxis*, edited by Sharlene Hesse-Biber, 173–97. Thousand Oaks, CA: Sage.

Devisch, René. 1996. "'Pillaging Jesus': Healing Churches and the Villagisation of Kinshasa." *Africa: Journal of the International African Institute* 66 (4): 555–86.

Drewal, Margaret Thompson. 1991. "The State of Research on Performance in Africa." *African Studies Review* 34 (3): 1–64.

Drewal, Margaret Thompson. 1992. *Yoruba Ritual*. Bloomington: Indiana University Press.

Dunn, Kevin. 2003. *Imagining the Congo: The International Relations of Identity*. New York: Palgrave MacMillan.

Durkheim, Emile. [1912] 1995. *The Elementary Forms of Religious Life*. New York: Free Press.

Durkheim, Emile. [1915] 1964. *The Elementary Forms of Religious Life*. London: George Allen and Unwin.

Ebron, Paulla. 2007. "Constituting Subjects through Performative Acts." In *Africa after Gender?*, edited by Catherine Cole, Takyiwaa Manuh, and Stephan Miescher, 171–90. Bloomington: Indiana University Press.

Edgell, Penny. 2012. "A Cultural Sociology of Religion: New Directions." *Annual Review of Sociology* 38: 247–65.

Edmondson, Laura. 2007. *Performance and Politics in Tanzania: The Nation on Stage.* Bloomington: Indiana University Press.

Eglise du Christ au Congo (ECC) 63 ème Communauté du Saint Esprit en Afrique (CSEA). n.d. *Les Grandes Lignes Doctrinale de la Communauté du Saint Esprit en Afrique.* Nzieta, Luozi, DRC.

Eley, Geoff, and Ronald Suny, eds. 1996. *Becoming National: A Reader.* New York: Oxford University Press.

Engelke, Matthew. 2007. *A Problem of Presence.* Berkeley: University of California Press.

Erlmann, Veit. 1996. *Nightsong: Performance, Power, and Practice in South Africa.* Chicago: University of Chicago Press.

Etambala, Mathieu Zana. 2004. "L'État colonial et les missions Catholiques face au mouvement Kimbanguiste à la veille de l'indépendance du Congo Belge 1944–1960." *Annales Aequatoria* 25: 95–149.

Ewing, Katherine. 2006. "Revealing and Concealing: Interpersonal Dynamics and the Negotiation of Identity in the Interview." *Ethos* 34 (1): 89–122.

Fabian, Johannes. 1990. *Power and Performance: Ethnographic Explorations through Proverbial Wisdom and Theater in Shaba, Zaire.* Madison: University of Wisconsin Press.

Fabian, Johannes. 1996. *Remembering the Present: Painting and Popular History in Zaire.* Berkeley: University of California Press.

Fanon, Frantz. 1967. *Black Skin, White Masks.* Translated by Charles Lam Markmann. New York: Grove.

Farnell, Brenda. 1995. *Do You See What I Mean? Plains Indians Sign Talk and the Embodiment of Action.* Austin: University of Texas Press.

Farnell, Brenda. 1999. "Moving Bodies, Acting Selves." *Annual Review of Anthropology* 28 (1): 341–73.

Farnell, Brenda. 2000. "Getting Out of Habitus: An Alternative Model of Dynamically Embodied Social Action." *Journal of the Royal Anthropological Institute* 6 (3): 397–418.

Feci, Damaso. 1972. *Vie cachée et vie publique de Simon Kimbangu selon la littérature colonial et missionnaire belge.* Brussels: CEDAF (Centre d'étude et de documentation africaines).

Feeley-Harnik, Gillian. 1985. "Issues in Divine Kingship." *Annual Review of Anthropology* 14: 273–313.

Fields, Karen E. 1985. *Revival and Rebellion in Colonial Central Africa.* Portsmouth, NH: Heinemann.

Fields-Black, Edda. 2008. *Deep Roots: Rice Farmers in West Africa and the African Diaspora.* Bloomington: Indiana University Press.

FORCAD. 1986. *Glossaire idéologique du MPR.* Kinshasa: Editions FORCAD.

Foucault, Michel. 1978. *The History of Sexuality: An Introduction.* Vol. 1. New York: Random House.

Foucault, Michel. 1980. "Two Lectures." In *Power/Knowledge: Selected Interviews and Other Writings, 1972–1977,* edited by Colin Gordon, 78–133. New York: Pantheon.

Foucault, Michel. 1984. "Nietzsche, Genealogy, History." In *The Foucault Reader*, edited by Paul Rabinow, 76–100. New York: Pantheon.

Foucault, Michel. 1991. "Governmentality." In *The Foucault Effect: Studies in Governmentality*, edited by Graham Burchell, Colin Gordon, and Peter Miller, 87–104. Chicago: University of Chicago Press.

Foucault, Michel. [1977] 1995. *Discipline and Punish: The Birth of the Prison*. Westminster, MD: Vintage.

Foucault, Michel. 2000. "The Subject and Power." In *Michel Foucault, Power*, edited by James Faubion, 326–48. New York: New Press.

Franklin, John Hope. 1985. *George Washington Williams: A Biography*. Chicago: University of Chicago Press.

Frederiksen, Bodil Folke. 1991. "Joe, the Sweetest Reading in Africa: Documentation and Discussion of a Popular Magazine in Kenya." *African Languages and Cultures* 4 (2): 135–55.

Fu-Kiau, A. kia Bunseki-Lumanisa. 1969. *N'Kongo ye nza yakun'zungidila; nza-Kôngo/ Le Mukongo et le monde qui l'entourait*. [The MuKongo and the world that surrounds him]. French translation by Zamenga Batukezanga. Kinshasa: National Office of Research and Development.

Fu-Kiau, A. kia Bunseki-Lumanisa. 2001. *African Cosmology of the Bantu-Kongo*. New York: Athelia Henrietta Press.

Furey, Constance. 2012. "Body, Society, and Subjectivity in Religious Studies." *Journal of the American Academy of Religion* 80 (1): 7–33.

Gast, Leon, and Taylor Hackford, dirs. 1997. *When We Were Kings*. 94 min. Gramercy Pictures: DAS Films.

Geuns, Andre. 1974. "Chronologie des Mouvements Religieux Indépendants au Bas-Zaire, particulièrement du Mouvement fondé par le Prophete Simon Kimbangu." *Journal of Religion in Africa* 6 (3): 187–222.

Geurts, Kathryn. 2002. *Culture and the Senses: Embodiment, Identity, and Well-Being in an African Community*. Berkeley: University of California Press.

Gilman, Lisa. 2001. "Purchasing Praise: Women, Dancing, and Patronage in Malawi Party Politics." *Africa Today* 48 (4): 43–64.

Gilman, Lisa. 2004. "The Traditionalization of Women's Dancing, Hegemony, and Politics in Malawi." *Journal of Folklore Research* 41 (1): 33–60.

Gilman, Lisa. 2009. *The Dance of Politics: Gender, Performance, and Democratization in Malawi*. Philadelphia: Temple University Press.

Gilroy, Paul. 1993. *The Black Atlantic: Modernity and Double Consciousness*. Cambridge, MA: Harvard University Press.

Goffman, Erving. 1959. *The Presentation of Self in Everyday Life*. Garden City, NY: Doubleday.

Goffman, Erving. 1961. *Encounters: Two Studies in the Sociology of Interaction*. Indianapolis: Bobbs-Merrill.

Goffman, Erving. 1967. *Interaction Ritual: Essays in Face-to-face Behavior*. Chicago: Aldine.

Goffman, Erving. 1983. "The Interaction Order: American Sociological Assoc., 1982 Presidential Address." *American Sociological Review* 48 (1): 1–17.

Gondola, Ch. Didier. 2002. *The History of Congo.* Westport, CT: Greenwood.

Gordon, Edmund. 1998. *Disparate Diasporas: Identity and Politics in an Afro-Nicaraguan Community.* Austin: University of Texas Press.

Gorr, Michael. 1986. "Toward a Theory of Coercion." *Canadian Journal of Philosophy* 16 (3): 383–405.

Gotink, Hugo. 1995. *Mangembo 1921–1942: Un regard sur l'evangelisation Catholique dans le Territoire de Luozi.* Kinshasa: Editions Centre de Vulgarisation Agricole.

Graham, R. H. C. 1921. "The Prophets: The Remarkable Movement in Lower Congo." *The Missionary Herald.*

Hall, David. 1997. *Lived Religion in America: Toward a History of Practice.* Princeton, NJ: Princeton University Press.

Harrison, Faye, ed. 1991. *Decolonizing Anthropology: Moving Further Toward an Anthropology for Liberation.* Washington, DC: Association of Black Anthropologists/American Anthropological Association.

Haviland, John B. 1998. "Early Pointing Gestures in Zincantan." *Journal of Linguistic Anthropology* 8 (2): 162–96.

Haviland, John B. 1999. "Gesture." *Journal of Linguistic Anthropology* 9 (1–2): 88–91.

Heywood, Linda, ed. 2002. *Central Africans and Cultural Transformations in the American Diaspora.* New York: Cambridge University Press.

Hilton, Anne. 1985. *The Kingdom of Kongo.* New York: Oxford University Press.

Hochschild, Adam. 1998. *King Leopold's Ghost: A Story of Greed, Terror, and Heroism in Colonial Africa.* Boston: Houghton Mifflin.

Hoskyns, Catherine. 1965. *The Congo since Independence: January 1960–December 1961.* Oxford: Oxford University Press.

Huckstep, Joan. 2005. "Embodied Nationalism 'Animation Politique' (Political Dance) in Zaire: A Case Study of the Dimensionality and Agency of Dance as the Spirit of Individual, Community, and National Identity." PhD diss., Temple University.

Human Rights Watch. 2008. *"We Will Crush You": The Restriction of Political Space in the Democratic Republic of Congo.* New York: Human Rights Watch.

Hunt, Nancy Rose. 1999. *A Colonial Lexicon of Birth Ritual, Medicalization, and Mobility in the Congo.* Durham, NC: Duke University Press.

Hurston, Zora Neale. 1938. *Tell My Horse: Voodoo and Life in Haiti and Jamaica.* Philadelphia: J. B. Lippincott.

Hurston, Zora Neale. [1942] 1991. *Dust Tracks on a Road.* New York: Harper Perennial.

Hymes, Dell. 1975. "Breakthrough into Performance." In *Folklore: Performance and Communication,* edited by Dan Ben-Amos and Kenneth Goldstein, 11–74. The Hague: Mouton.

Institut National de la Statistique. 1984. *Résultats provisoires du recensement scientifique de la population du 1er juillet 1984.* Kinshasa: Secrétariat national du recensement.

Jackson, John L. 2001. *Harlemworld: Doing Race and Class in Contemporary Black America.* Chicago: University of Chicago Press.

Jackson, Michael. 1989. *Paths toward a Clearing: Radical Empiricism and Ethnographic Inquiry*. Bloomington: Indiana University Press.

Jacobson-Widding, Anita. 1979. *Red—White—Black as a Mode of Thought: A Study of Triadic Classification by Colours in the Ritual Symbolism and Cognitive Thought of the Peoples of the Lower Congo*. Uppsala, Sweden: Almqvist and Wiksell.

Jadin, Louis. 1961. "Le Congo et la secte des Antoniens. Restauration du royaume sous Pedro IV et la 'Saint Antoine' congolaise (1694–1718)." *Bulletin de l'Institut Historique Belge de Rome* 33: 411–615.

Janzen, John. 1971. "Kongo Religious Renewal: Iconoclastic and Iconorthostic." *Canadian Journal of African Studies* 5 (2): 135–43.

Janzen, John. 1972. "Laman's Kongo Ethnography: Observations on Sources, Methodology, and Theory." *Africa: Journal of the International African Institute* 42 (4): 316–28.

Janzen, John. 1977. "The Tradition of Renewal in Kongo Religion." In *African Religions, A Symposium*, edited by Newell S. Booth Jr., 69–115. New York: Nok.

Janzen, John. 1978. *The Quest for Therapy in Lower Zaire*. Berkeley: University of California Press.

Janzen, John. 1982. *Lemba, 1650–1930: A Drum of Affliction in Africa and the New World*. New York: Garland.

Janzen, John. 1992. *Ngoma: Discourses of Healing in Central and Southern Africa*. Berkeley: University of California Press.

Janzen, John, and Wyatt MacGaffey. 1974. *An Anthology of Kongo Religion: Primary Texts from Lower Zaire*. Lawrence: University of Kansas Publications in Anthropology, no. 5.

Jewsiewicki, Bogumil, and V. Y. Mudimbe. 1993. "Africans' Memories and Contemporary History of Africa." *History and Theory* 32 (4): 1–11.

Johnson, E. Patrick. 2003. *Appropriating Blackness: Performance and the Politics of Authenticity*. Durham, NC: Duke University Press.

Jones, Donald, and Russell Richey, eds. 1990. *American Civil Religion*. San Francisco: Mellen Research University Press.

Joset, Paul-Ernest. 1968. "Quelques mouvements religieux au Bas-Congo et dans l'ex-Afrique Equatoriale Française." *Journal of Religion in Africa* 1 (2): 101–28.

Jules-Rosette, Bennetta. 1975a. *African Apostles: Ritual and Conversion in the Church of John Maranke*. Ithaca, NY: Cornell University Press.

Jules-Rosette, Bennetta. 1975b. "Song and Spirit: The Use of Songs in the Management of Ritual Contexts." *Africa: Journal of the International African Institute* 45 (2): 150–66.

Jules-Rosette, Bennetta. 1988. "Prophetic Performances: Apostolic Prophecy as Social Drama." *Theatre Drama Review* 32 (2): 140–59.

Jules-Rosette, Bennetta. 1994. "The Future of African Theologies—Situating New Religious Movements in an Epistemological Setting." *Social Compass* 41 (1): 46–95.

Kabuayi, Freddy Mulumba. 2006. "Ne Muanda Nsemi, chef spirituel de Bundu dia Kongo: Il faut absolutment un mini-dialogue avant le 30 juin 2006." *Le Potential*, May 15. Accessed February 29, 2008. http://www.lepotentiel.com/afficher_article.php?id_cdition=&id_articlc=27678.

Kannyo, Edward. 1979. "Post-colonial Politics in Zaire, 1960–79." In *Zaire: The Political Economy of Underdevelopment*, edited by Guy Gran, 54–68. New York: Praeger.

Kapalanga, Gazungil Sang'Amin. 1989. "Les spectacle d'animation politique en République du Zaire: Analyse des mécanismes de reprise, d'actualisation et de politisation des formes culturelles africaines dans les créations spectaculaires modernes." PhD diss., Centre d'Etudes Théâtrales, Université de Catholique de Louvain.

Kaplan, Irving. 1979. *Zaire: A Country Study*. Washington, DC: American University.

Kavenadiambuko Ngemba Ntime. 1999. *La Methode d'evangelisation des Redemptoristes Belges au Bas-Congo (1899–1919)*. Rome: Editrice Pontificia Universita Gregoriana.

Kayembe-Buba. 1970. *Histoire et signification de Djalelo*. Kinshasa: Impr. de Kinshasa.

Kendon, Adam. 1997. "Gesture." *Annual Review of Anthropology* 26: 109–28.

Kendon, Adam. 2004. *Gesture: Visible Action as Utterance*. New York: Cambridge University Press.

Kim, Suk-Young. 2010. *Illusive Utopia: Theater, Film, and Everyday Performance in North Korea*. Ann Arbor: University of Michigan Press.

Kodi, M. W. 1993. "The 1921 Pan-African Congress at Brussels: A Background to Belgian Pressures." In *Global Dimensions of the African Diaspora*, 2nd ed., edited by Joseph Harris, 263–88. Washington, DC: Howard University Press.

Koren, Henry J. 1958. *The Spiritans: A History of the Congregation of the Holy Ghost*. Pittsburgh: Duquesne University Press.

Kottak, Conrad. 2006. *Anthropology: The Exploration of Human Diversity*. 11th ed. New York: McGraw-Hill.

Kratz, Michaël. 1970. *La Mission des Rédemptoristes Belges au Bas-Congo: La Période des semailles (1899–1920)*. Brussels: Académie Royale des Sciences d'Outre-Mer.

Kurtz, Donald. 2001. *Political Anthropology: Paradigms and Power*. Boulder, CO: Westview.

La Fontaine, J. S. 1970. *City Politics: A Study of Leopoldville, 1962–1963*. Cambridge: Cambridge University Press.

Lagergren, David. 1970. *Mission and State in the Congo: A Study of the Relations between Protestant Missions and the Congo Independent State Authorities with Special Reference to the Equator District, 1885–1903*. Uppsala, Sweden: Almqvist and Wiksells.

Laman, Karl. 1957. *The Kongo* Vol. 2. Uppsala, Sweden: Almqvist and Wiksells.

Laman, Karl. 1962. *The Kongo* Vol. 3. Uppsala, Sweden: Almqvist and Wiksells.

Laman, Karl. [1936] 1964. *Dictionnaire KiKongo-Francais*. Ridgewood, NJ: Gregg.

Laman, Karl. 1968. *The Kongo* Vol. 4. Uppsala, Sweden: Almqvist and Wiksells.

Lambek, Michael. 1990. "Certain Knowledge, Contestable Authority: Power and Practice on the Islamic Periphery." *American Ethnologist* 17 (1): 23–40.

"Le député national élu de Luozi Ne Muanda Nsemi appelé à raffermir la paix au Bas-Congo." 2008. *Agence Congolaise de Presse*, February 19. Accessed February 29, 2008. http://www.digitalcongo.net/article/49911#.

Leese, Daniel. 2011. *Mao Cult: Rhetoric and Ritual in China's Cultural Revolution*. New York: Cambridge University Press.

Leiser, Burton. 2008. "On Coercion." *Amintaphil: The Philosophical Foundations of Law and Justice* 2 (1): 31–43.

Lemarchand, Rene. 1961. "The Bases of Nationalism among the BaKongo." *Africa: Journal of the International African Institute* 31 (4): 344–54.

Lerrigo, Peter Hugh James. 1922. *Rock-Breakers: Kingdom Building in Kongo Land*. Philadelphia: Judson.

Lewis, M. Paul, Gary F. Simons, and Charles D. Fennig, eds. 2015. "Koongo." *Ethnologue: Languages of the World, Eighteenth edition*. Dallas: SIL International. Accessed March 30, 2015. http://www.ethnologue.com/language/kon.

Lock, Margaret. 1993. "The Anthropology of the Body." *Annual Review of Anthropology* 22: 133–53.

Lutete, Celestin. 2008. "Affaire BDK: La MONUC promet de diligenter une enquête sur les violations des droits de l'homme au Bas-Congo." March 13. Accessed March 14, 2008. http://www.digitalcongo.net/article/50367.

Lutunu, Diawawana Mfumu. 1982. "Historique et structure de la Communauté du Saint-Esprit en Afrique (1961–1981)." Master's thesis, Protestant Faculty of Theology in Zaire.

Lyons, Maryinez. 1992. *The Colonial Disease: A Social History of Sleeping Sickness in Northern Zaire, 1900–1940*. Cambridge: Cambridge University Press.

Mabandu, Rachidi. 2008. "Révolte de Bundu dia Kongo: La sang continue à couler a Bas-Congo." *Forum des As*, March 5. Accessed March 5, 2008. http://www.digitalcongo.net/article/50216.

MacAloon, John, ed. 1984. *Rite, Drama, Festival, Spectacle: Rehearsals toward a Theory of Cultural Performance*. Philadelphia: Institute for the Study of Human Issues.

MacGaffey, Janet. 1988. "Evading Male Control: Women in the Second Economy in Zaire." In *Patriarchy and Class: African Women at Home and in the Workforce*, edited by Sharon Stichter and Jane Parpart, 161–76. Boulder, CO: Westview.

MacGaffey, Janet. 1991. *The Real Economy of Zaire: The Contribution of Smuggling and Other Unofficial Activities to National Wealth*. Philadelphia: University of Pennsylvania Press.

MacGaffey, Wyatt. 1968. "Kongo and the King of the Americans." *Journal of Modern African Studies* 6 (2): 171–81.

MacGaffey, Wyatt. 1970. *Custom and Government in the Lower Congo*. Berkeley: University of California Press.

MacGaffey, Wyatt. 1972. "Comparative Analysis of Central African Religions." *Africa* (42): 21–31.

MacGaffey, Wyatt. 1977. "Cultural Roots of Kongo Prophetism." *History of Religions* 17 (2): 177–93.

MacGaffey, Wyatt. 1983. *Modern Kongo Prophets: Religion in a Plural Society*. Bloomington: Indiana University Press.

MacGaffey, Wyatt. 1986a. "Ethnography and the Closing of the Frontier in Lower

Congo, 1885–1921." *Africa: Journal of the International African Institute* 56 (3): 263–79.

MacGaffey, Wyatt. 1986b. *Religion and Society in Central Africa: The BaKongo of Lower Zaire*. Chicago: University of Chicago Press.

MacGaffey, Wyatt. 1992. "Kimbanguism in the Independence Process." *Congo 1955–1960: Recueil D'études*, edited by A. Beyens, 329–42. Brussels: Académie Royale des Sciences d'Outre-Mer.

MacGaffey, Wyatt. 1998. "Am I Myself? Identities in Zaire, Then and Now." *Transactions of the Royal Historical Society* 8: 291–307.

Mackay, D. J. 1987. "Simon Kimbangu and the B.M.S. Tradition." *Journal of Religion in Africa* 17 (2): 113–71.

Mackay, Donald, and Daniel Ntoni-Nzinga. 1993. "Kimbangu's Interlocuter: Nyuvudi's 'Nsamu Miangunza (The Story of the Prophets).'" *Journal of Religion in Africa* 23 (3): 232–65.

Mahaniah, Kimpianga. 1975. "The Background of Prophetic Movements in the Belgian Congo: A Study of the Congolese Reaction to the Policies and Methods of Belgian Colonization and to the Evangelization of the Lower Congo by Catholic and Protestant Missionaries, from 1877 to 1921." PhD diss., Temple University.

Mahaniah, Kimpianga. 1982. *La Maladie et la guérison en milieu Kongo*. Kinshasa: Centre de Vulgarisation Agricole.

Mahaniah, Kimpianga. 1988. *L'Impact du Christianisme au Manianga*. Kinshasa: Editions Centre de Vulgarisation Agricole.

Mahaniah, Kimpianga. 1989. *Découvrir la zone de Luozi*. Kinshasa: Editions Centre de Vulgarisation Agricole.

Mahaniah, Kimpianga. 1993. "The Presence of Black Americans in the Lower Congo from 1878 to 1921." In *Global Dimensions of the African Diaspora, Second Edition*, edited by Joseph Harris, 405–20. Washington, DC: Howard University Press.

Mahema, Pastor Esther Luhunu. 2005. *La Femme vertueuse en milieu Africain*. Luozi, DRC: Presses de l'Université Libre de Luozi.

Markoff, John, and Daniel Regan. 1981. "The Rise and Fall of Civil Religion: Comparative Perspectives." *Sociological Analysis* 42 (4): 333–52.

Markowitz, Marvin. 1973. *Cross and Sword: The Political Role of Christian Missions in the Belgian Congo, 1908–1960*. Stanford, CA: Hoover Institution Press.

Marshall, Ruth. 2009. *Political Spiritualities: The Pentecostal Revolution in Nigeria*. Chicago: University of Chicago Press.

Martin, Marie-Louise. 1975. *Kimbangu: An African Prophet and His Church*. Oxford: Basil Blackwell.

Martin, Phyllis. 1995. *Leisure and Society in Colonial Brazzaville*. Cambridge: Cambridge University Press.

Martinez-Ruiz, Barbaro. 2009. "Kongo Atlantic Body Language." In *Performance, art, et anthropologie* (les actes). Accessed March 28, 2015. http://actesbranly.revues.org /462.

Martinez-Ruiz, Barbaro. 2013. *Kongo Graphic Writing and Other Narratives of the Sign*. Philadelphia: Temple University Press.

Masquelier, Adeline. 2001. *Prayer Has Spoiled Everything*. Durham, NC: Duke University Press.

Mauss, Marcel. [1934] 1979. "The Techniques of the Body." In *Sociology and Psychology, Essays*, 97–135. London: Routledge and Kegan Paul.

Mbemba, Rudy. 2002. *Le procès de Kimpa Vita: La Jeanne d'Arc congolaise*. Paris: Harmattan.

Mbembe, Achille. 1992. "The Banality of Power and the Aesthetics of Vulgarity in the Post-colony." *Public Culture* 4 (2): 1–30.

Mbembe, Achille. 2001. *On the Postcolony*. Berkeley: University of California Press.

Mbembe, Achille. 2002. "The Power of the Archive and Its Limits." In *Refiguring the Archive*, edited by Carolyn Hamilton, 19–27. Cape Town: David Phillip.

McCall, John C. 2000. *Dancing Histories: Heuristic Ethnography with the Ohafia Igbo*. Ann Arbor: University of Michigan Press.

McClintock, Anne. 1991. "No Longer in a Future Heaven": Women and Nationalism in South Africa. *Transition* 51: 104–23.

McEwan, Cheryl. 2000. "Engendering Citizenship: Gendered Spaces of Democracy in South Africa." *Political Geography* 19: 627–51.

McGreal, Chris. 1997. "Women Hope for Dictator's Demise." *Mail and Guardian*. Accessed April 7, 2015. http://mg.co.za/article/1997-04-18-women-hope-for-dictators-demise.

McGuire, Meredith. 1990. "Religion and the Body: Rematerializing the Human Body in the Social Sciences of Religion." *Journal for the Scientific Study of Religion* 29 (3): 283–96.

McGuire, Meredith. 2008. *Lived Religion: Faith and Practice in Everyday Life*. New York: Oxford University Press.

McLaurin, Irma. 1996. *Women of Belize: Gender and Change in Central America*. New Brunswick, NJ: Rutgers University Press.

McLaurin, Irma, ed. 2001. *Black Feminist Anthropology: Theory, Politics, Praxis, and Poetics*. New Brunswick, NJ: Rutgers University Press.

McNeil, David, ed. 2000. *Language and Gesture*. Cambridge: Cambridge University Press.

Meditz, Sandra, and Tim Merrill. 1994. *Zaire: A Country Study*. Washington, DC: Federal Research Division, Library of Congress.

Melzer, Sara, and Kathryn Norberg, eds. 1998. *From the Royal to the Republican Body: Incorporating the Political in Seventeenth and Eighteenth Century France*. Berkeley: University of California Press.

Mendoza, Zoila. 2000. *Shaping Society through Dance*. Chicago: University of Chicago Press.

Merleau-Ponty, Maurice. [1962] 1981. *The Phenomenology of Perception*. Translated by Colin Smith. London: Routledge.

Messick, Brinkley. 1993. *The Calligraphic State: Textual Domination and History in a Muslim Society*. Berkeley: University of California Press.

Meyer, Birgit. 2004. "Christianity in Africa: From African Independent to Pentecostal-Charismatic Churches." *Annual Review of Anthropology* 33: 447–74.

Mianda, Gertrude. 1995. "Dans l'ombre de la 'démocratie' au Zaïre: La Remise en question de l'émancipation Mobutiste de la femme." *Canadian Journal of African Studies* 29 (1): 51–78.

Mintz, Sidney W. 1986. *Sweetness and Power: The Place of Sugar in Modern History.* New York: Penguin.

Mitchell, Timothy. 1988. *Colonising Egypt.* Cambridge: Cambridge University Press.

Mobutu Sese Seko, Joseph-Désiré. 1975. *Discours, Allocations, et Messages.* Kinshasa: Publié par le Bureau du Président-Fondateur du MPR, Vol. 2.

Mobutu Sese Seko, Joseph-Désiré. 1983. *Discours, Allocations, et Messages.* Kinshasa: Publié par le Bureau du Président-Fondateur du MPR, Vol. 3.

Molyneux, Gordon. 1990. "The Place and Function of Hymns in the EJCSK (Eglise de Jésus-Christ sur terre par le Prophète Simon Kimbangu)." *Journal of Religion in Africa* 20 (2): 153–87.

Mona, Franck. 2007. "La Cei coupe court a la contestation par l'UN de l'election du gouverneur et vice-gouverneur du Bas-Congo." *Le Potential*, February 1. Accessed March 8, 2008. http://www.digitalcongo.net/article/40745.

Monteiro, Joachim John. 1875. *Angola and the River Congo (Volume II).* London: MacMillan and Co.

MONUC Human Rights Division. 2008. *Special Report: Special Inquiry into the Bas Congo Events of February and March 2008.* Office of the United Nations High Commissioner for Human Rights.

Moon, Seungsook. 2005. *Militarized Modernity and Gendered Citizenship in South Korea.* Durham, NC: Duke University Press.

Morel, E. D. 1907. *Red Rubber: The Story of the Rubber Slave Trade Flourishing on the Congo in the Year of Grace 1907.* London: T. F. Unwin.

MPR (Mouvement Populaire de la Revolution). 1967. *Manifeste de la N'sele.* Zaire: Mouvement populaire de la revolution.

Mudimbe, V. Y. 1988. *The Invention of Africa.* Bloomington: Indiana University Press.

Mudimbe, V. Y. 1994. *The Idea of Africa.* Bloomington: Indiana University Press.

Narayan, Kirin. 1993. "How Native Is a Native Anthropologist?" *American Anthropologist* 95 (3): 671–86.

Ndaywel è Nziem, Isidore. 1998. *Histoire gdu Congo.* Paris: De Boeck and Larcier.

Nicholaï, Henri. 1960. "Luozi: géographie régionale d'un pays du Bas-Congo." *Académie Royale des Sciences d'Outre-Mer, Classe des Sciences Naturelles et Médicales, Mémoires* 12 (5): 1–104.

Nkanga, Dieudonne Mbala. 1992. "'Radio Trottoir' in Central Africa." *Passages* 4: 4–5, 8.

Noland, Carrie. 2009. *Agency and Embodiment: Performing Gestures/Producing Culture.* Cambridge, MA: Harvard University Press.

Noland, Carrie, and Sally Ann Ness, eds. 2008. *Migrations of Gesture.* Minneapolis: University of Minnesota Press.

Nsemi, Ne Muanda. 1994a. *Le Culte Pan Africain.* Kinshasa: Editions Mpolo Ngimbi.

Nsemi, Ne Muanda. 1994b. *L'Espace culturel Kongo.* Kinshasa: Editions Mpolo Ngimbi.

Nsemi, Ne Muanda. 1995. *L'Union federale du Kongo.* Kinshasa: Editions Mpolo Ngimbi.

Nsemi, Ne Muanda. 1996. *Connaître le Kongo*. Kinshasa: Editions Mpolo Ngimbi.

Nsemi, Ne Muanda. n.d. *Les Enfants de Ne Kongo*. Kinshasa: Editions Mpolo Ngimbi.

Nzongola-Ntalaja, Georges. 2002. *The Congo from Leopold to Kabila: A People's History*. London: Zed.

Olesky, Elzbieta, Jeff Hearn, and Dorota Golanska, eds. 2011. *The Limits of Gendered Citizenship: Contexts and Complexities*. London: Routledge.

Ong, Aihwa. 1987. *Spirits of Resistance and Capitalist Discipline*. Albany: SUNY Press.

Parsons, Talcott. 1986. "Power and the Social System." In *Power*, edited by Steven Lukes, 94–143. Oxford: Basil Blackwell.

Pemberton, Jeremy. 1993. "The History of Simon Kimbangu, Prophet by the Writers Nfinangani and Nzungu 1921: An Introduction and Annotated Translation." *Journal of Religion in Africa* 23 (3): 194–231.

Pierre, Jemima. 2012. *The Predicament of Blackness: Postcolonial Ghana and the Politics of Race*. Chicago: University of Chicago Press.

Pruden, Wesley. 2009. "Obama Bows, the Nation Cringes." *Washington Times*, November 17: A4. Accessed October 5, 2010. http://www.washingtontimes.com/news/2009/nov/17/pruden-obama-bows-the-nation-cringes/?feat=home_headlines.

Pype, Katrien. 2007. "Fighting Boys, Strong Men, and Gorillas: Notes on the Imagination of Masculinities in Kinshasa." *Africa* 77 (2): 250–71.

Ranger, Terence. 1975. *Dance and Society in East Africa, 1890–1970: The Beni Ngoma*. Berkeley: University of California Press.

Ranger, Terence. 1986. "Religious Movements and Politics in Sub-Saharan Africa." *African Studies Review* 29: 1–69.

Reardon, Ruth Slade. 1968. "Catholics and Protestants in the Congo." In *Christianity in Tropical Africa*, edited by C. G. Baeta, 83–98. London: Oxford University Press.

Reed, Susan A. 1998. "The Politics and Poetics of Dance." *Annual Review of Anthropology*, no. 27: 503–32.

Remilleux, Jean-Louis, and Mobutu Sese Seko. 1989. *Dignité pour l'Afrique*. Paris: A. Michel.

Renne, Elisha. 2004. "Dressing in the Stuff of Dreams: Sacred Dress and Religious Authority in Southwestern Nigeria." *Dreaming* 14 (2–3): 120–35.

Roberts, Allen. 2013. *A Dance of Assassins: Performing Early Colonial Hegemony in the Congo*. Bloomington: Indiana University Press.

Rose, Tricia. 1994. *Black Noise: Rap Music and Black Culture in Contemporary America*. Hanover, NH: Wesleyan University Press.

Royce, Anya. 1977. *The Anthropology of Dance*. Bloomington: Indiana University Press.

Royce, Anya. 1984. *Movement and Meaning: Creativity and Interpretation in Ballet and Mime*. Bloomington: Indiana University Press.

Rushforth, Scott. 1994. "Political Resistance in a Contemporary Hunter-Gatherer Society: More about Bearlake Atapaskan Knowledge and Authority." *American Ethnologist* 21 (2): 335–52.

Ryckmans, André. 1970. *Les mouvements prophétiques Kongo en 1958*. Kinshasa: Bureau Organisation des Programmes Ruraux.

Schatzberg, Michael. 1978. "Fidélité au Guide: The J.M.P.R. in Zairian Schools." *Journal of Modern African Studies* 16 (3): 417–31.

Schatzberg, Michael. 1979. "The State and the Economy: The 'Radicalization of the Revolution' of Mobutu's Zaire." *Canadian Journal of African Studies* 14 (2): 239–57.

Schatzberg, Michael. 1988. *The Dialectics of Oppression in Zaire*. Bloomington: Indiana University Press.

Schatzberg, Michael. 2001. *Political Legitimacy in Middle Africa: Father, Family, Food*. Bloomington: Indiana University Press.

Schechner, Richard. 1985. *Between Theatre and Anthropology*. Philadelphia: University of Pennsylvania Press.

Schechner, Richard. 2013. *Performance Studies: An Introduction, 3rd edition*. London: Routledge.

Schepler, Susan. 2010. "Youth Music and Politics in Post-war Sierra Leone." *Journal of Modern African Studies* 48 (4): 627–42.

Schieffelin, Edward. 1997. "Problematizing Performance." In *Ritual, Performance, Media*, edited by Felicia Hughes-Freeland, 199–211. London: Routledge.

Schoepf, Brooke G. 2002. "'Mobutu's Disease': A Social History of AIDS in Kinshasa." *Review of African Political Economy* 29 (93/94): 561–73.

Scott, James. 1985. *Weapons of the Weak: Everyday Forms of Peasant Resistance*. New Haven, CT: Yale University Press.

Searle, John R. 1983. *Intentionality*. Cambridge: Cambridge University Press.

Searle, John R. 1992. *The Rediscovery of the Mind*. Cambridge, MA: MIT Press.

Shaw, Rosalind. 2002. *Memories of the Slave Trade: Ritual and the Historical Imagination in Sierra Leone*. Chicago: University of Chicago Press.

Simbandumwe, Samuel. 1992. "Understanding the Role of a Modern Prophet in Kimbanguist Hymns." *History of Religion* 32 (2): 165–83.

Simmons, Kimberly. 2009. *Reconstructing Racial Identity and the African Past in the Dominican Republic*. Gainesville: University Press of Florida.

Sinda, Martial. 1972. *Le Messianisme Congolais*. Paris: Payot.

Singer, Milton, ed. 1959. *Traditional India: Structure and Change*. Philadelphia: American Folklore Society.

Slade, Ruth. 1959. *English-Speaking Missions in the Congo Independent State (1878–1908)*. Brussels: 80 A rue de Livourne.

Slocum, Karla. 2001. "Negotiating Identity and Black Feminist Politics in Caribbean Research." In *Black Feminist Anthropology: Theory, Politics, Praxis, and Poetics*, edited by Irma McLaurin, 126–49. New Brunswick, NJ: Rutgers University Press.

Smith, Anthony. 1996. "The Origin of Nations." In *Becoming National: A Reader*, edited by Geoff Ely and Ronald Suny, 107–30. New York: Oxford University Press.

Smith, Anthony D. 2002. "When Is a Nation." *Geopolitics* 7 (2): 5–32.

Smith, Anthony. 2006. "Ethnicity and Nationalism." In *The Sage Handbook of Nations and Nationalism*, edited by Gerard Delanty and Krishan Kumar, 169–81. London: Sage.

Smith, Christian. 2003. *Moral, Believing Animals*. New York: Oxford University Press.

Stoler, Ann. 2002. "Colonial Archives and the Arts of Governance." *Archival Science* 2: 87–109.

Stoller, Paul. 1989. *Fusion of the Worlds: An Ethnography of Possession among the Songhay of Niger.* Chicago: University of Chicago Press.

Stoller, Paul. 1995. *Embodying Colonial Memories: Spirit Possession, Power, and the Hauka in West Africa.* New York: Routledge.

Stoller, Paul. 1997. *Sensuous Scholarship.* Philadelphia: University of Pennsylvania Press.

Straker, Jay. 2007. "Stories of 'Militant Theater' in the Guinean Forest: Demystifying the Motives and Moralities of a Revolutionary Nation-State." *Journal of African Cultural Studies* 19 (2): 207–33.

Straker, Jay. 2009. *Youth, Nationalism, and the Guinean Revolution.* Bloomington: Indiana University Press.

Strathern, Andrew. 1996. *Body Thoughts.* Ann Arbor: University of Michigan Press.

Strine, Mary, Beverly Whitaker Long, and Mary Frances Hopkins. 1990. "Research Trends in Interpretation and Performance Studies: Trends, Issues, Priorities." In *Speech Communication: Essays to Commemorate the Seventy-Fifth Anniversary of the Speech Communication Association,* edited by Gerald Philips and Julia Wood, 181–204. Carbondale: Southern Illinois University Press.

Swartz, Marc J., Victor W. Turner, and Arthur Tuden, eds. 1966. *Political Anthropology.* Chicago: Aldine.

Taylor, Diana. 2003. *The Archive and the Repertoire: Performing Cultural Memory in the Americas.* Durham, NC: Duke University Press.

"Terreur à Luozi et à Seke-Banza: Bundu dia Kongo défie l'autorité de l'Etat!" 2008. *Uhuru,* February 28. Accessed March 4, 2008. http://www.digitalcongo.net/article/50102.

Thassinda, uba Thassinda. 1992. *Zaire, les princes de l'invisible: L'Afrique noire bâillonnée par le parti unique.* Caen, France: Editions C'est-à-dire.

Thomas, Sir Keith. 1992. Introduction to *A Cultural History of Gesture,* edited by Jan Bremmer and Herman Roodenburg, 1–14. Ithaca, NY: Cornell University Press.

Thompson, Robert Farris. 1974. *African Art in Motion: Icon and Art in the Collection of Katherine Coryton White.* Los Angeles: University of California Press.

Thompson, Robert Farris. 1983. *Flash of the Spirit: African and Afro-American Art and Philosophy.* New York: Random House.

Thompson, Robert Farris. 2002. *Le Geste Kongo.* Paris: Museum Dapper.

Thompson, Robert Farris. 2005. *Tango: The Art History of Love.* New York: Pantheon Books.

Thompson, Robert Farris, and Joseph Cornet. 1981. *The Four Moments of the Sun: Kongo Art in Two Worlds.* Washington, DC: National Gallery of Art.

Thornton, John K. 1983. *The Kingdom of Kongo: Civil War and Transition, 1641–1718.* Madison: University of Wisconsin Press.

Thornton, John K. 1984. "The Development of an African Catholic Church in the Kingdom of Kongo, 1491–1750." *Journal of African History* 25 (2): 147–67.

Thornton, John K. 1991. "African Dimensions of the Stono Rebellion." *American Historical Review* 96 (4): 1101–13.

Thornton, John K. 1998. *The Kongolese Saint Anthony: Dona Beatriz Kimpa Vita and the Antonian Movement, 1684–1706.* Cambridge: Cambridge University Press.

Thornton, John K. 2001. "The Origins and Early History of the Kingdom of Kongo, c. 1350–1550." *International Journal of African Historical Studies* 34 (1) (2001): 1–31.

Thornton, John K. 2004. "Origin Traditions and History in Central Africa." *African Arts* 37 (1): 32–37, 93–94.

Toso, Carlo. 1984. *L'anarchia congolese nel sec. XVII : la relazione inedita di Marcellino d'Atri*. Genova: Bozzi.

Turner, Bryan. 1984. *The Body and Society*. Oxford: B. Blackwell.

Turner, Victor. 1987. *The Anthropology of Performance*. New York: PAJ Publications.

Ulysse, Gina. 2007. *Downtown Ladies: Informal Commercial Importers, A Haitian Anthropologist, and Self-Making in Jamaica*. Chicago: University of Chicago Press.

Van Wing, Joseph. 1937. "Les Danses Bakongo." *Congo: Revue générale de la Colonie Belge* 2 (2): 121–31.

Van Wing, Joseph. 1958. "Le Kibangisme vu par un temoin." *Zaire: Revue Congolaise* 12 (6): 563–618.

Van Wolputte, Steven. 2004. "Hang On to Your Self: Of Bodies, Embodiment, and Selves." *Annual Review of Anthropology* 33: 251–69.

Vansina, Jan. 1966. *Kingdoms of the Savanna*. Madison: University of Wisconsin Press.

Vansina, Jan. 1990. *Paths in the Rainforest: Toward a History of Political Tradition in Equatorial Africa*. Madison: University of Wisconsin Press.

Vansina, Jan, Willy de Craemer, and Renee Fox. 1976. "Religious Movements in Central Africa: A Theoretical Study." *Comparative Studies in Society and History* 18 (4): 458–75.

Vellut, Jean-Luc. 1987. "Résistances et espaces de liberté dans l'histoire coloniale du Zaïre: Avant la marche à L'Indépendance (ca. 1876–1945)." In *Rébellions-Révolutions au Zaïre, 1963–1965* Vol. 1, edited by Catherine Coquery-Vidrovitch, Alain Forest, and Herbert Weiss, 55–66. Paris: L'Harmattan.

Vellut, Jean-Luc, ed. 2005. *Simon Kimbangu 1921: De la predication à la deportation; Les Sources*. Vol. 1, *Fonds missionaries protestants (1), Alliance missionaire suédoise (Svenska Missionsförbundet, SMF)*. Brussels: Academie Royale des Sciences d'Outre Mer.

Vellut, Jean-Luc, ed. 2010. *Simon Kimbangu 1921: De la predication à la deportation; Les Sources*. Vol. 1, *Fonds missionaries protestants (2), Missions Baptistes et autres traditions évangéliques*. Brussels: Academie Royale des Sciences d'Outre Mer.

Verhaegen, Benoît. 1962. *ABAKO Documents, 1950–1960*. Brussels: Centre de Recherche et d'Information Socio-politiques (CRISP).

Verhaegen, Benoît. 2003. *L'ABAKO et l'indépendance du congo belge: dix ans de nationalisme kongo, 1950–1960*. Paris: L'Harmattan.

Wagner, Ann. 1997. *Adversaries of Dance*. Urbana: University of Illinois Press.

Wamba, Philippe. 1999. *Kinship: A Family's Journey in Africa and America*. New York: Dutton/Penguin.

Wamba-dia-Wamba, Ernest. 1999. "Bundu dia Kongo: A Kongolese Fundamentalist Religious Movement." In *East African Expressions of Christianity*, edited by Thomas Spear and Isaria Kimambo, 213–28. Athens: Ohio University Press.

Weber, Max. 1968. *Economy and Society: An Outline of Interpretive Sociology*. New York: Bedminster.

Wedeen, Lisa. 2008. *Peripheral Visions: Publics, Power, and Performance in Yemen*. Chicago: University of Chicago Press.

Weisenfeld, Judith. 2013. "Invisible Women: On Women and Gender in the Study of African American Religious History." *Journal of Africana Religions* 1 (1): 133–49.

Weiss, Gail. 1999. *Body Images: Embodiment as Intercorporeality*. New York: Routledge.

Werbner, Pnina, and Nira Yuval-Davis, eds. 1999. *Women, Citizenship, and Difference*. London: Zed.

West, Ellis. 1980. "Proposed Neutral Definition of Civil Religion." *Journal of Church and State* 22 (1): 23–40.

White, Bob. 2006. "L'Incroyable machine d'authenticité: L'animation politique et l'usage public de la culture dans le Zaire de Mobutu." *Anthropologie et Sociétés* 30 (2): 43–63.

White, Bob. 2008. *Rumba Rules: The Politics of Dance Music in Mobutu's Zaire*. Durham, NC: Duke University Press.

Wild-Wood, Emma. 2007. "'Se Débrouiller' or the Art of Serendipity in Historical Research." *History in Africa* 34 (1): 367–81.

Williams, Brackette. 1996. "Skinfolk, Not Kinfolk: Comparative Reflections of the Identity of Participant-Observation in Two Field Situations." In *Feminist Dilemmas in Fieldwork*, edited by Diane Wolf, 72–95. Boulder, CO: Westview.

Williams, Erica. 2013. *Sex Tourism in Bahia: Ambiguous Entanglements*. Urbana: University of Illinois Press.

Wolf, Diane, ed. 1996. *Feminist Dilemmas in Fieldwork*. Boulder, CO: Westview.

World Bank Databank. Gender Statistics (Democratic Republic of Congo). Accessed March 4, 2014. http://databank.worldbank.org/data/views/variableSelection /selectvariables.aspx?source=gender-statistics.

Young, Crawford. 1965. *Politics in the Congo: Decolonization and Independence*. Princeton, NJ: Princeton University Press.

Young, Crawford. 1983. "The Northern Republics, 1960–1980." In *History of Central Africa*, vol. 2, edited by David Birmingham and Phyllis Martin, 291–335. London: Longman.

Young, Crawford, and Thomas Turner. 1985. *The Rise and Decline of the Zairian State*. Madison: University of Wisconsin Press.

Young, Jason. 2007. *Rituals of Resistance: African Atlantic Religion in Kongo and the Lowcountry South in the Era of Slavery*. Baton Rouge: Louisiana State University Press.

Yuval-Davis, Nira. 1997. *Gender and Nation*. London: Sage.

Zagorin, Adam. 1993. "Leaving Fire in His Wake: Mobutu Sese Seko." *Time Magazine*, February 2. Accessed March 2, 2010. http: //content.time.com/time/magazine /article/0,9171,977788,00.html.

Zamenga, Batukezanga. 1979. *Un Croco a Luozi*. Kinshasa: Zabat.

Zinnbauer, Brian J., et al. 1997. "Religion and Spirituality: Unfuzzying the Fuzzy." *Journal for the Scientific Study of Religion* 36 (4): 549–64.

INDEX

Pages numbers followed by *f* indication illustratons and tables.

animation politique. *See* political animation

Anlo-Ewe ethnic group, 15

Ann Arbor, Michigan, 44, 239n5. *See also* University of Michigan

anthropology, 39, 44, 82, 133, 152, 217, 237n21; authority in, 236n16, 238n29; body in, 4, 18–19, 44; methodology and, 28–29, 54–68; performance in, 5, 7, 9, 20, 23, 140

Antonian Movement, 75, 229

Aragon, 227

Archives of the Redemptorist Fathers, 245n16

Argentina, 237n19

Aristotle, 7

art history, 17, 19

Askew, Kelly, 22–23

Association des BaKongo (ABAKO), 208

Atlanta, Georgia, 29, 44, 74

audiences, 5, 30, 91–92, 102, 156, 158, 214, 222, 227, 238n33, 246n18

Augouard, Prosper Phillipe, 78

Au Pays des Palmiers, 121

Austin, J. L., 9, 22

authenticity, 142–43, 149, 154, 157, 160–61, 178, 213

BaKongo. *See* BisiKongo ethnic group

Bakongo Renaissance, 251n27

BaLuba ethnic group, 62

Bana ba Tumi ethnic group, 206

Bangala ethnic group, 62, 208, 251n30

Bangoma, Ma, 165, 169–72, 180–81

bangunza, 24, 71–75, 84–99, 102, 104, 106–8, 122, 124–31, 162–63, 231, 240n4, 244n63. *See also* kingunza; Ngunzism

Bantu Migration, 206

baptism, 12, 25, 75, 83, 96, 104, 122, 229, 244n54

Baptist Missionary Society (BMS), 29, 32, 74, 76, 79, 83–85, 89, 101, 103–4, 130, 235n5, 241n9, 241n19

Baptists, 68. *See also* American Baptist Foreign Missionary Society; Baptist Missionary Society; Church and Missionary Alliance

basketball, 67, 240n21

Batikita, Ma, 122

Bauman, Richard, 237n18

Bayles, Michael, 141

Begler, Elsie, 236n16

Belgian colonialism. *See* Belgian Congo; Congo Free State

Belgian Congo, 5, 32–33, 60, 142, 200, 209, 240n4; dance in, 110–34, 229; kingunza in, 71–106

Belgian Redemptorists, 53, 76, 90, 120

Belgium, 28, 47, 60, 76, 78, 142, 157; Brussels, 29, 67, 74, 244n63; Louvain, 118; Tervuren, 29

Belize, 59

Bellah, Robert, 144, 238n32

Bemba, Chief, 97–98

Bena Kongo. *See* BisiKongo

Berlin conferences 1884–85, 76, 205

Bernhard, Wendy Lee, 250n10

A Better Chance program, 43

Bible, 1, 3, 26, 84, 93, 95, 100, 125, 199, 203–5, 210, 223

Bichini bia Congo, 44

Bierstedt, Robert, 236n16

bimpampa, 4, 17–19, 18*f,* 28–29, 31, 34, 211–12, 217, 219, 229–30, 237n19

BisiKongo ethnic group (BaKongo), 1–4, 11–12, 24, 32, 39, 62, 99, 133, 208–9, 238n36, 240n4, 242n29; dance and, 44, 111–13, 116–22, 120; definition, 236n7, 237n17, 251n30; gestures and, 19, 213; language and, 31, 188; marginalization of, 30, 225; MuKongo scholars, 19, 50, 78, 217, 250n10; political animation and, 151; religion and, 72, 75, 80, 84, 86, 94, 105, 194, 200, 202, 216, 240n4, 252n39; stereotypes about, 62

bisimbi, 85

Black Americans, 38–40, 56, 83, 105, 188, 193, 242n27. *See also* African Americans

Black communities, 2, 9, 11, 41, 43, 66–67, 88, 90, 114–16, 204, 210, 229. *See also* African diaspora; Afro-Caribbean communities; Pan-Africanism

Black Mission/Khaki Church. *See* Mpadism

Blackness, 2, 9, 41, 55–62, 65, 67–68, 101, 104, 192, 227, 229. *See also* African diaspora

Black Panthers, 192

Black Power: fist, 28; movement, 28, 192

Black Star Lines, 40

Bobangi (language), 208

body, 48, 110–11, 121–22, 191, 211–12, 223–25, 236n14, 237n19; body language, 19, 59, 239n13; as catalyst, 11, 34, 228, 231–32; as center, 4, 8, 10, 28, 34, 41, 54, 105, 228, 232; civil religion and, 24, 137–38, 146–47, 149, 158, 162–63, 173, 180, 182; as conduit, 10–11, 34, 228–30, 232; gender and, 166–68, 170, 173, 181–82; performance and, 1–22, 30; politics of the body, 44, 109, 133–34, 228; religion and, 24–28, 33–34, 75, 78, 80–81, 84–86, 89, 91–92, 98, 125, 127–34, 163, 193, 213, 216–22, 226, 245n1; of researcher, 32, 39, 41, 54–68, 229, 240n21; resistance through, 71–106. See also embodied performances; gesture; nitu; zakama

body hexis, 13–14

Bontinck, Pere, 29

bori, 26–27

Bourdieu, Pierre, 13–15, 22, 211, 236n10

Bowskill, Joseph, 103

Boyle, Patrick, 157

Bralima Brewery, 239n11, 248n1

Brazil, 60; Pernambuco, 229–30

Briggs, Charles, 237n18

Brown University: Afro-American Studies, 43; Program in Liberal Medical Education (PLME), 43

Buka, Ne Nganga, 219

BuKongo, 2, 197–99, 210, 214–17, 225, 231

bula makonko gesture, 2–3, 8, 12, 108, 190, 191f, 211–17, 214f, 216f, 219–20, 225–27, 230

Bundu dia Kongo (BDK), 2–3, 7–8, 29–30, 39, 62, 66, 68, 166, 187–226, 229, 231, 235n3, 249n4, 250nn7,8, 250n10, 250nn16,17, 251n20, 251n26, 252n41; 2008 violence, 34, 190, 193–94, 223–26, 252n41. See also Ne Muanda; Nsemi

Bundu dia Mayala, 190, 194

Bunseki, Fu-Kiau kia, 19, 217–18, 252n39

Butler, Judith, 9

Cabinda, 77f, 209

Callaghy, Thomas, 163, 247n10

Caltanisetta, Luca da, 212

Calvin, John, 245n11

Calvinists, 115

Cameroon, 32f, 140, 178, 206

Capuchins, 75

Caribbean, 43–44, 117. See also Afro-Caribbean communities; individual countries

Carlson, Marvin, 5

carnival, 43

Cartiaux, Léon, 39, 86–87, 97–99, 102, 104–5

Castaldi, Francesca, 23

Catholic Church, 25–26, 39, 58f, 132, 148, 158, 160–61, 198, 216, 219, 226, 246n17; dance and, 115–20, 125–26, 245n12. See also Holy See; missionaries; missionaries: Catholic missionaries; individual congregations

Catholic Redemptorist Fathers, 90, 245n16. See also Redemptorists

Central African Republic, 32f, 251n31

Centre d'Etudes pour l'Action Sociale (CEPAS), 29

Chad, 47, 251n31

Charles, 55–56

Cherubim and Seraphim African independent church, 245n1

China, 144, 147

Chirac, Jacques, 139f

Christian and Missionary Alliance (CMA), 76, 241n9

Christianity, 4, 75–78, 83, 129, 157, 192, 195, 216–17, 237n19, 245n10, 245n12, 249n10; BuKongo and, 2, 198, 202, 203–5, 219, 222–23, 225–26, 250n10; Christian prophetic movements, 3, 5, 20, 72, 84–85, 89–90, 94, 96, 102–3, 123, 131; dance within, 115–22, 124–27; Mobutu and, 147–48, 160–61, 178–81. See also Bible; Holy See; Holy Spirit; missionaries; individual denominations

Church of Jesus-Christ on Earth through the Prophet Simon Kimbangu, 132. See also Kimbanguist church

civil religion, 160, 164, 166, 178, 231; definition, 238n32; nationalism and, 32, 138–39, 142, 144–49, 158; political animation and, 24, 33, 151 civil society, 47–48, 174

Clark, Joseph, 101

class, 42, 43, 54, 57–58, 60–62, 64, 153, 179, 211, 220, 229, 240n20

coercion: gender and, 33–34, 166–72, 179, 182–83; political animation, 21, 24, 138–39, 141–42, 145–49, 157–58, 164

College Boboto, 29

Comaroff, Jean, 211, 238n31

Comaroff, John, 211

Communauté Evangelique du Congo (CEC), 29, 121, 129, 132f, 202, 216, 246n32

Congo Free State, 47, 60, 76–78, 113; Leopoldville, 47–48, 77f, 132–33, 142, 208, 241n10; Manianga, 53, 85, 109, 125, 128, 206; San Salvador, 76, 105, 241n19; Stanley Pool, 76, 79

Congolese civil wars, 20, 42, 46–47, 222

Congo News Letter, 89, 244n65

Congo River, 40, 47, 50, 53, 78, 104, 130, 206, 208, 224, 241n9, 244n65, 247n9, 251n26

Congregation for the Propagation of the Faith in Rome, 118

Connerton, Paul, 14–15

Conrad, Joseph: *Heart of Darkness,* 42

consciousness, 5–7, 14, 28, 91, 105, 134, 140, 149, 158, 219, 229

Cornet, Joseph, 217

cosmology, 6, 14, 78, 217–19, 218f, 252n39

Couldridge, Charles, 130–31

Counter-Reformation, 115

Cristi, Marcela, 145–46

Un croco à Luozi, 50

crocodiles, 49–51, 52f

Csordas, Thomas, 4, 8, 18, 236n14

Cuba, 67

cultural revitalization, 2–3, 193–94, 199, 202, 208–9, 213, 226

cultural studies, 17

Cuvelier, Monsignor Jean, 126; "Les Missions Catholiques en face des danses des Bakongo," 120

dance, 4–5, 15, 17, 18f, 23, 28–30, 43, 92–93, 107, 140, 144, 188, 228–30, 236n6, 236n12, 237n19, 239n5, 245n15, 247n7, 249n8;
in BisiKongo communities, 44, 111–13, 116–22, 226; Catholic views on, 115–20, 125–26, 245n12; dance clubs, 57, 64; dance music, 66, 247n9, 249n3, 252n40; dances of the hips, 19, 112; indigenous dances, 113; makinu ya nsi, 245n5; maringa, 117; ndosa dance, 112f, 245n5; political animation and, 7, 14, 21, 24, 33–34, 137–38, 145, 150–64, 166, 169–73, 176–78, 180–83, 231, 246n26, 248n2; Protestant views on, 112, 115–21, 161, 245n11, 246n18; religion and, 73, 108, 109f; saraband, 92, 243n52; secular dances, 33, 72, 110–27, 134; secret dances in the forest, 124

dancehalls, 44

dance studies, 17

"Les Danses Bakongo," 116–18

Dapper, Olfert, 82

Dapper Museum, 237n19

David (biblical figure), 1, 93

David (research assistant), 31, 188, 202

DeCapmaker, P., 118–19, 245n16

dekama, 165, 211, 213, 227, 237n20

Democratic Republic of Congo (DRC): Bamba, 87; Banana, 76, 77f; Bandundu, 32f, 108; Bangu, 103–4; Banza Manteke, 77f, 79, 241n9; Bas-Congo, 2, 29, 31, 32f, 43, 50, 52, 59, 63, 77f, 109, 118, 122–23, 128, 133, 139, 172, 193–94, 200, 223, 225, 235n1, 241n9; Belingo, 108; Bethelemi, 252n42; Boma, 32f, 52, 76, 77f, 78, 101, 113, 190, 241n9; Bu chefferie, 96; Bumba, 249n6; Congo-Brazzaville, 44, 77f, 131, 224–25, 236n7, 237n19; Congo-Kasai, 32f, 129, 142; Dembo, 96; Gombe, 12, 58f, 62, 64, 88; Inkisi, 172; Kamba, 88, 97; Kasangulu, 50; Kibentele, 77f, 85, 89, 241n9; Kibunzi, 77f, 85, 87, 103, 241n9; Kiesa, 97; Kimpaka, 99, 244n65; Kimpese, 50, 77f, 172, 241n9; Kimwenza, 29, 63; Kingoyi, 77f, 85, 116, 121, 124, 129, 241n9; Kinkenge, 77f, 86, 130, 241n9, 252n42; Kinkonzi, 77f, 241n19; Kinshasa, 2, 12, 20, 29–33, 41, 45, 47–50, 53–55, 58f, 59–67, 79, 81, 83, 104, 132, 137, 138, 139f, 142, 150–55, 158, 166, 168, 188–90, 199, 201–2, 208, 213, 219, 225, 236n7,

237n19, 239n8, 240n3, 240n16, 240n18, 240n20, 242n27, 247n9; Kintambo, 152; Kisangani, 32f, 158; Kisantu, 50, 77f, 119, 251n27; Kivunda, 168; Kongo Central, 52; Landana, 76; Lemba, 96; Loanda, 116–17, 120, 212; Lolo, 77f, 241n19; Londe, 241n19; Lower Congo, 1–3, 5, 8–9, 12, 15–17, 19, 24–27, 31, 33, 41, 52–53, 68, 72, 74–76, 78–80, 83, 86, 89, 91, 94, 103–5, 108, 110, 113, 116, 123–24, 126, 128–31, 161, 190, 194, 200–201, 210, 212, 216, 226, 235n1, 235n5, 236n7, 240n3, 241n9, 244n54, 251n27; Lubumbashi, 32f, 176; Lukunga, 77f, 79, 103, 241n9, 244n65; Luozi, 2, 12, 24–25, 29–33, 37–39, 45, 48–53, 54f, 60–61, 65–68, 74, 77f, 81, 84–85, 96, 104, 107–13, 116, 121–31, 132f, 139, 149, 151–52, 155–56, 159, 162–72, 176–78, 181–82, 187–89, 191f, 192–94, 197f, 198–202, 203f, 207f, 212–16, 220, 223–26, 236n12, 240n3, 242n38, 246n32, 252n37, 252n42; Madimba, 99; Magasin, 65–66, 240n19; Mai Stadium, 137; Masina, 67; Matadi, 32f, 47, 50, 52, 76, 77f, 79, 118–20, 130, 172, 190, 201, 241nn9,10; Mayidi, 29–30, 120; Mayombe, 97, 133, 241n9; Mayumbe, 128; Mbanza Manteke, 77f, 79, 94–95, 103, 241n9; Mbanza-Mona, 128, 156, 163, 169, 172; Mbanza-Mwembe, 156; Mbanza-Ngoyo, 53, 128; Mbanza-Ngungu, 50, 163, 172, 190; Mont-Ngafula, 166; Mpal-abala, 76, 77f, 80, 241n9; Mukimbungu, 77f, 121, 241n9; Mukimvika, 241n19; Ndan-danga, 76; Nganda, 77f, 241n19; Ngobila, 212; Ngombe-Kunsuka, 84; Nkamba, 1–2, 39, 77f, 83–85, 88–90, 92, 94, 100, 103, 105, 242n29, 244n61; Nkundi, 171; Northern Cataracts, 86, 96, 103; Nsona Mbata, 80, 89, 104, 241n18; Paka, 244n65; Palais de Peuple, 49f; Pangu, 97; Paroisse Sacre-Coeur, 58f; Pembo, 86–87; Saka, 111, 112f; Sankuru, 129; Sona Bata, 77f, 80, 84, 241n9; Southern Cataracts, 1, 52, 84, 88, 97, 104, 123; Soyo, 82; Thysville, 77f, 84, 89, 128, 130, 241n9; Tshumbiri, 104; Tumba, 77f, 90, 122–23; Upper Congo River, 122, 208, 247; Vungu, 77f, 241n19; Wathen, 77f, 83–85, 89, 103, 241n9, 241n19, 242n26; Zundu, 90, 93. *See also* Zaire

De Rossi, Judge, 100, 102

Derrida, Jacques, 28

Descartes, René, 19

Diangienda, Joseph, 132

Dibundu dia Mpeve ya Nlongo mu Afelika (DMNA), 25, 29, 37–38, 73, 81, 107–9, 161–63, 202, 216, 222, 236n12, 239n2, 252n37

Didier, 45–46, 63

Dieudonné, 128

discrimination, 41, 60, 62, 67, 118

"Djalelo," 248n15

domestic workers, 12

Dominicans, 43

Dosogne, Joseph, 126

Drewal, Margaret Thompson, 16–17, 231

Durkheim, Emile, 24, 237n25

Ebron, Paulla, 9, 236n15

Edmondson, Laura, 23

Eglise du Christ au Zaire, 160

Egypt, 26, 203–7; Cairo, 48

elections, 8, 20–21, 26, 47, 62, 68, 190, 192–94, 200–202, 209, 226, 237n23, 250n11, 252n32

Eley, Geoff, 167

embodied performances, 8–10, 16, 24, 28, 34, 73, 94, 108, 127, 133, 138, 140, 164, 166, 168, 191, 194, 213, 216–17, 219, 222, 225–26, 229–31

English (language), 46, 56, 193, 198–99, 203–4, 215, 220, 240n2, 248n14, 250n10; Pidgin English, 40

epilepsy, 84, 93–94. *See also* tuntuka

Esaie, Masamba, 108, 245n1

Ethiopia, 206

ethnography, 4, 28–31, 46, 50, 54, 58–68, 74, 111–12, 193; ethnographic texts, 22, 26–27, 142. *See also* participant observation

ethnohistory, 109

European Union, 252n34

everyday cultural performances, 3–4, 8, 10–12, 16–20, 22–25, 27–28, 38, 44, 72–73, 91, 108, 110, 133–34, 190–91, 211–26, 229–31, 236n13

Ewing, Katherine, 29

Kirkland, Robert, 104
Kizole, Tata, 6
Kodi, M. W., 40
Kongo, Ne Muanda, 216
Kongo/BaManianga ethnic group, 166, 209
Kongo dia Ntotila, 124, 200, 206–9, 251n29
Kongo Kingdom, 2–3, 5, 7–8, 19, 26, 75–76, 166, 188, 190, 194, 199–200, 202, 205–9, 211, 213, 219, 222, 225–30, 244n54, 246n32, 249n1, 249n6, 250n10, 250n17; Mbanza Kongo, 206, 212, 251n29
Kudada, Ma, 24–25
Kudia, Mama, 188, 224
Kumi, Ma, 221
Kunku, 97
Kuntilma, Makidi, 40
Kuyowa, Antoine, 103

Laman, Karl, 116, 236n11, 243n38
Lambek, Michael, 238n29
L'Association Musicale BaKongo (AMUBAKO), 208, 251nn27,28
Laurent, 166
Lebanon, 64
Léon, Papa, 50
Leopold II, King, 47–48, 60, 76–77, 157
Lerrigo, Peter Hugh James, 95–96
Libasa, Chief, 96–97
Liberia, 65, 206–7, 210, 251n26; Monrovia, 207
Library of Luozi, 29
Lingala (language), 45, 56, 143, 199, 208, 238n36, 247n9, 250n17, 251n30
linguistics, 5, 9, 17, 174, 208–9, 228, 237n18, 237n21
Livingstone Inland Mission (LIM), 76
Long, Beverly Whitaker, 236n9
Lovanium University, 195
Lucques, Laurent du, 82
Lumumba, Patrice, 142, 209, 252n32
Luozi River, 51
Lutherans, 115
Luyindula, Ne Nkamu, 30, 38–39, 122, 240n2, 247n4
Luzola, Ma, 81

Mabie, Catherine, 104
MacDiarmid, Peter, 104

MacGaffey, Wyatt, 39, 133, 217
Mahambu, 86
Mahaniah, Kimpianga, 30, 39–40, 50, 78, 107
Mahema, Esther Luhunu, 237n19
Maillet, J., 125–27
Makaba. See MaKongo
Makanda, Ma, 71–72
makinu. See dance
MaKongo, 199, 205–6, 207f
Malawi, 12, 23, 140, 168, 249n8
Malaysia, 11, 245n3
Maloba, Bombe, 86
Malula, Joseph Albert, 161
Mankenda Saba, Queen, 251n10
Mao Zedong, 144
Maquet-Tombu, Jeanne, 39
Marcellino d'Atri, Father, 227–28
marginalization, 2, 4, 18, 30, 139–40, 168, 182, 201, 220
Markoff, John, 146
marriage, 64–66, 104, 111, 165–66, 169, 176–79, 181–82, 206, 251n20
Marshall, Ruth, 26–27
Martin, Marie-Louise, 101–2
Martinez-Ruiz, Barbaro, 19
Masamba, 39
Masamba, Father, 120
masculinity, 178, 247n10
Masquelier, Adeline, 11, 26–27
Massamba, 40
Matadi, George, 151–52, 168–70
Mathieu, 31
Matswa movement, 128
Matuba, Samuel, 124
Mauss, Marcel, 8–9
Mavuela, J., 208
Mawri communities, 11, 27
Mayazola, Ma, 166, 169–72, 181–82
mayembo, 84
Mayidi Grant Seminary, 29
mazikua, 190, 192, 201–2, 203f, 213–16, 215f, 219, 224, 226, 249n4
Mbandila, 103
Mbandila, Kuyowa and Co., 103
Mbatshia, Simon Mbtashi, 200
Mbembe, Achille, 33, 140–41, 166–67, 171, 175, 178, 180–81, 183, 248n2

McClintock, Anne, 167

McLaurin, Irma, 59

media, 14, 48, 139, 145, 148, 150, 154, 161, 238n32, 248n12. *See also* music; television

medicine, 43–44, 79–80, 89, 94, 100–102

memory, 13–16, 26, 34, 39, 41, 111, 173, 211, 247n5

Mercer University, 29

Mere, Le Marquis de Maison, 220

Merleau-Ponty, Maurice, 6

methodology, 11, 28–32, 41–45, 73–75, 228. *See also* ethnography; nonprobability sampling; participant observation

Metzger, Peter, 104

Michel, Thierry: *Mobutu: King of Zaire,* 248n12

mind, 6–7, 19, 22, 229

missionaries, 16, 19–20, 29, 73–74, 92, 102, 106, 108, 110–11, 132–33, 148, 208, 217, 237n26, 242n30, 250n10; Catholic missionaries, 25, 39–40, 51, 63, 75–76, 77*f*, 82, 88–90, 99, 112, 116–20, 122–23, 125–26, 128, 130, 157, 211–12, 223, 227–31, 249n6, 251n27; Protestant missionaries, 2–3, 51, 61, 68, 75–80, 77*f*, 83–85, 88–89, 94, 97, 101, 103–4, 112, 115–17, 121–24, 126, 128–31, 134, 145, 235n5, 236n6, 241n9. *See also individual organizations and people*

Mission of Blacks. *See* Mpadism

"Les Missions Catholiques en face des danses des Bakongo," 120

Mobilization Propaganda and Political Animation (MOPAP), 154

Mobutisme, 153, 158

Mobutu: King of Zaire, 248n12

Mobutuism, 147

Mobutu Sese Seko, 47, 134, 139*f*, 190, 219, 247n4, 247n9, 248n15, 249n9, 252n32; civil religion and, 24, 27, 33, 138–39, 142, 144–49, 151, 158, 160, 164, 166, 178, 231, 238n32, 248n13; overthrow of, 193; political animation and, 7, 14, 19, 21, 24, 30, 33–34, 137–83, 229, 231, 235n3, 238n32, 246n26, 247n7, 249n6; Zaire naming, 50, 235n1, 247n2. *See also* People's Revolutionary Movement; Youth of the People's Revolutionary Movement; Zaire

MONUC, 223–24, 252nn41,42

Moody, Thomas, 84

Moonsammy, Patricia Van Leeuwaarde, 250n9

morality, 110

moral reform associations, 13

Morel, Léon-Georges, 1–2

Mosi, Ne, 159

moyo, 6

Mpadi, Simon, 128, 240n4

Mpadism, 39, 73, 128, 240n4

Mpanzu, 196, 202, 217, 251n20, 251n24

mpeve, 6, 38, 82–83, 92, 235n5. *See also* spirits

Mpongo, Léon Engulu Baanga, 148, 159

Mudimbe, V. Y., 29

Mukiese, Tata, 127–29

MuKongo people. *See* BisiKongo ethnic group

Munkukusa, 246n27

Muntanda, Chief, 97

musicians, 23, 30, 33, 127, 140, 142, 220, 249n3

Muzita, Kalebi, 129

Mvubi, Yoane (John the Baptist), 124

Namibia, 47, 206

Narayan, Kirin, 59

National Archives, 29, 138, 150–51

National Assembly, 8, 194, 201–2, 226

National Electric Company (SNEL), 159

National Institute of Arts, 29–30

nationalism, 10, 20, 23, 28, 32, 134, 193, 231, 242n27, 247n6, 248n3; definition, 22, 247n5; kingunza movement and, 72, 75, 102–6, 108–9, 122–23, 133; Kongo nationalism, 2–3, 30, 34, 41, 190, 198–99, 208–9, 219; political animation and, 14, 19, 24, 137–83, 229. *See also* Bundu dia Kongo

National Legislative Council, 157

National Library, 29, 45

National Museum, 29

Negro African Church, 201

Ne Kongo Kalunga. *See* Nzambi

Nelson, Bill, 32*f*, 77*f*

New World, 34, 230–32. *See also individual countries*

New York, 42, 45; Bronx, 32, 42–43, 49

Nfinangani, 242n30

nganga (singular)/banganga (plural), 5, 19, 25, 82, 84–85, 87, 89, 93, 120, 129, 244n54. *See also* mayembo

Ngolo, Ne Makinda, 219

Ngunzism, 73, 130–31. *See also* bangunza; kingunza

Nicaragua, 60

Niger, 11, 26–27

Nigeria, 15, 26, 206, 245n1; Lagos, 48

Nile River, 50

nitu, 6

Nkanga, Mbala, 43, 141, 173

Nkolele, Tata, 166, 177

Nkrumah, Kwame, 210, 252n34

Nkuku, Tata, 156, 178

Nkunku, Philippe, 124

Nkusu, Déo, 200

Nlamba, Yoane, 121

Noland, Carrie, 17–18

nongovernmental organizations (NGOs), 41, 177

nonprobability sampling, 30

North Carolina, 44

North Korea, 144

Nsaku, 196, 202, 217, 251n20

Nsafu, Mama, 121

Nsemi, Ne Muanda, 187, 190, 191f, 193–202, 205–6, 210, 223, 225–26, 250n10, 250n17, 251n20; *MaKongo*, 199, 205–6, 207f

nsikumusu, 130–31. *See also* Swedish Mission Covenant Church

Nsonde, Sebuloni, 124

Ntima, Ma, 165, 169, 171–72, 181–82

Nyerere, Julius, 237n24

Nzambi, 197, 214

Nzambi, Ne Fwani kia, 219

Nzambi, Ne kia kwa, 219

Nzambi 'a Kongo, 195–96

Nzambi 'a Mbumba, 195–96

Nzambi 'a Mpungu, 195–96

Nzambi Mpungu, 72, 85–86, 195, 198, 206, 215–16, 225

Nzeza-Landu, M. Edward, 208–9

Nzinga-Nkuwu (Joao I), 75, 196, 202–4, 217, 251n20

Nzongola-Ntalaja, Georges, 173–74

Nzungu, 242n29, 242n30

Obama, Barack, 11

obscenity, 113–14, 117, 119–20, 140, 177

oil industry, 40, 83

Olomide, Koffi, 220

"An Open Letter to His Serene Majesty Leopold II," 77–78

oral interpretation, 5

Organization of African Unity, 210

pagans, 20, 89, 115, 131

Palmaer, Georg, 89

Pan-Africanism, 40, 193–94, 209–10. *See also* Black communities; Blackness; United States of Africa

Panama: Portobelo, 43–44

Papa Joseph, 55

Parsons, Talcott, 236n16

participant observation, 28, 31

patriarchy, 172–80, 192

Patricia, 64

Paul, 50

Pedro IV, King, 227–28

penal colonies, 3, 101–2, 108, 113, 244n63

Pennsylvania, 43; Philadelphia, 247n7

Pentecostals, 26, 237n26

People's Republic of Zanzibar, 237n24

People's Revolutionary Movement (MPR), 137, 143, 147–49, 151–53, 156, 160–62, 172–75, 248n14. *See also* Youth of the People's Revolutionary Movement

Peres of Gand, 76

performance, 9, 15, 26, 30–31, 41, 65–66, 93–94, 96, 102, 120, 193–94, 238n29; coerced performances, 33–34, 125, 127, 137–83, 238n32; definition, 5–7, 236n9, 236n12; everyday cultural performances, 3–4, 8, 10–12, 16–20, 22–25, 27–28, 38, 44, 72–73, 91, 108, 110, 133–34, 190–91, 211–26, 229–31, 236n13; gender performance, 236n15; racial performance, 56–57; types of, 18f. *See also* dance; embodied performances; political animation

performance art, 15

performance studies, 5, 9, 15, 20, 23, 236n13

performative encounters, 4, 11, 24, 32–34,

Tshiluba (language), 238n36, 247n10
Tuden, Arthur, 236n16
tuntuka, 84
Turner, Victor, 7, 236n16
Tuzolana, Tata, 120

Uganda, 32f, 46–47, 112
Unibra, 239n11
United Kingdom, 28; Oxford, 29, 74. *See also*
   Great Britain
United States, 11–12, 28 29, 42, 45, 59, 63, 67,
   81, 144–46, 152, 188, 192, 250n17. *See also*
   individual states
United States of Africa, 210, 252n34. *See also*
   Pan-Africanism
l'Université Pédagogique National (UPN), 29
University of Ghana, 240n21
University of Michigan, 43–44, 188, 239n5
Unzola, Léonard Fuka, 200

Van Cleemput, Jean-Constant, 90
Van den Bosch, Monseigneur, 130
Van Hoof, Father, 119
Van Wing, Joseph, 39, 126–27; "Les Danses
   Bakongo," 116–19
Vives, Juan, 245n12
La Voix du Rédempteur, 90
Voluntary Corps of the Republic (CVR), 152
Von Rosle, Monsignor, 90

Walder, Andreas, 85
Wamba, Philippe, 68
Wamba-dia-Wamba, Ernest, 201, 250n10
Ward, Lincoln, 65, 67
Watchtower movement, 12
weapons of the weak, 110, 245n3
Weber, Max, 25, 236n16, 238n27
Wedeen, Lisa, 247n6
Weiss, Gail, 18
Werreson, 188, 249n3
When We Were Kings, 247n3
White, Bob, 23, 142, 144, 152, 159, 173

Whiteness, 2–3, 9, 11, 41, 43, 104–5, 205, 226–
   29; White privilege, 56–58, 60–62
White people, 11, 39, 64–66, 90, 96–97, 100–
   101, 117, 122, 123–25, 167, 192, 198, 213
Wild-Wood, Emma, 49
Williams, Brackette, 54
Williams, George Washington: "An Open
   Letter to His Serene Majesty Leopold II,"
   77–78
witchcraft, 6, 50, 246n27, 252n42. *See also*
   kindoki
witch doctors, 88–89
World Bank, 176
World War II, 39, 47

xenophobia, 46, 133

Yemen, 247n3
yinama, 211, 213, 217–19, 225, 226, 237n20
Young, Jason, 244n54
Youth of the People's Revolutionary Movement (JMPR), 156–58, 161, 169, 172, 177,
   179, 181

Zaire, 231, 247n7, 248n12; Bas-Zaire, 52, 139,
   150, 235n1; naming of, 21, 50, 137, 247n2;
   political animation in, 10, 23–24, 33,
   137–83, 139f, 249n5; Shaba, 23, 159. *See also*
   Democratic Republic of Congo
Zairian Coffee Bureau (OZACAF), 159
Zairianization, 159
Zakalia, Badiegisa. *See* Nsemi, Ne Muanda
zakama, 5, 10, 25, 27–29, 33–34, 108, 122, 128–
   32, 163; definition, 243n38; as everyday
   cultural performance, 4, 7, 17 20, 18f,
   72–73, 80–103, 110; Kimbangu and, 1–3,
   25, 231; terminology, 243n38. *See also* bangunza; kingunza; mayembo; sunsumuka;
   tuntuka
Zamenga, Batukezanga, 52
Zimbabwe, 47, 206, 239n7
Zole, Ne, 202, 215, 219